Adobe Photoshop

2025 Release

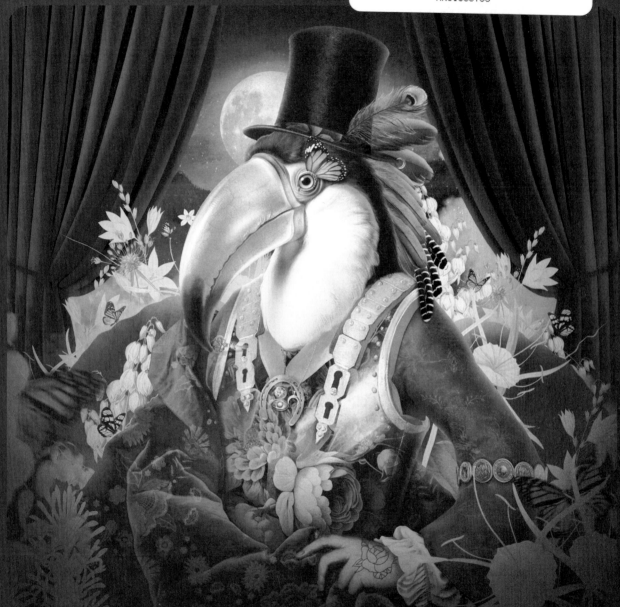

Classroom in a Book®
The official training workbook from Adobe

Conrad Chavez

WHERE ARE THE LESSON FILES?

Purchase of this Classroom in a Book in any format gives you access to the lesson files you'll need to complete the exercises in the book.

1   Go to peachpit.com/PhotoshopCIB2025.

2   Sign in or create a new account.

3   Click Submit.

● **Note:** If you encounter problems registering your product or accessing the lesson files or web edition, go to peachpit.com/support for assistance.

4   Answer the questions as proof of purchase.

5   The lesson files can be accessed through the Registered Products tab on your Account page.

6   Click the Access Bonus Content link below the title of your product to proceed to the download page. Click the lesson file links to download them to your computer.

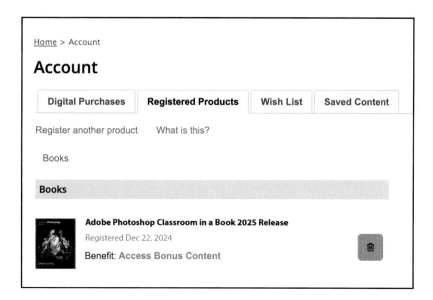

● **Note:** If you purchased a digital product directly from peachpit.com, your product will already be registered. Look for the Access Bonus Content link on the Registered Products tab in your account.

▶ **Warning:** For access to the lesson files, please register and download your files by December 31, 2029.

CONTENTS

GETTING STARTED

Adobe Photoshop, the benchmark for digital imaging excellence, provides professional image editing features enhanced by machine learning and cloud integration. Photoshop supports a wide range of workflows including print, web, and video. Photoshop gives you the digital editing tools you need to transform images more easily than ever before.

Photoshop works with other important tools that you'll use in this book. Adobe Camera Raw, included with Photoshop, helps you get the most quality out of camera raw images. Adobe Bridge is a digital asset manager that helps you browse and organize files you want to use with Photoshop and other Adobe Creative Cloud applications.

About Classroom in a Book

Adobe Photoshop Classroom in a Book 2025 Release is part of the official training series for Adobe graphics and publishing software, developed with the support of Adobe product experts. The lessons are designed to let you learn at your own pace. If you're new to Adobe Photoshop, you'll learn the fundamental concepts and features you'll need to master the program. If you haven't used Photoshop for several years, Classroom in a Book can help you get caught up with the many changes in recent versions.

Although each lesson provides step-by-step instructions for creating a specific project, there's room for exploration and experimentation. You can follow the book from start to finish or do only the lessons that match your interests.

What's new in this edition

This edition covers new features in Adobe Photoshop, such as new editing tools and more ways to use Adobe Firefly generative AI. This edition also expands coverage of optimizing images for web, social media, video, and print media, and includes many new and updated tips.

As in every edition, you'll learn best practices for organizing, managing, and showcasing your photos.

Prerequisites

Before you begin to use *Adobe Photoshop Classroom in a Book 2025 Release*, you should have a working knowledge of your computer and its operating system. Make sure that you know how to use the mouse and standard menus and commands and how to open, save, and close files. If you need to review these techniques, see the documentation for your Microsoft® Windows® PC or Apple® Mac® computer.

Note: The official version numbers of Adobe applications don't necessarily align with years because many existed before the year was part of the name. For example, Photoshop was released in 1990 as version 1, and the year did not appear in the name until Photoshop CC 2014, which is version 15.

To complete the lessons in this book, you'll need Adobe Photoshop 2025 and Adobe Bridge 2025 installed on your computer. The exact version number of the software is different than the year in the application name; this book was specifically tested using Photoshop version 25.0, Bridge version 14.0, and Camera Raw 17.0:

- To find the version of Photoshop that you are running, choose Help > System Info and look at the first line (Adobe Photoshop Version).

- To find the version of Bridge that you are running, choose Help > About Bridge (Windows) or Adobe Bridge > About Bridge (macOS) and look at the first line in the window that opens.

- To find the version of Camera Raw that you are running, look in the Camera Raw window title bar when Camera Raw is open.

If your versions of those applications are older, you may be able to get the versions matching this book by opening the Creative Cloud desktop application and clicking the Updates button. If newer versions don't appear in the Updates list, see if your computer meets the current system requirements because they may have changed.

If your versions are newer and don't match some of the steps in this book, you may be able to install a version matching this book; see "Installing a different version."

Installing Adobe Photoshop, Adobe Bridge, and Adobe Camera Raw

Before you begin using *Adobe Photoshop Classroom in a Book 2025 Release*, make sure that you've installed the required software. You must have an active license for Adobe Photoshop software, because it is not included with this book.

Many lessons in this book use Adobe Bridge, and one lesson uses Adobe Camera Raw. You install Photoshop and Bridge on your computer using the Adobe Creative Cloud desktop application, available at adobe.com/creativecloud/desktop-app.html; follow the onscreen instructions. Adobe Camera Raw is automatically installed when you install Photoshop.

Photoshop should run this book's lessons well on most recent computers. Your computer and its operating system software must meet Photoshop system requirements, which you can view at helpx.adobe.com/photoshop/system-requirements.html. For optimal performance, aim for the recommended, not minimum, specifications.

If your budget makes it challenging to meet the recommended level of Photoshop system requirements, focus on getting enough memory (also called *random access memory*, or RAM), and a system volume with enough storage capacity so that there's always at least 100GB of free space. A computer with fast components can slow to a crawl if the system volume has no more free space left. For most Photoshop work, it isn't necessary to pay for upgrades such as a central processing unit (CPU) with the most cores, or for the most powerful graphics processing unit (GPU).

Installing a different version

If your version of Photoshop, Bridge, or Camera Raw is newer than those used in this edition of Classroom in a Book and works differently than in the lessons, you may be able to install a compatible version using the Creative Cloud desktop application:

1   Start the Creative Cloud desktop application, and in the leftmost bar, click Apps. Find Photoshop in the list, click its … menu, and choose Other Versions.

Note: For Windows, a 64-bit operating system is required. (All supported versions of macOS are already 64-bit.)

Note: If you have a PC that runs Windows for ARM processors, you can install and run Photoshop natively, but some features may not be available yet. Also, performance may be affected by driver software that isn't fully optimized for ARM. For details, see helpx.adobe.com/photoshop/kb/windows-arm-support.html.

Note: You can use the Creative Cloud desktop application to install the two most recent major versions of an application; for example, if the current version is 25, you can install version 25 or 24.

2   Find the versions of the software listed in "Prerequisites," and click Install for each of those versions.

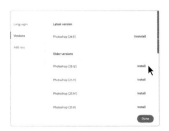

Adobe Camera Raw is not in the list because it's updated automatically. To install an older version of Camera Raw, download its installer from:

helpx.adobe.com/camera-raw/kb/camera-raw-plug-in-installer.html

Installing fonts

Some lessons in this book may suggest specific fonts. If a suggested font is not installed on your computer, you may be able to sync it to your computer using Adobe Fonts, which is part of a personal Creative Cloud subscription. (Adobe Fonts might not be included in some educational or organizational subscriptions.) To activate a font from Adobe Fonts and sync it to your computer while in Photoshop, choose Type > More from Adobe Fonts and follow the directions.

Starting Adobe Photoshop

You start Photoshop just as you do most software applications.

To start Adobe Photoshop in Windows: Click the Start button in the taskbar, and in the alphabetical list under A, click Adobe Photoshop 2025.

To start Adobe Photoshop on a Mac: Click the Adobe Photoshop 2025 icon in the Launchpad or Dock.

If you don't see Adobe Photoshop, type **Photoshop** into the search box in the taskbar (Windows) or in Spotlight search (macOS), and when the Adobe Photoshop 2025 application icon appears, select it, and press Enter or Return.

Online content

Your purchase of this Classroom in a Book includes the following online materials provided on your Account page on peachpit.com.

Lesson files

To work through the projects in this book, you will need to download the lesson files by following the instructions on the next page.

Web Edition

The Web Edition is an online interactive version of the book providing an enhanced learning experience. Your Web Edition can be accessed from any device with a connection to the Internet, and it contains:

* The complete text of the book
* Hours of instructional video keyed to the text
* Interactive quizzes

Accessing the lesson files and Web Edition

You must register your purchase on peachpit.com to access the online content:

1 Go to peachpit.com/PhotoshopCIB2025.

2 Sign in or create a new account.

3 Click Submit.

4 Answer the question as proof of purchase.

5 The lesson files can be accessed from the Registered Products tab on your Account page. Click the Access Bonus Content link below the title of your product to proceed to the download page. Click the lesson file link(s) to download them to your computer.

The Web Edition can be accessed from the Digital Purchases tab on your Account page. Click the Launch link to access the product.

Note: If you purchased a digital product directly from peachpit.com, your product will already be registered. Look for the Access Bonus Content link on the Registered Products tab in your account.

Warning: For access to the lesson files, please register and download your files by December 31, 2029.

Restoring default preferences

Like many applications, Adobe Photoshop stores various general settings in a document called a *preferences file*. Each time you quit Photoshop, certain workspace settings (such as the last-used options for some tools and commands) are recorded in the preferences file. Any changes you make in the Preferences dialog box are also saved in the preferences file.

To ensure that what you see onscreen matches the images and instructions in this book, you should restore the default preferences as described at the beginning of each lesson. If you choose to not reset your preferences, be aware that the tools, panels, and other settings in Photoshop may not match those described in this book.

If you have changed the settings in the Edit > Color Settings dialog box, those settings are saved in a different location than the Preferences file, so use the following procedure to save them as a preset before you start work using this book. When you want to restore your color settings, you can simply select the preset you created.

Tip: Color Settings can affect whether you see color profile alert messages when you open a document or paste content in Photoshop. One clue that color settings were altered is that profile alerts appear when they previously didn't, or they no longer appear when they used to.

To save your current color settings:

1   Start Adobe Photoshop.

2   Choose Edit > Color Settings.

3   Note what is selected in the Settings menu:

   •   If it is anything other than Custom, write down the name of the settings file, and click OK to close the dialog box. You do not need to perform steps 4–6 of this procedure.

   •   If Custom is selected in the Settings menu, click Save (*not* OK).

The Save dialog box opens. The default location is the Settings folder, which is where you want to save your file. The default filename extension is .csf (color settings file).

4   In the File Name field (Windows) or Save As field (macOS), type a descriptive name for your color settings, preserving the .csf file extension. Then click Save.

5   In the Color Settings Comment dialog box, type any descriptive text that will help you identify the color settings later, such as the date, specific settings, or your workgroup.

6   Click OK to close the Color Settings Comment dialog box, and again to close the Color Settings dialog box.

To restore your color settings:

1   Start Adobe Photoshop.

2   Choose Edit > Color Settings.

3   From the Settings menu in the Color Settings dialog box, choose the settings file you noted or saved in the previous procedure, and click OK.

Additional resources

Adobe Photoshop Classroom in a Book 2025 Release is not intended to replace help files or tutorials that you can open from the application, or to be a comprehensive reference for every feature. Only the commands and options used in the lessons are explained in this book. For comprehensive information about program features and tutorials, refer to these resources:

Home screen: In Photoshop, the Learn section of the Home screen offers tutorials.

Search command: Choose Edit > Search to open the Discover panel, which offers a wealth of tutorials, suggestions, and links before you even enter a search term. If you enter a term (such as **crop**) and press Enter or Return, the Discover panel can highlight relevant Photoshop tools and commands for you and provides links to more information.

▶ **Tip:** If you find that the Discover panel (Edit > Search) is useful, consider memorizing its keyboard shortcut in Photoshop: Press Ctrl+F (Windows) or Command+F (macOS). To close the panel, press the shortcut again.

Adobe Photoshop Help and Support: Choose Help > Photoshop Help to open the Discover panel with a list of online help resources including the User Guide and Support Community. You can also use your web browser to go to helpx.adobe.com/support/photoshop.html to find Help and Support content on Adobe.com.

Photoshop tutorials: Choose Help > Hands-On Tutorials to open the Discover panel with a list of guided lessons. Follow along in Photoshop with the provided sample documents. To find more tutorials online, go to helpx.adobe.com/photoshop/tutorials.html.

Photoshop blog: blog.adobe.com/en/topics/photoshop brings you tutorials, product news, and inspirational articles about using Photoshop.

Julieanne Kost's blog: jkost.com/blog is where veteran Adobe product evangelist Julieanne Kost posts useful tips and videos that introduce and provide valuable insights on the latest features in Photoshop and other Adobe photo applications.

Adobe Support Community: community.adobe.com lets you tap into user forums where you can ask questions about Photoshop and other Adobe applications.

Adobe Photoshop product home page: Find product information at adobe.com/products/photoshop.html.

Plug-ins menu: To find add-on "plug-in" software modules to extend and add features to your Creative Cloud tools, in Photoshop choose Plugins > Browse Plugins.

Creative Cloud desktop application: Click Discover to see tutorials, online streaming video, inspirational examples of creative work, and other links and resources for Photoshop and other Adobe applications you have installed.

Resources for educators: adobe.com/education and edex.adobe.com offer a treasure trove of information for instructors who teach classes on Adobe software. Find solutions for education at all levels, including free curricula that use an integrated approach to teaching Adobe software and can be used to prepare for the Adobe Certified Associate exams.

▶ **Tip:** You'll see the same Creative Cloud learning resources (and access to your work stored on Creative Cloud servers) when you use the Creative Cloud mobile app or when you're signed into creative.adobe.com.

1 GETTING TO KNOW THE WORK AREA

Lesson overview

In this lesson, you'll learn how to do the following:

- Open image files in Adobe Photoshop.

- Select and use tools in the Tools panel.

- Set options for a selected tool using the options bar.

- Use various methods to zoom in to and out from an image.

- Select, rearrange, and use panels.

- Choose commands in panel and context menus.

- Open and use a panel in the panel dock.

- Undo actions to correct mistakes or to make different choices.

- Export a copy with settings for a video thumbnail preview image.

This lesson will take about an hour to complete. To get the lesson files used in this chapter, download them from the web page for this book at peachpit.com/PhotoshopCIB2025. For more information, see "Accessing the lesson files and Web Edition" in the Getting Started section at the beginning of this book.

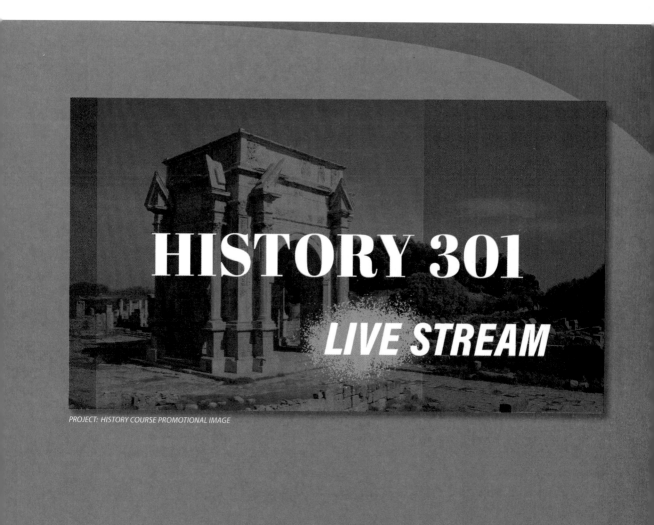

HISTORY 301
LIVE STREAM

PROJECT: HISTORY COURSE PROMOTIONAL IMAGE

As you work with Adobe Photoshop, you'll discover that you can often accomplish the same task in several ways. To make the best use of the extensive editing options available in Photoshop, it's important to become familiar with the work area.

Starting to work in Adobe Photoshop

The Adobe Photoshop work area includes menus, toolbars, and panels that give you quick access to tools and options for editing and adding elements to your image.

In Photoshop, you primarily work with bitmapped digital images: continuous-tone images that have been converted into a series of small squares, or picture elements, called *pixels*. You can also work with *vector graphics*, which are drawings made of smooth lines that retain their crispness when scaled. And you can add text, which is a form of vector graphics. You can create original artwork in Photoshop, or you can import and combine images from many sources, such as:

- Photographs from a digital camera or mobile phone
- Stock photography, such as images from the Adobe Stock service
- Scans of photographs, transparencies, negatives, graphics, or other documents
- Digital video clips
- Artwork created in drawing or painting programs
- Images created in Photoshop using Adobe Firefly generative AI

You'll learn about type in more detail in Lesson 7, and you'll learn about vector graphics in Lesson 8.

Starting Photoshop

⬤ **Note:** Typically, you won't need to reset defaults when you're working on your own projects. However, you'll reset the preferences before working on most lessons in this book to ensure that what you see onscreen matches the descriptions in the lessons. For more information, see "Restoring default preferences" on page 5.

To begin, you'll start Adobe Photoshop and reset the default preferences.

1 Click the Adobe Photoshop 2025 icon in your Start menu (Windows) or the Launchpad or Dock (macOS), and then simultaneously hold down Ctrl+Alt+Shift (Windows) or Command+Option+Shift (macOS) to reset the default settings.

If you don't see Adobe Photoshop 2025, type **Photoshop** into the search box in the taskbar (Windows) or in Spotlight (macOS), and when the Adobe Photoshop 2025 application icon appears, select it, and press Enter or Return.

2 When prompted, click Yes to confirm that you want to delete the Adobe Photoshop Settings file.

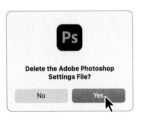

Using the Home screen

After starting Photoshop, the first thing you see is the Home screen, which gives you a number of ways to get started, as shown in the following illustration.

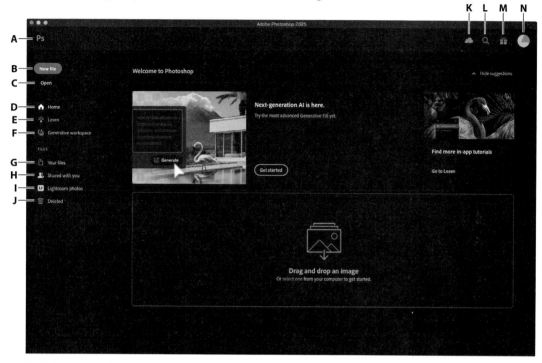

A. Switch to Photoshop workspace
B. Create new document
C. Open a document
D. Home screen content and recently opened local documents
E. Learn with tutorials
F. Generative Workspace for AI images
G. Cloud Documents you created on Windows, macOS, or iPad OS
H. Cloud Documents shared with you
I. Your photos in the Lightroom cloud
J. Deleted Cloud Documents
K. Cloud storage sync status
L. Search, Help, and Learn
M. What's New in Photoshop
N. Visit your Creative Cloud account in a web browser

On the left you see a list of view options:

- **Home** helps you use and learn about the current version and includes a tour. After you open at least one local or cloud document, a Recent section of previously opened documents appears at the bottom of the Home screen.

- **Learn** presents links to tutorials that open in Photoshop, where the Learn panel leads you through a lesson's steps that you follow using Photoshop itself.

- **Generative Workspace** opens a window that creates generative AI images more efficiently than using the Photoshop menu commands. You can generate multiple sets of variations at once, and it retains a history of your variations for later reference and reuse. (May not be available in all versions of Photoshop 2025.)

- **Your Files** lists Photoshop Cloud Documents, including those you edited on iPad using Photoshop or Adobe Fresco. You'll learn more about Cloud Documents

> **Tip:** To skip past the Home screen and go straight to the Photoshop application workspace, click the Photoshop icon in the upper-left corner.

in Lesson 3, "Working with Selections." Your Files doesn't list documents stored locally.

- **Shared with You** lists Cloud Documents that others made available to you for collaboration by using the File > Invite to Edit command.

- **Lightroom Photos** lists images synced to your Creative Cloud account's Lightroom online storage. This does not include Lightroom Classic local storage.

- **Deleted** lists Cloud Documents you've deleted, in case you change your mind and want to recover them (similar to the Recycle Bin or Trash on your computer desktop). This list includes Cloud Documents only, not files you deleted from Lightroom Photos or from your computer's local storage.

The Search icon in the upper-right corner can do different types of searches depending on where you start the search. When you click the Search icon and enter text on the Home screen, Photoshop looks for matching content in the Learn tutorials about Photoshop, in Adobe Stock images, and in your Lightroom cloud-synced images. When a document is open, the Search icon can find specific commands and tools in Photoshop, making it easier to learn where things are.

The Home screen automatically hides when you open a document, which is what you're going to do next. You can return to the Home screen by clicking the Home icon in the upper-left corner of the application window.

Open a document

You'll use the traditional Open command to view a Photoshop document.

1. Choose File > Open. (You can also click the Open button on the Home screen.) If a dialog box appears that says Open from Creative Cloud at the top, click On Your Computer at the bottom of the dialog box.

2. Navigate to the Lessons/Lesson01 folder that you copied to your hard drive from the peachpit.com website. (If you haven't downloaded the files, see "Accessing the lesson files and Web Edition" on page 4.)

3. Select the 01End.psd file, and click Open. Click OK if the Missing Profile dialog box appears, and click No if a message about updating text layers appears.

The 01End.psd file opens in its own window, in the default Photoshop workspace. You'll learn more about the workspace later in this lesson.

The end files in this book show you what you are creating in each project, and how it should look when it's completed. This one is a promotional image for a streaming video presentation. If you want, you can leave this file open to refer to, because you're about to build it.

4. If you don't want to leave the file open, choose File > Close. Do not close Photoshop, and don't save changes to the document.

Tip: To manage files in the Deleted list, click the ellipsis (…) button next to a file, and choose Restore or Permanently Delete.

Tip: If you want to change how dark or light the Photoshop workspace appears, open the Preferences dialog box, select the Interface panel, and select a different Color Theme.

Tip: If you drag and drop a compatible file anywhere on the Home screen, Photoshop will open it.

Starting a new document

You'll begin by creating the document you'll build in this lesson. How you start a document depends on the final delivery requirements of your project. For example, a document that will be printed usually has different requirements for color and resolution than a document that will be posted to a website or included in a video.

This document will promote a streaming video presentation on web pages, in streaming video applications, and on TV screens. It needs to use the pixel dimensions of the HDTV 1080p standard: 1920 pixels wide by 1080 pixels tall. That can later be scaled down to the smaller sizes used for video preview thumbnails on web pages and video apps.

Fortunately, Photoshop offers new document presets that help you more quickly create a document for common image sizes.

1 Choose File > New. (You can also click the New File button on the Home screen.)

2 In the New Document dialog box, click Film & Video.

Although the document you create in this lesson will be a still image, not a video, it does need to have HDTV 1080p pixel dimensions. The Film & Video category offers an HDTV 1080p preset, which lets you set up the document in one click.

When you click a New Document preset, the settings change in the Preset Details panel on the right. In this way you can inspect the settings used by any preset, and you can customize the New Document settings.

Tip: What do you do if you're not sure if the final document will be printed or displayed on screen? Create a high-resolution, full-color source document from which you can derive copies optimized for different media.

Tip: You don't have to start by selecting a preset. Instead, you can enter the settings you want in the Preset Details options.

Tip: If you frequently enter the same custom settings, you can save them as your own New Document preset. In the first row under Preset Details, name your preset and click the Save button (⬇) next to the name.

A. Preset categories   **B.** HDTV 1080p preset   **C.** Presets in current category   **D.** Preset Details

3 Click the preset HDTV 1080p, and then click Create.

Photoshop creates a new, blank, untitled document. It also includes guides, displayed in cyan. For this New Document preset, the guides are intended to help remind you to keep important video content away from frame edges, because some TVs (typically older ones) slightly crop the image. In your own projects, you can add guides to help align items in a design; you'll do this in later lessons.

4 Choose File > Save As, name the file **01Working.psd**, and click OK or Save.

Adding an image

With the new document created, you can now start adding to it. You'll import an image that will be the basis of the design.

1 Choose File > Place Embedded, and in the Lesson01 folder, select the file Arch.jpg and click Place.

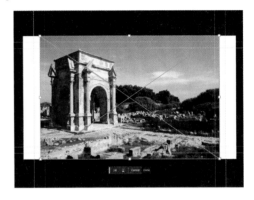

The image appears on the canvas, a bounding box with handles appears around the image, and the image was added as a new layer in the Layers panel. (You'll learn more about layers in Lesson 4.) Adding the image is not complete as long as the bounding box is active. Its handles give you an opportunity to *transform* (move, resize, or rotate) the image as you import it, and in this case, you want to take advantage of that right now and then finish the import.

2 Click and drag any handle on the bounding box so that the image covers the entire width of the canvas and so that the building is centered vertically within the canvas. To reposition the image, click and drag anywhere within it.

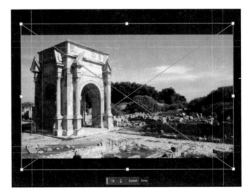

Notice that parts of the layer that extend beyond the canvas are not visible, but the bounding box handles indicate that those parts still exist. If you reposition or scale down the layer, areas beyond the canvas can become visible again.

3 In the options bar, click the check mark button (✔) to finish (commit) adding the image. The bounding box disappears.

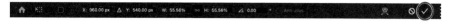

Note: Committing changes by pressing Enter or Return doesn't work when there's an active text cursor on a text layer so that Enter and Return can type a paragraph break character. Instead, commit type changes by clicking the check mark in the options bar or by clicking the canvas away from the type layer.

Some features in Photoshop happen in a special mode, such as the transformation bounding box you just used. Committing your changes exits that mode and returns you to the general Photoshop feature set. If you get tired of moving the mouse up to the options bar to click that check mark button, you can also commit changes by pressing the Enter or Return key.

Touring the Photoshop work area

As you work in Photoshop, you'll often have two questions:

* What is the state of the document or the selected item? (For example, what is the view magnification of the document? Or what is the font size of selected text?)

* What are the options for editing the document or selected item?

The following parts of the Photoshop workspace (shown on the next page) answer those questions:

Tools panel. This panel provides tools for creating and editing document elements.

Options bar. This panel offers options that customize the selected tool, so the options bar changes depending on which tool is selected in the Tools panel.

Document tab. When documents are open, one or more document windows also appear, which you can identify by the tabs across the top of the document window, similar to a web browser. The text in the tab displays information that can include the filename, magnification level, selected layer, and bit depth per channel.

Panels. Panels contain options for various tasks, objects, and attributes. For example, the Layers panel lists document layers and indicates which one is selected, and the Swatches panel lists color swatches that you can create, organize, and apply.

Properties panel. This panel offers options for the selected element, so what it shows changes depending on what's selected. It can consolidate options from multiple panels. For example, when a type layer is selected, the Properties panel can display Transform, Character, and Paragraph options at the same time, so that you can work there instead of looking at the options bar and three other panels. When nothing is selected, the Properties panel displays options for the entire document.

Contextual Task Bar. This floating bar suggests features that might be useful for the current task. It can help you become aware of relevant options that might normally be out of view in menus or in panels that aren't currently visible. This guidance makes the Contextual Task Bar useful for beginners.

Tip: The options bar, Properties panel, and Contextual Task Bar may seem similar but are different in important ways. The options bar is only about the selected tool, the Properties panel is about the selected layer(s), and the Contextual Task Bar also offers to help perform tasks for the selected layer.

Tip: If you see an asterisk (*) at the end of a document tab, the current document state is not saved. After you save the document, the asterisk disappears.

Document Status Bar. This displays information about the document. You can change what information it displays by clicking the arrow next to it. By default, the document Status Bar displays the document dimensions and resolution.

Search, Help, and Learn. This lets you enter a search term, which brings you a list of tools, commands, and tutorials. It's great for learning more about Photoshop or finding out where to find a tool or feature.

Workspaces menu. This menu offers different preset arrangements of panels.

Components such as the options bar, Properties panel, and Contextual Task Bar are constantly useful to refer to, so it's recommended that you keep them visible.

The Photoshop workspace is similar to those in Adobe Illustrator® and Adobe InDesign®, so learning how to use the tools and panels in one application makes it easier to learn and use the other applications. As in other applications, Photoshop features are distributed among tools, menu commands, and panels.

Each lesson will introduce you to more Photoshop features so that you can build a solid foundation for exploring other parts of Photoshop on your own.

Note: This illustration shows the macOS version of Photoshop. The arrangement is similar in Windows, but operating system styles may vary.

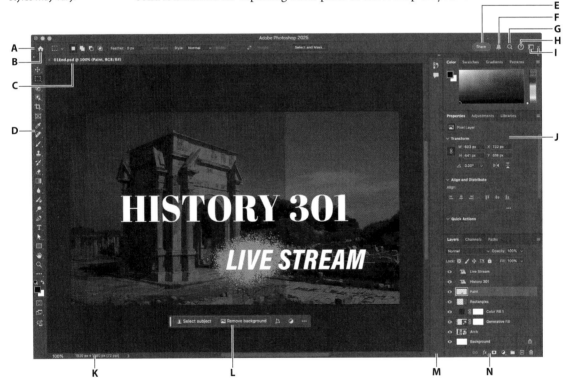

A. Options bar
B. Switch to Home screen
C. Document tab
D. Tools panel

E. Share button (for online review)
F. Notifications
G. Search, Help, and Learn
H. Tutorials
I. Workspaces menu

J. Properties panel
K. Document Status Bar
L. Contextual Task Bar
M. Panel stack collapsed
N. Panel stack expanded

Getting information and finding tools and options

There are so many tools, panels, and commands in Photoshop that it can be a challenge to get information about a selection or to find the options you need. To make Photoshop easier to use, keep the right information visible and know where to look.

Essential panels. If you work on a smaller screen and need to close panels to free up space to work, try to keep open the Layers panel, the options bar, the Properties panel, and the Contextual Task Bar. Together, they show you much of what you need to know most of the time and make it less necessary to open additional panels. You can show or hide any panel using the Window menu.

All in one: The Properties panel. We recommend keeping the Properties panel visible because it gives you information about the currently selected layer (such as layer dimensions or the currently applied font) and consolidates editing options so that you can leave many other panels closed. For example, for a type layer, it shows layer dimensions, paragraph options, and character options in one place.

For more information: The Info panel. For some workflows, the Info panel (Window > Info) is useful to keep visible. It displays information such as the color values under the pointer and the dimensions of a marquee selection, and if you customize it, it can show multiple types of Status Bar information. (The Status Bar can display only one type of information at a time.)

Just a click away. Menu commands can be inconvenient if you have to move the pointer a long way to reach them, especially on a large display. Remember that right-clicking (Windows) or Control-clicking (macOS) pops up a contextual menu under the pointer, typically listing commands useful for the item under the pointer.

If you think a feature exists but you can't find it in any of the panels or on the menus, choose Edit > Search.

> **Tip:** In macOS, you can enable right-click in System Settings > Mouse options. If you're using a trackpad, the Trackpad options provide more ways to open a context menu; look in the Secondary Click options for settings such as two-finger tap or bottom-right corner tap.

Using the tools

Photoshop tools are available in the Tools panel, the narrow strip along the left side of the application window. Generally, you select a tool when you want to create or edit by interacting directly with the image (by clicking and dragging the pointer).

The first tools you might need to use are those that let you change the view of the document without editing it. One of those is the Hand tool (🖐), an alternative to document window scroll bars. By dragging the Hand tool on the canvas, you pan (slide) the document within the document window.

The Zoom tool lets you change the view magnification interactively, and you'll explore that tool next. There's more to magnification than just dragging a tool; for example, you can first find out the current magnification.

Tip: The zoom percentage also appears in the document tab.

1 Examine the Status Bar near the bottom-left corner at the bottom of the document window, and notice the percentage displayed in the box to the left of the Status Bar. This represents the current view magnification, or zoom level.

Zoom level   Status Bar

100%   1920 px x 1080 px (72 ppi)

Zoom tool Z

Zoom in and out on an image. Learn more

Watch quick video

Tip: If the bottom of the Tools panel is cut off by the bottom of your screen, click the double arrows at the top of the Tools panel to display it as two shorter columns.

Now you'll select a tool.

2 Move the pointer over the Tools panel, and hover it (hold without clicking) over the magnifying-glass icon until a tool tip appears. The tool tip displays the tool's name (Zoom tool), keyboard shortcut (Z), a Learn More link, and a button that plays a short tutorial video.

3 Click the Zoom tool icon (Q) in the Tools panel to select it.

Tip: To select the Zoom tool using a keyboard shortcut, press the Z key. Tool shortcuts are single keys (do not press modifier keys such as Ctrl or Command). If a tool has a keyboard shortcut, you'll see it in the pop-up tool tip.

4 Move the pointer over the document window. The pointer now looks like a tiny magnifying glass with a plus sign in the center of the glass (⊕).

5 Click anywhere in the document window.

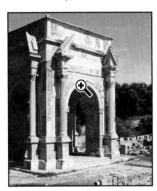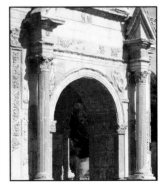

Each time you click, the Zoom tool magnifies by another level. If you want to know the current magnification percentage, look at the Status Bar or document tab.

6 Hold down the Alt key (Windows) or Option key (macOS) so that the Zoom tool pointer appears with a minus sign in the center of the magnifying glass (⊖), and then click anywhere in the image. Then release the Alt or Option key.

Now the view zooms out to a lower preset increment so you can see more of the image but in less detail. You can also drag the Zoom tool; you'll try that next.

About view magnifications

How do you know if an image is at the correct size for web pages, video, and print? The answer is different depending on the final delivery medium.

What 100% zoom percentage means. At 100% magnification in Photoshop, each image pixel is shown on one screen pixel, providing an accurate view of the image at the pixel level. However, 100% magnification does not represent how large the image will be reproduced when printed, because 100% isn't related to print resolution. How large 100% looks varies across displays with different DPI resolutions.

Previewing size for a web page or video frame. To preview image dimensions for on-screen media, first try 100% magnification. If 100% magnification in Photoshop displays an image at half the width and height that it appears in a web browser, your computer is probably using an HiDPI (Windows) or Retina (macOS) display. On these displays, try viewing web graphics in Photoshop at 200% magnification to match the size displayed in a web browser.

This happens because Retina/HiDPI displays typically have twice (2x) the pixel density (in dots per inch, or DPI) of older 1x displays, so pixels on those displays are half as wide and tall as on 1x displays. If a website is not specifically coded to handle images at 2x resolution on HiDPI/Retina displays, web browsers typically apply 2x scaling to graphics to prevent them from looking half as large as they should.

Previewing printed dimensions. To show an image on screen at the size that it will print, choose the View > Actual Size command. Actual Size detects the DPI resolution of the display, using that and the document resolution (in pixels per inch, or PPI) to calculate its print size in inches or centimeters.

Print Size. Although the View > Print Size command sounds like it should preview print dimensions, it's an older command that doesn't detect the resolution of the display. It can still be useful for previewing for arbitrary resolutions, but manually setting it up to do that is outside the scope of this book.

Note: Don't use the Actual Size command to preview image dimensions for a web page or mobile app. Actual Size is designed to calculate print dimensions only.

Note: You'll learn more about the difference between dots per inch (DPI) and pixels per inch (PPI) in Lesson 2.

7 Position the pointer anywhere on the canvas, and drag the Zoom tool to the right. The image enlarges from where you started dragging. Drag the Zoom tool to the left to zoom out.

This continuous magnification is called Scrubby Zoom and happens when the Scrubby Zoom setting is enabled in the options bar for the Zoom tool. When the setting is disabled, dragging the Zoom tool first creates a rectangle that indicates the canvas area that will fill the document window.

Note: In this book, any time a step tells you to *drag*, hold down the mouse button as you move the pointer. When you move the pointer without pressing the mouse button, that simply repositions the pointer on the screen.

8   Click Fit Screen in the options bar to see the entire image again.

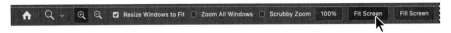

▶ **Tip:** On the View menu you can choose common magnification levels and the Zoom In, Zoom Out, and Fit on Screen commands. If you prefer to use keyboard shortcuts, those are shown next to those commands on the View menu.

As you work through the lessons in this book, feel free to use any combination of the different ways you changed magnification with the Zoom tool, such as clicking, holding down a modifier key while clicking, dragging left or right, and clicking a button in the options bar. You can also zoom using gestures, such as dragging the Zoom tool or pinching with two fingers on a trackpad, and you can enter a magnification percentage in the Status Bar. You also learned how to customize how a tool works by using options bar settings and modifier keys.

Zooming and scrolling with the Navigator panel

The Navigator panel (choose Window > Navigator to open it) is another speedy way to make large changes in the zoom level, especially when the exact percentage of magnification is unimportant. It's also a great way to inspect a magnified image, because the thumbnail shows you exactly what part of the image appears in the document window.

The slider under the image thumbnail in the Navigator panel enlarges the image when you drag to the right (toward the large mountain icon) and reduces it when you drag to the left.

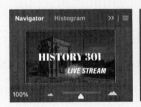 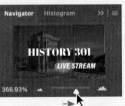

The red rectangular outline represents the area of the image that appears in the document window. When you zoom in far enough that the document window shows only part of the image, you can drag the red outline around the thumbnail area to see other areas of the image. This is also an excellent way to verify which part of an image you're working on when you work at high magnification.

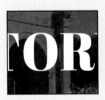 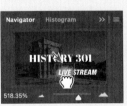 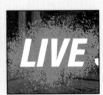

Using the Tools panel

You can save time by using the Tools panel efficiently.

Two-column mode. If the Tools panel is too tall for your display, click the double arrows at the top of the Tools panel to switch it to two-column mode.

Single-key shortcuts. Most tools have a single-key shortcut. For example, you can switch to the Move tool by pressing the V key. If a tool has a single-key shortcut, it's shown next to the tool name. Note that single-key shortcuts don't work when you're entering text.

Identifying tools. If you see a tool and want to know its name and single-key short-cut, hover the pointer over it in the Tools panel.

Grouped tools. To save space on your screen, multiple tools can be grouped into one slot in the Tools panel. The Tools panel shows only one of the tools in a group. If you see a small triangle in the lower-right corner of a tool, you know it's a tool group containing other tools that you can't currently see. To see the other tools and select one of them, hold down the mouse button on the visible tool, and in the 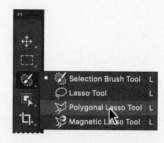 tool menu that pops out, select the tool you want. That tool becomes the visible tool. There are also two shortcuts for cycling through tools in a group:

- Alt-click (Windows) or Option-click (Mac) the visible tool until the tool you want becomes the visible tool.

- Add the Shift key to the single-key shortcut. For example, to cycle through the lasso selection tools, press Shift-L repeatedly.

Rearranging and hiding tools. If you want to arrange or group the tools differently, or to hide tools you never use, hold down the mouse button on the Tools panel ellipsis button (•••) and choose Edit Toolbar.

Include a custom Tools panel in a saved workspace. If you create your own work-space (see "About workspaces" on page 31), one option is Toolbar, which includes changes you make to the Tools panel. For example, in Lesson 10 you switch to the Painting workspace, which changes the Tools panel to put all the brush tools up front, hiding others. When you switch back to the Essentials (Default) workspace, the default Tools panel returns.

Combining elements using layers

There are more elements to add to this project. Next you'll create the colored rectangles. You'll start by creating a new pixel layer for the rectangle.

Creating a new layer

Note: If no layers are selected in the Layers panel, a new layer appears at the top of the layer stack.

Although you could create the colored rectangles directly on the Arch layer, that would permanently replace some of its original pixels. Instead, you'll add the rectangles on a separate layer so you can edit them without altering the Arch layer. For the orange rectangle, you want its layer to be visible in front of the Arch layer. A new layer is added in front of the selected layer, so first you'll select the Arch layer.

1 In the Layers panel, click the Arch layer to select it.

2 In the Layers panel, click the Create a New Layer button (⊞).

3 In the Layers panel, double-click the layer name, change it to **Rectangles**, and press Enter or Return.

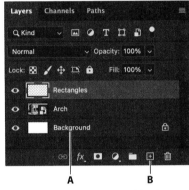

The new layer is now ready for you to fill with color. But first, make sure you're working in the correct unit of measure.

A. *Layer name* **B.** *Create a New Layer*

Setting the unit of measure

Tip: When rulers are displayed (View > Rulers), you can change the unit of measure by right-clicking (Windows) or Control-clicking (macOS) a ruler.

You can change the unit of measure you use to work in Photoshop. This graphic will be displayed on screens, so you'll work in pixels.

1 Choose Edit > Preferences > Units & Rulers (Windows) or Photoshop > Settings > Units & Rulers (macOS).

2 In the Rulers menu under Units, make sure Pixels is selected, and click OK.

Note: In macOS 12 or earlier, the Settings command is called Preferences.

Tip: If you can't remember where to find a preference setting, look for it using the Search Preferences field in the upper-right corner of the Preferences dialog box, in the title bar.

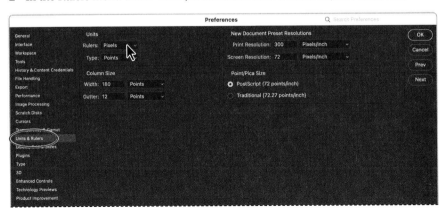

Selecting pixels

The 01End file shows that the orange rectangle covers only a narrow vertical strip along the left edge of the canvas. How will you restrict the color to that area? You'll mark pixels for editing by creating a *selection*. This selection will be a simple rectangle. You'll learn how to quickly create more complex selections, such as outlines of people, in Lessons 2, 3, and 6.

1   In the Tools panel, click the Rectangular Marquee tool to select it.

2   Position the pointer just beyond the upper-left corner of the canvas, and then drag it down and to the right to create a dashed line selection marquee; release the mouse button when the rectangular marquee snaps to the bottom of the canvas and the first vertical cyan guide. At that point, the indicator next to the pointer should report a width (W) of 96 pixels and a height (H) of 1080 pixels.

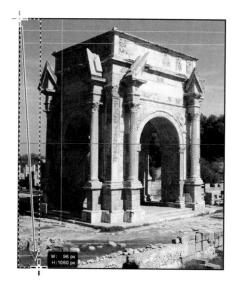

▶ **Tip:** If you hover the pointer over the Rectangular Marquee tool, a tool tip offers a Learn More link, and a button plays a short tutorial video.

A selection can exist only within the canvas, so even though you may have started dragging outside the canvas edges, the final selection is within the canvas edges.

Fill a selection with color

Now you'll complete the rectangle by applying a color fill to the selection.

1   In the Layers panel, make sure the Rectangles layer is selected so that the color you're about to create will be applied to that layer.

2   In the Contextual Task Bar, click the Fill Selection button, and choose Fill Color.

▶ **Tip:** If you want to know the dimensions of a selection after releasing the mouse button, open the Info panel (Window > Info), which displays width (W) and height (H) values for the current selection.

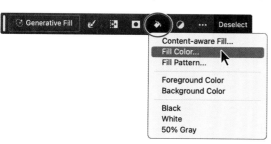

The Fill Selection button is a shortcut for the Edit > Fill command.

3 Create an orange color. We used the hexadecimal (hex) RGB value **ff7f00**, which you can enter into the # field near the bottom of the Color Picker dialog box. Hex color values are commonly used for web and mobile design.

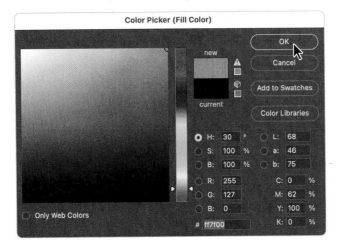

4 Click OK to close the Color Picker dialog box, and then click OK to close the Fill dialog box. The orange color fills the rectangular selection.

> **Tip:** If the selected pixels already had color, pressing the Delete key would remove the color.

5 Choose Select > Deselect, because you no longer need the selection. The selection marquee disappears.

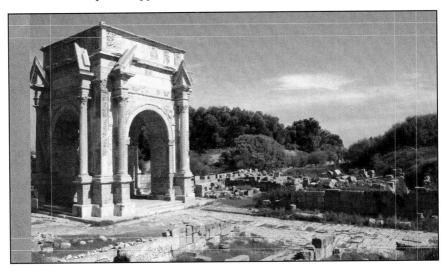

Create the blue rectangle

You'll create the blue rectangle the same way, with different pixel dimensions.

1   With the Rectangular Marquee tool, position the pointer just beyond the upper-right corner of the canvas, and then drag it down and to the left; release the mouse button when the transformation values next to the pointer report a width (W) of 660 pixels and a height (H) of 1080 pixels.

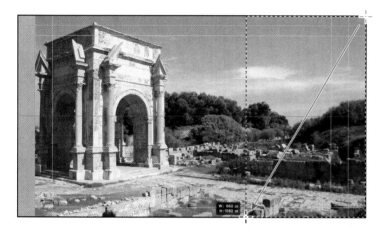

This time you'll open the Fill command using the actual menu command.

2   With the selection active and the Rectangles layer selected, choose Edit > Fill.

3   Click the Contents menu and choose Color, and then create a vivid blue color. We used the hexadecimal RGB value **0053b2**.

4   Click OK to close the Color Picker dialog box, and then click OK to close the Fill dialog box. The blue color fills the rectangular selection.

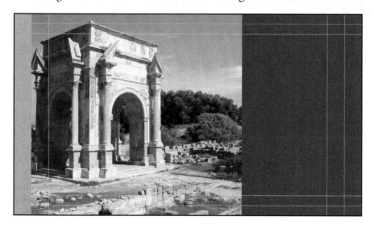

5   Choose Select > Deselect, and choose File > Save. Click OK in the Photoshop Format Options dialog box.

In the 01End file, you'll notice that the colors are not solid; the image shows through them. *Blending modes* are used to control how colors in the Rectangles layer combine with colors in underlying layers.

● **Note:** A layer's blending mode is separate from its opacity value, which you see next to the blending mode menu in the Layers panel. You can apply one or both.

6   In the Layers panel, make sure the Rectangles layer is selected, and choose Color from the blending modes menu.

The Color blending mode combines the hue and saturation values of the Rectangles layer with the luminance of the layers under it. You'll learn more about blending modes in Lesson 4. Feel free to try other blending modes.

Adding type

● **Note:** If a lesson in this book uses a font that isn't installed on your system, you may be able to install it from Adobe Fonts as part of your Creative Cloud subscription: In Photoshop, choose Type > More from Adobe Fonts. (Some educational or organizational Creative Cloud plans might not include Adobe Fonts.)

You'll need to add two lines of type to this graphic. Photoshop offers high-quality typographic tools; you'll learn more about them in Lesson 7. Type exists on its own layer. You'll set up the type specifications for the first type layer you'll add.

1   In the Tools panel, select the Horizontal Type tool (**T**).

The buttons and menus in the options bar now relate to the Type tool.

2   In the options bar, select a font from the first pop-up menu. We used Abril Fatface, which is available from Adobe Fonts, but you can select a different font.

3   Specify **210 pt** for the font size.

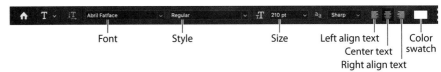

Font   Style   Size   Left align text   Color
                                           Center text   swatch
                                           Right align text

You can specify 210 points by typing directly in the font-size text box and pressing Enter or Return or by *scrubbing* the font-size menu label (see the tip in the margin). Scrubbing works with most labels for values in Photoshop panels. You can make the value change faster by holding down the Shift key as you drag.

Tip: To scrub a value, position the pointer over its label and drag horizontally.

4   In the options bar, click the Center Text button.

5   In the options bar, click the color swatch, specify solid white, and click OK.

6   Click the Horizontal Type tool slightly below the center of the canvas.

Tip: You can also change font size in the Character panel, and in the Contextual Task Bar when a type layer is selected.

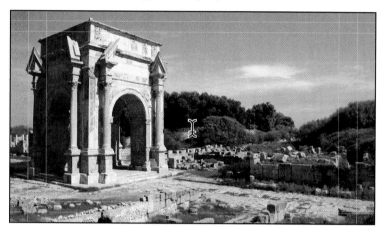

Tip: If you want to select just some of the text in a layer, drag the Horizontal Type tool over a range of characters.

A new type layer appears both on the canvas and in the Layers panel, with "Lorem Ipsum..." placeholder text selected so that you can preview the current settings. In the 01End file, this text is all capital letters, but instead of typing it that way, you can apply a type option.

7   If the Properties panel is not visible, click its tab or choose Window > Properties, scroll it down to the Type Options section, and click the first option, All Caps.

8   With the type still selected, type **History 301**. Because you applied the All Caps option, you don't need to use the Shift or Caps Lock keys.

Tip: The Properties panel shows type options because a type layer is selected in the Layers panel. You can also apply detailed type settings using the Character panel (Window > Character) and the Paragraph panel (Window > Paragraph).

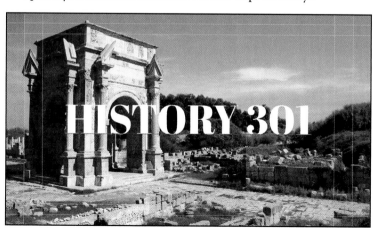

9 In the options bar, click the check mark button (✓) to commit editing the text.

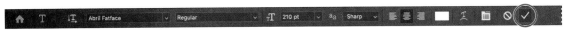

Tip: As you drag the Move tool, magenta lines called *Smart Guides* may appear. They help align the edges and centers of dragged content to other objects and guides. If they are getting in your way, you can disable them by deselecting the View > Show > Smart Guides command or by holding down the Control key as you drag.

10 If the type layer is not centered properly, drag it with the Move tool to center it.

Now add the other line of text.

11 Choose Select > Deselect Layers so that the options you set next don't affect the existing type layer.

12 Make sure the Horizontal Type tool is selected, and then in the options bar, select a font. We used Acumin Pro Condensed Black Italic (also available from Adobe Fonts), but you can select a different font.

13 In the options bar, specify **165 pt** for the font size, and in the options bar, click the Right Align Text button.

14 With the Horizontal Type tool, position the pointer at the inner vertical guide near the right edge of the canvas, click about two-thirds of the distance from the existing line of type and the bottom of the canvas, and type **Live Stream**. It should appear in all capital letters because the All Caps setting you applied in step 7 should still be in effect (if not, apply it).

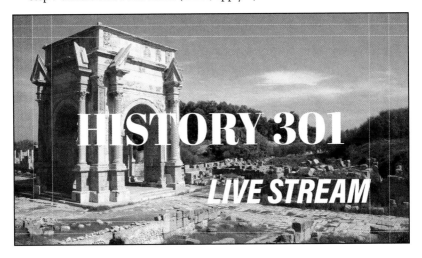

Tip: Another way to deselect a layer is clicking away from the layer, but before you click, move the pointer far enough that it's changed to a black arrow *without* the four-headed move arrows next to it.

15 In the options bar, click the check mark button (✓) to commit editing the text.

Great job so far! But there's a little more to do. The white type is difficult to read against the lighter tones of the image, and that's why the 01End file shows a dark green color across the image. You'll add that next.

Adding a solid color layer

You could fill a layer with green the same way you did earlier to create the rectangles, but now you'll quickly add a layer of solid color using a different method that lets you easily edit the color later.

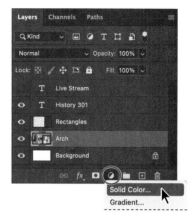

Tip: To edit a Solid Color fill layer later, simply double-click the layer's thumbnail in the Layers panel.

1 In the Layers panel, select the Arch layer so the next layer is created above it.

2 Click the Create New Fill or Adjustment Layer button at the bottom of the Layers panel, and choose Solid Color.

3 In the Color Picker, specify a dark green color; we used the hex RGB value **0c3303**. Click OK.

4 In the Layers panel, with the new Color Fill 1 layer selection, choose Hard Light from the blending mode menu. To lower the effect a little, next to the blending mode menu, change the layer Opacity value to 90%.

5 If the cyan guides are showing, choose View > Show > Guides to deselect it, hiding the guides. You won't need them for the rest of the lesson.

Layer blending mode   Layer opacity percentage

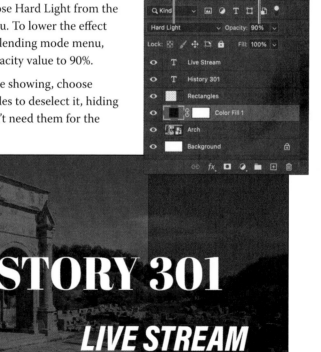

Using panels

Photoshop presents many important features in panels. If you can't find the panel you want, you can open it by choosing its name from the Window menu. To save space, less commonly used panels are hidden by default, and other panels are organized by grouping and docking.

Grouped panels. When panels are *grouped*, you see only the frontmost panel in the group. Panels behind it are indicated by a row of tabs across the top of the group, similar to tabbed documents or web pages. To bring forward a panel in a group, click its tab.

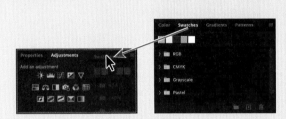 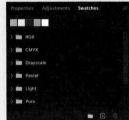

Docked panels. When panels are *docked*, they're joined at one or more edges, for example, side by side or as a vertical column.

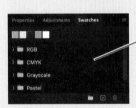 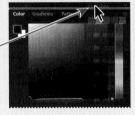 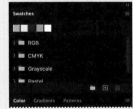

To add a panel to others, drag its tab over another panel or group, and release the mouse button when a blue line appears around the destination panel (to group) or along a panel edge (to dock). To move them, drag the bar across the top of the panels. To remove a panel from a panel group or docked panels, drag its tab away; now it's a *floating* panel. To resize a panel, drag an edge.

Docking to the application frame. To dock panels or a panel group to an edge of the Photoshop application frame, drag a panel tab or tab bar over the left, right, or bottom edge of the application frame, and release the mouse button when a blue line appears along that edge. Panel groups and the Tools panel can dock to the left and right edges, and the options bar can dock to the top edge.

Collapsing and expanding panels. To keep a panel available but free up space, collapse it by double-clicking its tab; expand it the same way. You can collapse or expand panels horizontally: Click the double arrows in the bar across the top of a panel. You can drag the side of collapsed panels inward to collapse it to icons only. In the default Essentials workspace, the inner docked panel group is collapsed to icons, and the outer group is fully expanded.

You can hide and show all panels by pressing the Tab key. When hidden this way, reveal panels docked to the left or right edge by positioning the pointer at that edge.

About workspaces

A workspace is a saved panel arrangement. Photoshop provides a number of built-in workspaces under the Window > Workspace menu. So far, you've been using the Essentials (Default) workspace. In some lessons in this book, you'll use a different workspace.

If you've arranged panels the way that you want, you can save it by choosing Window > Workspace > New Workspace. This adds it to the Window > Workspace menu.

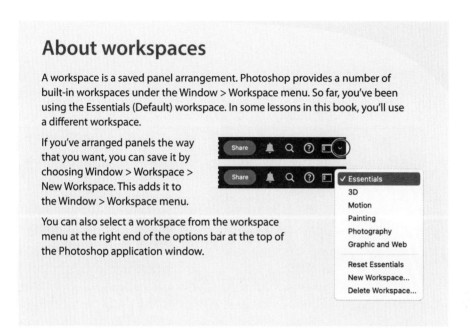

You can also select a workspace from the workspace menu at the right end of the options bar at the top of the Photoshop application window.

Painting a graphic element

The design for the 01End file includes a splash of color to help emphasize the word "Live." You'll create this by painting it with the Brush tool. First you'll set up the color.

Sampling a color

Photoshop maintains a *foreground color* and *background color*. Most of the time you'll pay attention to the foreground color, which is often the default color and is used to load a brush. The background color is used when a secondary color is needed. For example, the background color can be a second color for multi-color effects such as gradients, or the color that's revealed when you erase on the Background layer.

By default, the foreground color is black, and the background color is white. You can change the foreground and background colors by clicking their icons in the Tools panel. If you want to use a color that's already in the document, you can simply sample it with the Eyedropper tool, which loads it as the foreground color. You'll use that method to create a color based on the blue already in this document.

Tip: You can reset the foreground and background colors using the keyboard: To reset to default colors, press D. To exchange them, press X.

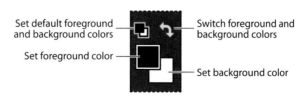

Set default foreground and background colors — Switch foreground and background colors — Set foreground color — Set background color

Note: If you have trouble finding the Eyedropper tool, click the Search icon near the top-right corner of the workspace, and type **eyedropper**. Click Eyedropper Tool in the search results; the tool will be selected in the Tools panel for you.

1   Select the Eyedropper tool (🖋) in the Tools panel.

2   With the Eyedropper tool, click a lighter blue area to sample a blue color.

3   In the Color panel (Window > Color), brighten the blue color for better contrast with the area under the word "Live." We used the hex RGB value **4099ff**; to enter this in the Color Panel choose Web Color Sliders from the Color panel menu.

▶ **Tip:** The Color panel and the Color Picker dialog box are alternate ways to set the foreground or background color. For step 3, you could instead open the Color Picker dialog box by clicking the foreground color swatch in the Tools panel.

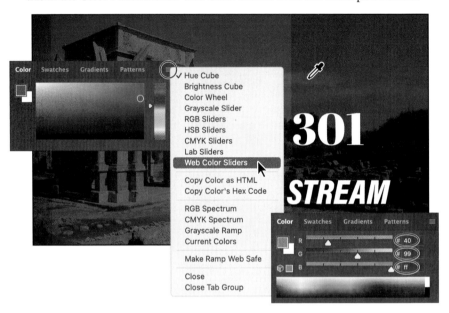

The foreground color changes in the Tools panel and the Color panel. Anything you paint will be this color until you change the foreground color again.

Painting with a brush

With the foreground color set, you can now paint. But first you'll create and name a layer to paint on, in the appropriate position in the layer stacking order.

1   In the Layers panel select the Rectangles layer, and then hold down Alt (Windows) or Option (macOS) as you click the Create a New Layer button (⊞).

That modifier key lets you name a layer as you create it, saving a step.

2   In the New Layer dialog box, for Name enter **Paint**, and click OK.

3   Select the Brush tool (🖌) in the Tools panel.

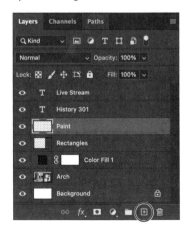

4 Choose Window > Brushes to open the Brushes panel. It may expand from a collapsed panel stack.

The Brushes panel contains brush presets, some of which are organized into groups (folders). Photoshop offers many types of brushes, from basic round and flat brushes to highly textured effects brushes. You'll use a brush that creates spattered paint.

5 In the Brushes panel, expand the Special Effects Brushes group, and select the first brush, Kyle's Spatter Brushes - Spatter Bot Tilt.

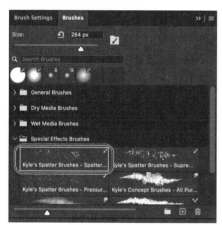

Tip: The Brushes panel stores brush presets. To make detailed changes to the current brush, use the Brush Settings panel (Window > Brush Settings). You'll learn more about brushes in Lesson 10.

6 Drag the Brush tool across the word "Live" to paint a few strokes, building up the spatter effect. The brush strokes may not match the size or shape of the spot in the 01End file, but you'll soon redo it, so don't be concerned about it for now.

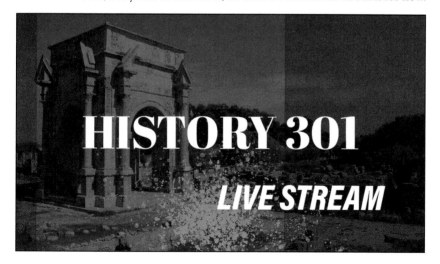

The brush strokes appear behind the word "Live." That's because you're painting on the Paint layer, which is behind the Live Stream text layer.

Tip: To rearrange the layer stacking order, simply drag layers up and down in the Layers panel.

Undoing and redoing steps

The Undo command is one of the greatest things about a computer: You can easily back out of a mistake. Photoshop offers three Undo/Redo commands, making it easier to experiment and do before/after comparisons. In this case, you'll undo the brush strokes you made so that you can do them over.

Tip: The keyboard shortcut for Edit > Undo is Ctrl+Z (Windows) or Command+Z (macOS). For Edit > Redo, it's Ctrl+Shift+Z (Windows) or Command+Shift+Z (macOS).

1 Choose Edit > Undo Brush Tool.

If you painted multiple brush strokes, you may have to repeat step 1 until they're all undone. If you need to repeat step 1, stop when the Undo command says Undo New Layer, because you don't want to undo that step.

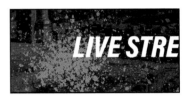

Tip: To see the steps you can undo and redo, look at the History panel (Window > History).

If you want to restore steps you undid, you can choose the command Edit > Redo Brush Tool, but you don't need to do that for this lesson. The Edit > Redo command is available until you perform a new step, because that starts a different history from that point, replacing all existing Redo steps.

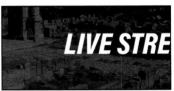

Now you'll paint another brush stroke after adjusting the brush size. Although you could do this using the Brush Settings panel where all brush settings are available, for quick access you'll use the Brush tool options bar.

Tip: Another shortcut for opening the Brush Presets picker is to right-click (Windows) or Control-click (macOS) the canvas when the Brush tool is selected.

2 With the Brush tool selected, in the options bar click the arrow next to the Brush Presets picker, set the Size to **80**, and click away from the brush picker to close it.

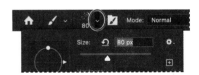

3 With the Paint layer selected, position the pointer over the Live text, and drag in a circular pattern to build up the brush stroke as a large spot behind the word.

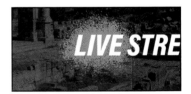

Now you'll quickly compare the layer state before and after the last step.

4 Choose Edit > Toggle Last State, look at the canvas, and then choose Edit > Toggle Last State again. Your painting step was undone and redone.

If you think you'll often use this, consider developing the habit of pressing the keyboard shortcut for the Toggle Last State command, because that's easier than repeatedly choosing its menu command with the mouse: Press Ctrl+Alt+Z (Windows) or Command+Option+Z (macOS).

5 Save the document.

About presets panels

As you work on more projects with Photoshop, you may find that you use certain graphics elements repeatedly, such as color swatches. Presets panels let you save your favorites for quick access and organize them. Presets panels include the Swatches, Gradients, Patterns, and Shapes panels.

To apply a preset, drag a preset from the panel, and drop it on a layer on the canvas. Or, select a layer, and then click a preset in a presets panel. The Shapes panel is an exception because it doesn't contain attributes, it contains graphics; so you drag one onto the canvas where it becomes a new layer.

Presets panels have common features.

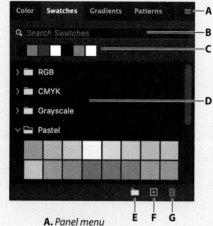

A. *Panel menu*
B. *Search field*
C. *Recently used presets*
D. *Presets list*
E. *Create a New Group button*
F. *Create a New Preset button*
G. *Delete Preset button*

Customizable. Options for viewing and managing presets, including some of the following options, are available on a presets panel menu.

Searchable. The first item in a presets panel is a search field so that you can search preset names.

Recents. The row under the search field lists recent presets you've applied, which is convenient if you want to continue applying presets you recently used.

List or thumbnail. You can display presets as a list with names, or as thumbnail icons, using thumbnail and list commands in the panel menu. When you see a preset displayed as a thumbnail, you can find out its name by hovering the mouse pointer over it.

Groups. You can organize presets into groups (folders) by dragging them in and out of groups in the panel. To create a new group, click the Create a New Group button at the bottom of a presets panel.

Import/export. A presets panel menu includes commands for importing and exporting presets, so that you can back them up separately, share them, or copy them to other computers.

Extending an image

The document now looks similar to the 01End lesson file. But there's one big difference: The photo of the arch is too far to the left. The composition would be more visually balanced if the Arch layer was moved closer to the center.

1   Select the Move tool, and in the options bar, deselect Auto-Select.

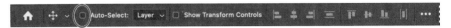

Auto-Select is often useful because it lets you select a layer by clicking it on the canvas. But that isn't useful for this step, because you want to move the Arch layer that is behind other layers. If Auto-Select is enabled, the Move tool will select one of the layers in front of the Arch layer. That's why you deselected Auto-Select. But when Auto-Select is disabled, you must manually select a layer.

2   In the Layers panel, select the Arch layer.

3   Position the Move tool over the canvas, and drag the Arch layer until it's centered within the green area.

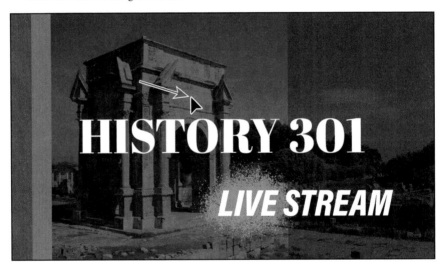

This looks better, except that when the arch is centered, the image does not extend to the left enough to cover the canvas. You can have Photoshop create content that fills that area using Generative Fill, an AI-powered feature. That will be easier if you hide all other layers first.

4 Hold down the Alt (Windows) or Option (macOS) key as you click the eye icon for the Arch layer in the Layers panel to hide all layers except Arch. Now you need to tell Photoshop which area to fill with generated content.

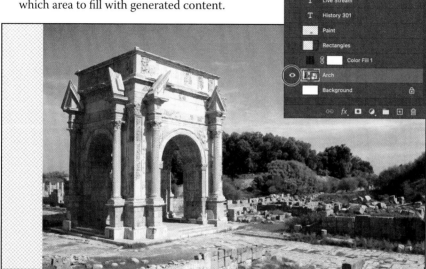

5 Select the Rectangular Marquee tool, and drag to create a selection marquee that covers all of the empty area between the left edge of the canvas and the left edge of the Arch layer; overlap the Arch layer slightly to ensure there won't be a gap.

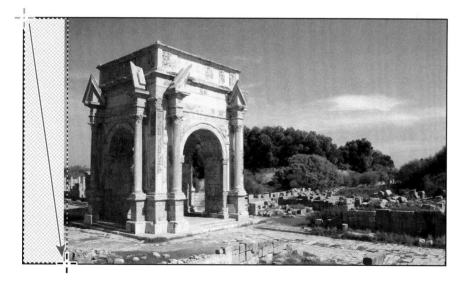

Note: Generative Fill can create almost any type of image. Adobe requires you to agree to the Generative Fill User Guidelines so that you agree to use the feature to generate images that are within the guidelines, and not images that are harmful, deceptive, or illegal.

6 In the Contextual Task Bar, click Generative Fill. The options on the bar change.

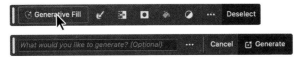

An empty text field appears in the Contextual Task Bar. It's there so that you can type a description of what you want to generate, but to simply fill the selection with content consistent with the existing image, leave it blank and continue.

7 Make sure the Arch layer is selected in the Layers panel, and then in the Contextual Task Bar, click Generate. If a message appears asking you to read and agree to the Generative Fill User Guidelines, click Agree when you're ready.

When it finishes, you'll see three new things:

- On the canvas, the empty selection is replaced with new content.

- In the Layers panel, a new Generative Fill layer was created above the Arch layer. This contains the new content so that it doesn't alter the original layer.

Note: If you don't see the Variations section, it may be out of view, especially on a smaller display. Try scrolling the Properties panel to bring the Variations panel up and into view.

- In the Properties panel, a Variations section offers alternatives you can click to try. The selected variation is the one you see on the canvas.

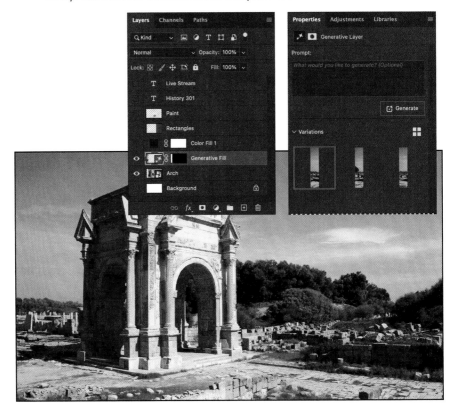

Note: When using Generative Fill, consider how the image will be used. As a graphic design illustration, it may not be important that the generated content doesn't exactly match the actual site. But if this image is intended to be used for news or reference (such as for historical research), don't include content that never actually existed.

8 In the Layers panel, right-click (Windows) or Control-click (macOS) the eye icon for the Generative Fill layer, and choose Show/Hide All Other Layers.

Now you can see how the content looks in the context of the total composition.

9 In the Properties panel, click each variation and select the one you like the most.

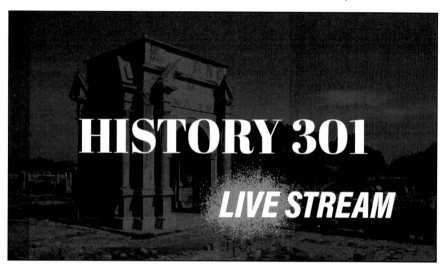

Exporting a copy for delivery

Now it's time to export a copy of this image as a thumbnail preview of the video it represents, to be uploaded to a video streaming service. For this lesson, let's suppose that a particular streaming service requires the following for thumbnail previews:

* Pixel dimensions: At least 1280 × 720 pixels.

* File format: JPEG or PNG.

* The file size of the image should be less than 2 megabytes.

In Photoshop, you can meet all of those requirements in one step. There's more than one way to do it in Photoshop; for this lesson you'll use the Export As command.

1 Choose File > Export > Export As.

In the Export As dialog box:

* The left pane previews the filename, file format, pixel dimensions, and file size of the exported copy. The reason you see "Scale All" and "Select All" is because Export As can export multiple images from a single document, but in this case you're exporting one image.

* The middle pane previews the image itself.

* The right pane lets you change export settings.

Note: Requirements for submitted images aren't the same on all services and social media sites, so before exporting a copy for upload, research the specific requirements for the service you're about to upload to.

Note: You'll use Export As to export multiple images from a single document in Lesson 12.

2 In File Settings in the right pane, set Format to JPG and Quality to 6, if they aren't already set that way.

3 In Image Size, set Width to 1280, and then apply the value by clicking outside the field or by pressing the Tab key. The Height automatically changes to 720 because Export As scales proportionally.

These adjustments ensure that the exported copy will meet the minimum submission requirements.

4 For Color Space, make sure Convert to sRGB and Embed Color Profile are enabled. These settings aren't stated in the submission requirements, but they help ensure consistent color across media.

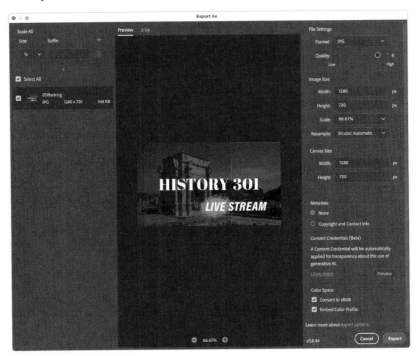

Notice that the left pane reports how your settings in the right pane affect the exported copy: The pixel dimensions are now 1280 × 720; and the file size is now under 350KB, safely within the 2MB file size limit. The preview in the middle updates to represent the resized pixel dimensions.

> **Tip:** If you want to verify the file format, dimensions, file size, and other properties of the copy after it's exported (it's named 01Working.jpg), you can inspect that file on your computer desktop or using Adobe Bridge.

5 Click Export, navigate to the Lesson01 folder, and click Save.

Congratulations! You've completed the graphic for the live stream by learning the basics of combining images, text, painted brush strokes, and other layers to create a composite Photoshop document, and you've exported a copy for delivery.

6 Close the document; if you are alerted to unsaved changes, click Save. If you left the 01End file open, close it without saving changes.

Review questions

1 Describe at least two types of images you can open or add to a document.

2 How do you select tools in Photoshop?

3 Describe two ways to zoom in to or out from an image.

4 How would you reverse the most recent change you made?

5 What are some ways to make panels use less space on your screen?

Review answers

1 You can use a photograph from a digital camera. You can also use a scanned image of a photographic print, a transparency or negative film frame, or a graphic. You can use images downloaded from the internet such as photography from Adobe Stock, or images uploaded to your Cloud Documents or your Lightroom photos. You can also create an image using Adobe Firefly generative AI.

2 To select a tool in Photoshop, click its icon in the Tools panel, or press the tool's keyboard shortcut. A selected tool remains active until you select a different tool. To select a hidden tool, either use a keyboard shortcut to toggle through the tools or click and hold the tool in the Tools panel to open a pop-up menu of the hidden tools.

3 Choose commands from the View menu to zoom in on or out from an image or to fit it onscreen, or use the zoom tools and click or drag over an image to enlarge or reduce the view. You can also use keyboard shortcuts or the Navigator panel to control the display of an image.

4 Choose Edit > Undo or Edit > Toggle Last State, or press its keyboard shortcut. (Another correct answer is to choose an earlier document state in the History panel, although that was not shown in this lesson.)

5 You can use any combination of grouping and docking panels together, collapsing them, or hiding them.

2 BASIC PHOTO CORRECTIONS

Lesson overview

In this lesson, you'll learn how to do the following:

- Understand image resolution and size.
- View and open files using Adobe Bridge.
- Straighten and crop an image.
- Adjust the tonal range of an image.
- Delete unwanted or distracting items using the Remove tool.
- Replace a large deleted area using Generative Fill.
- Apply the Smart Sharpen filter to finish retouching photos.

This lesson will take about an hour to complete. To get the lesson files used in this chapter, download them from the web page for this book at peachpit.com/PhotoshopCIB2025. For more information, see "Accessing the lesson files and Web Edition" in the Getting Started section at the beginning of this book.

As you work on this lesson, you'll preserve the start files. If you need to restore the start files, download them from your Account page.

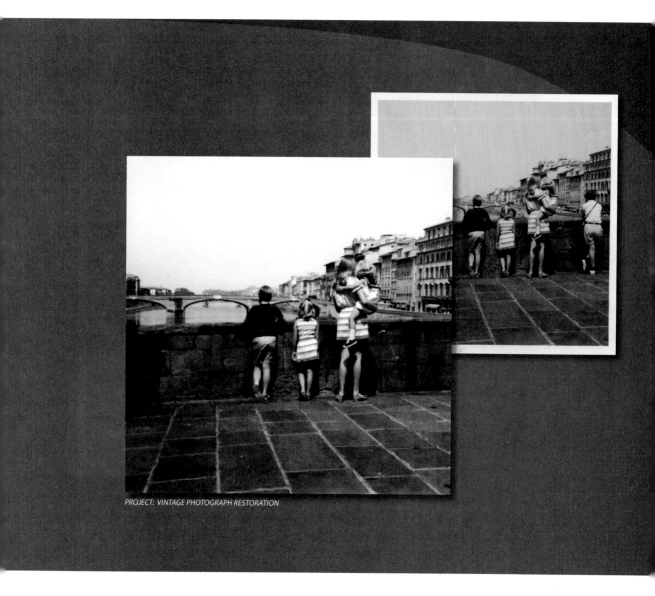

PROJECT: VINTAGE PHOTOGRAPH RESTORATION

Photoshop includes a variety of tools and commands
for improving the quality of a photographic image.
This lesson steps you through the process of cropping,
resizing, and retouching a vintage photograph.

Opening a file with Adobe Bridge

● **Note:** In this lesson, you retouch an image using Photoshop. For some images, such as those captured in camera raw format, it may be more efficient to edit in Adobe Camera Raw, which is installed with Photoshop. You'll learn about the tools Camera Raw has to offer in Lesson 12, "Working with Camera Raw."

For each lesson in this book, you can perform the steps using a specific folder of files. You may make copies of these files and save them under different names or locations, or you may work from the original files and then download them from the peachpit.com website again if you want a fresh start.

In this lesson, you'll retouch a scan of a damaged and discolored vintage photograph so it can be shared online, or printed 7 × 7 inches at 300 ppi.

In Lesson 1, you used the Open command to open a file. You'll start this lesson by comparing the original scan to the finished image in Adobe Bridge, a visual file browser that integrates with Photoshop and other Creative Cloud applications.

1 Start Photoshop, and then simultaneously hold down Ctrl+Alt+Shift (Windows) or Command+Option+Shift (macOS) to reset the default settings.

2 When prompted, click Yes to confirm that you want to delete the Adobe Photoshop Settings file.

● **Note:** If Bridge isn't installed, the File > Browse in Bridge command in Photoshop will start the Creative Cloud desktop app, which will download and install Bridge. After installation completes, you can start Bridge.

3 Choose File > Browse In Bridge. If you're prompted to enable the Photoshop extension in Bridge, click Yes or OK.

Adobe Bridge opens, displaying a collection of panels, menus, and buttons.

4 Select the Folders tab in the upper-left corner, and then browse to the Lessons folder you downloaded to your computer so that the lessons in the Lessons folder appear in the Content panel.

● **Note:** If Bridge asks you if you want to import preferences from a previous version of Bridge, select Don't Show Again, and click No.

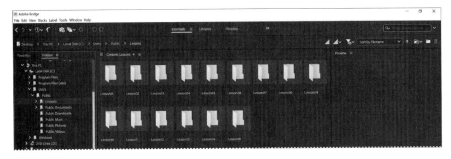

▶ **Tip:** In Bridge, if the Favorites panel list and a folder you want to add to Favorites are both visible, you can drag the folder and drop it in the Favorites panel. You can even drag and drop to add a folder from your computer desktop to the Favorites panel.

5 With the Lessons folder still selected in the Folders panel, choose File > Add To Favorites.

The Favorites panel lets you quickly access files, folders, applications, and other assets that you frequently use.

6 Click the Favorites tab to open the panel, and click the Lessons folder to open it. Then, in the Content panel, double-click the Lesson02 folder.

Thumbnail previews of the folder contents appear in the Content panel.

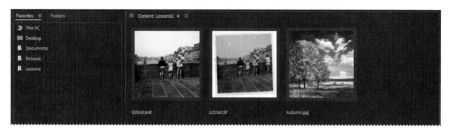

7 Compare the 02Start.tif and 02End.psd files. To enlarge the thumbnails in the Content panel, drag the thumbnail slider at the bottom of the Bridge window to the right.

In the 02Start.tif file, notice that the image is tilted, the colors are relatively dull, and the image has a green color cast and a distracting crease. You'll fix these problems in this lesson, and a few others.

8 Double-click the 02Start.tif thumbnail to open the file in Photoshop. Click OK if you see the Embedded Profile Mismatch dialog box, and close any messages that might appear about new features.

9 In Photoshop, choose File > Save As. Choose Photoshop from the Format menu, and name the file **02Working.psd**. Then click Save.

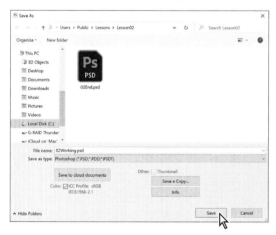

▶ **Tip:** In Bridge, you can see a larger preview of a selected item by using the Preview panel (choose Window > Preview). If that's not big enough, you can resize the Preview panel. Or, press the spacebar to see a full-screen preview of the selected item.

Note: If Photoshop displays a dialog box about the difference between saving to Cloud Documents and On Your Computer, click Save On Your Computer. You can also select Don't Show Again, but that setting will deselect after you reset Photoshop preferences.

Evaluating an image for editing

You can simply jump in and start editing, but it's often more efficient to first look over the image to understand what kind of editing it needs. As you gain experience with more Photoshop features, evaluating an image before editing can help you plan what work needs to be done, and in what order.

In the era when only film photography existed, it was common to make a test print and mark it up to indicate changes to make in a darkroom for the final version. Today, in a Photoshop document, you can add comments by using the Notes tool, add comments online with File > Share for Review, or add layers (that you can hide) to scribble or type on. You'll learn about those features later in the book.

The tasks you do, and in what order, vary depending on the project. It's usually best to correct tone and color first and then repair specific problem areas. The last steps include adjusting the pixel dimensions and sharpening for the final delivery medium. If an image will be used in different media, such as to be printed, shared online, and shown in a video, first edit to create a full-resolution high-quality source image. Then, for specific uses, export copies adjusted for different media.

This image needs straightening, tone and color correction, and some retouching. It's a faded print that was digitized by a family that would like to be able to reprint it 7 inches wide at 300 ppi. First, set up the Status Bar to show document dimensions. This will help you see if the document meets the print size requirement.

1   If the image dimensions aren't already displayed in the status area at the bottom of the application window, click the arrow there and choose Document Dimensions from the pop-up menu that appears.

The Status Bar says this image is 2160 × 2160 pixels at 240 ppi. This image is intended to be printed, so it will be better to set the unit of measure to inches.

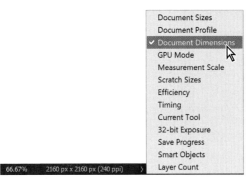

Tip: Another way to change the unit of measure is to right-click (Windows) or Control-click (macOS) the rulers and then choose a unit from the context menu that appears.

2   Choose View > Rulers to enable the Rulers command and display the rulers.

3   Double-click the rulers that appear along the top and left sides of the document window; this opens the Units & Rulers pane in the Preferences dialog box. Choose Inches from the Rulers menu in the Units section, and click OK.

You changed the unit of measure for the document, which affects the rulers and units in many panels and in the Status Bar. The Status Bar now shows that the document is 9 × 9 inches at 240 ppi. (2160 pixels divided by 240 pixels per inch equals 9 inches.)

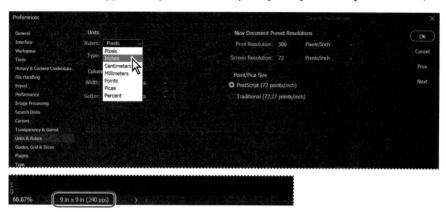

▶ **Tip:** Changing the unit of measure changes the units shown in the Status Bar, in the rulers, in panels, and in the Units/Rulers setting in the Photoshop Preferences dialog box's Units & Rulers pane.

Straightening and cropping the image

You'll start by using the Crop tool, which can also straighten an image.

1 In the Tools panel, select the Crop tool (⌗.). Crop handles appear.

2 In the options bar, choose W × H × Resolution from the Select A Preset Aspect Ratio or Crop Size menu. (Ratio is the default value.) A crop overlay appears.

3 In the options bar, type **7 in** into both the width and height fields, and enter **300** in the px/in field (Resolution).

7 × 7 inches at 300 ppi is fewer total pixels than the original 9 × 9 inches at 240 ppi. To achieve the new smaller dimensions, when you commit the Crop tool edit, pixels will be merged and removed as needed; if you had asked for larger dimensions, it would create new pixels instead. This is called *resampling* the image, and it's necessary when you enter values for resolution and at least one dimension.

▶ **Tip:** If the Crop tool is selected but the crop handles aren't visible, press the Enter or Return key. If they still aren't visible, click the View menu and make sure the Extras command is enabled.

▶ **Tip:** When you crop an image for the web or screens, in the options bar enter the required width and height in pixels (such as **800 px**), and leave the px/in resolution field empty. Inch units and px/in resolution are useful only for print.

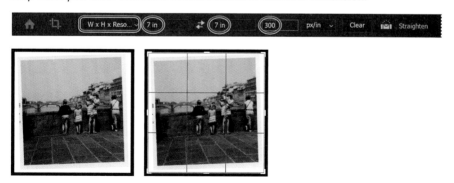

Next, you'll straighten the image.

Understanding image size and resolution

Resolution is a term that has different meanings depending on the medium. For video and electronic displays, resolution means *pixel dimensions*: the width and height of an image in *pixels*, the small squares that describe an image. For example, the resolution of a 4K video frame is 3840 × 2160 pixels. For print, resolution means *pixel density*, such as 300 pixels per inch (ppi).

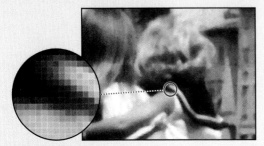

Pixels in a photographic image

In Photoshop, the most common ways to change image pixel dimensions are the Crop tool and the Image > Image Size command. To change pixel density (ppi), when using the Crop tool, enter a value in the Resolution field; or when using Image > Image Size, enable the Resample option.

How do you know how many pixels are in an image?

Multiply the width and height of an image, in pixels. For example, in this lesson you crop an image to 2100 × 2100 pixels, which equals 4,410,000 pixels or 4.41 *megapixels* (one million pixels equals one megapixel). Pixel dimensions affect file size and upload/download time.

How do you know an image's resolution in pixels per inch?

Divide an image's width or height in pixels by its number of inches. For example, if the 2100 × 2100 pixel image in this lesson is set to 7 inches wide, then each dimension is 2100 pixels divided by 7 inches, or 300 pixels per inch.

How much resolution is enough?

The requirements of a delivery medium determine how much resolution an image needs. For example, in video, if an image must fill every pixel of a 4K frame, it must be 3840 × 2160 pixels. For a print job, an image must have enough pixels to print at the required size with the required pixel density. For example, if an image must fill a space 7 inches wide and the production requirement for resolution is 300 ppi, then the image must be at least 2100 pixels wide (7 inches times 300 ppi).

How does physical reproduction size affect resolution?

Changing an image's reproduction size alters its *effective resolution*, because the same number of pixels now cover a smaller or larger area. For example, if you print this lesson's 7-inch wide image at 14 inches wide (double its original width), then its 2100 pixels divided by 14 inches equals 150 ppi.

Its effective resolution was halved because the same number of pixels is spread across twice the width. For this reason, when preparing images for print, knowing that they need to be 300 ppi is not enough. You also need to know at what size in inches each image needs to be 300 ppi.

Viewing distance influences the pixel density our eyes actually perceive, and this affects resolution requirements too. The traditional 300 ppi guideline for print is based on a viewing distance of roughly arm's length, like when you read a book. A very large photo print intended to be seen from several feet away can be printed at lower than 300 ppi, because beyond a certain viewing distance, your eyes see the pixels as dense enough to have a high effective resolution. For the same reason, a 50 ppi image can appear perfectly sharp on a highway billboard because it's seen from hundreds of feet away.

Does image resolution always have to match the resolution of the printer or display?

Because of the way display and output technologies work, an image file might not need to match the resolution of the hardware that reproduces the image. For example, some commercial printing plate-setters and photo-quality inkjet printers have a device resolution of 2400 dots per inch (dpi) or more, but the appropriate image resolution to send to those devices may be only 200 to 360 ppi for photos. This is because the 2400 dpi dots printed by the hardware are grouped into larger halftone cells or dot patterns that build tones and colors. Similarly, a 500-ppi smartphone display may not necessarily require 500-ppi images. Whatever your medium, ask your production team or output service provider to verify the pixel dimensions or ppi value they require in the final images you deliver.

What's considered high resolution?

For images reproduced on screens, one way to currently define *high resolution* is when an image has enough pixels to fill every pixel on a HiDPI (Windows/Android) or Retina (Apple) display. These displays generally have twice the pixel density of older displays.

For print, an image might be considered high resolution when its ppi value is around 240–360 ppi at its final reproduction size, because at that pixel density, it can reproduce enough detail to take advantage of the device resolutions of printing presses and professional photo printers.

Does changing resolution affect the storage size of a file?

Only when the pixel dimensions change. For example, this lesson's image has final pixel dimensions of 2100 × 2100 pixels set to 7 × 7 inches at 300 ppi. If you change either the size in inches or the ppi value (resolution) but keep the pixel dimensions at 2100 × 2100 pixels, the file size does not change. But if you change the size in inches without changing the ppi value (or vice versa), the pixel dimensions must change (this is called *resampling*), which changes the file size. For example, if this lesson's image is changed to 72 ppi while maintaining 7 × 7 inches, the pixel dimensions must change to 504 × 504 pixels, and the file size decreases accordingly.

It's important to remember that file size is determined by more than just the pixel dimensions. The file size of an image can also go up or down depending on its file type, bit depth, number of channels and layers, its compression method (if compressed), and more.

Tip: If you want the document to keep the pixels outside the crop area, deselect Delete Cropped Pixels in the options bar. That will let you reveal previously cropped areas by enlarging the Crop tool rectangle, which is useful if you change your mind later.

4 In the options bar click the Straighten icon. The pointer changes to the Straighten tool.

5 Position the pointer at the top-left corner of the image (where the sky ends), hold down the mouse button and drag to create a straight line following the top edge, and then release the mouse button.

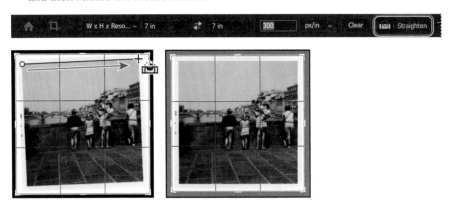

Tip: If you need to see crop edges more clearly, it's OK to change the view magnification while the crop rectangle is active.

Photoshop rotates the image using the angle at which you dragged the Straighten tool. In general, when you see something in an image that should be perfectly vertical or horizontal, such as the edge of a building, drag the Straighten tool along that.

A *crop shield* now dims the area outside the crop handles; it helps more clearly indicate what areas will be trimmed.

6 Drag the corners of the crop rectangle inward to crop out the white border. If you need to adjust the position of the photo inside the crop, position the pointer within the crop rectangle and drag the photo.

7 Press Enter or Return to apply the crop.

Tip: The Crop tool will continue to create a 7 × 7 inch, 300 ppi crop as long as those are the current options bar settings. If you want to crop with total freedom by resetting those options, click the Clear button in the Crop tool options bar.

The image was cropped, straightened, and resampled by the Crop tool options. The Status Bar should now show that the image is 7 × 7 in at 300 ppi.

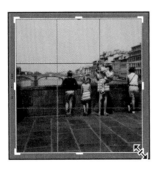
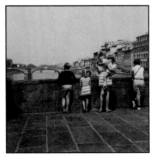

8 Choose File > Save to save your work. Click OK if you see the Photoshop Format Options dialog box.

9 You're done cropping, so in the Tools panel, select the Move tool.

Correcting tone and color

You'll use Curves and Levels adjustment layers to remove the color cast and adjust the color and tone in the image. The Curves or Levels options are powerful and may look complex, but don't be intimidated. Here you'll use them in a quick and easy way to brighten and adjust the tone of the image, you'll explore them more later.

1   In the Adjustments panel, scroll down to the Single Adjustments category. If it's collapsed, click the arrow to expand it, and click Curves. This adds a Curves adjustment layer; its controls appear in the Properties panel.

2   Select the White Point tool on the left side of the Properties panel.

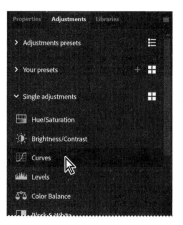 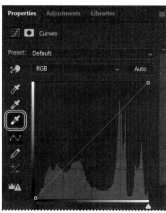

The White Point tool defines what color value should be made a neutral white. Once defined, all other colors and tones shift accordingly. This is a quick way to remove a color cast and correct image brightness. To properly set the white point, click an area of the image that should be the brightest neutral area of the image that contains detail—not a blown-out area like the sun or a lamp and not a specular highlight such as a reflection of sunlight on chrome.

3   Click a white stripe on the girl's dress to use it as the sample for white balancing.

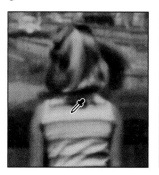 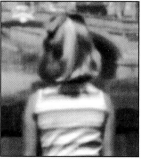

The White Point tool shifts color balance and brightness based on how different the sampled color is from neutral white; clicking another area may produce a different correction. The image looks sunny again, removing the color shift introduced by age-related print fading.

> **Note:** The color and tone edits in this lesson are relatively basic; it's possible to do them all using only Levels or Curves. For example, you can use the color balance eyedroppers and set the tonal range in both. Typically, the reason to use Curves is for a more precise or complex adjustment.

> **Tip:** On your own, experiment with the presets categories at the top of the Adjustments panel. They're useful for quick fixes, and you can learn how they're done by inspecting the layer group each preset adds to the document. In the Your Presets section, you can save adjustment layer combinations that you want to reuse in other documents.

> **Tip:** If you want to know the color values of the pixels that the pointer is positioned over, they're displayed in the Info panel (Window > Info).

Now you'll use a Levels adjustment layer to refine the tonal range of the image.

Tip: Settings for an adjustment layer are always in the Properties panel. The more you use adjustment layers (they're used three times in this lesson), the more you'll want the Properties panel to be open all the time in your Photoshop workspace.

4 In the Adjustments panel (if needed, click its tab to make it visible), in the Single Adjustments category click Levels (▟) to add a Levels adjustment layer.

For both Curves and Levels, the Properties panel displays a *histogram*—a graph displaying the distribution of tonal values in the image, from black on the left to white on the right. For Levels, the left triangle under the histogram represents the black point (the tonal level you want to set as the darkest in the image), the right triangle represents the white point (the tonal level you want to set as the lightest in the image), and the middle triangle represents the midtones.

5 Under the histogram, drag the left triangle (black point) to the right, and release it where the histogram indicates that significant shadow tones start to appear. Our value was **15**. All tones less than 15 become black.

Tip: If you're not sure what adjustments to make, try selecting a preset from the Presets menu near the top of the Properties panel. You'll see both how a preset changes the image, and what changes in the Properties panel created that look. This might help you decide how you want to change the settings.

6 Drag the middle triangle to the right to adjust the midtones. Our value was **.90**.

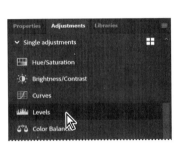
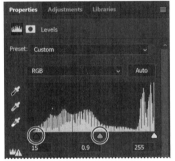

Note: Flattening also removes content preserved beyond the visible edge of the canvas. For example, if you used the Crop tool with the Delete Cropped Pixels option disabled, flattening removes the hidden pixels that the Crop tool preserved.

Now you'll *flatten* the image, which merges all layers into one Background layer. It's common to avoid flattening until you no longer need the flexibility of adjusting edits made using separate layers; many advanced Photoshop users flatten only the copy that's handed off to a client. If you're just getting started with Photoshop, flattening at this step makes it easier to work during the next phase, retouching.

7 Choose Layer > Flatten Image.

The appearance of the image did not change, and the Layers panel now shows only the Background layer.

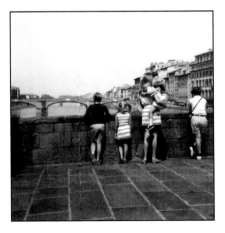

Repairing a damaged image

The next task is to repair surface damage that was on the original print. Photoshop offers a range of tools that can quickly remove blemishes and other imperfections, making a repair look consistent in content, tone, and color with the rest of the image. You'll try two of those tools: the Spot Healing Brush tool and the Remove tool.

1   In the Tools panel, select the Spot Healing Brush tool (🩹).

2   In the options bar, open the Brush pop-up panel, specify a brush with a Size of about **25** px and **100%** Hardness, and make sure Content-Aware is selected.

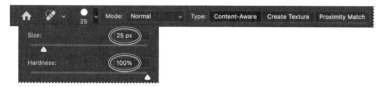

3   Zoom in to see the white hair in the upper-right area of the image.

4   In the document window, drag the Spot Healing Brush over the hair; when you release the mouse, the pixels where you dragged are "healed." If it's easier to repair the hair with multiple shorter strokes, that's OK.

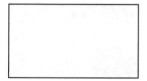  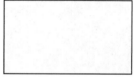

▶ **Tip:** When dragging any retouching tool, cover an area not much larger than the part you're trying to remove. Covering too large of an area might make a retouch more obvious.

5   In the sky, click the Spot Healing Brush wherever there are unwanted dust or dirt spots you want to heal. If needed, zoom in or out to see defects more clearly.

Next, you'll repair the long crease that runs through the image. You could use the Spot Healing Brush tool for this, but you'll try the more advanced Remove tool.

6   Zoom into the top half of the image to clearly see the vertical crease in the sky.

7   In the Tools panel, click and hold the mouse button on the Spot Healing Brush tool (🩹) to reveal the other retouching tools in its tool group, and select the Remove tool (🩹). If a message appears asking you to read and agree to the Generative AI User Guidelines, click Agree when you're ready.

8   In the options bar, set a brush Size of about **25** px, and make sure Remove After Each Stroke is selected.

▶ **Tip:** The Photo Restoration filter can reduce the amount of manual retouching that's needed. Choose Filter > Neural Filters, enable Photo Restoration, and adjust options. For black-and-white photos, Neural Filters also include a Colorize filter.

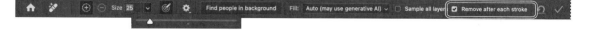

As owner of Gawain Weaver Art Conservation, Gawain Weaver has conserved and restored original works by artists ranging from Eadweard Muybridge to Man Ray and from Ansel Adams to Cindy Sherman. He teaches workshops internationally as well as online on the care and identification of photographs.

Find out more at gawainweaver.com.

Real-world photo restoration

The tools in Photoshop make restoration of old or damaged photographs seem like magic, giving virtually anyone the power to scan, retouch, print, and frame their photo collections.

However, when dealing with works by famous artists, museums, galleries, and collectors need to preserve original objects to the greatest degree possible despite deterioration or accidental damage. Professional art conservators are called upon to clean dust and soiling from print surfaces, remove discoloration and staining, repair tears, stabilize prints to prevent future damage, and even paint in missing areas of a work.

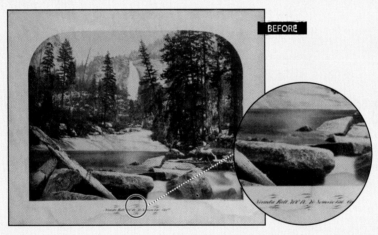

Carleton E. Watkins, Nevada Fall, 700 FT, Yosemite Valley, CA, mammoth albumen print, 15⅝" × 20¾". This print was removed from its mount to remove the stains and then remounted.

"Photograph conservation is both a science and an art," says Weaver. "We must apply what we know about the chemistry of the photograph, its mount, and any varnishes or other coatings in order to safely clean, preserve, and enhance the image. Since we cannot quickly 'undo' a step in a conservation treatment, we must always proceed with great caution and a healthy respect for the fragility of the photographic object, whether it's a 160-year-old salt print of Notre Dame or gelatin silver print of Half Dome from the 1970s."

Many of the manual tools of an art conservator have analogous digital versions in Photoshop:

 An art conservator might wash a photograph to remove the discolored components of the paper, or even use a mild bleaching process known as light-bleaching to oxidize and remove the colored components of a stain or overall discoloration. In Photoshop, you can use a Curves adjustment layer to remove the color cast from an image.

 A conservator working on a fine-art photograph might use special paints and fine brushes to manually "in-paint" damaged areas of a photograph. Likewise, you can use the Spot Healing Brush tool in Photoshop to spot out specks of dust or dirt on a scanned image.

 A conservator might use Japanese papers and wheat-starch paste to carefully repair and rebuild torn paper before finalizing the repair with some skillful in-painting. In Photoshop, you can remove a crease or repair a tear in a scanned image with a few clicks of the Clone Stamp tool.

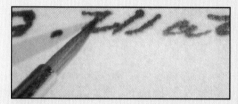 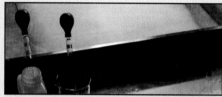

A fixative was applied to the artist's signature with a small brush to protect it when the mount was washed.

"Although our work has always been first and foremost about the preservation and restoration of the original photographic object, there are instances, especially with family photographs, where the use of Photoshop is more appropriate," says Weaver. "More dramatic results can be achieved in far less time. After digitization, the original print can be safely stored away, while the digital version can be copied or printed for many family members. Often, we first clean or unfold family photographs to safely reveal as much of the original image as possible, and then we repair the remaining discoloration, stains, and tears on the computer after digitization."

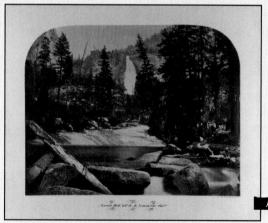

AFTER

▶ **Tip:** If you need to adjust the view, you don't have to switch tools. The scroll bars, View menu commands, and view keyboard shortcuts still work.

9 Position the Remove tool at the top of the crease in the sky, and then drag down along the crease, stopping just before the bridge. You can drag multiple smaller strokes. The Remove tool uses magenta to mark the areas where you dragged, compared to the black that the Spot Healing Brush used.

10 Continue removing the rest of the crease by dragging the Remove tool down along the crease until you reach the bottom of the image.

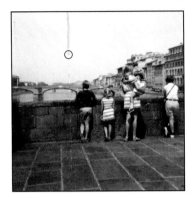
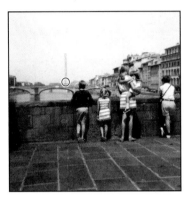
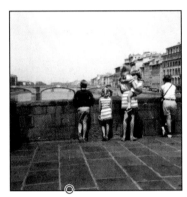

11 If you dragged multiple Remove Tool strokes on the bridge, the Remove tool may think that the unpainted remaining crease is a bridge feature to be preserved, and not remove it effectively. If that happens, then in the options bar, deselect Remove After Each Stroke. Now, when you drag multiple strokes, the Remove tool won't analyze and repair until you press Enter or Return, which you should do only after you finish marking the entire crease. Enabling Remove After Each Stroke lets the Remove tool see all strokes as the same single item to remove.

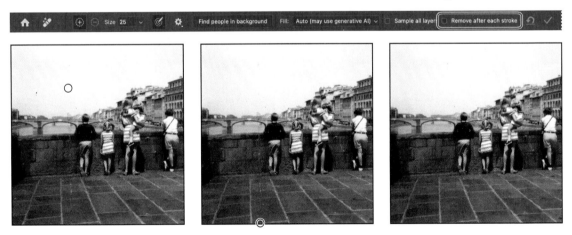

12 If you disabled Remove After Each Stroke, enable it again after you finish erasing all of the crease.

The boy at the right end of the bridge is not part of the same family, so you'll remove him from the photo.

13 In the options bar, set the brush Size to 100.

14 If necessary, zoom or scroll the view until you see the entire boy, and then drag the Remove tool to surround the boy, making sure to include the boy's shadow.

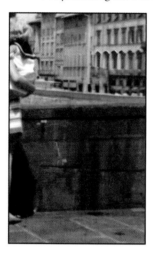

<aside>**Note:** The Remove tool may be smarter than the Spot Healing Brush tool, but the Spot Healing Brush tool can often be faster, and using the Remove tool can consume Generative Credits (see "About Adobe Firefly generative AI" on page 390).</aside>

How good the result looks can vary depending on the image and the area you covered with the Remove tool. If you'd like a better result, you have some options:

• Drag the Remove tool again to paint over the imperfections it created, because in many cases that refines and improves the result.

• Undo and try the Remove tool again, painting the area slightly differently.

• Undo and try a different method. In this lesson, you'll try Generative Fill next, so now you'll undo removing the boy so that you can start over.

15 Choose Edit > Undo Remove Tool to restore the boy.

16 Save your work so far.

Retouching a deleted area using Generative Fill

The Remove tool and Generative Fill are newer features based on recent advances in machine learning, so they're more likely to produce great-looking repairs more quickly than older tools. Generative Fill can solve a much wider range of image problems than the Remove tool. For example, you can use Generative Fill to create new objects and scenes. In this lesson, Generative Fill can remove the boy more effectively than the Remove tool, by offering more flexible options.

Before you can remove the boy, you must first create a selection around him to tell Photoshop what area you want to replace. The Object Selection tool can automatically detect objects, so you can draw a quick, rough selection instead of spending a lot of time to draw a precise selection.

▶ **Tip:** Like other selection tools, you can add to the results of Object Selection by holding down Shift as you drag the tool around areas that were missed. To exclude unwanted areas, Alt-drag (Windows) or Option-drag (macOS) the tool. Or, to draw a more precise initial selection, choose Lasso from the Mode menu in the options bar.

1 In the Tools panel, select the Object Selection tool (⬚), and hover it over each person in the photo, without clicking. Each person highlights when hovered.

As the Object Selection tool automatically detects an object, clicking the highlighted area selects it. The automatic highlight may not include the entire subject; in this case the automatic highlight around the boy might not include all of his shadow. To help ensure a more complete selection, you'll drag the tool instead.

2 Drag the Object Selection tool to draw a rectangle around the boy, and then release the mouse.

The resulting selection includes the entire boy and his shadow. The Contextual Task Bar appears below the selection.

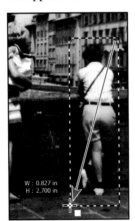
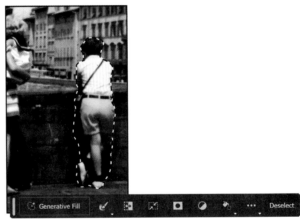

3 In the Contextual Task Bar, click the Generative Fill button.

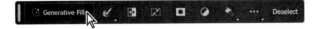

The Contextual Task Bar changes to display a field where you can enter text, followed by a Generate button. If you wanted to fill the selection with something specific, you could describe it by typing into the text field. In this case, you simply want to fill the selection with something consistent with the background, so you don't need to type anything before you continue.

4 Click Generate.

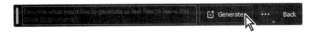

A progress bar appears, which may take longer on older computers. When it's done, the boy is replaced by new content that's consistent with the background. If it isn't a good fit, you're not stuck with what it gave you.

<ul>
<li>In the Layers panel, the result is a separate new layer named Generative Fill. If you click the layer's eyeball icon to hide it, the original content is visible again. This separate layer makes it possible for you to use just a portion of the results, or to restore the original content at any time.</li>
<li>When Generative Fill is selected in the Layers panel, the Properties panel shows options that let you change the result. The Variations section shows three versions. The highlighted variation is the one you see on the canvas.</li>
</ul>

Note: If a message appears asking you to read and agree to the Generative AI User Guidelines, click Agree when you're ready.

▶ **Tip:** When you hover the pointer over an item in the Variations list for Generative Layer properties, an ellipsis menu (…) appears. Clicking on it lets you rate or delete each variation. Rating helps improve the software.

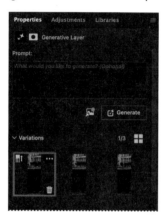

5 In the Properties panel, click each of the other variations, and select the one you think is the best, based on how well the background buildings and bridge wall are filled in. If you don't like any variation, click the Generate button to create more, until you like one well enough to select it.

Note: Generative Fill is one of the features that can consume Generative Credits (see "About Adobe Firefly generative AI" on page 390).

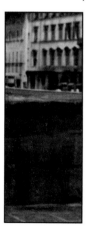 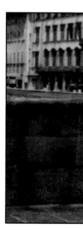 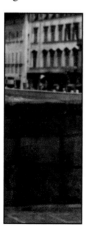

In the past, convincingly repairing such a large area used to require extensive, time-consuming manual retouching. Generative Fill gives you multiple variations in seconds.

▶ **Tip:** If you don't like how the Object Selection tool keeps highlighting as you move the pointer over the image, switch to another tool such as the Move tool or Hand tool.

Manual retouching with the healing and cloning tools

The rise of generative AI technology has led to powerful new retouching tools such as Generative Fill and the Remove tool. However, sometimes you may prefer to use the more traditional Photoshop healing and cloning tools instead. For example, some retouching tasks are specialized or simple enough that the traditional tools are faster, because their calculations aren't so complex. The older tools can also be useful when you're working on a project that doesn't allow using generative AI.

The easiest tools to use are those you can simply click or drag to repair an area, such as the Spot Healing Brush tool ( ) and the Remove tool ( ). Both try to fill in the repair area in a way that looks consistent with the content near where you click or drag the tool.

The Remove tool uses newer technology that can produce better results when repairing larger or more complex areas. Although the Remove tool can use generative AI, it doesn't have to. When the Remove tool is selected, the options bar displays a Fill menu that lets you control how a Remove tool repair is processed. For example, if you're not allowed to use AI for a project, you can set the Fill menu to "Never use generative AI."

Sometimes it works better to tell Photoshop to use a specific area as a source for filling in the area you're retouching. You can do that with the Clone Stamp tool ( ) and Healing Brush tool ( ). The Clone Stamp tool retouches by exactly copying pixels you sample from another area. The Healing Brush tool tries to blend sampled content into the area you're repairing. To use these tools, first click while holding down Alt (Windows) or Option (macOS) to sample an area, and then click or drag the tool to apply the sampled pixels to the area you want to retouch. For both tools, the Window > Clone Source panel offers more options that don't fit in the options bar.

The Patch tool ( ) is similar to the Spot Healing brush tool, but instead of setting the source by Alt/Option-clicking to sample a small area, you drag the Patch tool to select a region of any size or shape.

The Content-Aware Move tool ( ) is useful for moving or copying a selection to another area of an image and blending it into the new area. You can use the Content-Aware Move tool to extend content such as grass or a building, by selecting the Extend setting in the Mode menu in the options bar.

If you want to learn more about these tools, you can find the location of any Photoshop tool, and step-by-step instructions for it, by choosing Edit > Search. As with all tools, you can customize how they work by using the options bar to change settings for the current tool.

Sharpening the image

Typically, sharpening is one of the last editing steps. Photoshop offers many ways to sharpen, from basic to advanced. You'll use the Smart Sharpen filter because it produces good results while also being relatively easy to use.

1   Choose Layer > Flatten Image. Merging layers is necessary so that the upcoming sharpening step affects the entire image, not just the selected layer.

2   Choose Filter > Sharpen > Smart Sharpen.

3   In the Smart Sharpen dialog box, make sure that Preview is selected so you can see the effect of settings you adjust in the document window.

> **Tip:** For a before/after comparison of your changes, toggle the Preview option. It displays the result in the document window, not just in the dialog box. You'll find the Preview option in many dialog boxes in Photoshop.

You can drag inside the preview window in the dialog box to see different parts of the image, or you can click the magnification buttons below the thumbnail.

4   Make sure Lens Blur is chosen in the Remove menu.

You can choose to remove Lens Blur, Gaussian Blur, or Motion Blur in the Smart Sharpen dialog box. Lens Blur is good for general sharpening. Gaussian Blur is similar to the older Unsharp Mask filter. Motion Blur helps reduce streaks from the camera or subject moving in one direction when the photo was taken.

5   Drag the Amount (of sharpening) slider to about **100**%.

6   Drag the Radius slider to about **3**.

The Radius value determines the number of pixels surrounding the edge pixels that affect the sharpening. If an image starts out relatively sharp, a typical Radius value is 1 pixel. In this image the finest details are not sharp, so a higher Radius value helps.

> **Tip:** Images with coarse details or slight blur may benefit from a larger Radius setting. Images showing very fine details and no blur may benefit from a smaller Radius value.

7   When you're satisfied with the results, click OK to apply the Smart Sharpen filter.

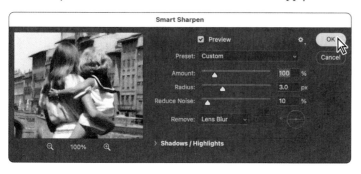

8   Choose File > Save, and then close the project file.

Your image is ready to share or print!

Extra credit

Creatively converting a color image to black and white

You can control how a color image converts to black and white to get the look you want. The lightness of colors is not the same. For example, at maximum saturation, yellow is much lighter than blue. When you convert using the Black & White adjustment layer, you can control the lightness of different colors. For example, if the original sky is light blue, lowering the Blue value in the Black & White adjustment layer darkens the sky in the black-and-white version. This technique started in film photography, where a photographer would attach a color filter to the front of the lens to change the lightness of the sky, foliage, or portrait skin relative to the other original colors in the image.

1   Choose File > Open, navigate to the Autumn.jpg file in the Lesson02 folder, and click Open.

2   In the Adjustments panel, scroll down to the Single Adjustments category, and click the Black & White button. A new Black & White adjustment layer appears in the Layers panel, and the options for it appear in the Properties panel.

3   In the Properties panel, adjust the color sliders to change the lightness of different colors until you create the tonal relationships you want.

You can experiment with options from the Preset menu, such as Darker or Infrared. Or, select the on-image adjustment tool (☝) in the upper-left corner of the Properties panel, position it in the image over a color you want to adjust, and drag horizontally. The tool moves the sliders associated with the original color of the image where you started dragging; for example, dragging on the yellow leaves adjusts the lightness of all yellow areas.

4   If you want to colorize the entire photo with a single hue, select Tint in the Properties panel, click the color swatch, and select a tint color. You can continue to adjust the color sliders.

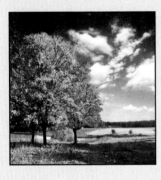
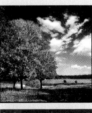
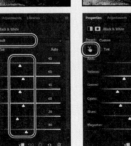
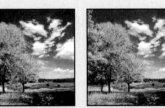
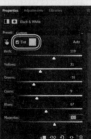

Review questions

1 What does *resolution* mean?

2 What are some ways to use the Crop tool to improve an image?

3 How can you adjust the tone and color of an image in Photoshop?

4 How can you instantly create a precise selection of an irregularly shaped object?

5 What tools can you use to remove blemishes and unwanted content in an image?

6 What are some ways Generative Fill can help retouch an image?

Review answers

1 For media such as print, the term *resolution* refers to the number of pixels per unit of physical width or height in an image, such as pixels per inch (ppi). Printer resolution may be expressed in dots per inch (dpi), because device dots do not always correspond to image pixels. For media measured in pixels, such as web and video, resolution typically refers to pixel dimensions (height and width), not pixels per inch.

2 You can use the Crop tool to trim, straighten, resize, and change the resolution of an image.

3 You can adjust the tone and color of an image in Photoshop using the Curves and Levels adjustment layers.

4 The Object Selection Tool recognizes objects in an image. You can click a highlighted object you want to select, or drag around it, and the resulting selection will follow the outline of the object.

5 In this lesson, you used the Spot Healing Brush tool, Remove tool, and Generative Fill. Many other healing/cloning/patching tools are also available in Photoshop.

6 Generative Fill can be effective at filling large deleted areas in a convincing way, either by matching the background or generating new objects. It also generates variations so that you can choose from alternative solutions.

3 WORKING WITH SELECTIONS

Lesson overview

In this lesson, you'll learn how to do the following:

- Make specific areas of an image active using selection tools.

- Reposition a selection marquee.

- Move, rotate, and duplicate the contents of a selection.

- Use keyboard-mouse combinations that save time and hand motions.

- Deselect a selection.

- Adjust the position of a selected area using the arrow keys.

- Add to and subtract from a selection.

- Use multiple selection tools to make a complex selection.

- Save your work as a Photoshop cloud document you can easily open in Photoshop on other devices, and for online collaboration.

 This lesson will take about an hour to complete. To get the lesson files used in this chapter, download them from the web page for this book at peachpit.com/PhotoshopCIB2025. For more information, see "Accessing the lesson files and Web Edition" in the Getting Started section at the beginning of this book. The lesson steps that use Adobe Cloud Documents require Internet access.

As you work on this lesson, you'll preserve the start files. If you need to restore the start files, download them from your Account page.

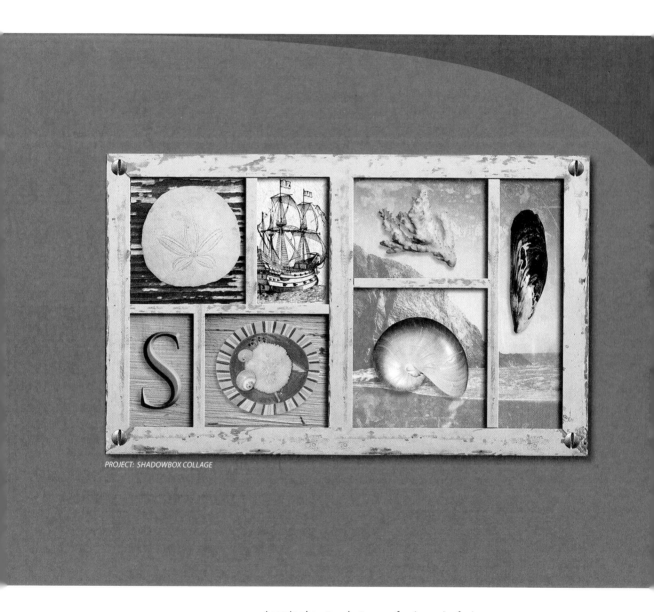

PROJECT: SHADOWBOX COLLAGE

Learning how to select areas of an image is of primary importance—you must first select what you want to affect. As long as a selection is active, only the area within the selection can be edited.

About selecting and pixel selection tools

Tip: The concept of selecting the content you want to change is common across many image-editing applications. As soon as you understand how selections work in one application, you can use that knowledge in other similar applications.

When you want to edit just an area of a pixel layer, you use a two-step process. First, *select* (mark) the area you want to change, using one of the selection tools. Then use another tool, filter, or other feature to make the changes, such as moving the selected pixels to another location or applying a filter. When a selection is active on a pixel layer, changes you make apply only to the selected area; other areas are unaffected. Similar pixel selection tools are grouped in the Tools panel:

Content- and edge-based selections. The Object Selection tool (![icon]) uses machine learning to identify subjects that you select with a simple click or drag; this is a quick and easy way to select people, animals, and other non-geometric shapes (you used the Object Selection tool in Lesson 2). The Quick Selection tool (![icon]) quickly expands the area you drag by looking for distinct regions of content in the image.

Color-based selections. The Magic Wand tool (![icon]) selects parts of an image based on similarity in pixel color. It's useful for selecting odd-shaped areas that share a specific range of colors or tones.

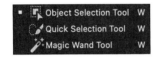

Note: This lesson focuses on basic tools and techniques for selecting areas of pixels. In many cases you might save time and effort by using more automated selection features; see the sidebar "More ways to select pixels" on page 84.

Geometric selections. The Rectangular Marquee tool (![icon]) selects a rectangular area. The Elliptical Marquee tool (![icon]) selects an elliptical area. The Single Row Marquee tool (![icon]) and Single Column Marquee tool (![icon]) select either a 1-pixel-high row or a 1-pixel-wide column, respectively.

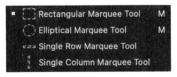

Tip: The Selection Brush is useful when you think it would be easier to paint the area you want to select rather than to draw an outline around it.

Freehand selections. The Selection Brush tool (![icon]) lets you mark the intended selection area using paint; when you switch to another tool, the area you painted becomes a marquee selection. The Lasso tool (![icon]) traces a freehand selection around an area. The Polygonal Lasso tool (![icon]) lays down straight-line segments around an area. The Magnetic Lasso tool (![icon]) automatically follows edges, typically giving the best results when the area you want is well defined by contrast, such as a visible color break or line that it can follow.

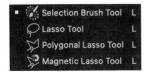

Getting started

First, you'll look at the image you will create as you explore the selection tools in Photoshop.

1   Start Photoshop, and then simultaneously hold down Ctrl+Alt+Shift (Windows) or Command+Option+Shift (macOS) to restore the default preferences. (See "Restoring default preferences" on page 5.)

2   When prompted, click Yes to confirm that you want to delete the Adobe Photoshop Settings file.

3   Choose File > Browse In Bridge to open Adobe Bridge.

4   In the Favorites panel, click the Lessons folder. Then double-click the Lesson03 folder in the Content panel to see its contents.

5   Study the 03End.psd file. Move the thumbnail slider to the right if you want to see the image in more detail.

The project is a shadow box that includes a piece of coral, a sand dollar, a mussel, a nautilus, and a plate of small shells. The challenge in this lesson is to arrange these elements, which were scanned together on the single page you see in the 03Start.psd file.

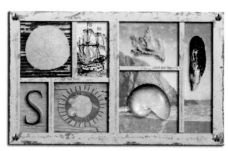

Note: If Bridge isn't installed, the File > Browse In Bridge command in Photoshop will start the Creative Cloud desktop app, which will download and install Bridge. After installation completes, you can start Bridge.

Note: If Bridge asks you if you want to import preferences from a previous version of Bridge, click No.

Using cloud documents

Photoshop document sizes can become large, especially for high-resolution images that use many layers. When you work with documents stored online, large file sizes upload and download more slowly; on a limited data plan you may reach the data limit more quickly. Adobe cloud documents help you edit online documents efficiently by using file formats optimized for networks. For example, editing a Photoshop file as a cloud document means only the parts affected by an edit are transmitted, instead of the entire file.

Cloud documents are constantly synced and also easily accessible from the Home screen in Photoshop. For example, if you use Photoshop on both a computer and an Apple iPad and you save an image as a cloud document, you'll find it on the Photoshop Home screen on both devices, updated with the changes you made on the most recent device you used to edit the document.

▶ **Tip:** Using cloud documents can be more efficient than putting a Photoshop file on a cloud-based file syncing service. A cloud document transfers only the parts of a file that change, and you can open it in one click on the Photoshop Home screen.

Converting a Photoshop local document to a cloud document is easy; the only thing you have to do is save it to cloud documents instead of to your computer.

1 In Bridge, double-click the 03Start.psd thumbnail to open the image file in Photoshop. Close any messages that appear about new features. You've opened the document from your local storage.

2 Choose File > Save As, and click Save to Creative Cloud. If you see the standard Save As dialog box, first click the Save To Cloud Documents button.

3 Rename the file **03WorkingCloud**, and click Save. If a message appears about the file being uploaded to Cloud Documents, you may dismiss it. In the document window tab, a cloud icon appears before the filename, which now ends with the extension .psdc to indicate that it's a cloud document.

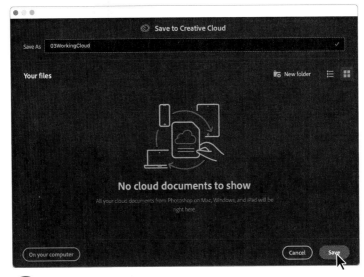

4 Close the document.

You can now open the cloud document from the Home screen in Photoshop on any supported platform, including Windows, macOS, iPad OS, and the Photoshop web app in supported web browsers. However, these lessons won't work in the iPad OS and web browser versions of Photoshop because they have smaller feature sets that are organized differently than the Windows and macOS versions of Photoshop that these lessons are designed for.

Now you'll open the cloud document. Again, this will be slightly different than opening a document from local storage.

1 In the Photoshop Home screen, select Your Files on the left side. It lists cloud documents you uploaded using your Adobe ID. You can also select Home, where the Recent list shows local and cloud documents you recently opened.

▶ **Tip:** You can organize your cloud documents in folders on the server. When viewing Your Files on the Photoshop Home screen, click the folder icon near the top to create a new folder.

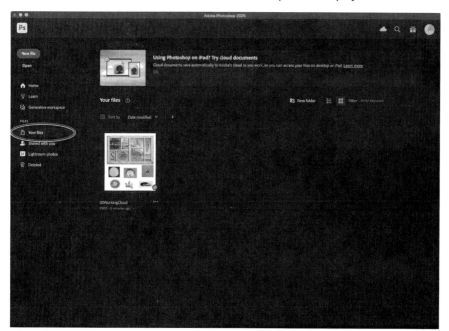

▶ **Tip:** If you want to manage a cloud document, such as renaming or deleting it, click the document's ellipsis (…) button in the Your Files list on the Photoshop Home screen, and choose a command from the menu that appears.

2 Click 03WorkingCloud, the file you just saved. This downloads the file to your computer and opens it in Photoshop.

If you're editing a Photoshop Cloud (PSDC) Document, how can you provide that file to a client who requires a PSD file? By saving the cloud document to your own local storage. Again, the conversion is automatic, so it's easy and seamless.

1 Choose File > Save As. If you see the Save to Creative Cloud dialog box, click On Your Computer at the bottom to see the conventional Save As dialog box. Notice that the filename extension is now .psd, because you are saving this document to your local storage, not Cloud Documents.

2 Name the document **03Working.psd**, and save it into the Lesson03 folder. Now you have your own local PSD format copy that you can distribute and back up traditionally (without cloud services).

For this lesson, you can continue with your local copy (03Working.psd), or you can close the local PSD copy and instead open and work with your cloud documents copy (03WorkingCloud.psdc).

● **Note:** You can't find a cloud document on your computer by looking through folders on your desktop; you see cloud documents in the Home screen in Photoshop. A cloud document is stored on Adobe servers and cached only to your local storage. If you need a local copy of a cloud document, choose File > Save As and save it to your computer as described to the left.

Using the Magic Wand tool

The Magic Wand tool selects pixels of a specific color range. It's most useful when the area you want to select is relatively uniform in tone or color.

The Tolerance option sets the range of tonal levels the Magic Wand tool selects, starting from the pixel you click. The default tolerance value of 32 selects the color you click plus 32 lighter and 32 darker tones of that color. If the Magic Wand tool doesn't select the entire area you expect, try increasing the Tolerance value. If the tool selects too much, try decreasing the Tolerance value.

1 Select the Zoom tool in the Tools panel, and then zoom in so that you can see the entire sand dollar in detail.

2 Select the Magic Wand tool (🪄), hidden under the Object Selection tool (🔲).

3 In the options bar, confirm that the Tolerance value is **32**. This value determines the range of colors the wand selects.

Tip: If a Magic Wand tool selection picks up too many similar colors outside the area you want to select, try enabling the Contiguous option in the options bar.

4 Click the Magic Wand tool on the red background outside the sand dollar.

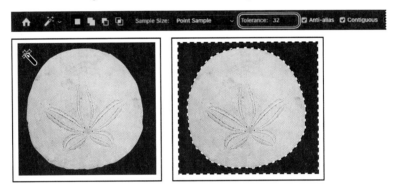

The Magic Wand tool perfectly selected the red background, because all of the background colors are similar enough to the pixel you clicked (within the 32 levels specified in the Tolerance setting). But it's the shell we want, so let's start over.

Tip: Another convenient way to deselect pixels is to click the Deselect button in the Contextual Task Bar. If it's hidden, choose Window > Contextual Task Bar to show it.

5 Choose Select > Deselect.

6 Position the Magic Wand tool over the sand dollar, and click.

Look carefully at the animated selection marquee that appears over the sand dollar. If this was a perfect selection, the selection marquee would tightly follow the outer edge of the sand dollar. But notice that some interior areas of the sand dollar show selection marquees, because their colors differ from the color you clicked by more than 32 levels (the Tolerance setting). The current selection doesn't include all interior colors.

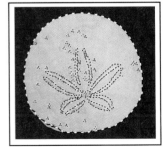

When you want to select a subject that is mostly the same color and value, against a relatively solid background, you can often solve this by increasing the Tolerance value. But the more complex the subject or background, the more likely a wide Tolerance value will also select unwanted parts of the background. In that case, it's usually better to use a different selection tool, such as the Quick Selection tool. You'll do that next, but first let's deselect the current selection.

7 Choose Select > Deselect.

Using the Quick Selection tool

To use the Quick Selection tool you simply click or drag it within a subject, and the tool looks for the subject's edges. You can add or subtract areas of the selection until you have exactly the area you want. This works better than the Magic Wand tool because the Quick Selection tool is more aware of image content, instead of relying on color similarity alone. Let's see if the Quick Selection tool does a better job selecting the sand dollar.

▶ **Tip:** Notice that the Quick Selection tool looks for a subject outward from where you click or drag the tool, and the Object Selection tool looks for a subject inside the area you drag with that tool.

1 Select the Quick Selection tool (◔✎) in the Tools panel. It's grouped with the Object Selection tool (▦) and Magic Wand tool (✦).

2 Select Enhance Edge in the options bar.

Selecting Enhance Edge should improve the quality of the selection, with edges that are truer to the object. If you're using a slower or older computer, you might notice a slight delay when using Enhance Edge.

3 Click or drag within the sand dollar (do not cross over into the background).

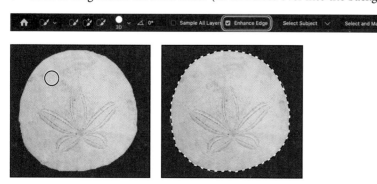

The Quick Selection tool looks at what content is probably connected to the area where you clicked or dragged and finds the full edge automatically, selecting the entire sand dollar. The sand dollar is simple enough that the Quick Selection tool can isolate it instantly. When the Quick Selection tool doesn't complete the selection initially, click or drag over areas you want to add to the selection.

Leave the selection active so that you can use it in the next exercise.

▶ **Tip:** If the Quick Selection tool includes areas outside the subject, you can remove unwanted areas from the selection by clicking or dragging over them while holding down the Alt (Windows) or Option (macOS) key. That's the shortcut for selecting the Subtract From Selection icon in the options bar.

Moving a selected area

Once you've made a selection, any changes you make apply exclusively to the pixels within the selection. The rest of the image is not affected by those changes.

To move the selected area to another part of the composition, you use the Move tool. This image has only one layer, so the pixels you move will replace the pixels beneath them. This change is not permanent until you deselect the moved pixels, so you can try different locations for the selection you're moving before you commit it.

Tip: If you deselect an area by accident, you may be able to restore the selection by choosing Edit > Undo or Select > Reselect.

1 If the sand dollar is not still selected, repeat the previous exercise to select it.

2 Zoom out so you can see both the shadow box and the sand dollar.

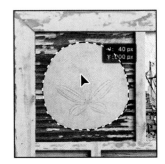

3 Select the Move tool (✛). Notice that the sand dollar remains selected.

4 Drag the selected area (the sand dollar) to the upper-left area of the frame, which is labeled "A." Position it over the silhouette in the frame, leaving the lower-left part of the silhouette showing as a shadow.

5 Choose Select > Deselect, and then choose File > Save.

Tip: In some cases you can deselect pixels by clicking outside the current selection, but be careful … depending on which tool is selected, clicking elsewhere on the canvas might start a new selection.

There's more than one way to deselect a selection. You can choose Select > Deselect, press the keyboard shortcut shown next to the command, or click the Deselect button on the Contextual Task Bar.

Adding to and subtracting from pixel selections

If a pixel selection isn't quite right, you can edit it. When a selection tool is active, its options bar displays icons that change how your next action affects the existing selection. The options are New (■), Add (◼), Subtract (◻), and Intersect (▣). New replaces the current selection, Add extends it, Subtract removes an area from it, and Intersect keeps the area in common between the current selection and your next selection tool action. If you want, you can make an initial selection with one tool and then add to or subtract from that selection using a different tool.

The Quick Selection tool works like a brush, so its options are New (⊘), Add (⊘), and Subtract (⊘).

For adding and subtracting, you can hold down modifier keys instead of clicking a button. Hold down Shift to add, and hold down Alt (Windows) or Option (macOS) to subtract. For example, if you want to use the Lasso tool to remove a few pixels from a pixel selection, hold down the Alt or Option key as you drag the tool.

Using the Object Selection tool

To use the Object Selection tool, all you have to do is draw a rough selection around the object you want to select, and the Object Selection tool identifies the object and creates a tight selection for it. For an object that has a complicated outline, such as the coral, the Object Selection tool will typically be much faster than trying to draw that irregular outline by hand.

1   Select the Object Selection tool (▨), which is grouped with the Quick Selection tool (◔) and Magic Wand tool (✦).

2   Drag a selection around the piece of coral. It doesn't have to be precise or centered. What's important is that it's a relatively tight selection with a small amount of space between the coral and the edges of the selection marquee. You're simply showing Photoshop which object you want to select.

Note: A colored highlight may appear over an object when you hover over it with the Object Selection tool. The highlight indicates that it's automatically identifying a potential selection. If the area you want to select is highlighted, just click.

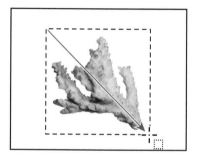
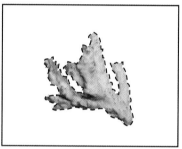

The Object Selection tool analyzes the area inside the rectangular selection, finds the object, and creates a selection marquee along its complicated edge.

3   Select the Move tool (✛), and drag the coral to the area of the shadow box labeled "B," positioning it so that a shadow appears to the left of and below the coral.

4   Choose Select > Deselect, and then save your work.

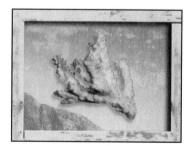

Tip: If the Object Selection tool creates a selection that's too tight, choose Select > Modify > Expand and enter a pixel value; usually 1 to 3 is enough. As with other selection tools, you can add missed bits to the selection (by Shift-dragging the tool around the missed parts). Or subtract from the selection by holding down Alt (Windows) or Option (macOS) as you drag the tool around the area to remove.

Manipulating selections

You can move a selection marquee (not the pixels), reposition it as you create it, and even duplicate it. In this section, you'll learn several ways to adjust selection marquees as you create them with the marquee selection and lasso selection tools. One of the most useful things you may learn about in this section are the modifier keys that work with many tools to save you time and steps.

Repositioning a selection marquee while creating it

Selecting ellipses and rectangles can be tricky. Sometimes the selection will be off-center or the ratio of width to height won't match what you need. In this exercise, you'll learn techniques such as two important keyboard-mouse combinations that can make your Photoshop work much easier.

As you perform this exercise, be careful to follow the directions about keeping the mouse button or specific keys pressed. If you accidentally release the mouse button at the wrong time, simply start the exercise again from step 1.

1   Select the Zoom tool (Q), and click or drag it until the plate of shells at the bottom of the document window is at least 100% magnification (use 200% if the entire plate of shells still fits in the document window).

2   Select the Elliptical Marquee tool (◯), hidden under the Rectangular Marquee tool (▭).

Note: You don't have to include every pixel in the plate of shells, but the selection should be the shape of the plate and should contain the shells comfortably.

3   Move the pointer over the plate of shells, and drag diagonally across the oval plate to create a selection, but *do not release the mouse button*. It's OK if your selection does not match the plate shape yet.

If you accidentally release the mouse button, draw the selection again. In most cases—including this one—the new selection replaces the previous one.

4   Still holding down the mouse button, hold down the spacebar, and continue to drag the selection. Instead of resizing the selection, now you're moving it. Position the selection so that it more closely aligns with the plate.

Tip: The technique of holding down the spacebar to reposition as you draw also works with other drawing tools in Photoshop, such as the shape tools and the Pen tool.

5   Carefully release the spacebar (but not the mouse button) and continue to drag, trying to make the size and shape of the selection match the oval plate of shells as closely as possible. If necessary, hold down the spacebar again, and drag to move the selection marquee into position around the plate of shells.

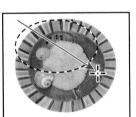
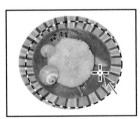
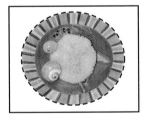

Begin dragging a selection.   *Press the spacebar to move it.*   *Complete the selection.*

6   When the selection border is positioned appropriately, release the mouse button.

Tip: If you want to resize a selection after releasing the mouse button, choose Select > Transform Selection.

7   Choose View > Fit On Screen or use the slider in the Navigator panel to reduce the zoom view so that you can see all of the objects in the document window.

Leave the Elliptical Marquee tool and the selection active for the next exercise.

Moving selected pixels with a keyboard shortcut

Now you'll use a modifier key to move the selected pixels onto the shadow box. The shortcut temporarily switches the active tool to the Move tool, so you don't need to select it from the Tools panel.

1 If the plate of shells is not still selected, repeat the previous exercise to select it.

2 With the Elliptical Marquee tool (○) selected in the Tools panel, and hold down the Ctrl (Windows) or Command (macOS) as you hover the pointer within the selection. Continue to hold down the key for the next step.

The pointer icon now includes a pair of scissors (▶✄), indicating that the selection will be cut from its current location.

3 While continuing to hold down the Ctrl or Command key, drag the plate of shells onto the area of the shadow box labeled "C." (You'll use another technique to nudge the oval plate into the exact position in a minute.)

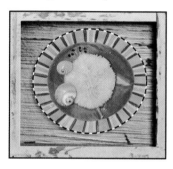

4 Release the mouse button and the key, but don't deselect the plate of shells.

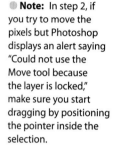

Note: In step 2, if you try to move the pixels but Photoshop displays an alert saying "Could not use the Move tool because the layer is locked," make sure you start dragging by positioning the pointer inside the selection.

Moving a selection with the arrow keys

You can make minor adjustments to the position of selected pixels by using the arrow keys. You can nudge the selection in increments of 1 pixel or 10 pixels.

When a selection tool is active in the Tools panel, the arrow keys nudge the selection border, but not the contents. When the Move tool is active, the arrow keys move both the selection border and its contents.

You'll use the arrow keys to nudge the plate of shells. Before you begin, make sure that the plate of shells is still selected in the document window.

1 Select the Move tool (✛), and press the Up Arrow key (⬆) on your keyboard a few times to move the oval upward.

Notice that each time you press the arrow key, the plate of shells moves 1 pixel. Experiment by pressing the other arrow keys to see how they affect the selection.

Tip: If a selection becomes deselected accidentally, choose Select > Reselect.

Softening the edges of a selection

To smooth the hard edges of a selection, you can apply anti-aliasing or feathering or use the Select and Mask option.

Anti-aliasing smooths the jagged edges of a selection by softening the color transition between edge pixels and background pixels. Since only the edge pixels change, detail loss is minimal. Anti-aliasing is useful when you cut, copy, and paste selections to create composite images.

Anti-aliasing is available for the Lasso, Polygonal Lasso, Magnetic Lasso, Elliptical Marquee, and Magic Wand tools. (Select the tool to display its options in the options bar.) To apply anti-aliasing, you must select the option before making the selection. Once a selection is made, you cannot add anti-aliasing to it.

Feathering blurs edges by building a transition at the boundary between the selection and its surrounding pixels. This can blur detail at the edge of the selection.

You can define feathering for the marquee and lasso tools as you use them, or you can add feathering to an existing selection. Feathering effects become apparent when you move, cut, or copy the selection.

- To feather a selection edge using the Select and Mask option, make a selection, and then click Select and Mask in the options bar to open its dialog box. In there you can smooth the outline, feather it, or contract or expand it.

- To anti-alias a selection edge, select a lasso tool, or the Elliptical Marquee or Magic Wand tool, and select Anti-alias in the options bar.

- To define a feathered edge for a selection you're about to draw, select any of the lasso or marquee tools. Enter a Feather value in the options bar. This value defines the width of the feathered edge and can range from 1 to 250 pixels.

- To define a feathered edge for an existing selection, choose Select > Modify > Feather. Enter a value for the Feather Radius, and click OK.

2   Hold down the Shift key as you press an arrow key.

When you hold down the Shift key, the selected pixels move 10 pixels every time you press an arrow key.

> **Tip:** Selection edges, guidelines, and other visible items that aren't actual objects are called *extras*, so another way to hide the selection edges is to deselect the View > Extras command or press its keyboard shortcut, Ctrl+H (Windows) or Command+H (macOS).

Sometimes the selection marquee can distract you as you make adjustments. You can hide the edges of a selection temporarily without actually deselecting and then display the selection marquee once you've completed the adjustments.

3   Choose View > Show > Selection Edges to deselect the command, hiding the selection marquee around the plate of shells.

4   Use the arrow keys to nudge the plate of shells until it's positioned over the silhouette so that there's a shadow on the left and bottom of the plate. Then choose View > Show > Selection Edges to reveal the selection border again.

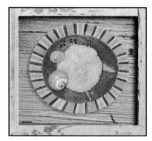
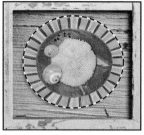

Hidden selection edges.   Visible selection edges.

Tip: A selection marquee (animated dashed border) is different than the transform controls (rectangle with handles on it). If transform controls are visible and you want to hide them, in the options bar with the Move tool selected, deselect Show Transform Controls.

5   Choose Select > Deselect, or click the Deselect button in the Contextual Task Bar.

6   Choose File > Save to save your work so far.

Selecting with the lasso tools

Photoshop includes three lasso tools: the Lasso tool, the Polygonal Lasso tool, and the Magnetic Lasso tool. You can use the Lasso tool to make selections that require both freehand and straight lines, using keyboard shortcuts to move back and forth between the Lasso tool and the Polygonal Lasso tool. You'll use the Lasso tool to select the mussel. It takes a bit of practice to alternate between straight-line and freehand selections—if you make a mistake while you're selecting the mussel, simply deselect and start again.

Tip: Because the lasso tools are manual, they can be the most time-consuming way to create a selection. They are typically most useful for selecting simple shapes or adjusting an existing selection.

1   Select the Zoom tool (Q), and click or drag to zoom into the mussel image at the bottom of the canvas so that you can see it more clearly.

2   Select the Lasso tool (Q), hidden under the Selection Brush tool (⁂). Starting at the lower-left section of the mussel, drag around the rounded end of the mussel, tracing the shape as closely as possible. *Do not release the mouse button.*

Tip: You'll try the Selection Brush tool in Lesson 9.

3   When you reach a corner or straight part of the edge, press the Alt (Windows) or Option (macOS) key, and then release the mouse button so that the lasso pointer changes to the polygonal lasso shape (⋈). *Do not release the Alt or Option key.*

4   Begin clicking along the end of the mussel to place anchor points, following the contours of the mussel. Be sure to hold down the Alt or Option key throughout this process. This lets you create perfectly straight segments along the selection.

Tip: Go slowly until you become comfortable with the Lasso tool. If you make a mistake or accidentally release the mouse button during steps 2–8, choose Edit > Undo, and start again at step 2.

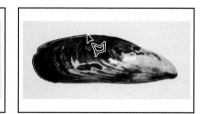

Drag with the Lasso tool.   Click with the Polygonal Lasso tool.

The selection border automatically stretches like a rubber band between anchor points.

5 When you reach the tip of the mussel, hold down the mouse button as you release the Alt or Option key. The pointer again appears as the lasso icon.

6 Carefully drag around the tip of the mussel, holding down the mouse button.

7 When you finish tracing the tip and reach the straight segments along the lower side of the mussel, first press Alt or Option again, and then release the mouse button. Click along the straight segments of the lower side of the mussel as needed. Continue to trace the straight and curved mussel edges until you arrive back at the starting point of your selection at the left end of the mussel.

● **Note:** To make sure that the selection is the shape you want when you use the Lasso tool, end the selection by dragging across the starting point of the selection. If you start and stop the selection at different points, Photoshop draws a straight line between the start and end points of the selection.

8 Click the starting point of the selection, and then release Alt or Option. The mussel is now entirely selected. Leave the mussel selected for the next exercise.

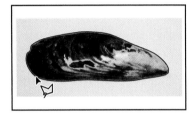 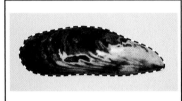

Rotating selected pixels

Now you'll rotate the mussel.

Before you begin, make sure that the mussel is still selected.

1 Choose View > Fit On Screen so that the entire canvas fits on your screen.

2 Position the pointer inside the mussel selection marquee, and then hold down Ctrl (Windows) or Command (macOS) as you drag the selected mussel to the section of the shadow box labeled "D."

The pointer changes to the Move tool icon when you press Ctrl (Windows) or Command (macOS).

3 Choose Edit > Transform > Rotate.

The mussel and selection marquee are bounded by transform controls and handles.

▶ **Tip:** You can constrain rotation to common angles such as 90 degrees by holding down the Shift key as you drag the bounding box.

4 Move the pointer outside the transform controls so that it becomes a curved, two-headed arrow (↰). Drag to rotate the mussel to a 90-degree angle. You can verify the angle in the transformation values display next to the pointer, or in the Rotate box in the options bar. Press Enter or Return to commit the transformation.

5   If necessary, use the Move tool (✛), and drag to reposition the mussel, leaving a shadow to match the others. When you're satisfied, choose Select > Deselect.

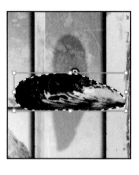

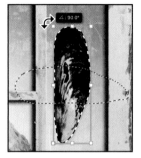

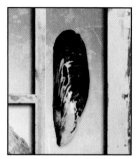

> **Tip:** Remember that you can also reposition a selection by pressing arrow keys when the Move tool is selected.

6   Choose File > Save.

Selecting with the Magnetic Lasso tool

You can use the Magnetic Lasso tool to make freehand selections of areas with high-contrast edges. When you draw with the Magnetic Lasso tool, the selection border automatically snaps to the edge between areas of contrast. You can also control the selection path by occasionally clicking the mouse to place anchor points in the selection border.

You'll use the Magnetic Lasso tool to select the nautilus so that you can move it to the shadow box.

1   Select the Zoom tool (🔍), and click or drag to zoom in on the nautilus.

2   Select the Magnetic Lasso tool (✍), hidden under the Lasso tool (◯).

3   Click once along the left edge of the nautilus, and then hover the Magnetic Lasso tool along the edge to trace its outline.

> **Tip:** In low-contrast areas, you may want to click to place your own fastening points. You can add as many as you need. To remove the most recent fastening point, press Delete, and then move the mouse back to the remaining fastening point and continue selecting.

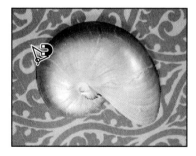

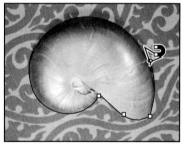

Even if you don't hold down the mouse button, the tool snaps to the edge of the nautilus and automatically adds fastening points.

4 When you reach the left side of the nautilus again, double-click to return the Magnetic Lasso tool to the starting point, closing the selection. Or you can move the Magnetic Lasso tool over the starting point and click once.

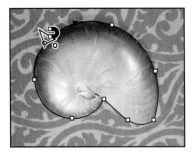 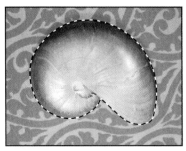

5 Double-click the Hand tool (🖐) to fit the entire image in the window.

6 Select the Move tool (✛), and drag the nautilus onto its silhouette in the section of the frame labeled "E," leaving a shadow below it and on the left side.

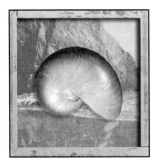

7 Choose Select > Deselect, and then choose File > Save.

Selecting from a center point

In some cases, it's easier to make elliptical or rectangular selections by drawing a selection from an object's center point. You'll use this technique to select the head of the screw for the shadow box corners.

1 Select the Zoom tool (🔍), and zoom in on the screw to a magnification of about 300%. Make sure that the entire screw head is visible in your document window.

2 Select the Elliptical Marquee tool (⬭) in the Tools panel.

3 Move the pointer to the approximate center of the screw.

4 Click and begin dragging. Then, without releasing the mouse button, hold down the Alt (Windows) or Option (macOS) key as you continue dragging the selection to the outer edge of the screw.

The selection is centered over its starting point.

5   When you have the entire screw head selected, release the mouse button first, and then release Alt or Option (and the Shift key if you used it). Do not deselect, because you'll use this selection in the next exercise.

> **Tip:** To select a perfect circle, press Shift as you drag. Hold down Shift while dragging the Rectangular Marquee tool to select a perfect square.

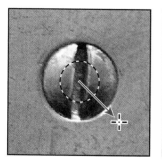 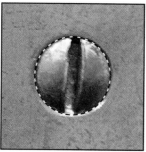

6   If necessary, reposition the selection border using one of the methods you learned earlier. If you accidentally released the Alt or Option key before you released the mouse button, select the screw again.

Resizing and copying a selection

Now you'll move the screw to the lower-right corner of the wooden shadow box and then duplicate it for the other corners.

Resizing the contents of a selection

You'll start by moving the screw, but it's too large for the space. You'll need to resize it as well.

Before you begin, make sure that the screw is still selected. If it's not, reselect it by completing the previous exercise.

1   Choose View > Fit On Screen so that the entire image fits within the document window.

2   Select the Move tool (✛) in the Tools panel.

3   Position the pointer within the screw selection.

The pointer becomes an arrow with a pair of scissors (➤), indicating that dragging the selection will cut it from its current location and move it to the new location.

4   Drag the screw onto the lower-right corner of the shadow box.

Tip: If the screw won't move or resize smoothly, as if it gets "stuck," hold down the Control key to temporarily disable snapping to magenta Smart Guides as you drag. Or permanently disable them by deselecting the View > Show > Smart Guides command.

5   Choose Edit > Transform > Scale. Transform controls appear around the screw.

6   Drag one of the corner points inward to reduce the screw to about 40% of its original size or until it is small enough to sit on the shadow box frame.

As you resize the object, the selection marquee resizes, too. Both resize proportionally by default.

7   Press Enter or Return to commit the change.

8   Use the Move tool to reposition the screw after resizing it so that it is centered in the corner of the shadow box frame.

Tip: If you don't want to maintain original proportions while resizing, press the Shift key as you drag a corner handle of a transformation bounding box.

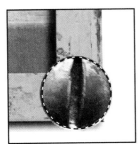 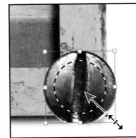 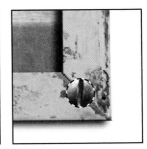

9   Leaving the screw selected, choose File > Save to save your work.

Moving and duplicating a selection simultaneously

You can move and duplicate a selection at the same time. You'll copy the screw for the other three corners of the frame. If the screw is no longer selected, reselect it now, using the techniques you learned earlier.

1   With the Move tool (✛) selected, press Alt (Windows) or Option (macOS) as you position the pointer inside the screw selection.

The pointer changes, displaying the usual black arrow and an additional white arrow, which indicates that a duplicate will be made when you move the selection.

Tip: Pay attention to where the pointer is and how it looks. If you begin dragging when the pointer is over a transform handle or if the pointer does not look like a black/white arrow pair, instead of being duplicated the selection might be edited in a way you didn't expect.

2   Continue holding down the Alt or Option key as you drag a duplicate of the screw straight up to the top-right corner of the frame. Release the mouse button and the Alt or Option key, but don't deselect the duplicate image.

3   Hold down Alt+Shift (Windows) or Option+Shift (macOS), and drag a new copy of the screw straight left to the upper-left corner of the frame.

Pressing the Shift key as you move a selection constrains the movement horizontally or vertically in 45-degree increments.

4 Repeat step 3 to drag a fourth screw to the lower-left corner of the frame.

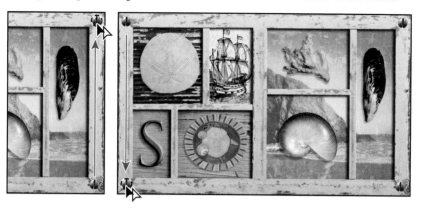

5 When you're satisfied with the position of the fourth screw, choose Select > Deselect, and then choose File > Save.

Copying selected pixels

You can use the Move tool to copy selected pixels as you drag them within or between images, or you can copy and move selections using commands on the Edit menu. The Move tool uses less memory, because it doesn't use the clipboard.

Photoshop has several copy and paste commands on the Edit menu:

- **Copy** takes the selected area on the active layer and puts it on the clipboard.
- **Copy Merged** creates a merged copy of all the visible layers in the selected area.
- **Paste** inserts the clipboard contents at the center of the image. If you paste into another image, the pasted content becomes a new layer.

On the Edit > Paste Special submenu, Photoshop also provides specialized pasting commands to give you more options in certain situations:

- **Paste without Formatting** pastes text without the formatting it may have been copied with, such as font and size. It helps ensure that text pasted from another document or application matches the formatting of a Photoshop text layer.
- **Paste in Place** pastes clipboard content at the location it had in the original image, instead of at the center of the document.
- **Paste Into** pastes clipboard content inside the active selection in the same or a different image. The source selection is pasted onto a new layer, and the area outside the selection is converted into a layer mask.
- **Paste Outside** is the same as Paste Into except that Photoshop pastes the content outside the active selection and converts the area inside the selection to a layer mask.

If two documents have different pixel dimensions, content you paste between them may appear to change size. This is because content maintains its pixel dimensions when pasted into a document with different pixel dimensions. You can resize a pasted selection, but the image quality of the selection may decrease if enlarged.

More ways to select pixels

If it's too difficult or time-consuming to select the area you want by clicking or dragging a selection tool (such as the Lasso tool), see if it could be done faster using a smarter selection tool or technique.

Selecting specific kinds of content

On the Select menu, use the Subject or Sky command to select a main subject or the sky, respectively. The Object Selection tool (⌧) can detect and select individual items; click what you want or drag the tool around it. For the Remove tool (✐), the options bar offers the Find Distractions menu which selects people in the background or wires in the sky; you can then delete them using, for example, generative fill. Similarly, the Select > People in Background command selects less prominent people.

If you want to edit only the in-focus part of an image, choose Select > Focus Area and set options. When you click OK, the area you defined as "in focus" becomes a selection.

Selecting by tone or color

Some selection techniques help you edit only specific color or tonal ranges throughout the image.

Color Range command. Choose Select > Color Range and specify a range of colors to select. You can click the image to sample a color, or choose a Select preset such as Skin Tones or Shadows.

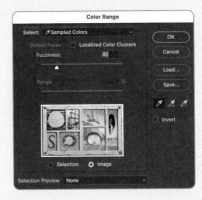

Thumbnail previews. In the Layers or Channels panel, Ctrl-click (Windows) or Command-click (macOS) a thumbnail preview to select based on pixel values. For example, in the Layers panel this technique selects all non-transparent pixels. In the Channels panel, this creates a selection based on luminance (brightness), used in advanced techniques such as creating a luminance mask. Ctrl/Command-clicking the composite channel selects composite luminance, and Ctrl/Command-clicking one channel (such as the Blue channel of an RGB image) selects that channel's luminance.

Selecting by painting

When drawing a marquee is too challenging for a manual selection, it can be easier to use a brush to mark the area you want to select. The Selection Brush tool (✕) is one way to do this; paint an area with it and when you switch to another tool, the area you painted becomes a selection marquee.

QuickMask is another way. In the Tools panel, click the QuickMask icon (▣), and start painting with a brush tool. To exit QuickMask mode click the Quick Mask icon again and the area you painted becomes a pixel selection. To enter and exit QuickMask mode with a single key, press the Q key.

Creating a refined selection with Select and Mask

For selections with fuzzy edges such as hair, try the specialized tools and options in the Select and Mask workspace. You'll learn more about Select and Mask in Lesson 6.

Selecting different kinds of content

This lesson focuses on selecting the pixels you want to edit. In Photoshop you will also work with non-pixel items, so it's useful to know how to select them too:

Pixels. An area of selected pixels is also called a *marquee* selection, which appears as an animated "marching ants" border. You can select pixels by using tools in the marquee and lasso tool groups, the Object Selection, Quick Selection, and Magic Wand tools, and by using commands on the Select menu. You can also use the methods in the sidebar "More ways to select pixels" in this lesson.

List items in panels. Some features affect only what's selected in a panel list, such as in the Layers and Paths panels. For example, many Photoshop commands, and many settings in the Properties panel, affect only the layer selected in the Layers panel.

Type. You can select a type layer in the Layers panel. To select specific characters on that type layer, use a text tool. You'll learn more about working with text in Lesson 7.

Paths. When you work with paths, they're vector objects (not pixels), so select them in the Paths panel, select subpaths using the Path Selection Tool, and select path points and segments with the Direct Selection tool. Shape layers are paths you can export and print, and you select shape layers in the Layers panel. You'll learn more about paths and shape layers in Lesson 8.

Using different kinds of selections together

For some features, you might need to use a specific kind of selection or multiple kinds of selection simultaneously. For example, to apply a filter to an entire layer, first select that layer in the Layers panel list; and to apply that filter only to a specific area on that layer, also select an area of pixels.

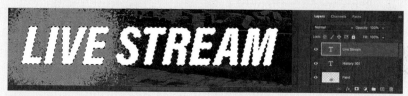

Marquee selecting pixels on the layer selected in the Layers panel.

Converting between pixel selections and paths

It can be useful to convert between different kinds of selections. For example, sometimes it's faster to draw the intended area using a shape tool or Pen tool instead of with a lasso selection tool and then convert the path into a pixel selection. You can convert either way using the Paths panel:

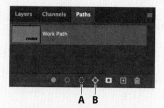

- To convert a path to a pixel selection, click the Load Path as a Selection button.

- To convert a pixel selection to a path, click the Make Work Path from Selection button.

A. *Load Path as a Selection button*
B. *Make Work Path from Selection button*

Cropping an image

Now that your composition is in place, you'll crop the image to a final size. You can use either the Crop tool or the Crop command to crop an image.

1 Select the Crop tool (⌐), or press C to switch from the current tool to the Crop tool. Photoshop displays a crop boundary around the entire image.

2 In the options bar, make sure Ratio is selected in the Preset pop-up menu and that there are no ratio values specified. (If there are, click Clear.) Then confirm that Delete Cropped Pixels is selected.

When Ratio is selected but no ratio values are specified, you can freely crop the image to any proportions.

▶ **Tip:** To crop an image with its original proportions intact, choose Original Ratio from the Preset pop-up menu in the options bar.

3 Drag the crop handles so that the shadow box is in the highlighted area, omitting the backgrounds from the original objects at the bottom of the image. Crop the frame so that there's an even area of white around it.

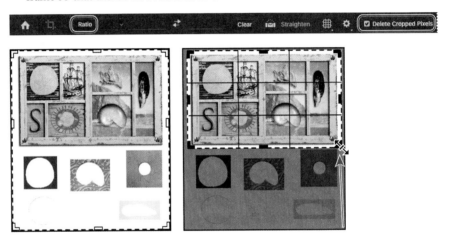

▶ **Tip:** You can also apply the crop by clicking the Commit Current Crop Operation button (✔) in the options bar. The button may not appear on narrower displays or at lower resolution display settings.

4 When you're satisfied with the position of the crop area, press the Enter or Return key to apply the crop.

5 Choose File > Save to save your work.

You've used several different selection tools to move all the seashells into place. The shadow box is complete!

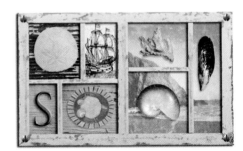

Review questions

1 Once you've made a selection, what area of the image can be edited?

2 How do you add to and subtract from a selection when using a tool such as the Quick Selection or Lasso tool?

3 How can you move a selection while you're creating it?

4 What is the difference between the Quick Selection tool and the Object Selection tool?

5 How does the Magic Wand tool determine which areas of an image to select? What is tolerance, and how does it affect a selection?

Review answers

1 When a selection is active, edits apply only within that selection.

2 To add to a selection, click the Add To Selection button in the options bar, and then click the area you want to add. To subtract from a selection, click the Subtract From Selection button in the options bar, and then click the area you want to subtract. You can also add to a selection by pressing Shift as you drag or click; to subtract, press Alt (Windows) or Option (macOS) as you drag or click.

3 To reposition a selection as you're creating it, keep holding down the mouse button as you also hold down the spacebar and drag.

4 The Quick Selection tool attempts to detect content edges, while the Object Selection tool attempts to recognize subjects (such as people) and objects in the image.

5 The Magic Wand tool selects adjacent pixels based on their similarity in color. The Tolerance value determines how many color tones the Magic Wand tool will select. The higher the tolerance setting, the more tones are selected.

4 LAYER BASICS

Lesson overview

In this lesson, you'll learn how to do the following:

- Organize artwork on layers.

- Create, view, hide, and select layers.

- Rearrange layers to change the stacking order of artwork.

- Apply blending modes to layers.

- Resize and rotate layers.

- Apply a gradient to a layer.

- Apply a filter to a layer.

- Add text and layer effects to a layer.

- Add an adjustment layer.

- Save a copy of the file with the layers flattened.

 This lesson will take less than an hour to complete. To get the lesson files used in this chapter, download them from the web page for this book at peachpit.com/PhotoshopCIB2025. For more information, see "Accessing the lesson files and Web Edition" in the Getting Started section at the beginning of this book.

As you work on this lesson, you'll preserve the start files. If you need to restore the start files, download them from your Account page.

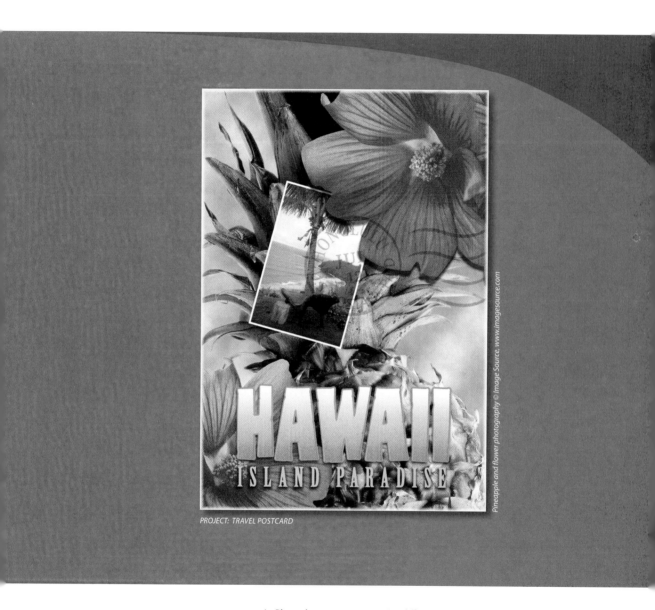

PROJECT: TRAVEL POSTCARD

In Photoshop, you can organize different parts of an image using layers. Each layer can then be edited as discrete artwork, giving you tremendous flexibility as you compose and revise an image.

About layers

Note: Some file formats, such as JPEG and GIF, don't support layers. To save those images with layers, you must save them in Photoshop or TIFF format. Also, some color modes (on the Image > Mode submenu), such as Bitmap and Indexed Color, don't support layers. The lesson files in this lesson are Photoshop documents in RGB color mode.

Every Photoshop file contains one or more *layers*. All new layers in an image are transparent until you add text or artwork. Working with layers is analogous to placing portions of a drawing on clear sheets of film, such as those viewed with an overhead projector: Individual sheets may be edited, repositioned, and deleted without affecting the other sheets. When the sheets are stacked, the entire composition is visible.

Many of the lesson files for this book have a *background layer*, a layer behind all others that is always completely opaque. Photoshop documents intended for print, digital camera images, and scanned images typically have a background layer. Photoshop documents created for mobile devices and websites might not have a background layer; for example, website graphics may need transparent areas that won't block a web page's background or other elements. To learn more about the background layer, see "About the background layer" on page 92.

Getting started

You'll start the lesson by viewing an image of the final composition.

1   Start Photoshop, and then simultaneously hold down Ctrl+Alt+Shift (Windows) or Command+Option+Shift (macOS) to restore the default preferences. (See "Restoring default preferences" on page 5.)

2   When prompted, click Yes to delete the Adobe Photoshop Settings file.

3   Choose File > Browse In Bridge to open Adobe Bridge.

Note: If Bridge isn't installed, you'll be prompted to install it. For more information, see page 3.

4   In the Favorites panel, click the Lessons folder. Then double-click the Lesson04 folder in the Content panel to see its contents.

5   Study the 04End.psd file. Move the thumbnail slider to the right if you want to see the image in more detail, or enlarge the Preview panel.

This layered composite represents a postcard. You will assemble it in this lesson as you learn how to create, edit, and manage layers.

6   Double-click the 04Start.psd file to open it in Photoshop. Close any messages that appear about new features.

Note: If Photoshop displays a dialog box telling you about the difference between saving to Cloud Documents and On Your Computer, click Save On Your Computer. You can also select Don't Show Again, but that setting will deselect after you reset Photoshop preferences.

7   Choose File > Save As, rename the file **04Working.psd**, and click Save. Click OK if you see the Photoshop Format Options dialog box.

Saving another version of the start file frees you to make changes without worrying about overwriting the original.

Using the Layers panel

In this lesson, you'll use many features of the Layers panel. The Layers panel lists all the layers in an image, displaying the layer names and thumbnail previews of the content on each layer. You can use the Layers panel to hide, view, reposition, delete, rename, and merge layers. The layer thumbnails are automatically updated as you edit the layers.

1   If the Layers panel is not visible in the work area, choose Window > Layers.

The Layers panel lists five layers for the 04Working.psd file (from top to bottom): Postage, HAWAII, Flower, Pineapple, and Background. If you can't see all of the layers at once, drag the top edge of the Layers panel to make it taller.

2   Select the Background layer to make it active (if it's not already selected). Notice the layer thumbnail and the icons shown for the Background layer:

▶ **Tip:** Use the context menu to hide or resize the layer thumbnail (the small preview picture next to the layer name). Right-click (Windows) or Control-click (macOS) a thumbnail in the Layers panel to open the context menu, and then choose a thumbnail size.

*   The lock icon (🔒) indicates that the layer is protected from layer changes. That's why the options above the layer list are unavailable. However, it's still possible to edit the layer content itself, such as painting on it.

*   The eye icon (👁) indicates that the layer is visible in the document window. If you click the eye, the document window no longer displays that layer.

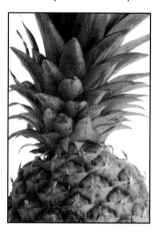
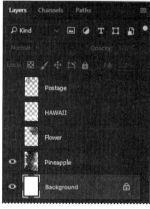

The first task for this project is to add a photo of the beach to the postcard. First, you'll open the beach image in Photoshop.

3 In Photoshop, choose File > Open, navigate to the Lesson04 folder, and then double-click the Beach.psd file to open it.

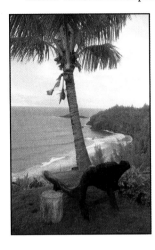
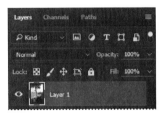

The Layers panel changes to display the layer information for the active Beach.psd file. Notice that only one layer appears in the Beach.psd image: Layer 1. It's not a Background layer, so it can use layer features such as transparency.

About the background layer

If you see a layer named Background at the bottom of the Layers panel and it displays a lock icon, it's a *background layer*, which does not act like other layers. You can't change a background layer's position in the stacking order, and it's always opaque (no transparent areas). When you flatten the layers of a Photoshop document, the document contains only a background layer.

You can convert a background layer to a regular layer or create a document without a background layer. When a Photoshop document has no background layer, any pixels that don't contain content can be transparent. That makes it possible for the content in a Photoshop document to have a non-rectangular shape when placed over another background in Photoshop or in other applications.

To convert a background layer into a regular layer:

Click the lock icon next to the Background layer name. It changes to a default layer name. (Or, double-click the Background layer, set options, and click OK.)

To convert a regular layer into a background layer:

1 Select a layer in the Layers panel.

2 Choose Layer > New > Background From Layer.

Renaming and copying a layer

To add content, drag and drop one or more files or Photoshop layers into a Photoshop document window. You can drag layers from a source document window, drag them from the Layers panel, or drag a compatible file from the desktop. Each item you drop into a Photoshop document is added as a separate layer.

You'll drag the Beach.psd image onto the 04Working.psd file. Before you begin, make sure that both the 04Working.psd and Beach.psd files are open and that the Beach.psd file is selected.

First, you'll give Layer 1 a more descriptive name.

1   In the Layers panel, double-click the name Layer 1, type **Beach**, and then press Enter or Return. Keep the layer selected.

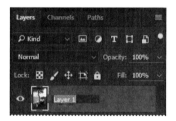 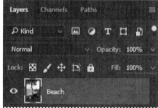

2   Choose Window > Arrange > 2-Up Vertical. Photoshop displays both of the open image files. Select the Beach.psd image so that it is the active file.

3   Select the Move tool (⊕), and use it to drag the Beach.psd image onto the 04Working.psd document window.

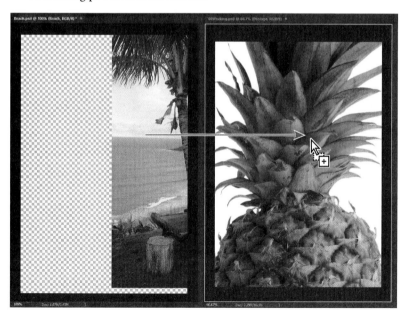

> **Tip:** Dragging many layers to another document can be easier if you combine them into a layer group first. Select them in the Layers panel, and then choose Layer > Group Layers. Now you have only one thing to drag: the layer group (which uses a folder icon).

● **Note:** When you rename a layer, make sure you double-click the layer name text. If you double-click outside the name, other layer options may appear instead.

> **Tip:** When the Move tool is selected, a rectangle with transform controls appears around the layer. Square handles let you resize the layer by dragging. You can rotate the layer by dragging just outside the box (when the pointer appears as a curved two-headed arrow).

> **Tip:** You can also transfer layers between documents by copying and pasting: Select layers in the Layers panel, choose Edit > Copy, switch to another document, and choose Edit > Paste.

> **Tip:** If you hold down Shift as you drop a dragged image into a Photoshop document, the dragged image automatically centers itself in the target image window.

The Beach layer now appears in the 04Working.psd file document window and its Layers panel, between the Background and Pineapple layers. Photoshop always adds new layers directly above the selected layer; you selected the Background layer earlier.

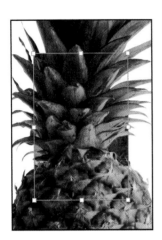 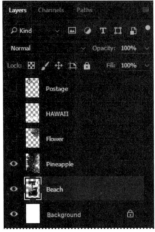

4   Close the Beach.psd file without saving changes to it.

Viewing individual layers

> **Tip:** To center a layer that's already added, drag it near the center of the document, and magenta Smart Guides appear when a layer is snapped to the horizontal and vertical document center.

The 04Working.psd file now contains six layers. Some of the layers are visible, and some are hidden. The eye icon (👁) next to a layer thumbnail in the Layers panel indicates that the layer is visible.

1   Click the eye icon (👁) next to the Pineapple layer to hide the image of the pineapple.

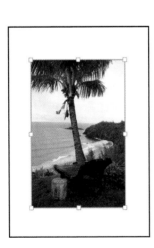 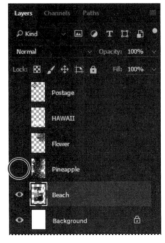

You can hide or show a layer by clicking this icon or clicking in its column, also called the Show/Hide Visibility column.

2   Click again in the Show/Hide Visibility column to display the pineapple.

Adding a border using the Stroke layer style

Now you'll add a white border around the Beach layer to create the impression that it's an old photograph.

1   Select the Beach layer. (To select the layer, click the layer name in the Layers panel.)

The layer is highlighted, indicating that it is active. Changes you make in the document window affect the active layer.

2   To make the opaque areas on this layer more obvious, hide all layers except the Beach layer: Press Alt (Windows) or Option (macOS) as you click the eye icon (👁) next to the Beach layer.

▶ **Tip:** Need images for a project like this one? In Photoshop, choose File > Search Adobe Stock to download low-resolution placeholder images from the Adobe Stock online photo library. If you license the images, Photoshop replaces the placeholders with high-resolution images.

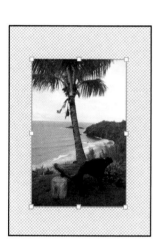
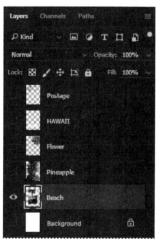

The white background and other objects in the image disappear, leaving only the beach image against a checkerboard background. The checkerboard indicates transparent areas of the active layer.

3   Choose Layer > Layer Style > Stroke.

The Layer Style dialog box opens. Now you'll select the options for the white stroke around the beach image.

▶ **Tip:** When the Preview option is enabled in a dialog box such as Layer Style, you can watch the selected layer change as you adjust the options.

4 Specify the following settings:

- Size: **5** px

- Position: Inside

- Blend Mode: Normal

- Opacity: **100**%

- Color: White. Click the Color swatch, select white, and click OK.

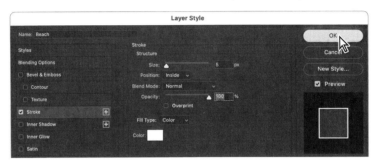

● **Note:** Layer styles apply to the opaque pixels of a layer only. For example, the Stroke layer style draws its line around the opaque pixels of the Beach layer and doesn't change the transparent pixels.

5 Click OK to commit the effect to the layer.

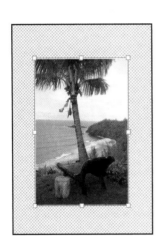
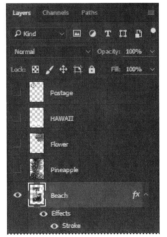

Rearranging layers

The order in which the layers of an image are organized is called the *stacking order*. Stacking order determines how the image is viewed—you can change the order to make certain parts of the image appear in front of or behind other layers.

You'll rearrange the layers so that the beach image is in front of another image that is currently hidden in the file.

1   Make the Postage, HAWAII, Flower, Pineapple, and Background layers visible
    by clicking the Show/Hide Visibility column next to their layer names.

▶ **Tip:** When you
want to hide or show
a continuous series
of layers, you can also
drag through their
eye icons in the Show/
Hide Visibility column,
instead of clicking each
eye icon separately.

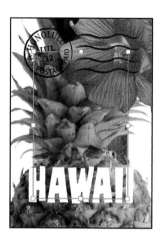
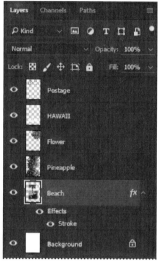

The beach image is almost entirely blocked by images on other layers.

2   In the Layers panel, drag the Beach layer up so that it is positioned between the
    Pineapple and Flower layers—as you drag, a blue line indicates where it will be
    dropped—and then release the mouse button.

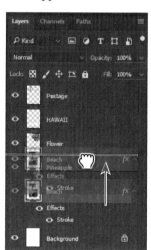
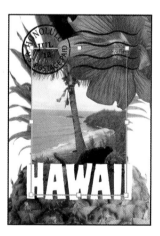

▶ **Tip:** You can also
control the stacking
order of layered
images by selecting
them in the Layers
panel, choosing
Layer > Arrange, and
then choosing Bring
To Front, Bring Forward,
Send Backward, or
Send To Back.

The Beach layer moves up one level in the stacking order, and the beach image
appears on top of the pineapple and background images but under the postmark,
flower, and the word "HAWAII."

Changing the opacity of a layer

You can reduce the opacity of any layer to reveal the layers below it. In this case, the postmark is too dark on the flower. You'll edit the opacity of the Postage layer to let the flower and other images show through.

1   Select the Postage layer, and then in the Layers panel, click the arrow next to the Opacity field to display the Opacity slider. Drag the slider to 25%. You can also type **25** in the Opacity box or scrub the Opacity label.

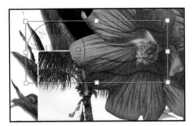 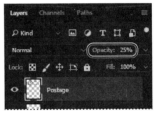

The Postage layer becomes partially transparent so you can better see the layers underneath. Notice that the change in opacity affects only the content of the Postage layer. The Pineapple, Beach, Flower, and HAWAII layers remain opaque.

2   Choose File > Save to save your work.

Duplicating a layer and changing the blending mode

You can apply different blending modes to a layer. *Blending modes* affect how the color values of pixels on a layer mix with pixels on the layers behind it (see the "Blending modes" sidebar on page 100). First you'll use blending modes to increase the intensity of the image on the Pineapple layer so that it doesn't look so dull. Then you'll change the blending mode on the Postage layer. (Currently, the blending mode for both layers is Normal.)

1   Click the eye icons next to the HAWAII, Flower, and Beach layers to hide them.

Tip: If you prefer using the menu bar, Duplicate Layer is also available by choosing Layer > Duplicate Layer.

2   Right-click or Control-click the Pineapple layer name, and choose Duplicate Layer from the context menu. (Make sure you click the layer name; other areas may display a different context menu.) Click OK in the Duplicate Layer dialog box.

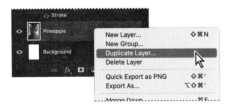

A layer called "Pineapple copy" appears above the Pineapple layer in the Layers panel.

3 With the Pineapple copy layer selected, choose Overlay from the Blending Modes menu in the Layers panel.

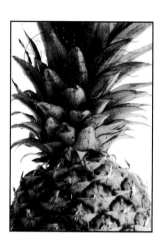
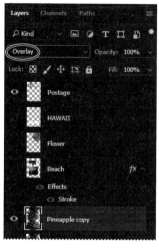

▶ **Tip:** Notice that the image changes as you move the mouse over the options in the Blending Modes menu. This is a quick way to preview which one will do what you want.

The Overlay blending mode blends the Pineapple copy layer with the Pineapple layer beneath it to create a vibrant, more colorful pineapple with deeper shadows and brighter highlights.

▶ **Tip:** If the effect of a blending mode is too strong, reduce the Opacity of that layer.

4 Select the Postage layer, and choose Multiply from the Blending Modes menu.

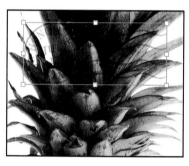
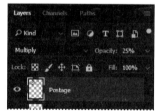

▶ **Tip:** As the list of layers becomes longer, it can be difficult to locate the layer you want. You can use the filter field at the top of the Layers panel to limit the layer list by attributes such as layer kind, layer name, effect, and more.

The Multiply blending mode multiplies the color values of its layer with those of the underlying layers. In this example, areas of the postmark that are over the pineapple are darkened using the tonal values of the pineapple.

Each blending mode uses different math to combine a layer with the layers behind it. Overlay tends to increase contrast; Multiply tends to darken its layer.

5 Choose File > Save to save your work.

▶ **Tip:** In the Layers panel list, you can display the selected layers only and hide the rest: Choose Select > Isolate Layers. When you do this, the filter switch in the Layers panel turns red to let you know that some layers are hidden in the list.

Blending modes

Blending modes affect how the color pixels on a layer mix with pixels on the layers behind them. The default blending mode, Normal, hides pixels beneath the top layer unless the top layer is partially or completely transparent. Each of the other blending modes uses a different method to mix a layer's color values with the layers behind it.

Often, the best way to see how a blending mode affects your image is simply to try it. You can easily experiment with various blending modes in the Layers panel, watching the image change as you move the mouse over the options in the Blending Modes menu. As you experiment, keep in mind how different groups of blending modes affect an image:

- To darken underlying layers, try Darken, Multiply, Color Burn, Linear Burn, or Darker Color.
- To lighten underlying layers, try Lighten, Screen, Color Dodge, Linear Dodge, or Lighter Color.
- To increase the contrast between layers, try Overlay, Soft Light, Hard Light, Vivid Light, Linear Light, Pin Light, or Hard Mix.
- To change the color values of the image, try Hue, Saturation, Color, or Luminosity.
- To create an inversion effect, try Difference or Exclusion.

The following blending modes tend to be used more often and are good ways to start experimenting:

- **Multiply** does what the name implies: It multiplies the selected layer's color values with the color values of underlying layers.

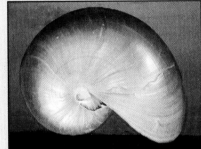

- **Lighten** uses the lightest color value it finds after comparing pixels on the selected layer to underlying layers.

Multiply

- **Overlay** increases contrast in underlying layers, especially in light and dark areas. The difference is smaller the closer the selected layer's color value is to middle gray, which applies no change to underlying layers.

Lighten

- **Luminosity** replaces the luminance of underlying pixels, using the selected layer.

Overlay   Luminosity   Difference

- **Difference** subtracts darker colors from lighter ones. It's a great way to visually identify the differences between two nearly identical images on separate layers.

When you apply different blending modes to multiple layers, you can change the effect by applying the blending modes in a different order in the layer stack. Also, applying a blending mode to a layer group gives you a different result than applying the same blending mode to each layer in the group.

Resizing and rotating layers

Changing the position, size, and angle of layers gives you many creative possibilities. In Photoshop, these kinds of edits are called *transformations*. You performed transformations in Lesson 3 with selections, and they also apply to layers.

1   Click the Visibility column on the Beach layer to make the layer visible.

2   Select the Beach layer in the Layers panel, and choose Edit > Free Transform.

When Free Transform mode is active, the options bar changes to show transformation values instead of tool options. This gives you more control than the transform controls on the Move tool rectangle.

First, you'll resize and angle the layer.

3   Drag the lower-right corner handle inward to scale down the beach photo by about 50%. (Watch the Width and Height percentages in the options bar.)

4   With the transform controls rectangle still active, position the pointer just outside that rectangle until the pointer becomes a curved double arrow. Drag clockwise to rotate the beach image approximately 15 degrees. You can also enter **15** in the Set Rotation box in the options bar.

▶ **Tip:** The Edit > Free Transform command is so useful that you may want to memorize its keyboard shortcut: Ctrl+T (Windows) or Command+T (macOS).

A   B   C

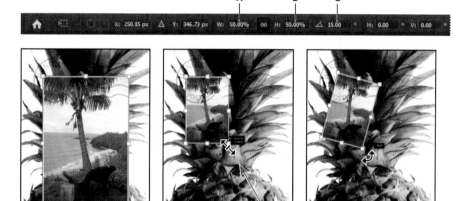

A. *Width value*
B. *Height value*
C. *Set Rotation box*

5   Click the Commit Transform button (✓) in the options bar, or press the Enter or Return key.

6   Make the Flower layer visible. Then select the Move tool (✛), and drag the beach photo so that its corner is tucked neatly beneath the flower, as in the illustration after step 7.

▶ **Tip:** Here's another way to commit a transformation: Position the pointer far enough outside the transform controls rectangle so that the pointer looks like an arrow (not a curved rotation arrow), then click.

Tip: If the transform controls rectangle gets in your way when the Move tool is selected, deselect Show Transform Controls in the options bar. When you want to transform by dragging, you can either enable that option or choose Edit > Free Transform.

7   Choose File > Save.

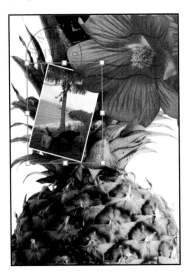

Using a filter to create artwork

Next, you'll create a new layer with no artwork on it yet. (Adding empty layers to a file is like adding blank sheets of clear film to a stack of images.) You'll use this layer to add realistic-looking clouds to the sky with a Photoshop filter.

1   In the Layers panel, select the Background layer to make it active, and then click the Create A New Layer button (⊞) at the bottom of the Layers panel.

A new layer, named Layer 1, appears between the Background and Pineapple layers. The layer has no content, so it has no effect on the image.

Note: You can also create a new layer by choosing Layer > New > Layer or by choosing New Layer from the Layers panel menu.

2   Double-click the name Layer 1, type **Clouds**, and press Enter or Return to rename the layer.

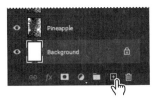 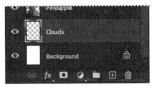

3 In the Tools panel, click the foreground color swatch, select a sky blue color from the Color Picker, and click OK. We selected a color with the following values: R=48, G=138, B=174. The Background Color remains white.

4 With the Clouds layer still active, choose Filter > Render > Clouds.

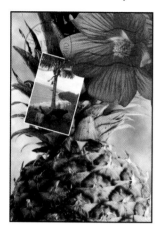

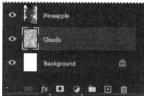

Tip: If you expect to use a certain color frequently in multiple documents, add it to your Creative Cloud Libraries. Create a color in the Color panel, and then in the Libraries panel, click the Add Elements button (+) and choose Foreground Color. Now that color is available to any Photoshop document that you open.

Realistic-looking clouds appear behind the image.

5 Choose File > Save.

Dragging to add a new layer

You can add a layer to an image by dragging an image file from Bridge or from the desktop in Explorer (Windows) or the Finder (macOS). You'll add another flower to the postcard now.

1 If Photoshop fills your monitor, reduce the size of the Photoshop window:

- On Windows, click the Restore button (⧉) in the upper-right corner, and then drag any corner of the Photoshop window to make it smaller.

- On a Mac, click the green Maximize/Restore button (●) in the upper-left corner of the document window, or drag any corner of the Photoshop window to make it smaller.

2 In Photoshop, select the Pineapple copy layer in the Layers panel to make it the active layer.

Tip: If you're adding artwork from a Creative Cloud library, you can simply drag and drop it from the Libraries panel into a Photoshop document. You can also do this with Adobe Stock images stored in your Creative Cloud Libraries.

3 In Explorer (Windows) or the Finder (macOS), navigate to the Lessons folder you downloaded to your computer. Then navigate to the Lesson04 folder, and position that window so you can see its contents next to the Photoshop window.

4 Select Flower2.psd, drag it from Explorer or the Finder, and drop it into the 04Working.psd document window in Photoshop.

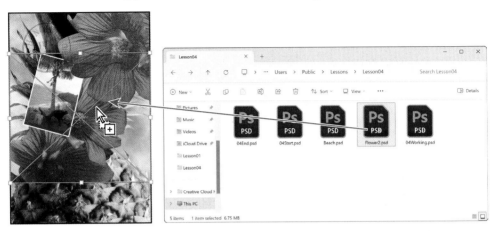

▶ **Tip:** You can drag images from a Bridge window to Photoshop as easily as you can drag from the Windows or Mac desktop.

The Flower2 layer appears in the Layers panel, above the Pineapple copy layer.

5 Now that you are done importing, you can make the Photoshop application window larger again if it will give you more room to work comfortably.

6 Position the Flower2 layer in the lower-left corner of the postcard so that about half of the top flower is visible.

● **Note:** If you don't see the Commit Transform button in the options bar, the Photoshop application window may be too narrow. Either resize the window to be wider or press the Enter or Return keyboard shortcut for committing an edit.

7 Click the Commit Transform button (✔) in the options bar to accept the layer. Its layer icon indicates that Photoshop placed the image as a Smart Object, which is a layer you can edit without making permanent changes. You'll work more extensively with Smart Objects in Lesson 5.

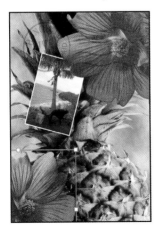

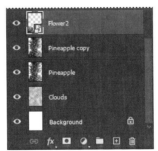

Adding text

Now you're ready to create some type using the Horizontal Type tool, which places the text on its own type layer. You'll then edit the text and apply a special effect.

1 Make the HAWAII layer visible. You'll add text just below this layer and apply special effects to both layers.

2 Choose Select > Deselect Layers to ensure that no layers are selected.

3 In the Tools panel, select the Horizontal Type tool (**T**). Then choose Window > Character to open the Character panel. Do the following in the Character panel:

- Select a condensed font (we used Birch Std, which you can add from Adobe Fonts; if you use a different font, adjust other settings accordingly).

- Select a font style (we used Regular).

- Select a large font size (we used 36 points).

- Select a large tracking value (🖾) (we used 250).

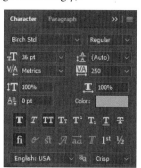

- Click the color swatch, select a shade of grassy green in the Color Picker, and click OK to close the Color Picker.

- If the font does not have a bold variant, click the Faux Bold button (**T**).

- Click the All Caps button (**TT**).

- Select Crisp from the Anti-aliasing menu (ªₐ).

4 In the options bar or Paragraph panel, click the Center Text icon (≡).

5 Click just below the "W" in the word "HAWAII," and type **Island Paradise**, replacing the selected placeholder text that appears. Then click the Commit Any Current Edits button (✔) in the options bar.

▶ **Tip:** If a font has a bold variant, always choose that instead of applying the Faux Bold option. True bold fonts are precisely crafted to be typographically consistent and well designed; Faux Bold is computer generated.

As you type, the text expands out from the center because you selected centered text alignment. The Layers panel now includes a layer named Island Paradise with a "T" thumbnail, indicating that it is a type layer. This layer is at the top of the layer stack because no layers were selected when it was created.

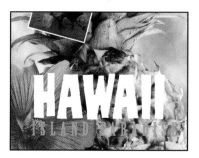

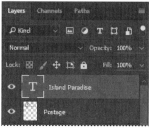

6 If the text is slightly off center relative to the "HAWAII" text, select the Move tool (✛), and drag to reposition the "Island Paradise" text layer as needed.

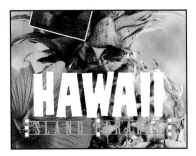

Applying a gradient to a layer

You'll apply a gradient to the "HAWAII" layer to make it more colorful. The general workflow for adding a gradient is to set the gradient type and initial colors, apply the gradient, and then adjust if needed.

1 Select the HAWAII layer in the Layers panel to make it active.

● Note: Make sure you click the thumbnail, rather than the layer name, or you'll see a different context menu.

2 Right-click or Control-click the thumbnail in the HAWAII layer, and choose Select Pixels.

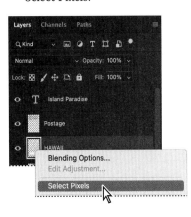

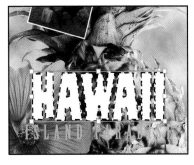

● Note: Though the layer contains the word "HAWAII," it is no longer an editable type layer. The text was rasterized (converted to pixels).

All non-transparent pixels on the HAWAII layer (the white lettering) are selected. Now that you've selected the area to fill, you'll apply a gradient.

3 In the Tools panel, select the Gradient tool (▢).

4 In the options bar, make sure that the Linear Gradient (▢) style is selected.

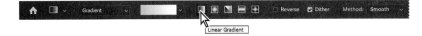

5 Click the Foreground Color swatch in the Tools panel, select a bright shade of orange in the Color Picker, and click OK. The Background Color should still be white.

6 Click the Gradients panel tab to bring it forward, or if it isn't visible, choose Window > Gradients to open it.

7 In the Gradients panel, expand the Basics group, and click the Foreground to Background gradient preset (the first one in the Basics group). This preset uses the foreground and background colors you set in step 5. (You can also drag the gradient preset swatch and drop it on a layer.)

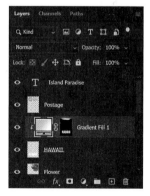

Tip: To list the gradient options by name rather than by sample, click the menu button in the Gradient Picker, and choose either Small List or Large List. Or, hover the pointer over a thumbnail until a tool tip appears, showing the gradient name.

The gradient is applied within the selected pixels, starting with orange at the bottom and gradually blending to white at the top. In the Layers panel, a new Gradient Fill 1 layer was created above the HAWAII layer, appearing in the list indented with an arrow because it's added as a clipping mask attached to the HAWAII layer. (You'll learn more about clipping masks in Lesson 6.) A gradient is not always applied as a Gradient Fill clipping mask; how a gradient is applied depends on what's selected.

You see gradient controls appear on the canvas over the "HAWAII" text, because the Gradient tool is selected and a Gradient Fill layer is selected in the Layers panel. A white bar indicates the gradient distance. The bar distance matches the height of the "HAWAII" text because the gradient length was based on the pixel selection you created in step 2. You can drag the controls to adjust those gradient settings.

Tip: Two more ways to apply a gradient: Drag a preset from the Gradients panel and drop it on the non-transparent pixels of a layer on the canvas, or drag the Gradient tool across the canvas.

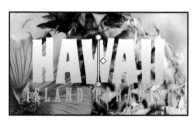

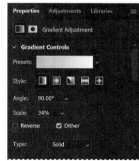

For more information about creating and editing gradients, see the sidebar "About gradients," later in this lesson.

8 Save the work you've done so far.

About gradients

Gradients can add interest and dimension to your designs; recent versions of Photoshop have greatly expanded their power and flexibility. With many options for creating and editing gradients, knowing a few basic ideas will save you a lot of time.

The key features for working with gradients are the Gradients panel, the Properties panel, the Gradient tool, and the options bar when the Gradient tool is selected. You don't always need all of them, but it's important to know how they work together.

Setting up a new gradient

To set the type of gradient and its options before applying it, use the options bar when the Gradient tool is selected. Of the five gradient types, the most commonly used are the Linear Gradient and the Radial Gradient.

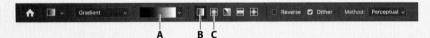

A. *Gradient presets*
B. *Linear gradient type*
C. *Radial gradient type*

To set a gradient's colors before creating it, set the Foreground and Background colors in the Tools panel, and then in the Gradients panel, select the Foreground to Background gradient preset (it's in the Basic presets group). In the Gradients panel, you manage and apply presets in the same way as in the other preset panels (Swatches, Shapes, and Patterns).

Applying a gradient to a layer

Applying a gradient to a layer is as simple as dragging a gradient preset swatch from the Gradients panel and dropping it on a non-Background layer on the canvas or in the Layers panel. How Photoshop applies the gradient depends on the layer type:

- For a pixel layer, such as brush strokes or a photo, a gradient is applied as a Gradient Fill layer clipping mask, which displays that layer only on the pixel layer's non-transparent pixels. To edit it, double-click that Gradient Fill layer. (For more about clipping masks, see page 115.)

- For a shape layer, such as a vector circle or polygon, a gradient is applied as a Gradient Fill (not a Gradient Fill layer). To edit it, select the layer and edit the Fill option in the Appearance section of the Properties panel, or in the options bar when a shape or pen tool is selected.

- For a type layer, a gradient is applied as a Gradient Overlay layer effect. To edit it, in the Layers panel double-click Gradient Overlay in the layer where it's applied.

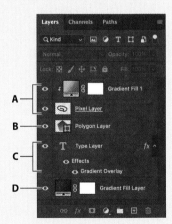

A. *Gradient applied to layer as Gradient Fill clipping mask*
B. *Shape with gradient applied as Gradient Fill*
C. *Type layer with gradient applied as Gradient Overlay*
D. *Gradient Fill layer*

Adding a new Gradient Fill layer

When you want to create a gradient as an entire adjustable layer of its own,
add a new Gradient Fill layer by doing one of the following:

• With no layers selected, drag the Gradient tool to set the distance and angle of the gradient.

• Choose Layer > New Fill Layer > Gradient.

Editing a gradient using on-canvas controls

When a Gradient Fill is selected in the Layers panel and the Gradient tool is also selected, gradient controls appear on the canvas. A white bar indicates the gradient distance. You can adjust the gradient distance and angle by dragging the circular handles (color stops) at the ends of the bar. You can add a new circular color handle along the gradient by positioning the pointer near (not on) the gradient bar, and when the pointer appears as an arrow with a plus sign (⯈₊), click. Color handles are circular, a diamond-shaped midpoint stop appears when a color stop is selected. You can change any color stop by double-clicking its circular handle, and you can change the position of a color or midpoint stop by dragging it.

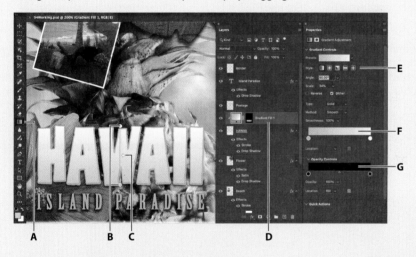

A. Gradient tool
B. Color stops
C. Midpoint stop
D. Gradient Fill layer
   selected
E. Gradient Presets, Style,
   Angle, and more
F. Gradient proxy and
   color stops
G. Opacity proxy and
   opacity stops

Editing a gradient using the Properties panel

When a Gradient Fill layer is selected in the Layers panel, the Properties panel displays a Gradient Controls section where you can make detailed adjustments. For example, you can change the gradient Style and Angle, and you can use the gradient proxy to edit color stops along the gradient. You can also vary opacity along the gradient by editing and adding opacity stops in Opacity Controls.

Similar gradient options are also available in the Gradient Fill dialog box that opens when you double-click a Gradient Fill layer or Gradient Overlay effect in the Layers panel.

Applying a layer style

You can enhance a layer by adding a shadow, stroke, satin sheen, or other special effect from a collection of automated and editable layer styles. These styles are easy to apply, and they link directly to the layer you specify.

Like layers, layer styles can be hidden by clicking their eye icons (👁) in the Layers panel. Layer styles are nondestructive, so you can edit or remove them at any time.

Earlier, you used a layer style to add a stroke to the beach photo. Now, you'll add drop shadows to the text to make it stand out.

▶ **Tip:** You can also open the Layer Style dialog box by clicking the Add A Layer Style button at the bottom of the Layers panel and then choosing Drop Shadow or another layer style from the pop-up menu.

1 In the Layers panel, select the Island Paradise layer, and then choose Layer > Layer Style > Drop Shadow.

2 In the Layer Style dialog box, make sure that the Preview option is selected, and then, if necessary, move the dialog box so that you can see the "Island Paradise" text in the image window. A drop shadow is now applied.

3 In the Structure area, select Use Global Light, and then specify the following settings:

- Blend Mode: Multiply
- Opacity: **75**%
- Angle: **78** degrees
- Distance: **5** px
- Spread: **30**%
- Size: **10** px

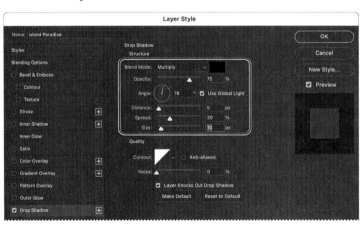

▶ **Tip:** You can also change Global Light settings by choosing Layer > Layer Style > Global Light.

When Use Global Light is selected, a *global* (shared) lighting angle is available in many layer effects that use shading. If you set a lighting angle in one of these effects, every other effect with Use Global Light selected inherits the same angle setting.

Angle determines the lighting angle at which the effect is applied to the layer. Distance determines the offset distance for a shadow or satin effect. Spread determines how gradually the shadow fades toward the edges. Size determines how far the shadow extends.

Because the Preview option is selected, as you make changes Photoshop updates the drop shadow preview in the document window.

4 Click OK to accept the settings and close the Layer Style dialog box.

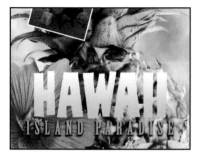 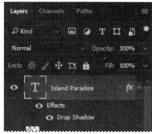

In the Layers panel, the layer style appears nested in the Island Paradise layer. An Effects heading is listed first, and under that, the layer styles applied to the layer appear. An eye icon (👁) appears next to the effect category and next to each effect. To turn off an effect, click its eye icon. Click the visibility column again to restore the effect. To hide all layer styles for that layer, click the eye icon next to Effects. To collapse the list of effects, click the arrow to the right of the layer name.

5 Make sure that eye icons appear for both items nested in the Island Paradise layer.

6 Press Alt (Windows) or Option (macOS), and in the Layers panel, drag the Effects listing or the fx symbol (*fx*) for the Island Paradise layer onto the HAWAII layer.

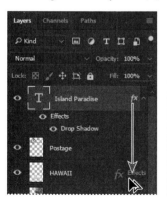 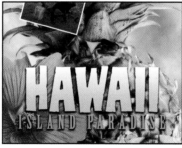

► Tip: If you expect to use a layer style frequently in multiple documents, add it to your Creative Cloud Libraries. First create or open a library. In the document, select a layer that uses the style, click the Add Content button (+.) at the bottom of the Libraries panel, and then click Layer Style. Now you can apply that style to any open Photoshop document.

The Drop Shadow layer style is applied to the HAWAII layer, copying the settings you applied to the Island Paradise layer. Now you'll add a green stroke around the word "HAWAII."

7 Select the HAWAII layer in the Layers panel, click the Add A Layer Style button (*fx*) at the bottom of the panel, and then choose Stroke from the pop-up menu.

8 In the Structure area of the Layer Style dialog box, specify the following settings:

- Size: **4** px

- Position: Outside

- Blend Mode: Normal

- Opacity: **100**%

▶ **Tip:** Here's a quick way to match the color of the "Island Paradise" text. When the Color Picker is open for the Stroke Color, position the pointer outside the Color Picker dialog box so that it changes into an eyedropper icon. Click the "Island Paradise" text to sample its green color, loading it into the Color Picker.

- Color: Green. Click the Color swatch, select a color consistent with the one used for the "Island Paradise" text, and then click OK to close the Color Picker.

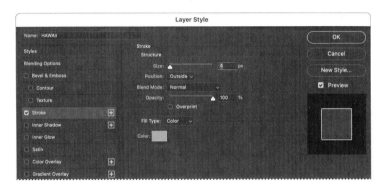

9 Click OK to apply the stroke.

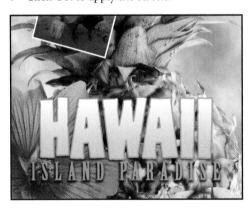

Now you'll add a drop shadow and a satin sheen to the flower.

10 Select the Flower layer, and choose Layer > Layer Style > Drop Shadow. Then change the following settings in the Structure area:

- Opacity: **60**%

- Distance: **13** px

- Spread: **9**%

- Make sure Use Global Light is selected and that the Blend Mode is Multiply. Do not click OK.

▶ **Tip:** As the Layers panel list of layers and effects becomes longer, you may want to give the Layers panel more room by hiding unneeded panels in the same stack. For example, if the Gradients panel is still visible, collapse it by double-clicking its panel tab.

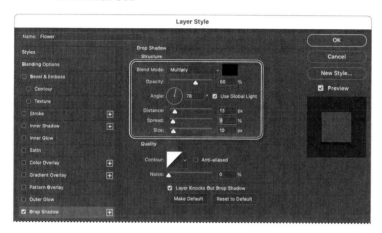

11 With the Layer Style dialog box still open, click the word "Satin" on the left to select it and display its options. Then make sure Invert is selected, and apply the following settings:

- Color (next to Blend Mode): Click the color swatch, choose a color that enhances the flower color, such as a fuchsia hue, and click OK to close the Color Picker.

- Opacity: **20**%

- Distance: **22** px

Note: Be sure to click the word "Satin." If you click only the check box, Photoshop applies the layer style with its default settings, but you won't see the options.

The Satin layer effect applies interior shading to create a satiny finish. The contour controls the shape of the effect; Invert flips the contour curve.

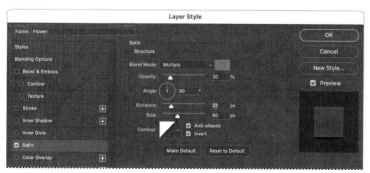

Tip: You just added two different layer styles to the same layer, but you can also add multiple instances of the same layer style. For example, you can add multiple strokes to one layer. This works for any layer effect that has a [+] button next to its name in the Layer Styles dialog box.

12 Click OK to apply both layer styles. In the Layers panel you can see the two layer styles applied to the Flower layer, and you can use the eye icons to see what the Flower layer looks like with and without the layer styles applied.

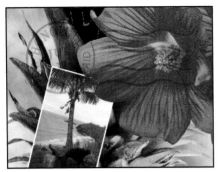
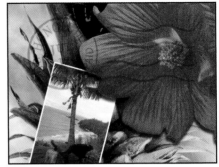

Before applying layer styles.

The flower with the drop shadow and satin layer styles applied.

Adding an adjustment layer

You can add adjustment layers to apply color and tonal adjustments without permanently changing the pixel values in the image. For example, if you add a Color Balance adjustment layer to an image, you can experiment with different colors repeatedly, because the change occurs only on the adjustment layer. If you decide to return to the original pixel values, you can hide or delete the adjustment layer.

You've used adjustment layers in other lessons. Here, you'll add a Hue/Saturation adjustment layer to change the color of the purple flower. An adjustment layer affects all layers below it in the image's stacking order unless a selection is active when you create it or you create a clipping mask.

1 Select the Flower2 layer in the Layers panel.

2 In the Adjustments panel, scroll to the Single Adjustments list and click Hue/Saturation, to add a Hue/Saturation adjustment layer.

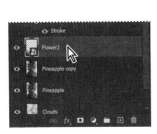
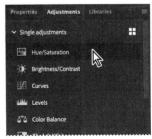

3 In the Properties panel, apply the following settings:

- Hue: **43**
- Saturation: **19**
- Lightness: **0**

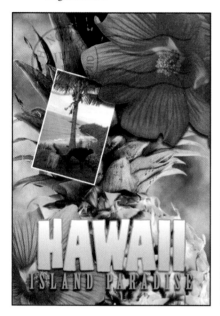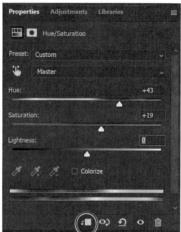

The changes affect the Flower2, Pineapple Copy, Pineapple, Clouds, and Background layers. The effect is interesting, but you want to change only the Flower2 layer.

4 In the Properties panel, click the Create Clipping Mask button (⬓⬜). It's the first button along the bottom of the panel, and you see it when the Properties panel displays options for a layer that can become a clipping mask, such as an adjustment layer.

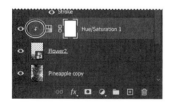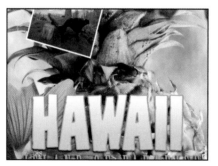

▶ **Tip:** You can also find the Create Clipping Mask and Release Clipping Mask commands (and their keyboard shortcut) on the Layer menu, on the Layers panel menu, and by right-clicking the layer name. You can also create a clipping mask for a layer by Alt-clicking (Windows) or Option-clicking (macOS) the line under that layer in the Layers panel.

An arrow appears in the Layers panel, indicating that the adjustment layer applies only to the Flower2 layer. You'll learn more about clipping masks in Lesson 6 and Lesson 7.

Updating layer effects

Layer effects are automatically updated when you make changes to a layer. You can edit the text and watch how the layer effect updates to match.

1 Select the Island Paradise layer in the Layers panel.

2 In the Tools panel, select the Horizontal Type tool (**T**).

3 In the options bar, change the Size by a few points, and press Enter or Return.

You changed the settings for the entire type layer, even though you didn't select the text by highlighting the characters (as you would have to do in a word processing program). This worked because in Photoshop, you can change settings for an entire type layer by selecting it in the Layers panel, as long as a type tool is selected.

If you add more text to a layer that has a layer effect applied to it, the new text takes on the same layer effect. Changing the type size may leave too little space above the Island Paradise and HAWAII type layers, so if you need to, you can adjust that.

4 Select the Move tool (✛), and drag the Island Paradise type layer as needed.

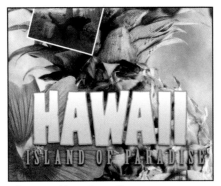
When you add text, layer effects are automatically applied to the new characters.

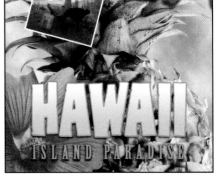
Reposition the text beneath the word "HAWAII."

5 Choose File > Save.

Note: The Auto-Select option can save time by letting you select a layer by clicking it with the Move tool, instead of having to select it in the Layers panel. But in documents where many layers overlap, if clicking keeps selecting the wrong layer, try turning off Auto-Select.

Creating a border from a selection

The Hawaii postcard is nearly done. The elements are almost all arranged correctly in the composition. You'll finish up by positioning the postmark and then adding a white postcard border.

1 Select the Move tool, and in the options bar, make sure Auto-Select is disabled.

2 Select the Postage layer, and then use the Move tool (✛) to drag it to the middle right of the image, as in the illustration.

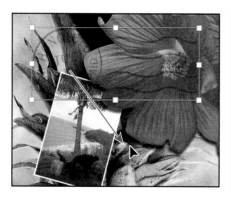 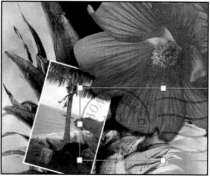

3 Select the Island Paradise layer in the Layers panel, and then click the Create A New Layer button (⊞) at the bottom of the panel.

4 Choose Select > All.

5 Choose Select > Modify > Border. In the Border Selection dialog box, type **10** pixels for the Width, and click OK.

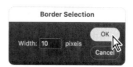

A 10-pixel border is selected around the entire image. Now, you'll fill it with white.

6 In the Tools panel or Color panel, set the Foreground Color to white, and then choose Edit > Fill.

7 In the Fill dialog box, choose Foreground Color from the Contents menu, and click OK.

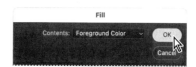

8 Choose Select > Deselect.

9 Double-click the Layer 1 name in the Layers panel, and rename the layer **Border**.

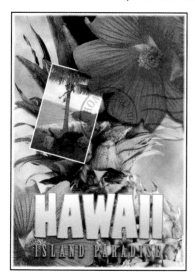 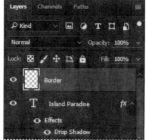

Use layer comps to store and switch among design ideas

The Layer Comps panel (choose Window > Layer Comps) lets you store different views of a multilayered image file. A layer comp is simply a saved state of the settings in the Layers panel. Whenever you want to preserve a specific combination of layer properties, create a new layer comp. Then, by switching from one layer comp to another, you can quickly review the two designs. The beauty of layer comps becomes apparent when you want to demonstrate a number of possible design arrangements. When you've created a few layer comps, you can review the design variations without having to tediously select and deselect eye icons or change settings in the Layers panel.

For example, suppose you're designing a brochure, and you're producing a version in English as well as in French. You might have the French text on one layer and the English text on another in the same image file. To create two different layer comps, you would simply turn on visibility for the French layer and turn off visibility for the English layer and then click the Create New Layer Comp button in the Layer Comps panel. Then you'd do the inverse—turn on visibility for the English layer, turn off visibility for the French layer, and click the Create New Layer Comp button—to create an English layer comp. To view the different layer comps, click the Layer Comp box for each comp in the Layer Comps panel in turn.

Layer comps can be especially valuable when you want to save complex combinations of states of multiple layers. If some aspects need to stay consistent among layer comps, you can change the visibility, position, or appearance of one of its layers and then sync it to see that change reflected in all the other layer comps.

Flattening and saving files

When you finish editing all the layers in your image, you can merge or *flatten* layers to reduce the file size. Flattening combines all the layers into a single background layer. However, you cannot edit layers once you've flattened them, so you shouldn't flatten an image until you are certain that you're satisfied with all your design decisions. Rather than flattening your original PSD files, it's a good idea to save a copy of the file with its layers intact, in case you need to edit a layer later.

● **Note:** If the sizes do not appear in the Status Bar, click the Status Bar pop-up menu arrow, and choose Document Sizes.

To appreciate what flattening does, notice the two numbers for the file size in the Status Bar at the bottom of the document window. The first number represents

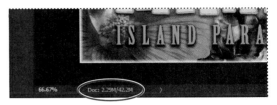

what the file size would be if you flattened the image. The second number represents the file size without flattening. This lesson file, if flattened, would be 2–3MB, but the current file is much larger. So flattening is well worth it in this case.

1 Select any tool except the Type tool (**T**) to be sure that you're not in text-editing mode. Then choose File > Save (if it is available) to be sure that all your changes have been saved in the file.

2 Choose Image > Duplicate.

3 In the Duplicate Image dialog box, name the file **04Flat.psd**, and click OK.

4 Leave the 04Flat.psd file open, but close the 04Working.psd file.

5 Choose Layer > Flatten Image.

Only one layer, named Background, remains in the Layers panel.

▶ **Tip:** The Flatten Image command is also on the Layer menu and on the context menu when you right-click/Control-click a layer name.

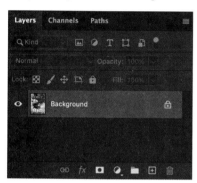

6 Choose File > Save. Even though you chose Save rather than Save As, the Save As dialog box appears, because this document has not yet been saved to storage.

7 Make sure the location is on your computer in the Lessons/Lesson04 folder, and then click Save to accept the default settings and save the flattened file.

You have saved two versions of the file: a one-layer, flattened copy as well as the original file, in which all the layers remain intact.

You've created a colorful, attractive postcard. This lesson only begins to explore the vast possibilities and the flexibility you gain when you master the art of using Photoshop layers. You'll get more experience and try different techniques for layers in almost every lesson as you move forward in this book.

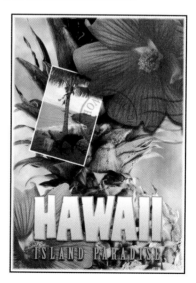

▶ **Tip:** Flattening always means merging all layers into one, with an opaque background. If you want to merge only some of the layers in a file, in the Layers panel select just those layer and choose Layer > Merge Layers.

Extra credit

Exploring design options with Adobe Stock

Visualizing different ideas for a design project is easier when you can experiment with images. The Libraries panel in Photoshop gives you direct access to millions of Adobe Stock images. We'll add a stock image of a ukulele to this lesson's composition.

1   In the Lesson04 folder, open 04End.psd. Save it as **04End_Stock**.

2   In the Layers panel, select the Beach layer.

3   In the Libraries panel, open or create a library, type **ukulele** into the search field, set the search field menu (⌄) to Adobe Stock, and locate any vertical image of a ukulele on a white background. Hover the pointer over the ukulele image you want, and click the plus button (+) to add that image's preview to the current library.

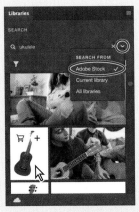

Adobe Stock search results.

4   Drag the ukulele image into the document. Drag a corner handle to proportionally scale the image to be about as tall as the Beach layer. Apply the changes to finish importing the image.

5   Now remove the background. With the ukulele layer selected, click the Remove Background button in the Contextual Task Bar. Notice that this created a mask for the ukulele layer in the Layers panel.

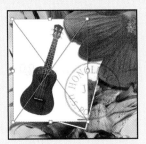

Stock image in document.

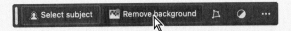

6   With the Move tool, drag the ukulele to the upper-left corner so that it partially overlaps the small photo of the beach view. You've just added an Adobe Stock photo to your postcard image!

Licensing an image

Until it's licensed, the ukulele image is a low-resolution version with an Adobe Stock watermark. You don't have to license the ukulele image for this lesson, but you must license images used in a real project. With the ukulele layer (not mask) selected in the Layers panel, click License Asset in the Properties panel and follow the prompts. After licensing, the image is automatically replaced with a high-resolution version without a watermark. If you plan to license many images, consider an Adobe Stock monthly plan or a pack of credits.

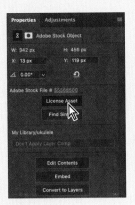

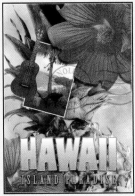

You've added a new element to your postcard using Adobe Stock!

Review questions

1 What is the advantage of using layers?

2 When you create a new layer, where does it appear in the Layers panel stack?

3 How can you make artwork on one layer appear in front of artwork on another layer?

4 How can you apply a layer style?

5 To edit a Gradient Fill layer by dragging on-canvas controls, what two things should you make sure to do?

6 Where can you see detailed options for editing a Gradient Fill layer?

Review answers

1 Layers let you move and edit different parts of an image as discrete objects. You can also hide individual layers as you work on other layers.

2 In the Layers panel, a new layer always appears immediately above the selected layer. If no layer is selected, a new layer appears at the top of the layer list.

3 You can make artwork on one layer appear in front of artwork on another layer by dragging layers up or down the stacking order in the Layers panel or by using the Layer > Arrange commands—Bring To Front, Bring Forward, Send Backward, and Send To Back. However, you can't change the layer position of a background layer unless you convert it to a regular layer (unlock it or double-click to rename it).

4 To apply a layer style, select the layer, and then click the Add A Layer Style button in the Layers panel, or choose Layer > Layer Style > [style].

5 Make sure the Gradient Fill layer is selected, and if you also make sure the Gradient tool is selected, the on-canvas gradient editor appears.

6 Detailed options for a Gradient Fill layer are displayed in the Gradient Controls section of the Properties panel, when a Gradient Fill layer is selected.

5 QUICK FIXES

Lesson overview

In this lesson, you'll learn how to do the following:

- Remove red eye.

- Brighten an image.

- Adjust the features of a face.

- Combine images to create a panorama.

- Crop and straighten an image and fill in any resulting empty areas.

- Add different types of blur to simulate motion in an image.

- Merge images to extend depth of field (focus stack).

- Apply optical lens correction to a distorted image.

- Adjust the perspective of an image to match another image.

 This lesson will take about an hour to complete. To get the lesson files used in this chapter, download them from the web page for this book at peachpit.com/PhotoshopCIB2025. For more information, see "Accessing the lesson files and Web Edition" in the Getting Started section at the beginning of this book.

As you work on this lesson, you'll preserve the start files. If you need to restore the start files, download them from your Account page.

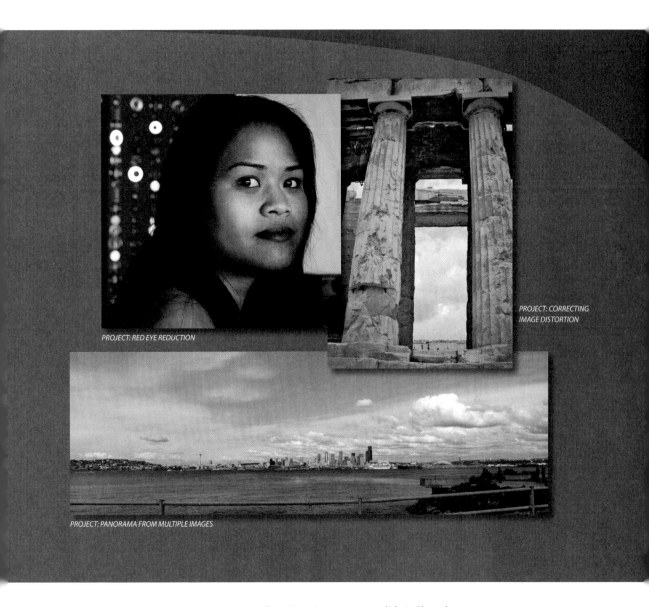

PROJECT: RED EYE REDUCTION

PROJECT: CORRECTING IMAGE DISTORTION

PROJECT: PANORAMA FROM MULTIPLE IMAGES

Sometimes just one or two clicks in Photoshop can turn an image from so-so (or worse) to awesome. Quick fixes get you the results you want without a lot of fuss.

Getting started

Not every image requires a complicated makeover using advanced features in Photoshop. In fact, once you're familiar with Photoshop, you can often improve an image quickly. The trick is to know what's possible and how to find what you need.

In this lesson, you'll make quick fixes to several images using a variety of tools and techniques. You can use these techniques individually or team them up when you're working with an image that needs just a little more help.

1   Start Photoshop, and then immediately hold down Ctrl+Alt+Shift (Windows) or Command+Option+Shift (macOS) to restore the default preferences. (See "Restoring default preferences" on page 5.)

2   When prompted, click Yes to delete the Adobe Photoshop Settings file.

Improving a snapshot

If you're sharing a snapshot with family and friends, you may not need it to look professional. But you probably don't want glowing eyes, and it would be good if the picture isn't too dark to show important detail. Photoshop gives you the tools to make quick changes to a snapshot or when the expression on a model's face needs a subtle adjustment.

Correcting red eye

Red eye occurs when the retina of a subject's eye is reflected by the light of a flash on the camera. It commonly occurs in flash photographs taken in a dark room, because the subject's irises are wide open. Fortunately, red eye is easy to fix in Photoshop. In this exercise, you will remove the red eye from the woman's eyes in the portrait.

You'll start by viewing the before and after images in Adobe Bridge.

1   Choose File > Browse In Bridge to open Adobe Bridge.

2   In the Favorites panel in Bridge, click the Lessons folder. Then, in the Content panel, double-click the Lesson05 folder to open it.

3   Adjust the thumbnail slider, if necessary, so that you can see the thumbnail previews clearly. Then look at the RedEye_Start.jpg and RedEye_End.psd files.

● **Note:** If you haven't installed Bridge, you'll be prompted to do so when you choose Browse In Bridge. For more information, see page 3.

● **Note:** If Bridge asks you if you want to import preferences from a previous version of Bridge, click No.

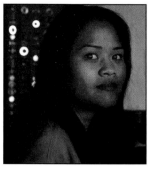
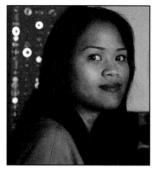

RedEye_Start.jpg RedEye_End.psd

Red eye is not the only problem with the image; it's also underexposed. Both are easy to correct in Photoshop.

4 Double-click the RedEye_Start.jpg file to open it in Photoshop. Close any messages that appear about new features.

5 Choose File > Save As, choose Photoshop for the Format, name the file **RedEye_Working.psd**, and click Save.

6 Select the Zoom tool (Q), and then drag to zoom in to see the woman's eyes. If Scrubby Zoom isn't selected, drag a marquee around the eyes to zoom in.

7 Select the Red Eye tool (⁺☉), hidden under the Spot Healing Brush tool (🩹).

8 In the options bar, reduce the Pupil Size to **23%** and the Darken Amount to **62%**.

The Darken Amount specifies how dark the pupil should be.

9 Click the pupil in the woman's left eye. The red reflection disappears.

10 Click the pupil in the woman's right eye to remove the red reflection there, too.

> **Note:** If Photoshop displays a dialog box telling you about the difference between saving to Cloud Documents and On Your Computer, click Save On Your Computer. You can also select Don't Show Again, but that setting will deselect after you reset Photoshop preferences.

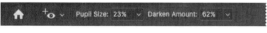

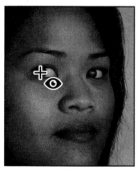
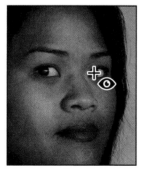
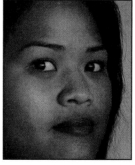

If the red reflection is directly over the pupil, clicking the pupil usually removes it. If it doesn't, you can try clicking the highlight or try dragging the Red Eye tool around the entire pupil.

11 Choose View > Fit On Screen to see the entire image, and save your work.

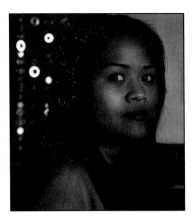

Brightening an image

The woman's eyes no longer glow red, but the overall image is a bit dark. You can brighten an image in several different ways, as you've already seen. You can try adding adjustment layers for Brightness/Contrast, Levels, and Curves, depending on the degree of adjustment you want to make. For a quick fix or a good starting point, try the Auto button or the presets, which are available in both the Levels and Curves adjustments. Let's try a Curves adjustment layer for this image.

1 In the Adjustments panel, in the Single Adjustments list click Curves.
A Curves adjustment layer is added to the Layers panel, and the settings for the Curves adjustment layer now appear in the Properties panel.

2 Click Auto. In this example, the automatic correction adds a midpoint on the curve and raises its value, lightening the image mostly around the midtones.

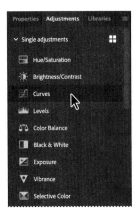 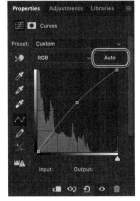 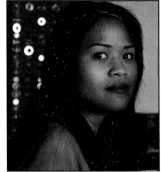

3 Choose Lighter (RGB) from the Preset menu. The curve changes slightly. The difference is that a preset applies the same curve to every image, while Auto analyzes the layer and creates a curve customized for it.

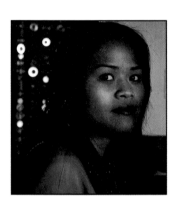
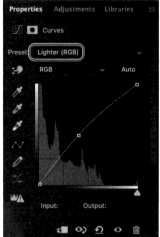

4 Click the Reset To Adjustment Defaults button (↺) at the bottom of the Properties panel to revert to the unadjusted image.

5 Select the on-image adjustment tool (☝) in the Curves panel, and then click the center of the forehead and drag up. Clicking with that tool adds a curve point that corresponds to the tonal level you clicked in the image. When you drag up, you raise that point and the curve, brightening the image from that tonal level.

> **Tip:** If you want to use the Auto button or the white point or black point samplers (eyedropper icons) in the Curves or Levels adjustments, use them before applying manual adjustments. Like presets, adjustments by those tools replace manual adjustments.

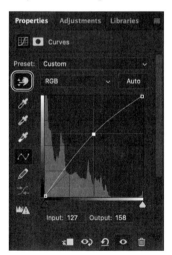
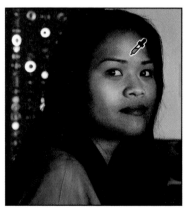

> **Tip:** To see how much you've brightened the image, hide the Curves layer, and then show it again.

You've just tried three different ways to adjust brightness using Curves.

6 Choose Layer > Flatten Image, and save the file.

Adjusting facial features with Liquify

The Liquify filter is useful when you want to distort only part of an image. It includes Face-Aware Liquify options that can automatically recognize faces in images and then lets you easily adjust facial features such as the size of or distance between the eyes. This can be useful for photos used in advertising and fashion, when portraying a certain look or expression may be more important than faithfully representing a specific person.

1   With RedEye_Working.psd still open, choose Filter > Liquify.

2   In the Properties panel, if the Face-Aware Liquify options are collapsed (hidden), click the right-facing triangle to expand them.

3   Make sure the Eyes section is expanded and that the link icon (🔗) is selected for both Eye Size and Eye Height. Enter **32** for Eye Size and **10** for Eye Height.

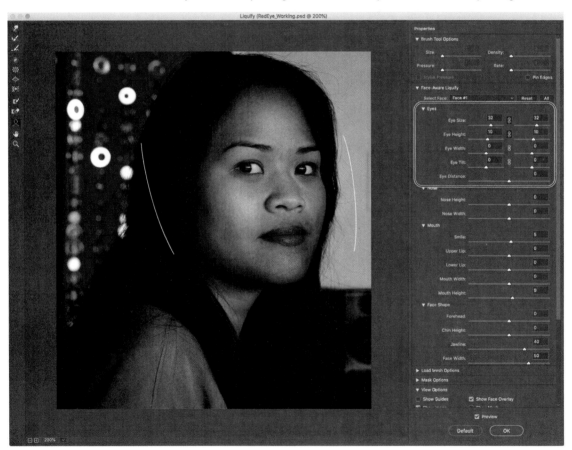

▶ **Tip:** When the Face tool ( ) is selected in the Liquify toolbar, handles appear as you hover the pointer over different parts of the face. You can drag those handles to adjust different parts of the face directly, as an alternative to dragging the Face-Aware Liquify sliders.

When the link icon (🔗) is not selected for an Eyes option, you can set different values for the left and right eyes.

Tip: A keyboard shortcut for toggling the Preview option is to press the P key.

4   Make sure the Mouth section is expanded, and then enter **5** for Smile and **9** for Mouth Height.

5   Make sure the Face Shape section is expanded, and then enter **40** for Jawline and **50** for Face Width.

6   Deselect and reselect the Preview option to compare the image before and after your changes.

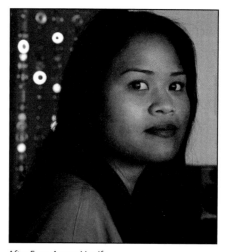

Before Face-Aware Liquify   After Face-Aware Liquify

Tip: The Face-Aware Liquify options have a limited range because they're designed for subtle, believable distortions. If you want to exaggerate faces into caricatures or extreme expressions, try the more advanced manual tools along the left side of the Liquify dialog box. Or try the face-altering filters in Filter > Neural Filters.

Feel free to experiment with any of the Face-Aware Liquify options to get a better sense of the possibilities for quick, easy alterations.

7   Click OK to exit Liquify. Close the document, and save your changes.

The Face-Aware Liquify features are available only when Photoshop recognizes a face in an image. It may not recognize a face that is turned too far away from the camera or partially covered by hair, sunglasses, or a hat shadow.

When a workspace totally changes

Some Photoshop features, such as Liquify, open a dedicated workspace—a maximized dialog box covering most of the screen. If you're new to Photoshop, this can be confusing, because panels that were open may be temporarily inaccessible. For example, if panels such as Layers and Color were open before using Liquify, the dedicated Liquify workspace covers those panels as long as Liquify is open.

When a dedicated workspace is open, how do you restore the regular workspace? Look for OK and Cancel buttons. For example, when your Liquify edits are complete, click OK to apply your changes and return to the normal Photoshop workspace.

Blur Gallery

The Blur Gallery includes five interactive blurs: Field Blur, Iris Blur, Tilt-Shift, Path Blur, and Spin Blur. Each gives you on-image selective motion blur tools, with an initial blur pin. You can create additional blur pins by clicking on the image. You can apply a single blur or a combination of blurs, and you can create a strobe effect for path and spin blurs.

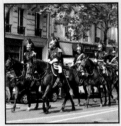 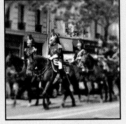

Before   *After*

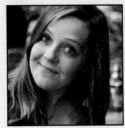 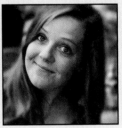

Before   *After*

Field Blur applies a gradient blur to areas of the image, defined by pins you create and settings you specify for each. When you first apply Field Blur, a pin is placed in the center of the image. You can adjust the blur relative to that point by dragging the blur handle or specifying a value in the Blur Tools panel; you can also drag the pin to a different location.

Iris Blur progressively blurs everything outside the focus ring. Adjust the ellipse handles, feather handles, and blur amount to customize the iris blur. It can be a quick way to approximate a shallow depth-of-field blur effect.

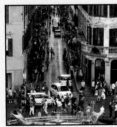 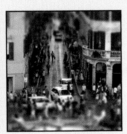

Before   *After*

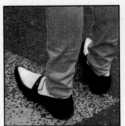 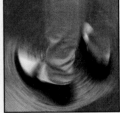

Before   *After*

Tilt-Shift simulates an image taken with a tilt-shift lens, where the image has very shallow depth of field with the focus point in the distance. This blur defines a plane of sharpness and then fades outward to a blur. You can use this effect to simulate photos of miniature objects.

Spin Blur is a radial-style blur measured in degrees. You can change the size and shape of the ellipse, re-center the rotation point by pressing Alt or Option as you click and drag, and adjust the blur angle. You can also specify the blur angle in the Blur Tools panel. Multiple spin blurs can overlap. This blur can be useful for illustrating the rotation of propellers, wheels, or gears.

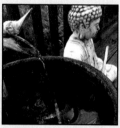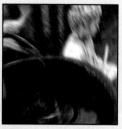

Before   *After*

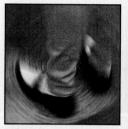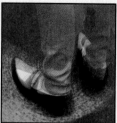

Before   *After*

Path Blur creates motion blurs along paths you draw. You control the shape and amount of the blur.

When you first apply a Path Blur, a default path appears. Drag the end point to reposition it. Click the center point and drag to change the curve. Click to add additional curve points. The arrow on the path indicates the blur's direction.

You can also create a multiple-point path or a shape. Blur shapes describe the local motion blurs, similar to camera shake. The Speed slider in the Blur Tools panel determines the speed for all the path blurs. The Centered Blur option ensures that the blur shape for any pixel is centered on that pixel, resulting in more stable-feeling motion blurs; to make the motion appear more fluid, deselect this option.

If you wanted to illustrate the blurs of individual animal legs moving in different directions, you could add a separate instance of Path Blur to each leg.

Some blur types provide additional options in the Effects tab, where you specify the bokeh parameters to control the appearance of blurred areas. Light Bokeh brightens the blurred areas; Bokeh Color adds more vivid colors to lightened areas that aren't blown out to white; Light Range determines the range of tones that the settings affect.

You can add a **strobe effect** to spin and path blurs. Select the Motion Effects tab to bring its panel forward. The Strobe Strength slider determines how much blur shows between flash exposures (0% gives no strobe effect; 100% gives full strobe effect with little blur between exposures). Strobe Flashes determines the number of exposures.

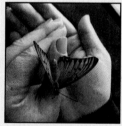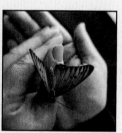

Before   *After*

Applying a blur will smooth out visible digital image noise or film grain that's in the original image, and this mismatch between the original and blurred areas can make the blur appear artificial. You can use the Noise tab to restore noise or grain so that blurred areas match up with unblurred areas. Start with the Amount slider, and then use the other Noise options to match the character of the original grain. Increase the Color value if the original has visible color noise, and lower the Highlights value if you need to balance the noise level in the highlights compared to the shadows.

Using Blur Gallery effects

The interactive blurs in the Blur Gallery let you customize a blur as you preview it on your image. You'll apply blur effects to simulate two different kinds of motion.

You'll start by looking at the start and end files in Bridge.

1 Choose File > Browse In Bridge to open Adobe Bridge.

2 In the Favorites panel in Bridge, click the Lessons folder. Then, in the Content panel, double-click the Lesson05 folder to open it.

3 Compare the Car_Start.jpg and Car_End.psd thumbnail previews. Blur effects added to the Car_End.psd image make it look like it's racing at high speed.

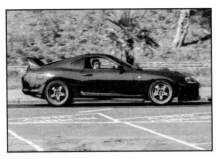 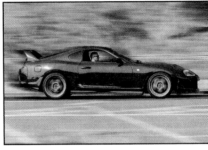

Car_Start.jpg.   Car_End.psd.

4 Choose File > Return To Adobe Photoshop, and choose File > Open.

5 Select the Car_Start.jpg file in the Lesson05 folder, and click OK or Open.

6 Choose File > Save As, choose Photoshop for the Format, name the file **Car_Working.psd**, and click Save.

You want to blur the background but not the car, so you'll copy the car to a new layer and isolate the car there.

7 Choose Layer > New > Layer Via Copy. The new layer copy is named Layer 1.

8 In the Layers panel, double-click Layer 1 and rename it **Car**.

Tip: Copying a selected layer is a step in many techniques, so experienced users save mouse clicks by pressing the keyboard shortcut for the Layer > Layer Via Copy command: Press Ctrl-J (Windows) or Command-J (macOS). If you also created a marquee selection, only that area is copied to a new layer. Some remember the J letter of the shortcut by thinking of this as "jumping" a selection to a new layer.

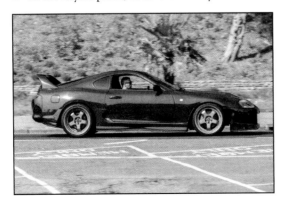 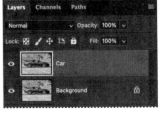

9 With the Object Selection tool (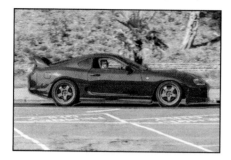), hover the pointer over the car, and when the magenta outline appears around the car, click to select it. The selection may take longer to appear on an older or slower computer, and the final selection may be more precise than the rough magenta highlight.

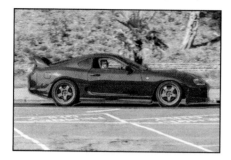
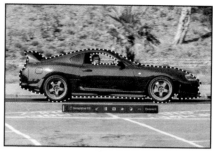

10 In the Layers panel, click the Add Layer Mask button. Although there is no visible change, the selection was converted to a layer mask that hides the area outside the car so you now see a new layer mask thumbnail in the Layers panel.

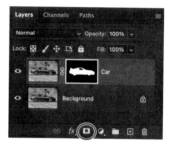

Applying Path Blur

You'll create the impression of speed by blurring the background. You'll apply this blur as a Smart Filter so that you can change it later if needed.

1 In the Layers panel, select the Background layer, and choose Filter > Convert for Smart Filters. Click OK if you're asked to confirm the conversion.

2 In the Layers panel, double-click Layer 0 and name it **Background Blur**.

3 Choose Filter > Blur Gallery > Path Blur. The Blur Gallery task space opens, the selected layer becomes blurred horizontally, and a blue arrow appears.

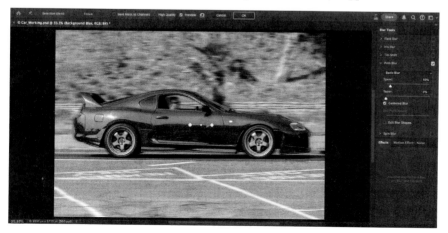

The blue arrow shows the direction of the Path Blur, which is currently horizontal. On the blue arrow, the large circular handles let you control the path direction and the small handle in the middle controls the path shape, in case you want the blur to be something other than a straight line. You don't need to change the path shape for this lesson, because the default straight horizontal blur is already appropriate.

The blur amount is the Speed value applied in the Path Blur options in the Blur Tools panel.

▶ **Tip:** When the Path Blur pointer has a plus sign next to it (✦+), clicking adds a new blur path, and clicking a blur path adds a control point. If you don't want to add those, don't click when the pointer displays a plus sign.

4   In the Path Blur section of the Blur Tools panel, change the Speed value to **200%**.

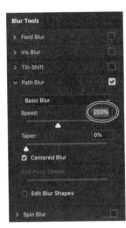 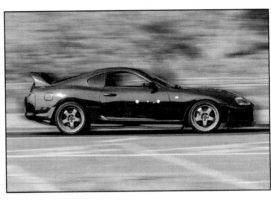

Increasing the Speed value makes the background blur more dramatic, but the blur extends both behind and in front of the car because the blur is centered in the image. You'll correct that now.

5   In the Path Blur section of the Blur Tools panel, deselect Centered Blur.

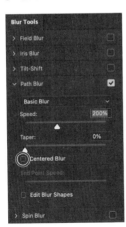 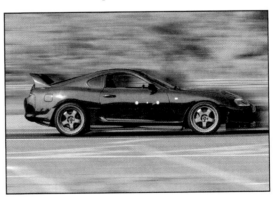

But now the blur only happens in front of the car. This is because the blue arrow points to the right.

6 Position the pointer over the handle over the blue arrow, and drag the handle to the left so that the arrow points behind the car. Now the blur is behind the car.

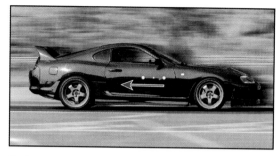

7 Click OK to close Blur Gallery. (The OK button is at the top of the task space.)

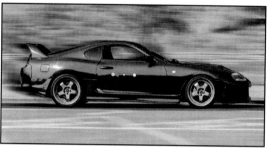

When applying effects, always look at the entire image for details that might spoil the effect. In this image, you might notice some problems. The driver has gone missing because they were affected by the blur effect. Also, the wheels aren't blurred very much. You'll address both of these issues next.

8 Save your work, and click OK in the Photoshop Format Options dialog box.

Editing a mask

The reason Path Blur affected the driver is because the Object Selection tool did not select the driver when it selected the car. You'll correct this with a quick mask edit.

▶ **Tip:** If you notice that an area was missed after clicking the Object Selection tool, you can add the area by holding down the Shift key as you drag the Object Selection tool around the missed area. To remove an unwanted area, hold down the Alt key (Windows) or the Option key (macOS) as you drag the tool.

1 In the Layers panel, click the Car layer mask thumbnail (not the layer thumbnail). The Contextual Task Bar changes to show mask editing options.

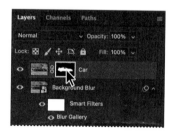

2 In the Contextual Task Bar, click Add To Mask, and in the options bar, set the Brush tool Size to **30 px** and the Hardness to **50%**. (Clicking Add To Mask switches to the Brush tool.)

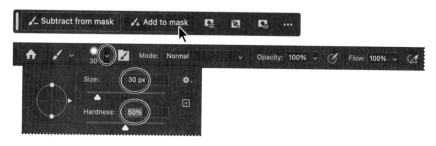

3   Position the pointer near the back of the open car window, where the driver was. Drag the Brush tool to edit the mask and reveal the driver.

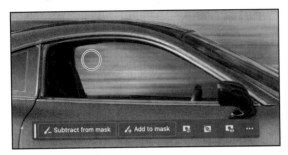 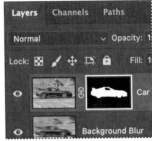

▶ **Tip:** If you dragged the brush outside the driver, un-blurring the background, in the Contextual Task Bar click Subtract From Mask and paint over the area you need to correct.

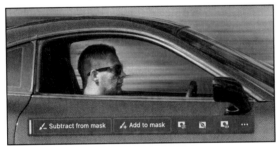 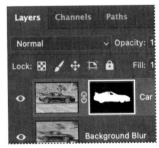

Next you'll add blur to the wheels to be more consistent with speed implied by the background blur. It would take a lot of work to shape Path Blurs into circles, so instead you'll apply Spin Blur. First you must isolate the wheels onto their own layer.

Using the Selection Brush tool

▶ **Tip:** In many cases the fastest way to select something is with the Object Selection tool or a command such as Select > Subject or Select > Sky. When the automatic methods don't easily select what you want, that's when you might want to try drawing or painting the selection manually.

By this lesson you should be familiar with marking a selection by drawing a marquee (animated dashed outline), such as when you drag the Rectangular Marquee tool or Lasso tool. Sometimes it's easier to mark a selection by painting, and in this lesson you'll use the Selection Brush tool to select the car wheels.

1   In the Layers panel, hold down the Alt key (Windows) or the Option key (macOS) as you drag the Car layer to the Create a New Layer button (⊞) .

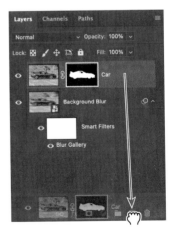

Dragging to the button is a shortcut for the Layer > New > Layer Via Copy command, and adding the Alt or Option modifier key opens the Duplicate Layer dialog box so you can set options for the new layer, such as its name.

2 In the Duplicate Layer dialog box, name the layer **Wheels** and click OK.

Now you need to delete the existing mask, because you'll create a new mask based on the wheels selection you're about to make.

3 In the Layers panel, drag the Wheels layer mask thumbnail (not the layer) to the Delete icon (🗑), and when asked if you want to apply the mask, click Delete. Don't be concerned that the background is no longer blurred; it will be masked out soon.

4 In the Tools panel, select the Selection Brush tool (✏).

5 In the options bar, set the brush Size to **50 px** and the Hardness to **100%**.

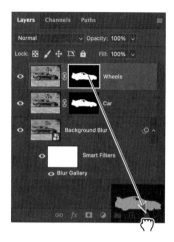

▶ **Tip:** If you need to paint a selection in a perfectly straight line, click the Selection Brush tool to start the line, then Shift-click the Selection Brush tool to end the line.

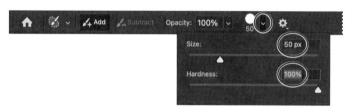

6 Drag the Selection Brush tool to paint over the car's wheels and tires. Areas you paint appear magenta by default and will be selected. Don't paint over the wheel wells or car body. Because this area will be blurred, don't worry about painting perfectly precise curves or edges.

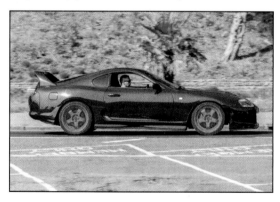

▶ **Tip:** If you paint an area by mistake with the Selection Brush tool, in the options bar click Subtract and then drag to remove unwanted areas. Or, to set Subtract mode temporarily, hold down the Option (Windows) or Alt (macOS) key as you paint with the tool.

7 In the Layers panel, click the Add Layer Mask button. A new layer mask is created based on the selection you painted with the Selection Brush tool.

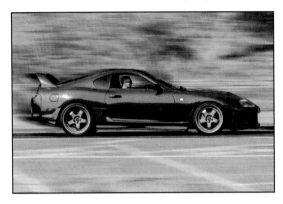 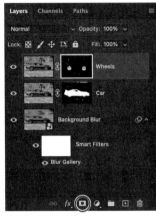

⬤ **Note:** When you convert the Wheels layer to a Smart Object, the mask disappears and the layer thumbnail has a transparent background. This is because the layer mask is now inside the Smart Object; to edit the mask double-click the Smart Object to open it. If you prefer the mask to be available in the Layers panel, convert the layer to a Smart Object before selecting the wheels and creating a layer mask.

Applying Spin Blur

With the wheels now isolated by a mask, applying a blur to this layer will now affect only the wheels. You'll apply Spin Blur as a Smart Filter, as you did before.

1 With the Wheels layer (not its mask) selected in the Layers panel, choose Filter > Convert for Smart Filters (click OK if a confirmation message appears), and then choose Filter > Blur Gallery > Spin Blur.

When the Blur Gallery task space opens this time, the Spin Blur section is expanded in the Blur Tools panel, a blue circle with handles appears at the center of the image, and part of the area inside the circle is blurred. This circle is one Spin Blur instance.

2 Hover the pointer over the blue circle; this reveals more controls. Position the pointer within the circle but not over any controls, and drag to reposition the circle so that it's centered over the front wheel.

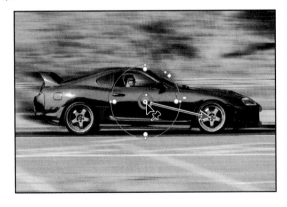 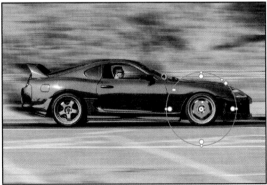

3 Position the pointer near the center of the front wheel blur instance, revealing the ring around the center handle, and drag the ring to adjust the blur (we set it to 50 degrees). This is the same as changing the Blur Angle value in the Spin Blur section of the Blur Tools panel.

4 Position the pointer over the center of the rear wheel, and click. A new instance of Spin Blur appears where you clicked.

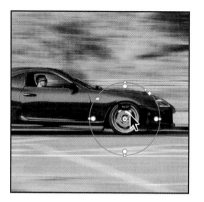

▶ **Tip:** When you hover the pointer over a Spin Blur instance, you see two sets of circular handles around the edge. The outer, smaller circles change the size, proportions, or rotation angle of the blur shape. The inner, larger circles change the feather amount. Dragging the center circle (not the ring) moves the blur.

When you move the pointer well outside of any blur circles, it appears as an "add pin" icon (✦₊), letting you know that if you click, it will add a new blur instance.

5 Adjust the rear wheel blur as you did in step 3, either by dragging the ring around the blur center or by changing the Blur Angle value.

6 When you're satisfied with your work, click OK to close the Blur Gallery task space and apply the blurs to the Wheels layer.

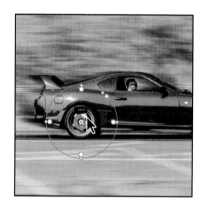

You can inspect how the layers were combined to make the final image by hiding and showing different layers and effects in the Layers panel.

7 The car now looks a lot faster! Close the document, and save changes.

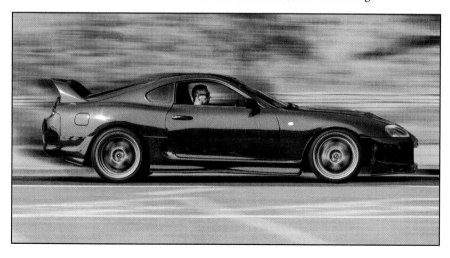

Creating a panorama

Sometimes a vista is too large for a single shot. Photoshop makes it easy to combine multiple images into a panorama so that your viewers can get the full effect.

Once again, you'll take a look at the end file first to see where you're going.

1 Choose File > Browse In Bridge.

Tip: In Bridge, you can preview a selected image in full-screen mode by pressing the spacebar. This is useful for previewing detailed or large images such as a panorama. Press the spacebar again to close the preview.

2 Navigate to the Lesson05 folder, if you're not there already. Then, look at the Skyline_End.psd thumbnail preview.

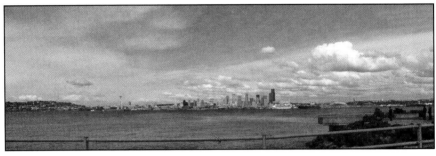

Skyline_End.psd.

You'll combine four shots of the Seattle skyline into a single wide panorama image so that viewers get a sense of the whole scene. Creating a panorama from multiple images requires only a few clicks. Photoshop does the rest.

Tip: You can also open selected images from Bridge directly into Photomerge by choosing Tools > Photoshop > Photomerge.

3 Choose File > Return to Adobe Photoshop.

4 Choose File > Automate > Photomerge.

5 In the Source Files area, click Browse, and navigate to the Lesson05/Files For Panorama folder.

6 Shift-select all the images in the folder, and click OK or Open.

7 In the Layout area of the Photomerge dialog box, select Perspective.

The best option for merging photos isn't always Perspective; it depends on how the originals were photographed. If you're not completely happy with the result of a particular merge, you can always try again with a different Layout option. If you're not sure which one to use, you can simply click Auto.

8 At the bottom of the Photomerge dialog box, select Blend Images Together, Vignette Removal, Geometric Distortion Correction, and Content Aware Fill Transparent Areas. Then click OK.

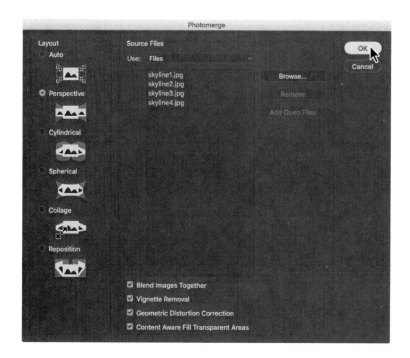

Blend Images Together blends images based on the optimal borders between them, instead of creating a simple rectangular merge. Vignette Removal helps ensure consistent brightness when merging images that are darker around their edges. Geometric Distortion Correction compensates for barrel, pincushion, or fish-eye distortion. Content Aware Fill Transparent Areas automatically patches the empty areas between the merged image edges and the sides of the canvas.

Photoshop creates the panorama image. It's a complex process, so you may have to wait a few moments while Photoshop works. When it's finished, you'll see the full vista in the document window with five layers in the Layers panel. The bottom four layers are the original four images you selected. Photoshop identified the overlapping areas of the images and matched them, correcting any angular discrepancies. The top layer, containing "(merged)" in the layer name, is a single panorama image blended from all of the images you selected, combined with formerly empty areas filled in by Content Aware Fill. Those areas are indicated by the selection.

Note: Photomerge requires more time when you merge more images, or images with large pixel dimensions. Photomerge works faster on computers that are newer or that have more RAM.

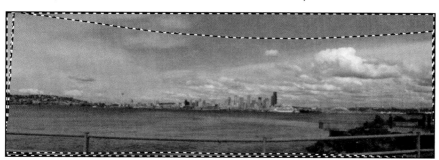

Tip: If you want to see how the panorama looks without the areas created by Content Aware Fill, hide the top layer.

Getting the best results with Photomerge

If you know you're going to create a panorama when you take your shots, keep the following guidelines in mind to get the best result:

Overlap images by 15% to 40%. Sufficient overlap helps Photomerge blend edges seamlessly. Over 50% overlap won't help and makes you take too many images.

Use a consistent focal length. If you use a zoom lens, keep the focal length the same for all the pictures in the panorama. Avoid extreme focal lengths.

Stay level. Keep the horizon at the same vertical position in each frame to avoid a tilted panorama. If your camera has a level indicator in the viewfinder, use it.

Use a tripod if possible. You'll get the best results if the camera is at the same height for each shot. A tripod with a rotating head makes that easier.

Take the photos from the same position. If you're not using a tripod with a rotating head, try to stay in the same position as you take the photos so that they are taken from the same viewpoint.

Use the same exposure and aperture. Images blend more smoothly if the exposure is consistent across frames; auto-exposure may create unexpected exposure variations. Using the same aperture setting maintains consistent depth of field.

Try different layout options. If you don't like the results, try again using a different layout option. Often, Auto selects the appropriate option, but sometimes you'll get a better image with one of the other options.

▶ **Tip:** If you plan to create panoramas of interiors or with objects close to the camera, rotating a camera by hand or on a tripod may introduce parallax errors where items don't line up. You can avoid such errors by using a tripod attachment (sometimes called a *nodal slide*) that precisely rotates the camera around the entrance pupil of the specific lens you use.

9   In the Tools panel, select the Hand tool. If the Object Selection tool is still selected, its selection highlight can be distracting when you're not trying to select.

10 Choose Select > Deselect.

11 Choose Layer > Flatten Image.

▶ **Tip:** In the finished panorama files, the layers created from the original images have masks. Photoshop created the masks to blend the edges where adjacent images match. You can edit those masks, but if you won't need to, flattening the image results in a smaller file size.

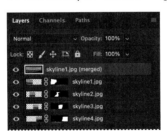
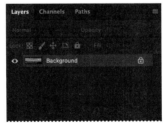

12 Choose File > Save As. Choose Photoshop for the Format, and name the file **Skyline_Working.psd**. Save the file in the Lesson05 folder. Click Save.

The panorama looks great, but it's a little dark. You'll add a Levels adjustment layer to brighten it a little bit.

13 In the Adjustments panel, in the Single Adjustments list click Levels to add a Levels adjustment layer.

14 Select the White Point eyedropper in the Properties panel, and then click a white area of the clouds.

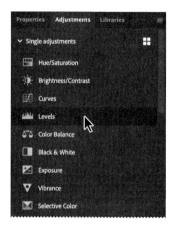 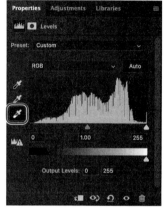

● **Note:** Step 14 works when you click an area that is close to, but not exactly, pure white. If an image doesn't change when you click it with the White Point eyedropper, you probably clicked an area that can't become any whiter and there is no color cast to correct. That happens when the pixel values where you clicked are already pure white in all color channels (such as RGB 255,255,255).

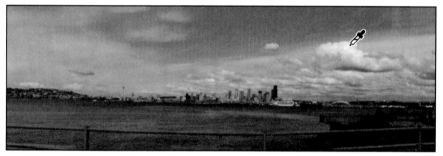

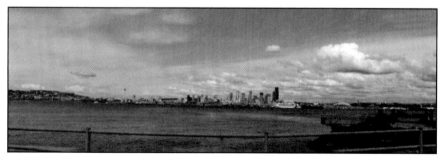

The entire image brightens. The sky appears more blue, because the image was originally a little warm. The White Point eyedropper neutralized the warm cast.

15 Save your work. Click OK in the Photoshop Format Options dialog box.

It's that easy to create a panorama!

● **Note:** In step 15, the Photoshop Format Options alert may appear because a layer was added. The Photoshop Format Options dialog box usually won't appear for Photoshop documents containing only a Background layer.

Filling empty areas when cropping

The panorama image looks great except for two things: The horizon is slightly tilted, and the lower handrail is incomplete where the rocks on the right descend into the water. If you were to rotate the image, empty areas might appear at the corners, requiring a tighter crop and losing parts of the image. Fortunately, the Crop tool offers ways to fill in empty areas that can result from straightening and cropping. You'll try the Generative Expand option.

1   Make sure **Skyline_Working.psd** is open, and make sure the Background layer is selected in the Layers panel.

2   Choose Layer > Flatten Image.

3   In the Tools panel, select the Crop tool. The crop rectangle and its handles appear around the image. If a message appears to let you know about the Generative Expand feature, you can read it or ignore it; you're about to try it.

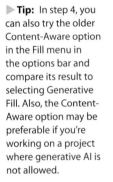

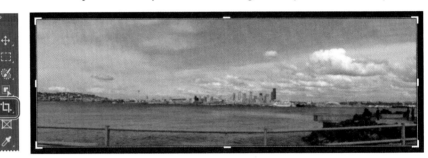

Tip: In step 4, you can also try the older Content-Aware option in the Fill menu in the options bar and compare its result to selecting Generative Fill. Also, the Content-Aware option may be preferable if you're working on a project where generative AI is not allowed.

4   In the options bar, select the Straighten icon (▭), and in the Fill menu, make sure Generative Expand is selected.

Generative Expand will intelligently fill empty areas when you apply the crop.

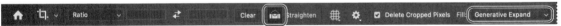

5   Position the Straighten pointer on the horizon at the left edge of the image, and drag to the right to create a Straighten line that's aligned with the horizon; release the mouse button when you reach the end of the horizon at the right edge of the image.

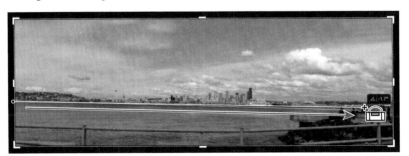

Straightening the image rotated it, creating empty space at the top-left and bottom-right corners. Those will be filled by the Fill option you chose in step 4.

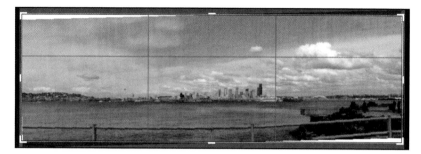

6 Click the Commit button (✔) in the options bar to apply the crop settings. If you don't see that button, press the Enter or Return key instead. If a message appears asking you to read and agree to the Generative Fill User Guidelines, click Agree when you're ready.

● **Note:** If the Commit button (✔) doesn't appear in the options bar, the options bar might be too short. There's room to show all options bar settings when it's at least 1920 pixels wide at 100% UI scaling, meeting the Recommended level for a display according to the Photoshop system requirements. The Enter or Return key work as a shortcut for the Commit button even if the button isn't visible.

A progress bar appears as Generative Expand creates alternatives for filling in the empty corners. When it's finished, the Layers panel includes a new Generative Expand layer, and the Properties panel displays the three Variations created by Generative Expand. The selected Variation is the one currently applied to the Generative Expand layer.

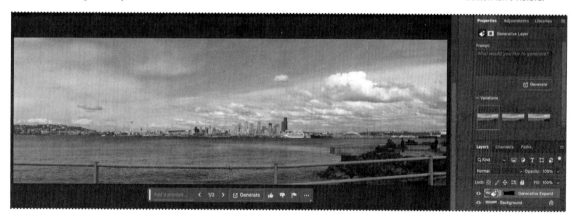

7 In the Properties panel, click each of the three Variations while watching the top-left and bottom-right corners, and select the variation you think is the best.

If you don't like any of them, click Generate to create three more variations, and select one of those.

That's how easy it is to fill in empty areas created by cropping!

8 Switch to the Move tool, so that the Crop tool rectangle won't distract you in later steps.

9 Save your changes, and close the document.

Replacing a sky

When you find the right subject for a photo illustration or composite but it doesn't have quite the right sky to match the mood or time of day you want to convey, you can easily swap out the sky in Photoshop. Sky Replacement does many of the tough parts for you, such as creating a mask for the sky and making colors more consistent between the photo and the new sky.

1   In the Lesson05 folder, open the document Skyline_End.psd, and then choose Edit > Sky Replacement.

2   Select an image from the Sky list. The sky updates in the document; you can compare the original and new sky by clicking the Preview option. To use your own sky image, click the gear icon in the Sky list and choose Get More Skies > Import Images.

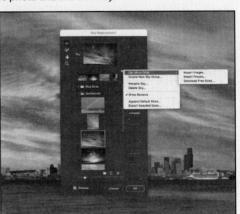

3   Check the quality of the automatically composited image. Are the colors of the two images consistent? Do you see any issues with the edge quality of the automatic sky mask? You can zoom in to check edges.

4   If you notice problems, use the Sky Replacement options. For example, you can reposition the sky image with the Sky Move tool, edit the mask edge with the Sky Brush tool, or change the Scale value in Sky Adjustments.

5   When you are satisfied with the Sky Replacement settings, make sure New Layers is selected in the Output To menu, and click OK.

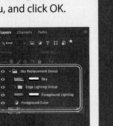

If Output is set to New Layers, notice in the Layers panel that Sky Replacement automatically created layers to add the new sky and adjustments separately from the original layer. After you click OK in Sky Replacement, you can edit the layers and masks it created (you'll learn more about layer masks in Lesson 6, "Masks and Patterns"). Hiding the new layers reveals the original sky.

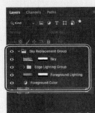

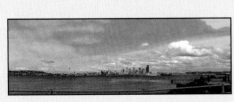

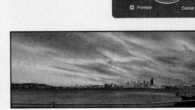

Correcting image distortion

The Lens Correction filter fixes common camera lens flaws, such as barrel and pincushion distortion, chromatic aberration, and vignetting. *Barrel distortion* is a lens defect that causes straight lines to bow out toward the edges of the image. *Pincushion distortion* is the opposite effect, causing straight lines to bend inward. *Chromatic aberration* appears as a color fringe along the edges of image objects. *Vignetting* occurs when the edges of an image, especially the corners, are darker than the center.

The Lens Correction filter contains an Auto Correction tab, which can automatically correct for some combinations of camera models and lenses. If your camera or lens isn't listed or if you want more control, you can use the Custom tab, which contains options that can compensate for many types of lens distortions such as geometric distortion, chromatic aberration, and vignetting.

Tip: If you capture photos with your camera set to save raw files, the Adobe Camera Raw plug-in module (for processing raw files in Photoshop and Bridge) has similar lens correction options in its Optics panel. Also, many more lens profiles are available for camera raw images than for Photoshop documents. You'll learn more about this in Lesson 12, "Working with Camera Raw."

1   Choose File > Browse In Bridge.

2   Navigate to the Lesson05 folder if you're not already there, and then look at the Columns_Start.psd and Columns_End.psd thumbnail previews.

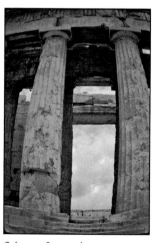

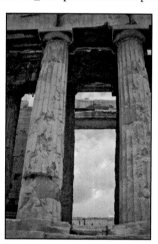

Columns_Start.psd.   *Columns_End.psd.*

In this case, the original image of a Greek temple is distorted, with the columns appearing to be bowed. This photo was shot at a range that was too close with a wide-angle lens. You'll quickly correct the lens barrel distortion.

Tip: If the crop rectangle from the previous exercise is still visible and distracting, switch to a tool such as the Hand tool.

3   Double-click the Columns_Start.psd file to open it in Photoshop.

4   Choose File > Save As. In the Save As dialog box, name the file **Columns_Working.psd**, and save it in the Lesson05 folder. Click OK if the Photoshop Format Options dialog box appears.

5   Choose Filter > Lens Correction. The Lens Correction dialog box opens.

6 At the bottom of the dialog box, make sure Show Grid and Preview are selected.

An alignment grid overlays the image. To the right are options for automatic corrections based on lens profiles. In the Custom tab are manual controls for correcting distortion, chromatic aberration, and perspective.

▶ **Tip:** At the bottom of the Lens Correction dialog box, Camera Model, Lens Model, and Camera Settings are blank if the shot metadata for the original image is not present in the file. If that metadata is in the file, those values are filled in, and values in the Search Criteria section may be pre-selected using that metadata, as a better starting point.

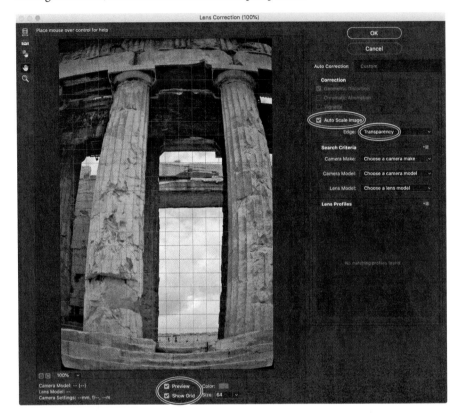

The Lens Correction dialog box includes auto-correction options. You'll adjust one setting in the Auto Correction tab and then customize the settings.

7 In the Correction area of the Auto Correction tab, make sure Auto Scale Image is selected and that Transparency is selected from the Edge menu.

8 Select the Custom tab.

▶ **Tip:** Watch the alignment grid as you make these changes so that you can see when the vertical columns are straightened in the image.

9 In the Custom tab, drag the Remove Distortion slider to about **+52.00** to remove the barrel distortion in the image. Alternatively, you could select the Remove Distortion tool (▦) and drag in the image preview area until the columns are straight. The adjustment causes the image borders to bow inward. Because you selected Auto Scale Image, the Lens Correction filter automatically scales the image to adjust the borders.

10 The horizontal lines aren't parallel with the edges of the frame, so drag the Horizontal Perspective slider to about **+14**.

11 Deselect the Preview option to review how the image looked before these corrections, and then select the Preview option again to see how well the corrections improved the image.

The curving distortion caused by the wide-angle lens and low shooting angle is reduced.

12 Click OK to apply your changes and close the Lens Correction dialog box.

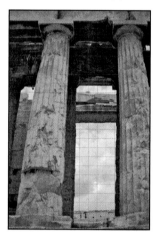
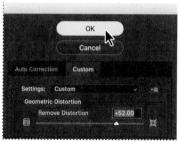

13 Choose File > Save to save your changes, click OK if the Photoshop Format Options dialog box appears, and then close the image.

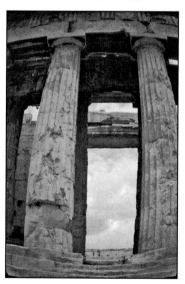
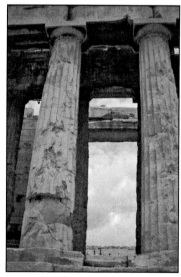

The temple looks much more stable now!

Extending depth of field

Sometimes you have to choose to focus on either the background or the foreground of a scene because the *depth of field*—the range of distances in focus—is narrow. If you want more depth of field but it isn't possible because of limitations of the equipment or the location, you can take a set of photos focused along the range of distances you want to appear sharp. You can merge the photos in Photoshop using a process sometimes called *focus stacking*. This produces a single image with the combined depth of field of the image set.

▶ **Tip:** See if your camera has a feature with a name such as "focus bracketing" that, with a single press of the shutter button, takes multiple shots focused at a series of distances. This feature makes it easier to photograph a consistent image set for focus stacking.

Because you'll need to align the images exactly, it's helpful to use a tripod to keep the camera steady. You might still be able to get good results with a handheld camera if you compose the images consistently. In this exercise, you'll add depth of field to an image of a wine glass in front of a beach.

1   Choose File > Browse In Bridge.

2   Navigate to the Lesson05 folder, if you're not there already, and then look at the Glass_Start.psd and Glass_End.psd thumbnail previews.

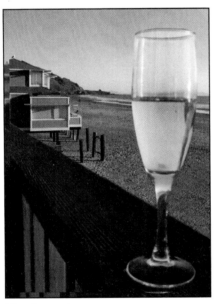

Glass_Start.psd.

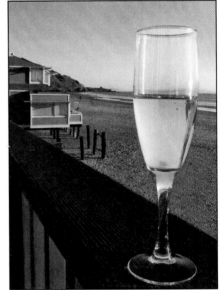

Glass_End.psd.

The first image has two layers. Depending on which layer is visible, either the glass in the foreground or the beach in the background is in focus. You'll extend the depth of field to make both clear.

3   Double-click the Glass_Start.psd file to open it.

4   Choose File > Save As. Name the file **Glass_Working.psd**, and save it in the Lesson05 folder. Click OK if the Photoshop Format Options dialog box appears.

5   In the Layers panel, hide the Beach layer so that only the Glass layer is visible. The glass is in focus, but the background is blurred. Then, show the Beach layer again. Now the beach is in focus, but the glass is blurred.

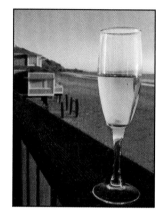
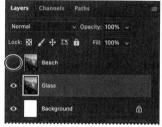

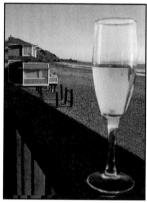
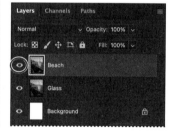

You'll merge the layers, using the part of each layer that is in focus. First, you need to align the layers.

6   In the Layers panel, Shift-click to select both of the layers.

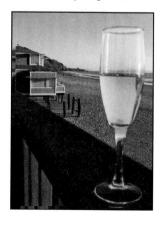
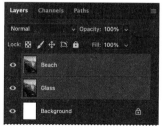

7 Choose Edit > Auto-Align Layers.

Because these images were shot from the same angle, Auto will work just fine.

Tip: When aligning layers that are not involved in a panorama, Reposition is often the best alignment option to use. In this exercise, Reposition is the projection that the Auto option chose.

8 Select Auto, if it isn't already selected. Make sure neither Vignette Removal nor Geometric Distortion is selected. Then click OK to align the layers.

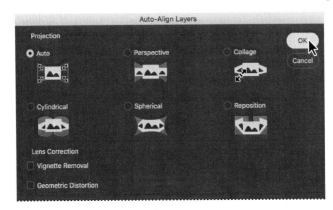

Now that the layers are perfectly aligned, you're ready to blend them.

9 Make sure both layers are still selected in the Layers panel. Then choose Edit > Auto-Blend Layers.

Tip: The technique in this exercise, called *focus stacking*, is useful for macro photography, where depth of field is typically very shallow. Multiple images with shallow depth of field are shot at different focus distances and then merged.

10 Select Stack Images and Seamless Tones And Colors, if they aren't already selected. Make sure Content Aware Fill Transparent Areas is not selected, and then click OK.

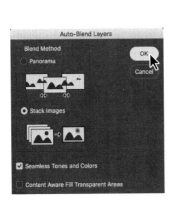 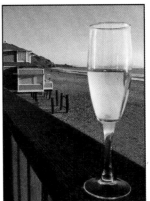

Both the wine glass and the beach behind it are in focus, because Auto-Blend Layers combined the sharpest parts of each image. In the Layers panel, notice that both original layers are preserved, and the blending is achieved by masks that hide the out-of-focus areas of each image so that only the sharp areas of each are visible.

11 Save your work, and close the file.

Adjusting perspective in an image

The Perspective Warp feature lets you adjust the way objects in your image relate to the scene. You can correct distortions, change the angle from which an object appears to be viewed, or shift the perspective of an object so that it merges smoothly with a new background.

Using the Perspective Warp feature is a two-step process: defining the planes and adjusting them. You start in Layout mode, drawing *quads* to define two or more planes; it's a good idea to align the edges of the quads so that they are parallel with the lines of the original object. Then you switch to Warp mode and manipulate the planes you defined.

You'll use Perspective Warp to merge images with different perspectives.

1 Choose File > Browse In Bridge.

2 Navigate to the Lesson05 folder, if you're not there already, and then look at the Bridge_Start.psd and Bridge_End.psd thumbnail previews.

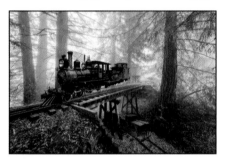
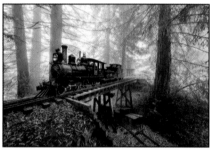

Bridge_Start.psd.   *Bridge_End.psd.*

In the Bridge_Start.psd file, the image of the train has been combined with the image of a trestle bridge, but their perspectives don't match. If you're illustrating a story about a flying train that's landing on a trestle bridge, this might be perfect. But if you want a more realistic image, you'll need to adjust the perspective of the train to put it firmly on the tracks. You'll use Perspective Warp to do just that.

3 Double-click the Bridge_Start.psd file to open it in Photoshop.

4 Choose File > Save As, and rename the file **Bridge_Working.psd**. Click OK in the Photoshop Format Options dialog box.

5 Select the Train layer.

The tracks are on the Background layer. The train is on the Train layer. Because the Train layer is a Smart Object, you can apply Perspective Warp and then modify the results if you're not satisfied.

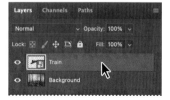

Note: Perspective Warp can work faster on a computer that qualifies for graphics acceleration. To see if your computer qualifies, see the "Getting Started" section for a link to the Photoshop system requirements.

6 Choose Edit > Perspective Warp.

A small animated tutorial appears, showing you how to draw a quad, which defines a plane.

7 Watch the animation, and then close it.

Now you'll create quads to define the planes of the train image.

8 Draw the quad for the side of the train: Click above the top of the smokestack, drag down to the railroad tie below the front wheel, and then drag across to the end of the caboose.

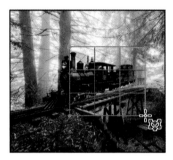

9 Drag a second quad for the front of the train, dragging across the cowcatcher at the bottom and into the trees at the top. Drag it to the right until it attaches to the left edge of the first quad. If a tip appears to help you use the feature, you can read it and dismiss it.

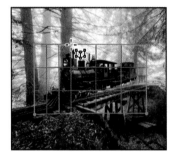

Tip: Not sure if you've properly drawn the perspective of quads around a subject? They should look like a shipping container fitted to the subject.

10 Drag the corners of the planes to match the angles of the train. The bottom line of the side plane should be consistent with the bottom of the train wheels; the top edge should follow the top of the caboose. The front plane should follow the lines of the top of the cowcatcher and the top of the light.

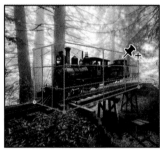

Now that the quads are drawn, you're ready for the second step: warping.

11 Click Warp in the options bar. Close the tutorial window that appears.

12 Click the Automatically Straighten Near Vertical Lines button, next to Warp in the options bar.

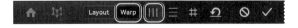

Lines close to vertical are made vertical, making it easier to adjust its perspective.

13 Drag the handles to manipulate the planes, moving the back end of the train down and into perspective with the tracks.

14 Warp other parts of the train as needed. You may need to adjust the front of the train. Pay attention to the wheels; make sure you don't distort them as you warp the perspective.

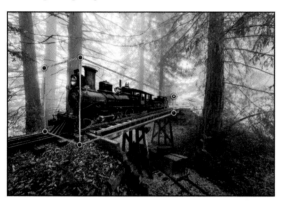

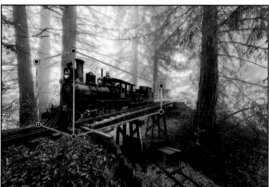

While there are precise ways to adjust perspective, in many cases you may need to trust your eyes to tell you when it looks right. Remember that you can return to tweak it again later, because you're applying Perspective Warp as a Smart Filter.

15 When you're satisfied with the perspective, click the Commit Perspective Warp button (✔) in the options bar.

16 To compare the changed image with the original, hide the Perspective Warp filter in the Layers panel. Then show the filter again.

If you want to make further adjustments, double-click the Perspective Warp filter in the Layers panel. You can continue to adjust the existing planes or click Layout in the options bar to reshape them. Remember to click the Commit Perspective Warp button to apply your changes.

17 Save your work, and close the file.

Changing the perspective of a building

In the exercise, you applied Perspective Warp to one layer to change its relationship with another. But you can also use Perspective Warp to change the perspective of an object in relationship to others in the same layer. For example, you can shift the angle from which you view a building.

In this case, you apply Perspective Warp the same way: In Layout mode, draw the planes of the object you want to affect. In Warp mode, manipulate those planes. Of course, because you're shifting angles within a layer, other objects on the layer will change too, so you need to watch for any irregularities.

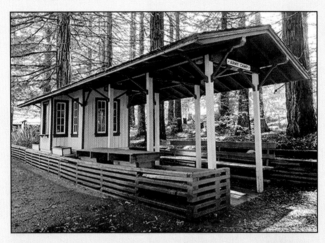

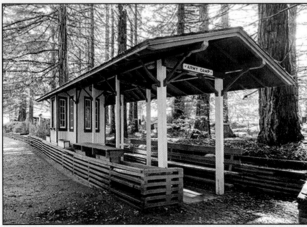

In this image, as the perspective of the building shifts, so does the perspective of the trees surrounding it.

Extra credit

Transformations with the Content-Aware Move tool

With the Content-Aware Move tool, you need only a few quick steps to duplicate a thistle so that it combines seamlessly with the background and is also different enough that it doesn't look like an exact copy of the original.

1   Open Thistle.psd in your Lesson05/Extra Credit folder, and save it as **Thistle_Working.psd**.

2   Select the Content-Aware Move tool (✄) (grouped with the healing brush and Red Eye tools).

3   In the options bar, choose Extend from the Mode menu. Choosing Extend duplicates the thistle; if you just want to reposition the single thistle, you would choose Move.

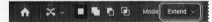

4   With the Content-Aware Move tool, draw a selection around the thistle, with a margin large enough to include a little of the grass around it.

5   Drag the selection to the left, and drop it in the empty area of grass.

6   Right-click (Windows) or Control-click (macOS) the dragged thistle, and choose Flip Horizontal.

7   Drag the top-left transformation handle to make the thistle smaller. If you think the copy of the thistle should be farther from the original, position the pointer inside the transformation rectangle and drag the thistle copy slightly to the left.

8   Press Enter or Return to apply the transformations. Leave the content selected so you can adjust the Structure and Color options in the Options bar to improve how the duplicated thistle blends with the background.

9   Choose Select > Deselect, save your changes, and close the document.

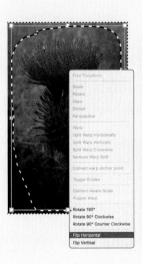
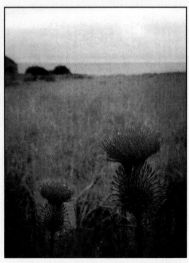

Tips for using the Content-Aware Move tool

The Content-Aware Move tool defaults to the Move mode, which helps blend moved selections into their new background (see "Extra credit" on page 157).

When set to Extend mode, the Content-Aware Move tool can expand areas of regular or randomized visual repetition such as meadows, solid-colored walls, sky, wood grains, or water. The Extend mode can also be useful with architectural subjects, especially when they're shot on a plane parallel to the camera; it's less effective for subjects shot at an angle.

If you're working with an image that has multiple layers, select Sample All Layers in the options bar to include them all in the selection.

The Structure and Color options define how closely the results reflect the existing image patterns. In the Structure settings, 1 is the loosest and 7 the strictest. The Color settings range from 0 (no color adaptation) to 10 (matching the color as closely as possible). Experiment with the options while the object is still selected to see which give you the best results in a particular image. You may want to hide the selection edges (choose View > Show > Selection Edges or View > Extras) to see how the object integrates into its new position.

Review questions

1 What is red eye, and how do you correct it in Photoshop?

2 Why might some parts of the Photoshop workspace become inaccessible or hidden, such as the Color and Layers panels? And how do you return to the normal workspace?

3 How can you create a panorama from multiple images?

4 Which common camera lens flaws can the Lens Correction filter fix?

Review answers

1 Red eye occurs when a camera flash is reflected in the retinas of a subject's eyes. To correct red eye in Photoshop, zoom in to the subject's eyes, select the Red Eye tool, and then click or drag around each eye.

2 If standard panels can't be opened, you are probably working in a dedicated workspace that provides options only for a specific task, such as applying Liquify or Blur Gallery effects. Many menu commands and panels aren't available in a dedicated workspace. To exit a dedicated workspace and keep the edits you made in it, look for an OK button and click it. (When not in a dedicated workspace, panels can be opened and hidden using the Window menu or by a preset on the Window > Workspace menu.)

3 To blend multiple images into a panorama, choose File > Automate > Photomerge, select the files you want to combine, and click OK.

4 The Lens Correction filter can fix common camera lens flaws such as barrel and pincushion distortion, in which straight lines bow out toward the edges of the image (barrel) or bend inward (pincushion); chromatic aberration, where a color fringe appears along the edges of image objects; and vignetting at the edges of an image, especially corners, that are darker than the center.

6 MASKS AND PATTERNS

Lesson overview

In this lesson, you'll learn how to do the following:

- Select a subject in one click.

- Use Select and Mask to remove the background around a subject.

- Refine a mask to include complex edges.

- Manipulate an image using Puppet Warp.

- Create a star by customizing a vector shape layer.

- Create an adjustable pattern from a vector shape layer.

This lesson will take about an hour to complete. To get the lesson files used in this chapter, download them from the web page for this book at peachpit.com/PhotoshopCIB2025. For more information, see "Accessing the lesson files and Web Edition" in the Getting Started section at the beginning of this book.

As you work on this lesson, you'll preserve the start files. If you need to restore the start files, download them from your Account page.

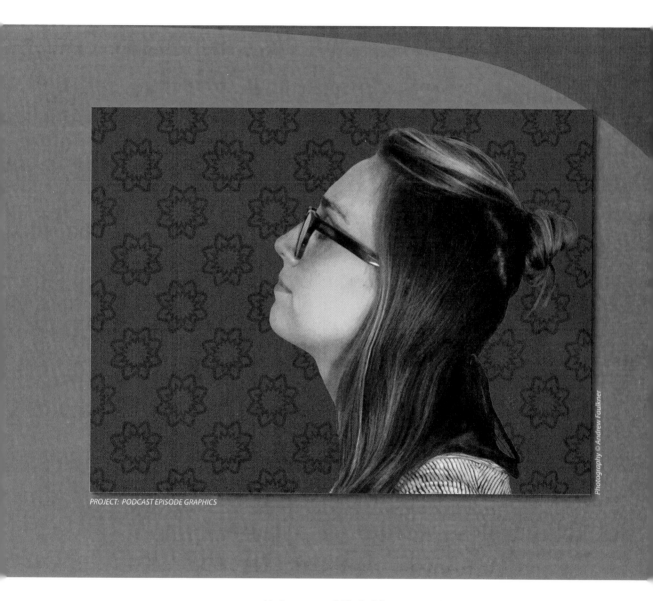

PROJECT: *PODCAST EPISODE GRAPHICS*

Masks are essential for building a composite image. Create masks to hide unwanted areas of each layer, such as backgrounds, so that what's visible on the layers are only the subjects you want to composite.

Why masks are useful

Out of the camera, a digital image is an opaque rectangle. To composite that image with others, you need to hide unwanted areas. Or you might want an adjustment layer or filter to be visible only on some areas of a layer. The recommended way to do both is by using a *mask*, a way to mark areas of a layer as transparent.

Using a mask is more useful than deleting or erasing unwanted areas of a layer, because a mask is reversible. For example, if you accidentally trimmed off part of the subject with a mask, editing the mask lets you restore the trimmed area.

A mask is similar to a selection, but there are important differences. A selection is temporary, affects only the selected layer, and is lost when you close a document. In contrast, one layer (pixel) mask and one vector mask can be saved with each layer. You can easily convert a selection to a mask, and vice versa.

Getting started

First, you'll view the image that you'll create using masks.

1   Start Photoshop, and then simultaneously hold down Ctrl+Alt+Shift (Windows) or Command+Option+Shift (macOS) to restore the default preferences. (See "Restoring default preferences" on page 5.)

2   When prompted, click Yes to delete the Adobe Photoshop Settings file.

3   Choose File > Browse In Bridge to open Adobe Bridge.

4   Click the Favorites tab on the left side of the Bridge window. Select the Lessons folder, and then double-click the Lesson06 folder in the Content panel.

5   Study the 06End.psd file. To enlarge the thumbnail so that you can see it more clearly, move the thumbnail slider at the bottom of the Bridge window to the right.

In this lesson, you'll create a graphic for a podcast. The model was photographed in front of a different background. You'll use Select And Mask to quickly isolate the model over the final background. You'll also tilt the model's head up a little more and create a pattern for the background.

6   Double-click the 06Start.psd thumbnail to open it in Photoshop. Click OK if you see an Embedded Profile Mismatch dialog box, and close any messages that appear about new features.

7   Choose File > Save As, rename the file to **06Working.psd**, and click Save. Click OK if the Photoshop Format Options dialog box appears.

Saving a working copy of the file lets you preserve the original, if you need it later.

About masks and channels

Alpha channels, quick masks, clipping masks, layer masks, vector masks—what's the difference? They're all variations of the same idea: an image overlay that uses white, black, and gray areas to control which areas of a layer are visible or transparent. Choose the right one by understanding the following important differences:

- A **color channel** stores one of the visible components of a color image. For example, an RGB image has three color channels: red, green, and blue.

- An **alpha channel** stores a selection as a grayscale image. You can convert alpha channels to and from selections, masks, and vector paths. In some file formats such as PNG, an alpha channel marks transparent areas of an image in a way that other applications can recognize and use.

- A **layer mask** is an alpha channel attached to a specific layer in Photoshop, controlling which parts of the layer are revealed or hidden. It appears as a white thumbnail next to the layer thumbnail in the Layers panel until you paint black in it; an outline around the layer mask thumbnail indicates that it's selected.

- A **vector mask** is a layer mask made of resolution-independent vector objects, not pixels. It's useful for creating a geometrically precise mask edge faster than painting it with a brush. You create vector masks using the commands on the Layer > Vector Mask submenu and using the Pen tool or shape tools.

- A **clipping mask** uses one layer's content to mask another layer. For example, if you want to fill type characters with an image, setting up the type characters as a clipping mask shows the image only inside the characters.

- A **channel mask** is a mask manually built using tones from one or more color channels, such as the green channel in an RGB image. Channel masks are useful in advanced techniques for masking, color correction, and sharpening. For example, the edge between trees and sky may be clearest in the blue channel.

- A **quick mask** is a temporary mask you create to restrict painting or other edits to a specific area of a layer. It's a selection in pixel form; instead of editing the selection marquee, you edit a quick mask using painting tools.

▶ **Tip:** Because masks mark which areas of a layer are visible, they also control where your edits are visible. For example, if you paint a masked layer with the Brush tool, the brush strokes are visible only on the unmasked (white) areas of a layer.

Using Select And Mask and Select Subject

Photoshop provides a set of tools focused on creating and refining masks, collected in a task space called Select And Mask. Inside Select And Mask, you'll use the Select Subject tool to get a fast head start on the mask that will separate the model from the background. Then you'll refine the mask using other Select And Mask tools, such as the Quick Selection tool.

1 In the Layers panel, make sure both layers are visible and the Model layer is selected.

2 Choose Select > Select And Mask.

▶ **Tip:** When any selection tool is active, the Select And Mask button is available in the options bar. You can choose Select > Select and Mask when the Select and Mask button is not shown.

Tip: The first time you use Select And Mask, a tutorial tip may pop up. You may view it before you continue with the lesson, or you can click Later or Close.

The image opens in the Select And Mask task space (notice how the panels changed). A semitransparent "onion skin" overlay indicates masked areas, currently covering the entire image because nothing is revealed by the mask yet.

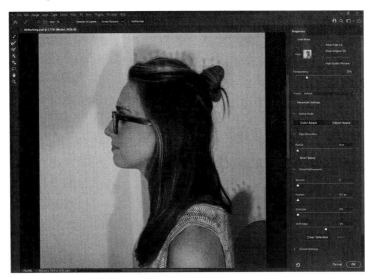

Tip: When a selection tool is active, you can also open Select And Mask by clicking the Select And Mask button in the options bar, instead of having to find the command in the menus.

3 Click the View menu in the View Mode section of the Properties panel, and choose Overlay. The masked area is now shown as a semitransparent red color instead of the onion skin. It's solid because nothing is masked yet.

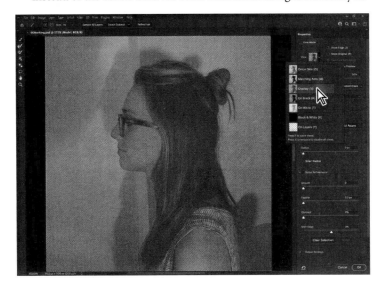

Tip: Quickly cycle through the View Modes by pressing the F key. Viewing different modes helps you spot selection mistakes that might not be obvious in other modes. Also, the View Mode menu lists a single-key shortcut for each mode.

The different View Modes are provided so that you can see the mask more easily over various backgrounds. In this case, the red overlay will make it easier to see missed areas and edges later, where edges and loose hair aren't properly masked.

4 In the options bar, click the Select Subject button.

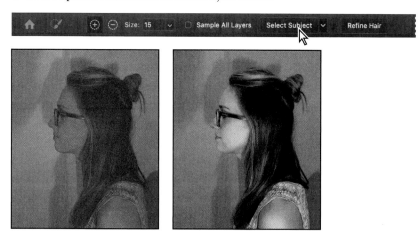

Tip: You don't have to be in the Select And Mask dialog box to use the Select > Subject command. Also, it's OK to use Select Subject first and then enter Select And Mask to refine the selection. Or, if Select Subject doesn't work, try the Object Selection tool.

Using advanced machine learning technology, the Select Subject feature is trained to identify typical subjects of a photo, including people, animals, and objects, and then create a selection. The selection may not be perfect, but it's often close enough for you to refine easily and rapidly with other selection tools.

5 Click the View menu in the View Mode section of the Properties panel, and choose Black & White. This View Mode helps make the mask edge easier to see.

6 Click the View menu in the View Mode section of the Properties panel, and choose Overlay to better compare the edge to the actual image.

Notice that there are a few areas over the chest that were missed by Select Subject. You can easily add them to the selection using the Quick Selection tool.

7 Make sure the Quick Selection tool (⚡) is selected. In the options bar, set up a brush with a size of **15** px.

8 Drag the Quick Selection tool over the missed areas (without dragging into the background) to add the missed areas to the selection. Notice that the Quick Selection tool fills in the selection as it detects content edges, so you don't have to be exact. It's okay if you release the mouse button and drag more than once.

Tip: If you don't like the initial selection, you can try Select Subject in different ways. One way is to click the menu next to the Select Subject button and compare Cloud and Device processing. Another way is to try a different Refine Mode in the Properties panel; compare Color Aware and Object Aware and see which works better.

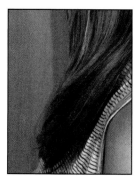
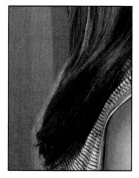

Tip: When editing a
selection, increase the
magnification if it helps
you see missed areas.

Where you drag teaches the Quick Selection tool which areas should be revealed
and are not part of the mask. Do not drag the Quick Selection tool over or past the
model's edge to the background, because that would teach the Quick Selection tool
to include part of the background in the mask. If you accidentally add unwanted
areas to the mask, either choose Edit > Undo or reverse the edit by painting over it
with the Quick Selection tool in Subtract mode. To enable Subtract mode for the
Quick Selection tool, click the Subtract From Selection icon (⊖) in the options bar.

Tip: You can adjust
the opacity of the onion
skin by dragging the
Transparency slider
under the View Mode
options.

As you drag the Quick Selection tool over the model, the overlay disappears from
the areas that you are marking to be revealed. Don't worry about perfection yet.

9   Click the View menu in the View Mode section again, and choose On Layers.
    This shows you how the current Select And Mask settings look over any layers
    that are behind this layer. In this case, you're previewing how the current settings
    will mask the Model layer over the Episode Background layer.

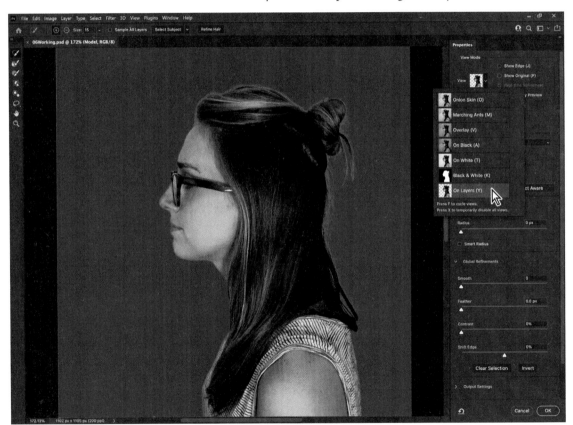

Inspect the edges around the model at a high magnification, such as 400%. Some of the original light background may still show between the model's edge and the podcast background, but overall the Select Subject and Quick Selection tools should have created clean edges for the shirt and face. Don't be concerned about edge gaps or imperfect hair edges, because you'll take care of those next.

Getting better and faster results with Select And Mask

When using Select And Mask, it's important to use different tools for image areas that should be fully revealed, for areas that should be fully masked, and for partially masked edges (such as fuzzy dog hair). Try these recommendations:

- The Select Subject button can be a fast way to create an initial selection.

- Next to the Select Subject button is a drop-down list letting you choose a way to process Select Subject. Cloud processing may produce more detailed results by sending the image to more powerful Adobe computers. Device processing (on your computer) is usually faster, but less precise. Changing this setting affects only the next time you click the Select Subject button; you can set the method permanently in the Image Processing panel of the Preferences dialog box.

- The Quick Selection tool is useful for rapidly touching up a selection produced by Select Subject or for creating an initial selection. As you drag the tool, it uses edge detection technology to find mask edges automatically. Don't drag it on or over a mask edge; keep it fully inside (in Add mode) or outside (in Subtract mode) the areas that should be revealed.

- To paint solid mask edges manually (without using automatic edge detection), use the Brush, Lasso, or Polygonal Lasso tool. These have an Add mode for marking revealed areas and a Subtract mode for marking masked areas.

- Instead of having to switch between Add and Subtract modes with the options bar, you can leave a tool in Add mode, and when you want to temporarily use the tool in Subtract mode, hold down the Alt (Windows) or Option (macOS) key.

- To improve the mask along edges containing complex transitions such as hair, drag the Refine Edge Brush along those edges. Do not drag the Refine Edge brush over areas that should be fully revealed or fully masked.

- You don't have to do all of the work inside Select And Mask. For example, if you've already created a selection with another tool such as Color Range, leave that selection active, and then if you want to clean up the selection, click Select > Select And Mask in the options bar.

▶ **Tip:** In Select And Mask, the Polygonal Lasso tool is grouped with the Lasso tool.

Refining a mask

The mask is pretty good so far. The Select Subject mask even correctly masked the hole within the loop of hair over the back of the shirt. But just above that loop is another gap within hair, and that gap should also be part of the mask so that the blue background shows through. In Select And Mask, the Refine Edge Brush tool can help mask areas and edges that are fuzzy.

1   At a magnification of 300% or higher, inspect the empty areas within the hair, comparing the large hole inside the lower hair loop with the smaller gap in the hair above it.

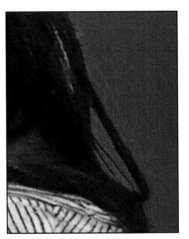

The blue background should also be showing through the upper gap, but the gap is currently not masked out. This gap would not be easy to mask with a normal (solid color) brush tool because of the fine hairs along its edges, but the Refine Edge Brush tool is designed to recognize and mask these types of subtle edges.

Julieanne Kost is an official Adobe Photoshop evangelist.

Tool tips from the Photoshop evangelist

Zoom tool shortcuts

Often when editing an image, you'll need to zoom in to work on a detail and then zoom out again to see the changes in context. Here are several keyboard shortcuts that make zooming faster and easier:

*   With any tool selected, press Ctrl (Windows) or Command (macOS) with the plus sign (+) to zoom in, or with the minus sign (−) to zoom out.

*   Double-click the Zoom tool in the Tools panel to return the image to 100% view.

*   When Scrubby Zoom is selected in the options bar, just drag the Zoom tool to the left to zoom out or to the right to zoom in.

*   Press Alt (Windows) or Option (macOS) to change the Zoom In tool to the Zoom Out tool, and click the image. Each Alt/Option-click reduces the image by the next preset increment, centering the image where you clicked.

2 Select the Refine Edge Brush tool (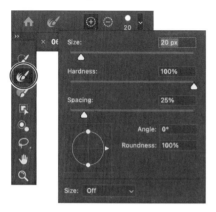). In the options bar, set up a brush with a size of **20** px and Hardness of **100%**.

▶ **Tip:** Depending on the image, clicking the Refine Hair button can reduce the amount of manual brushing you need to do with the Refine Edge Brush tool.

3 Drag the Refine Edge Brush tool over the enclosed area that should be transparent. Gaps in the hair should become masked as transparent, and fine hairs are added to the visible edge.

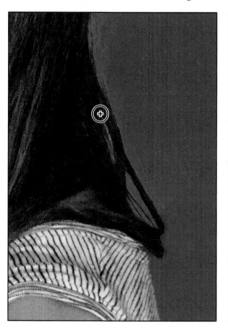
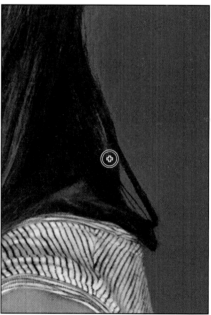

4 Click the View option, and choose Black & White to clearly evaluate the current mask edge. Inspect the mask at different magnifications. When you're done, on the menu bar choose View > Fit On Screen. Black areas indicate transparency.

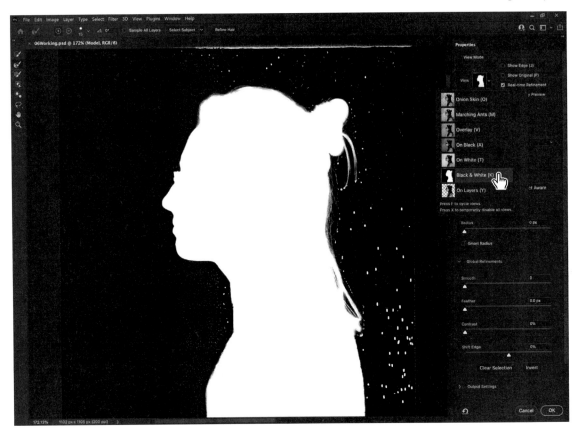

If you see hairs or other details that should be more visible, drag the Refine Edge brush over them. The finer the details you want to mask, the smaller you should set the Refine Edge brush size. It's okay if the brush size is slightly larger than the details you want to mask, and you don't have to drag the Refine Edge Brush tool precisely.

If you see Refine Edge Brush tool mistakes that need to be erased, such as inner areas incorrectly added to the mask, drag the Refine Edge Brush tool over the mistakes while holding down the Alt (Windows) or Option (macOS) key.

If you see individual spots or discrete areas that need to be fully visible or fully transparent, you can paint them out using the Brush tool, the third one down in the toolbox. To make areas visible, paint them with white; to make areas hidden, paint them with black. You can also drag the Lasso tool to enclose any areas you want to add, subtract, or intersect with the mask, depending on its mode in the options bar.

Adjusting Global Refinements

At this point the mask is good but needs to be tightened up a little. You can tune the overall appearance of the mask edge by adjusting the Global Refinements settings.

1 Click the View menu in the View Mode section of the Properties panel, and choose On Layers. This lets you preview adjustments over the Episode Background layer, which is behind the Model layer.

2 In the Global Refinements section, move the sliders to create a smooth, unfeathered edge along the face. The optimal settings depend on the selection you created, but they'll probably be similar to ours. We moved the Smooth slider to 1 to reduce the roughness of the outline, Contrast to 20% to sharpen the transitions along the selection border, and Shift Edge to −15% to tighten the mask by moving the selection edge inward. (Adjusting Shift Edge to a positive number would move the border outward.)

Note: Pay attention to details while using Global Refinements. For example, if you adjust Smooth and the mask edge starts to round corners or grind down important details, that means Smooth is set too high. Similarly, setting Feather too high can create unsightly halos along the edge.

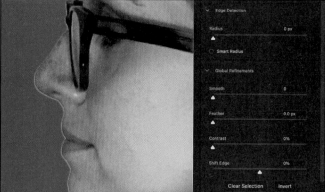

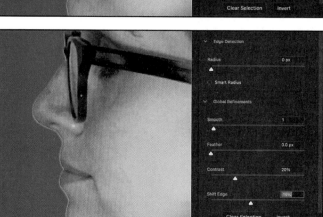

3 Take one more look at this preview of the current mask over the background layer, and make any remaining corrections as needed.

Completing the mask

▶ **Tip:** If you mask many images that need similar Properties panel settings in Select and Mask, click the Preset menu and choose Save Preset to create a named preset that you can apply at any time.

When you're satisfied with the mask, you can apply it to the document as a selection, a layer with transparency, a layer mask, or a new document. For this project, we want to use this as a layer mask on the Model layer, which was selected when you entered Select And Mask.

1 If the Output Settings are hidden, click the disclosure icon (⟩) to reveal them.

2 Zoom in to 200% or more so that you can more easily see the light fringing around the face edge that's due to the Model layer's original background color seeping in behind the mask.

3 Select Decontaminate Colors to suppress those color fringes. If Decontaminate Colors creates unwanted artifacts, reduce the Amount until the effect looks the way you want. We set Amount to 25%.

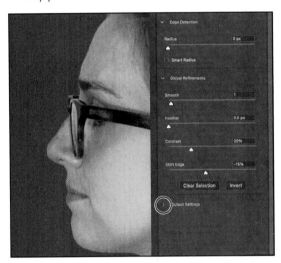

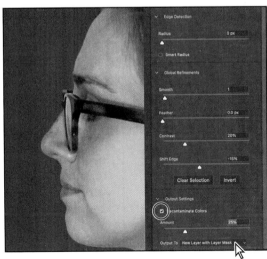

4 Choose New Layer With Layer Mask from the Output To menu. Then, in the lower-right corner of the Select and Mask workspace, click OK.

Photoshop applies your masking adjustments and closes the Select and Mask dialog box, returning you to the normal Photoshop workspace.

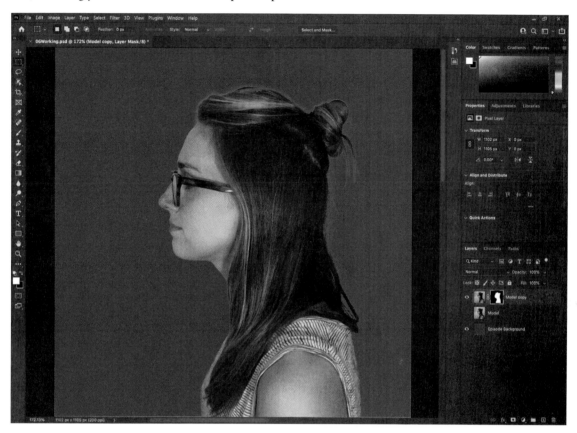

5 In the Layers panel, the Model Copy layer now has a layer mask (pixel mask) that was generated by Select And Mask.

The layer was copied because using the Decontaminate Colors option requires generating new pixels. The original Model layer is preserved and automatically hidden. If you wanted to start over, you could delete the Model Copy layer, make the original Model layer visible again and selected, and open Select And Mask again.

If the mask isn't perfect, you can continue to edit it at any time. When a layer mask thumbnail is selected in the Layers panel, you can click the Select And Mask button in the Properties panel, click it in the options bar (if a selection tool is active), or choose Select > Select And Mask.

● **Note:** If you had not selected Decontaminate Colors, it would have been possible to choose a Layer Mask output option that would have added a layer mask to the Model layer without copying it.

6 Save your work.

Manipulating an image with Puppet Warp

Note: Photoshop provides several different ways to warp a layer. You'll use Puppet Warp because it's the easiest way to pivot part of an image, such as tilting the head back in this example.

The Puppet Warp feature gives you flexibility in manipulating an image. You can reposition areas, such as hair or an arm, just as you might pull the strings on a puppet. Place pins wherever you want to control movement. You'll use Puppet Warp to tilt the model's head back so she appears to be looking up.

1 Zoom out so you can see the entire model.

2 With the Model Copy layer selected in the Layers panel, choose Edit > Puppet Warp.

A mesh appears over the visible areas in the layer—in this case, the model. On the mesh, you'll place pins where you want to control movement (or to ensure there is no movement).

Note: It's OK if your mesh pin positions are slightly different than what is shown here.

3 Click to add pins around the body and along the base of the head, as shown below. Each time you click, Puppet Warp adds a pin. About 10 to 12 pins should work.

The pins you've added around the shirt will keep it in place as you tilt the head.

Tip: The ability of Puppet Warp to pivot part of a layer makes it different than the other Photoshop distortion tools, such as Filter > Liquify and the Edit > Transform submenu commands.

4 Click the pin at the nape of the neck to select it. A blue dot appears in the center of the pin to indicate that it's selected.

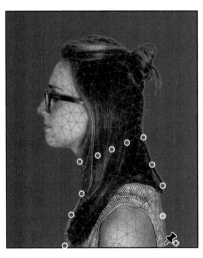
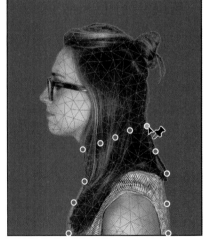

5 Press Alt (Windows) or Option (macOS). A larger circle appears around the pin, and a curved double arrow appears next to it. Continue pressing Alt or Option as you drag the pointer to rotate the head backwards. You can see the angle of rotation in the options bar; you can enter **170** there to rotate the head back.

6 When you're satisfied with the rotation, click the Commit Puppet Warp button (✓) in the options bar, or press Enter or Return.

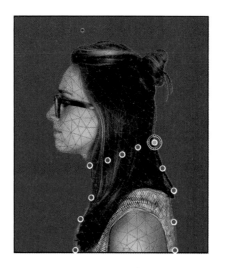

Note: Be careful not to Alt-click or Option-click the dot itself, because that deletes the pin.

▶ **Tip:** On your own, you can compare the difference between dragging the pin itself, and Alt/Option-dragging to pivot the layer around the pin.

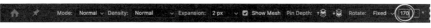

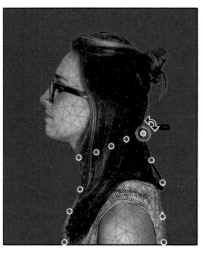
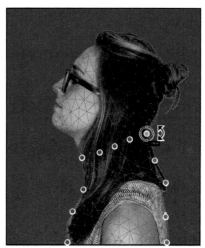

7 Delete the Model layer (the one without the mask). It's no longer needed.

8 Choose File > Save to save your work so far.

Creating a pattern for the background

The design for the episode graphic incorporates a pattern into the background. You'll quickly create the pattern by customizing a vector graphic shape.

Customizing a polygon shape

The background is based on star shapes. There is no star tool in Photoshop, but you can easily create a star by customizing a shape drawn with the Polygon tool.

1 In the Lesson06 folder, open the document 06Pattern.psd. It opens in a separate document tab.

2 Select the Polygon tool (⬠), which is grouped with the Rectangle tool. In the options bar, make sure the tool is set to **Shape**.

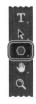

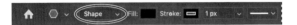

3 Hold down Shift and draw a polygon shape about 340 pixels wide. If it isn't centered on the canvas, after drawing you can reposition it with the Move tool.

4 With the shape layer still selected, in the Appearance section of the Properties panel set the Fill swatch to No Color, set the Stroke to **20px**, and apply a blue Stroke color slightly darker than the background; we used R=23, G=49, B=153.

5 In the Appearance section of the Properties panel, set the polygon Number Of Sides to **8**, and set the Star Ratio to **70%**. When the Star Ratio is less than 100%, the number of sides becomes the number of points.

A. *Rotate angle*
B. *Number of sides*
C. *Star ratio*

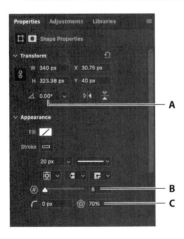

6 In the Layers panel, duplicate the star shape layer by dragging and dropping it on the Create A New Layer button.

7 In the Transform section of the Properties panel, change the Rotate angle to **24**.

8 Choose Edit > Free Transform Path, and hold down the Alt (Windows) or Option (macOS) key as you drag a corner handle to shrink the duplicate star layer to fit inside the larger star. Press Enter or Return to apply the transformation.

Tip: The Edit > Free Transform Path command may appear as Free Transform if you switched to the Move tool in step 3. The command is Free Transform Path when the current tool can edit paths or shapes.

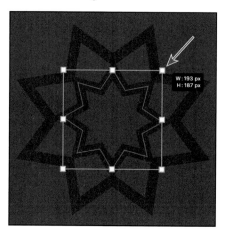

Tip: In step 8, the reason you hold down the Alt or Option key is to scale the shape from its center.

9 Choose View > Pattern Preview to see how the design looks as a pattern. If a message appears, click OK. Only the original shape on the canvas is editable, but Pattern Preview updates to account for any changes you make.

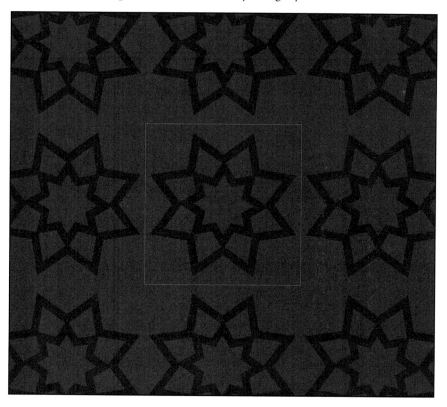

10 Select the Move tool, select Polygon 1 (the large star) in the Layers panel, and look for a small circular handle inside the top-right star point. If you don't see the handle, make sure Show Transform Controls is selected in the options bar, and increase the view magnification.

11 Drag the handle to change the sharp star points to rounded points. We used a radius of 20 pixels. The pattern preview updates.

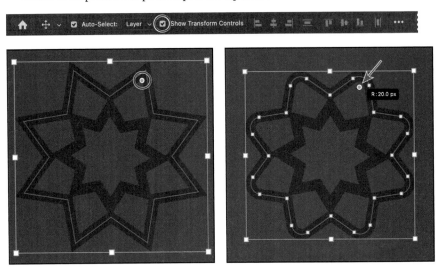

12 In the Layers panel, select Polygon 1 copy (the small star). In the Properties panel, set the Number Of Points to **15** and reduce the Stroke Width to **15 px**.

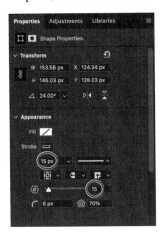

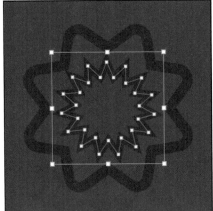

13 Click the eye icon for the Background layer to hide it so that the pattern will have a transparent background.

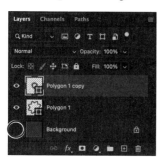

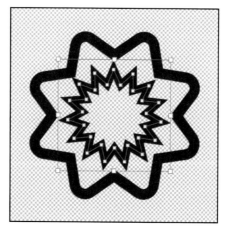

Tip: If you wanted this pattern to always have its own blue background, blocking layers behind it, you'd leave the Background layer visible when defining the pattern.

14 Choose Edit > Define Pattern, name it **Podcast Pattern**, and click OK. This creates a pattern preset that you can use in any Photoshop document.

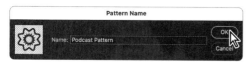

15 Choose File > Save As, rename the file to 06Pattern_Working.psd, and click Save. Click OK if the Photoshop Format Options dialog box appears.

16 Switch to 06Working.psd, and select the Episode Background layer.

17 In the Layers panel, click the Create New Fill Or Adjustment Layer button, and choose Pattern.

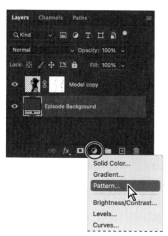

Tip: If you want to create a pattern from just an area of a document, use the Rectangular Marquee tool to draw a selection before choosing Edit > Define Pattern.

18 In the Pattern Fill dialog box, click the pattern picker, and at the bottom of the list, select the blue pattern you created. Set Angle to **45** degrees, set Scale to **35%**, and click OK.

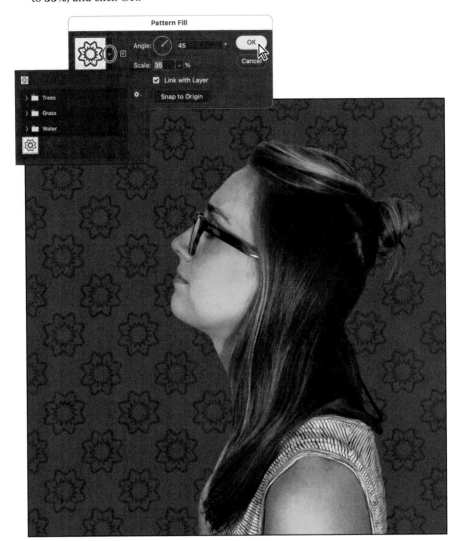

▶ **Tip:** If you want a pattern to cover a partial area of the document, apply a mask to the pattern fill layer. Or, select an area of a layer, choose Edit > Fill, and choose Pattern from the Contents pop-up menu.

▶ **Tip:** This example creates a pattern using vector shape layers, but you can also create a pattern that includes other kinds of layers, such as photos, type, and paintings.

19 Save your work. Your podcast background is ready for the next stage!

Review questions

1 How is a mask similar to and different than a selection?

2 What's a quick way to precisely select the most prominent item in an image?

3 Why is Select and Mask useful?

4 How do you use a layer mask to make parts of a layer transparent?

5 After you define a pattern, how do you apply it to the image as an adjustable pattern?

Review answers

1 A mask and a selection both let you mark areas of a layer to restrict visibility or edits. A mask belongs to a specific layer and is saved with the document; a selection is temporary and is lost when a document is closed.

2 Select Subject identifies an image's main subject and creates a precise selection around the subject in one click.

3 Select and Mask offers specialized tools to improve the edge of a selection or mask.

4 You make parts of a layer transparent (hidden) by painting black in a layer mask. White areas mark layer areas that are to be opaque (visible), and gray shades indicate semi-transparent areas.

5 Apply a pattern to the image by creating a pattern fill layer.

7 TYPOGRAPHIC DESIGN

Lesson overview

In this lesson, you'll learn how to do the following:

- Use guides to position text in a composition.

- Make a clipping mask from type.

- Merge type with other layers.

- Preview fonts.

- Format text.

- Flow text along a path.

- Control type and positioning using advanced features.

This lesson will take less than an hour to complete. To get the lesson files used in this chapter, download them from the web page for this book at peachpit.com/PhotoshopCIB2025. For more information, see "Accessing the lesson files and Web Edition" in the Getting Started section at the beginning of this book.

As you work on this lesson, you'll preserve the start files. If you need to restore the start files, download them from your Account page.

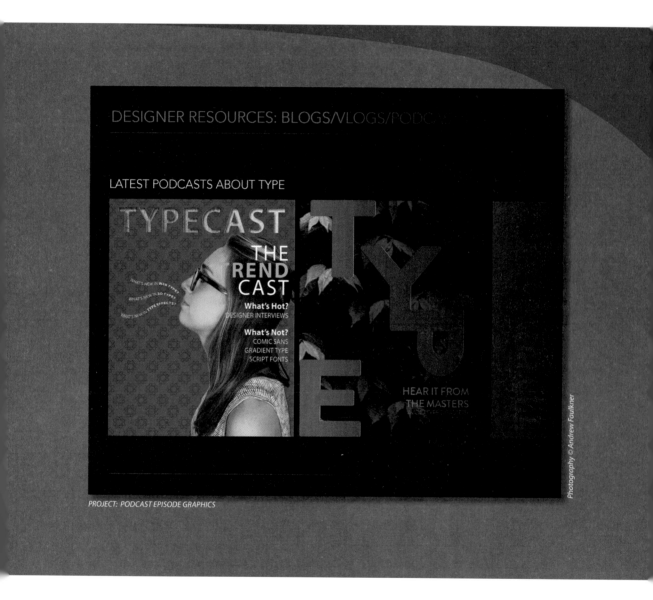

PROJECT: PODCAST EPISODE GRAPHICS

Photoshop provides powerful, flexible text tools so you can add type to your images with great control and creativity.

About type

Note: If some fonts installed on your computer aren't available in Photoshop, check to see if they are PostScript Type 1 fonts, which are an old font format that is no longer supported. Consider licensing OpenType versions of those fonts, which may be available as Adobe Fonts.

A Photoshop type layer consists of vector-based shapes that describe the letters, numbers, and symbols of a typeface. Many typefaces are available in more than one format. The TrueType format is widely used, and the OpenType format is preferred by professionals (see "OpenType in Photoshop" on page 201, later in this lesson).

Photoshop preserves the vector-based character outlines, so type renders at the full resolution of the Photoshop document as you edit, scale, or resize type layers. However, the pixel dimensions of the document limit how sharp type can be. As you magnify a document, jagged type edges appear sooner in a document with smaller pixel dimensions, such as in low-resolution graphics designed for websites.

Getting started

Note: Though this lesson starts where Lesson 6 left off, use the 07Start.psd file. We've included a path and a sticky note in the start file that won't be in the 06Working.psd file you saved.

In this lesson, you'll work on a design that represents an episode of a podcast series about typography. You'll start with the artwork you created in Lesson 6: The episode artwork has a model, her shadow, and the blue background. You'll add and stylize type for the episode artwork, including warping the text.

You'll start the lesson by viewing an image of the final composition.

1   Start Photoshop, and then simultaneously hold down Ctrl+Alt+Shift (Windows) or Command+Option+Shift (macOS) to restore the default preferences. (See "Restoring default preferences" on page 5.)

2   When prompted, click Yes to delete the Adobe Photoshop Settings file.

Note: If Bridge is not installed, you'll be prompted to download and install it. See page 3 for more information.

3   Choose File > Browse In Bridge to open Adobe Bridge.

4   In the Favorites panel on the left side of Bridge, click the Lessons folder, and then double-click the Lesson07 folder in the Content panel.

5   Select the 07End.psd file. Increase the thumbnail size to see the image clearly by dragging the thumbnail slider to the right.

You'll apply the type treatment in Photoshop to finish the episode artwork. All of the type controls you need are available in Photoshop, so you don't have to switch to another application to complete the project.

Note: If Photoshop displays a dialog box telling you about the difference between saving to Cloud Documents and On Your Computer, click Save On Your Computer. You can also select Don't Show Again, but that setting will deselect after you reset Photoshop preferences.

6   Double-click the 07Start.psd file to open it in Photoshop. Click OK if you see an Embedded Profile Mismatch dialog box, and close any messages that appear about new features.

7   Choose File > Save As, rename the file **07Working.psd**, and click Save.

8   Click OK in the Photoshop Format Options dialog box.

9 Choose Graphic and Web from the Workspace Switcher in the options bar.

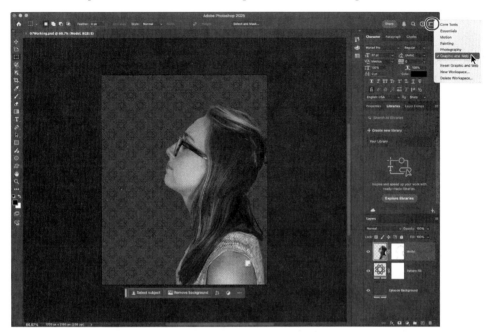

The Graphic and Web workspace displays the Character and Paragraph panels that you'll use in this lesson, along with the Glyphs and Layers panels. The Tools panel may look different than it has in other lessons, because the Graphic and Web workspace includes a customized Tools panel.

▶ **Tip:** You can easily customize the Tools panel for your needs. Choose Edit > Toolbar and then hide, show, or arrange the tools the way you want.

Creating a clipping mask from type

A *clipping mask* is an object or a group of objects whose shape masks other artwork so that only areas within the clipping mask are visible. In effect, you clip the artwork to the visible pixels of the layer. In Photoshop, you can create a clipping mask from shapes or letters. In this exercise, you'll use letters as a clipping mask to allow an image in another layer to show through.

Adding guides to position type

You'll be adding multiple type layers that need to line up on the canvas. To simplify alignment, you'll start by adding nonprinting guides to help position the type.

1 Choose View > Fit On Screen to see the whole canvas clearly.

2 Choose View > Rulers to display rulers along the left and top borders of the document window.

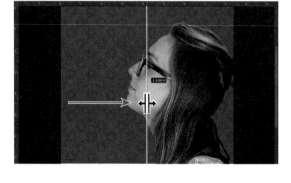

3 If the rulers aren't displaying in inches, right-click (Windows) or Control-click (macOS) the rulers, and choose Inches.

4 Position the pointer over the left ruler; then drag a vertical guide out of the left ruler and drop it in the center of the document (4.25").

Adding point type

Now you're ready to add type to the composition. You can enter *point type* (short text anchored to a point) or *paragraph type* (multiple lines that can recompose as you resize their text container). First, you'll create point type.

1 In the Layers panel, select the Pattern Fill layer.

2 Select the Horizontal Type tool (**T**), and, in the options bar, do the following:

- Choose a serif typeface, such as Minion Pro Regular, from the Font Family pop-up menu.

- Type **115 pt** for the Size, and press Enter or Return.

- Click the Center Text button.

3 In the Character panel, change the Tracking value to **50**.

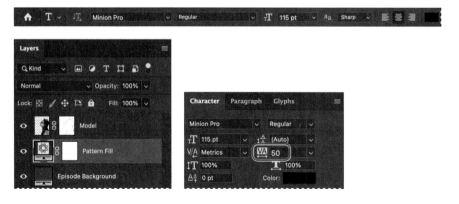

Tracking specifies the space between selected letters, which affects type density.

4   Position the pointer over the center guide you added to set an insertion point, roughly where the guide crosses the edge of the model's face, click, and then type **TYPECAST** in all capital letters. Then click the Commit Any Current Edits button (✔) in the options bar.

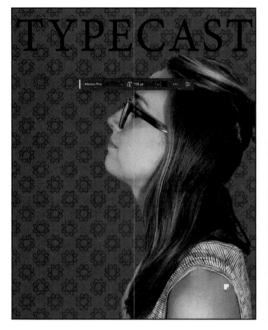

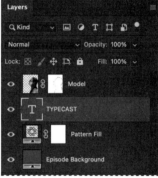

● **Note:** After you type, you must commit your editing in the layer by clicking the Commit Any Current Edits button, switching to another tool or layer, or clicking away from the text layer. You cannot commit to current edits by pressing Enter or Return; doing so would create a new line of type.

The word "TYPECAST" is added, and it appears in the Layers panel as a new type layer named TYPECAST. You can edit and manage the type layer as you would any other layer. You can add or change the text, change the orientation of the type, apply anti-aliasing, apply layer styles and transformations, and create masks. You can move, restack, and copy a type layer, or edit its layer options, just as you would for any other layer.

The text is big enough, but not modern enough, for this design. Try a different font:

5   Double-click the "TYPECAST" text to edit it.

6   In the options bar or Contextual Task Bar, open the Font Family pop-up menu by clicking the arrow to the right of the font name. Hover the pointer over items in the font list.

When the pointer is over a font name, Photoshop temporarily applies that font to the selected text so you can preview the font in context.

▶ **Tip:** When a type layer is selected in the Layers panel, the Properties panel displays type settings—another place you can change type options such as the font.

● **Note:** If a lesson in this book uses a font that isn't installed on your system, you may be able to install it from Adobe Fonts as part of your Creative Cloud subscription: In Photoshop, choose Type > More from Adobe Fonts. (Some educational or organizational Creative Cloud plans might not include Adobe Fonts.)

7 Select Myriad Pro Semibold or a similar font, and then click the Commit Any Current Edits button (✓) in the options bar.

That's much more appropriate.

8 If needed, use the Move tool to drag the "TYPECAST" text to adjust its position close to the top of the design.

9 Choose File > Save to save your work so far.

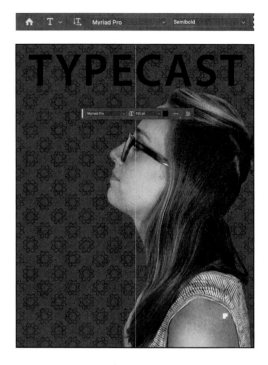

Making a clipping mask and applying a shadow

You added the letters in black, the default text color. However, you want the letters to appear to be filled with a texture from an image, so you'll use the letters to make a clipping mask that will allow another image layer to show through.

1 In the Layers panel, make sure the TYPECAST layer is selected.

2 Choose File > Place Embedded, navigate to the Lesson07 folder, and double-click the Metal.tif file. It appears with a bounding box so that you can scale it or move it into place.

3 With the bounding box still active, drag the Metal layer up until it's aligned with the top of the canvas. Then press Enter or Return to finish placing the file.

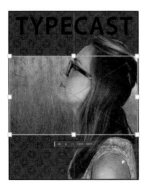 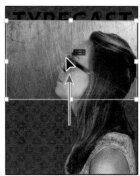 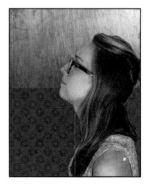

4 With the Metal layer selected, choose Layer > Create Clipping Mask.

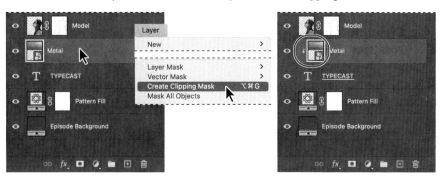

Tip: You can also create a clipping mask by holding down the Alt (Windows) or Option (macOS) key and clicking between the Metal and TYPECAST type layers. Or, choose Layer > Create Clipping Mask when the Metal layer is selected.

Creating a clipping mask restricts the Metal layer to the non-transparent areas of the next layer down (the TYPECAST layer). In the Layers panel, a small arrow and an underlined layer name indicate the two layers used in the clipping mask.

Next, you'll add an inner shadow to give the letters depth.

5 Select the TYPECAST layer. Then, click the Add A Layer Style button (*fx*) at the bottom of the Layers panel, and choose Inner Shadow from the pop-up menu.

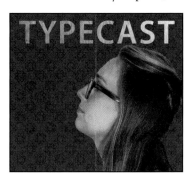 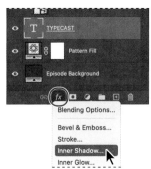

6 In the Layer Style dialog box, set the Blend Mode to Multiply, and set Opacity to **48**%, Angle to **120°**, Distance to **18**, Choke to **0**, and Size to **16**. Then click OK.

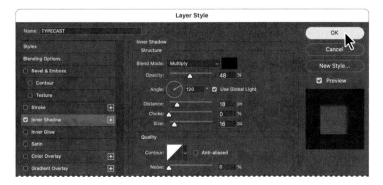

The Inner Shadow option adds a sense of dimension to the title text.

7 Choose File > Save to save your work so far.

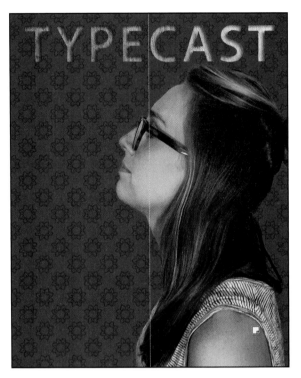

Julieanne Kost is an official Adobe Photoshop evangelist.

Tool tips from the Photoshop evangelist

Type tool tricks

- If clicking a type tool isn't creating a new type layer because it's activating an existing type layer nearby, Shift-click the tool to create the new type layer.

- To select all of the characters on a type layer, in the Layers panel double-click the layer's thumbnail icon.

- To check spelling across all type layers, choose Edit > Check Spelling. You can also choose Check Spelling from the context menu that appears when you right-click (Windows) or Control-click (macOS) a type tool on the canvas.

Paragraph and character styles

If you need to consistently format a large amount of type in a Photoshop document, you can use paragraph and character styles to consistently format more text in less time. Use a paragraph style to apply a named preset of type options to one or more paragraphs with a single click. Use a character style to apply a preset of type options to one or more selected characters. You can use these styles by opening their panels: Choose Window > Paragraph Styles and Window > Character Styles.

Type styles in Photoshop are similar to type styles in page layout applications such as Adobe InDesign and word-processing applications such as Microsoft Word, but there are a few differences in Photoshop. For the best results working with type styles in Photoshop, keep the following in mind:

- By default, all text you create in Photoshop has the Basic Paragraph style applied. The Basic Paragraph style is defined by your text defaults, but you can change the style definition by double-clicking the style name.

- Deselect all layers before you create a new style.

- If the selected text was changed from the current paragraph style (usually the Basic Paragraph style), those changes (considered overrides) persist even when you apply a new style. To ensure that all the attributes of a paragraph style are applied to text, apply the style, and then click the Clear Override button (↻) in the Paragraph Styles panel.

- Want to use the styles from another Photoshop document? Open the Paragraph Styles or Character Styles panel menu, choose Load Styles, and select the document containing the styles you want. To save the current styles as defaults for all new documents, choose Type > Save Default Type Styles. To use your default styles in an existing document, choose Type > Load Default Type Styles.

Creating type on a path

In Photoshop, you can create type that follows along a path that you draw with a pen or shape tool. The direction the type flows depends on the order in which anchor points were added to the path. When you use the Horizontal Type tool to add text to a path, the letters are perpendicular to the baseline of the path. If you change the location or shape of the path, the type moves with it.

> **Tip:** To learn about drawing paths with the Pen tool, see Lesson 8.

You'll create type on a path to make it look as if questions are coming from the model's mouth. We've already created the path for you; we stored it in the Paths panel.

1   In the Layers panel, select the Model layer.

2   Choose Window > Paths to show the Paths panel.

3 In the Paths panel, select Speech Path to make it active and visible.

The path appears to be coming out of the model's mouth.

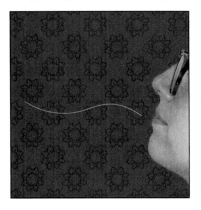 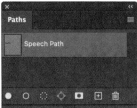

4 Select the Horizontal Type tool.

5 In the options bar, click the Right Align Text button.

6 In the Character panel, select the following settings:

- Font Family: Myriad Pro
- Font Style: Regular
- Font Size (↳T): **14** pt
- Tracking (ⱽₐ): **−10**
- Color: White
- All Caps (**TT**)

Note: The path won't print or export because it isn't a shape layer—it exists only in the Paths panel. But the text on the path is a type layer, so the type will print and export.

7 Move the Horizontal Type tool over the path. When a small curved line appears across the I-bar, click near the end of the path closest to the model's mouth, and type **What's new in 3D type?**.

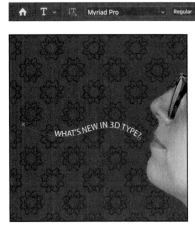 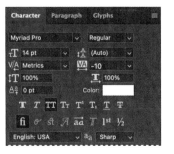

As you type on the path, the text is added from the right because Right Align Text was selected in step 5.

8 With the Horizontal Type too, select "3D TYPE?" and change its font style to Bold. Click the Commit Any Current Edits button (✔) in the options bar.

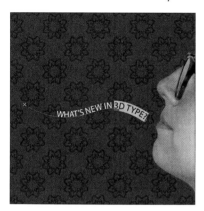 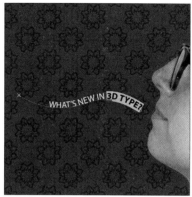

9 In the Layers panel, select the What's new in 3D type? layer, choose Layer > Duplicate Layer, and click OK.

You can't see the duplicate text layer yet, because it's exactly on top of the original text layer. But the Layers panel shows that the duplicate layer has the word "copy" at the end of the layer name. You'll move the copy away from the original.

10 Choose Edit > Free Transform Path. Rotate the path approximately 15 degrees, and then shift the path up above the first path and a little to the right, as in the following figure. Click the Commit Transform button in the options bar.

11 With the Type tool, select "3D" in the upper copy of the text layer, and replace it with **web**. Click the Commit Any Current Edits button in the options bar.

When you edit the characters on a text layer, the layer name automatically updates to match. (The layer name will not update if you edited the layer name to differ from the actual text on the layer.)

● **Note:** For step 10, if you can't remember how to rotate using a transform bounding box, position the pointer slightly outside the transform bounding box until the pointer changes to a rotate icon (an arc with two arrows), and drag. Or, you can enter a rotation value in the options bar.

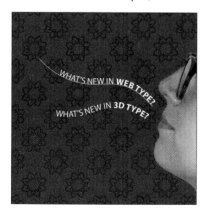 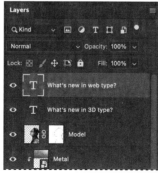

12 Repeat steps 9–11, replacing the words "3D type" with **type effects**. Rotate the left side of the path about –15 degrees, and move it below the original path.

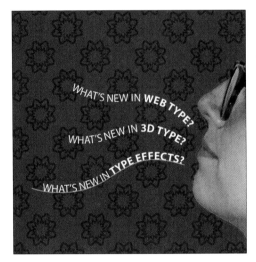
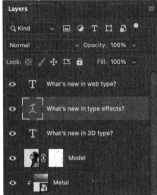

13 Choose File > Save to save your work so far.

Warping point type

The text on a curvy path is more interesting than straight lines would be, but you'll warp the text to make it more playful. *Warping* lets you distort type into a variety of shapes, such as an arc or a wave. The warp style you select is an attribute of the type layer—you can change a layer's warp style at any time to change the overall shape of the warp. Warping options give you precise control over the orientation and perspective of the warp effect.

1 If necessary, zoom or scroll to move the visible area of the document window so that the sentences to the left of the model are in the center of the screen.

2 Select the What's new in 3D type? layer.

Note: You can also choose Warp Text from the context menu that appears when you right-click/Control-click a type layer (not the layer thumbnail) in the Layers panel.

3 Choose Type > Warp Text.

4 In the Warp Text dialog box, choose Wave from the Style menu, and select the Horizontal option. Specify the following values: Bend, +**33**%; Horizontal Distortion, –**23**%; and Vertical Distortion, +**5**%. Then click OK.

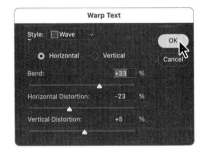

The Bend slider specifies how much warp is applied. Horizontal Distortion and Vertical Distortion determine the perspective of the warp.

Tip: Do you want to simulate type wrapping around a beverage can? With a type layer selected, choose Edit > Transform > Warp, and then choose Cylinder from the Warp pop-up menu in the options bar.

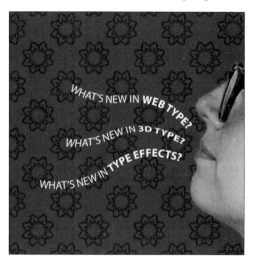

The words "What's new in 3D type?" appear to float like a wave on the design.

5 Repeat steps 3 and 4 to warp the other two text layers you typed on a path. Feel free to try different settings.

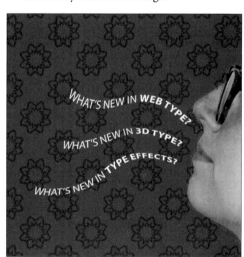

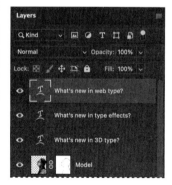

6 Save your work.

Designing paragraphs of type

All of the text you've added so far has been point type because it's a single line. However, many designs call for full paragraphs of text. You can add paragraph type and apply paragraph styles. You don't have to switch to a dedicated page layout program for sophisticated paragraph type controls.

Using guides for positioning

You will add paragraphs to the design. First, you'll add some guides to the work area to help you position the paragraphs.

1 If necessary, zoom or scroll so that you can see the entire top half of the document.

2 Drag a guide from the left vertical ruler, placing it approximately ¼" from the right edge of the canvas.

3 Drag a guide down from the top horizontal ruler, placing it approximately 2" from the top of the canvas.

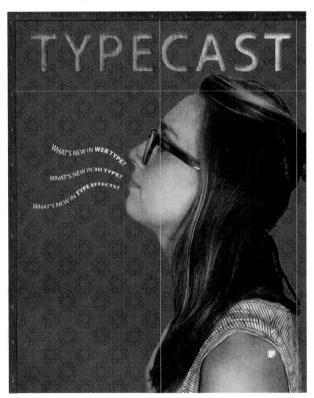

Adding paragraph type from a sticky note

You're ready to add the text. In a real-world design environment, text might be provided to you in a comment (in an online Photoshop review using File > Share for Review) or in an email message. It's also possible for someone to open the document and enter text into a sticky note, as we've done for you here.

1   Position the Move tool near the edge of the yellow sticky note in the lower-right corner of the image window, and when it appears as a black pointer only (▸), double-click to open the Notes panel.

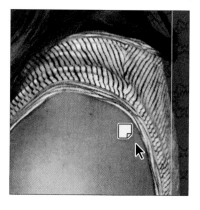 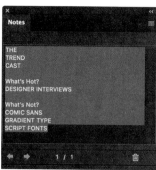

Tip: You create notes using the Note tool, which is hidden when the Graphics and Web workspace is active. You can find the Note tool quickly by choosing Edit > Search. However, if you want to collect comments from multiple people, it may be easier to use the cloud-based Share for Review online comment feature (choose File > Share for Review).

2   All nine lines of the text should be selected; if they aren't, click in the note text and choose Select > All. Choose Edit > Copy, and close the Notes panel.

3   Select the Model layer. Then, select the Horizontal Type tool (**T**).

4   Position the pointer where the guides intersect at about ¼" from the right edge and 2" from the top of the canvas. Hold down the Shift key as you start to drag a text box down and to the left. Then release the Shift key, and continue dragging until the box is about 4 inches wide by 6 inches high. The new text layer is created in front of the Model layer that was selected (above the Model layer in the Layers panel).

5   Choose Edit > Paste to add the text from the note.

6   Select the first three lines ("The Trend Cast"), and then apply the following settings in the Character panel:

   • Font Family: Myriad Pro (or another sans serif font)

   • Font Style: Regular

   • Font Size (⁑T): **70** pt

   • Leading (↕⁑): **55** pt

   • Tracking (ᴠ⁄ᴀ): **50**

   • Color: White

Tip: In step 4, the reason you press Shift is to make sure you create a new type layer. If you don't press Shift, the Horizontal Type tool might instead select text in the nearby text layer containing the "TYPECAST" headline.

Note: If the text isn't visible, make sure the new type layer is above the Model layer in the Layers panel.

Tip: If you paste text and it includes unwanted formatting, you can instead choose the Edit > Paste Special > Paste Without Formatting command in Photoshop to remove all formatting from the pasted text.

7 With the text still selected, make sure Right Align Text button is selected in the options bar or Paragraph panel.

8 Select just the word "Trend," and change the Font Style to Bold.

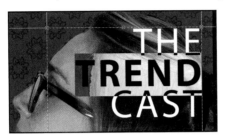

You've formatted the title. Now you'll format the rest of the text.

9 Select the rest of the text you pasted. In the Character panel, select the following:

- Font Family: Myriad Pro

- Font Style: Regular

- Font Size: **22** pt

- Leading: **28** pt

- Tracking: **0**

- Deselect All Caps (**TT**)

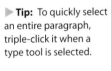

● **Note:** *Leading* (pronounced "ledding") determines the vertical space between lines.

The text looks good, but it's all the same. You'll make the headlines stand out more.

10 Select the "What's Hot?" text, change the following in the Character panel, and then press Enter or Return:

- Font Style: Bold

- Font Size: **28** pt

▶ **Tip:** To quickly select an entire paragraph, triple-click it when a type tool is selected.

11 Repeat step 10 for the "What's Not!" subhead.

12 Select the word "TREND." Then, in the Character panel, change the text color to blue. We used R=0, G=174, B=239 (or #00aeef in hexadecimal RGB).

13 Click the Commit Any Current Edits button in the options bar.

14 Save your changes.

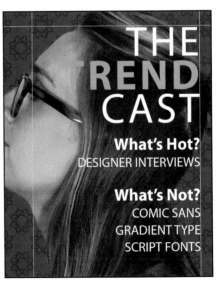

Saving as Photoshop PDF

The type you've added consists of vector-based outlines, which remain crisp and clear as you zoom in or resize them. However, if you save the file as a JPEG or TIFF image, Photoshop rasterizes the type, so you lose that flexibility. When you save a Photoshop PDF file, vector type is preserved. However, type resolution is always limited to the document resolution. For example, in a 300 × 200 px document even a vector type layer is likely to look jaggy because a document of those pixel dimensions simply doesn't have many pixels for resolving curves and details.

You can preserve other Photoshop editing capabilities in a Photoshop PDF file too. For example, you can retain layers, color information, and even notes.

To ensure you can edit the document later, select Preserve Photoshop Editing Capabilities in the Save Adobe PDF dialog box. This will result in a larger PDF file.

To preserve any notes in the file and convert them to Acrobat comments when you save to PDF, select Notes in the Save area of the Save As dialog box.

You can open a Photoshop PDF file in Acrobat or Photoshop, place it in another application, print it, or upload it to a website. For more information, see "Saving the Image as Photoshop PDF" in Lesson 14, "Producing and Printing Consistent Color."

Finishing up

Now, you'll clean up a bit before saving the finished project.

1   With the Move tool, right-click (Windows) or Control-click (macOS) near the top-left corner of the yellow note icon, and choose Delete Note from the context menu; click Yes to confirm that you want to delete the note.

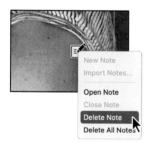

2   Hide the guides: Choose View > Show > Guides to deselect the command. Then choose View > Fit on Screen to get a nice look at your work.

3   Choose File > Save.

Congratulations! You've added and stylized all of the type. Now that the design is ready to go, you'll export a copy to upload to the podcast service.

▶ **Tip:** Want a design to have a familiar look but not with the exact font that look is known for? Try Font Similarity. Choose a font in the Font Family menu in either the Type tool options bar or the Character panel. You'll see options at the top of the font list; click the Show Similar Fonts button.

The font list will now show the 20 most similar fonts available either on your system or from Adobe Fonts.

▶ **Tip:** The keyboard shortcut for hiding and showing guides (View > Show > Guides) is Ctrl+; (Windows) or Command+; (macOS).

The Glyphs panel

The Glyphs panel (Window > Glyphs) lists all characters available for a font, including specialized characters and alternate versions such as swashes. At the top is a row of recently used glyphs (empty if you haven't used any glyphs yet). Use the menu below the font name to specify a writing system such as Arabic, or a category such as punctuation. To use a glyph, position a flashing text cursor in a text layer and then double-click a glyph. A black dot in the bottom-right corner of a glyph's box indicates that alternates are available; click and hold the mouse on that box to view or select alternate glyphs.

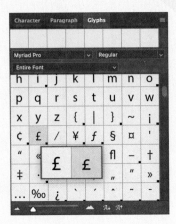

4 Choose File > Export > Export As, choose JPG from the Format menu, leave the rest of the settings as they are, and click Export. Change the filename to **07Upload.jpg**, go to the Lesson07 folder, and click Save.

5 Close the document window and save any changes.

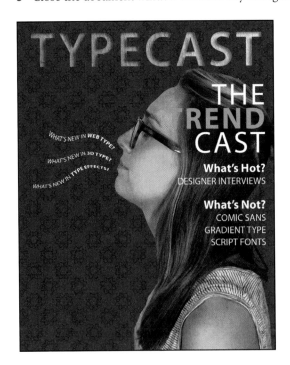

OpenType in Photoshop

OpenType is a cross-platform font file format developed jointly by Adobe and Microsoft. The format uses a single font file for both Mac and Windows, so you can move files from one platform to another without font substitution or reflowed text. OpenType offers expanded character sets and layout features, such as swashes and discretionary ligatures, that aren't available in traditional PostScript and TrueType fonts. This, in turn, provides richer linguistic support and advanced typography control. You can identify OpenType fonts in the Photoshop font menu because they appear with an OpenType icon (O). Here are some highlights of OpenType:

The OpenType menu. The Character panel menu includes an OpenType submenu that displays all available features for a selected OpenType font, including ligatures, alternates, and fractions. Dimmed features are unavailable for that typeface; check marks appear next to features that have been applied.

Discretionary ligatures. To add a discretionary ligature to two OpenType letters, such as to "th" in the Bickham Script Standard typeface, select them in the file, and choose OpenType > Discretionary Ligatures from the Character panel menu.

Swashes. Adding swashes or alternate characters works the same way as discretionary ligatures: Select the letter, such as a capital "T" in Bickham Script, and choose OpenType > Swash to change the ordinary capital into an ornate (swash) "T."

True fractions. To create true fractions, type the fraction's characters—for example, 1/2. Then, select the characters, and from the Character panel menu, choose OpenType > Fractions. Photoshop applies the true fraction (½).

Color fonts. While you can apply a color to a font in Photoshop, a format called OpenType-SVG allows multiple colors and gradients to be part of the font design itself. For example, a color font may provide the letter "A" in solid blue as well as solid red and in a blue-to-green gradient.

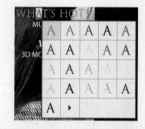

Emoji fonts. Another example of OpenType-SVG fonts are emoji fonts, made possible because OpenType-SVG allows vector graphics to be used as font characters. The Photoshop font family menu indicates color and emoji fonts with an OpenType SVG icon ( ).

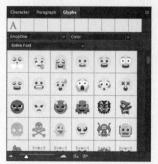

Variable fonts. When you want a certain font weight but Regular is too thin and Bold is too thick, you can use a variable font that lets you customize attributes such as weight, width, and slant in the Properties panel. The Photoshop font family menu indicates variable fonts with an OpenType VAR icon ( ).

Note that some OpenType fonts have more options than others.

> ▶ **Tip:** Want to know if a character has OpenType alternates? Just select it. If a thick bar appears under a selected character, right-click (Windows) or Control-click (macOS) the bar and select Show Alternatives for Selection to reveal the alternate glyphs available for that character in the font applied to it. You can select from those glyphs just as you can in the Glyphs panel, or you can click a triangle to open the Glyphs panel.

Extra credit

Using Match Fonts to keep your projects consistent

We want to identify a font that was used in another design and apply it to text that says "Premiere Episode" (see the file MatchFont.jpg in the Lesson07 folder). We'd like to use that font for another episode. But the only available file is flattened, so the original type layer is lost. Because no type layer is available, it's impossible to select the text to find out which font was used. Fortunately, you don't have to guess which font is in the image because, in Photoshop, you can let the Match Font feature figure it out for you. Thanks to the magic of intelligent imaging analysis, using just a picture of a Latin font, Photoshop can use machine learning to detect which font it is. Match Font then shows you a list of similar fonts. Match Font is also useful for identifying fonts in photos, such as in the text on a sign in a street scene.

1. Open MatchFont.jpg in the Lesson07 folder.

2. Use the Rectangular Marquee tool to tightly select the area containing the mystery font.

3. Choose Type > Match Font. Photoshop displays a list of fonts similar to the font in the image, including active fonts on your system and Adobe Fonts.

4. To list only the fonts on your computer, deselect Show Fonts Available To Add From Adobe Fonts.

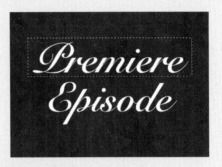

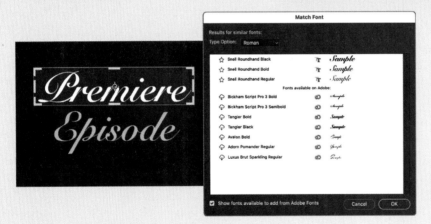

5. Select a script font that most closely resembles the font in the image from the list of fonts that Match Font determined to be similar. Your Match Font results may look different than ours.

6. Click OK. Photoshop selects the font you clicked, so you can now create new text with it.

Review questions

1 How is a Photoshop text layer different than a pixel (image) layer?

2 What are the two kinds of text layers in Photoshop? How are they different?

3 What is a clipping mask, and how do you make one from type?

4 If you want to add an inner shadow to type, will you find that effect by looking at adjustment layers, layer styles, or filter?

Review answers

1 A Photoshop text layer consists of vector-based shapes that describe the letters, numbers, and symbols of a typeface. When you add type to an image in Photoshop, the characters appear on a text layer at the same resolution as the document. As long as it's a type layer, Photoshop preserves the type outlines so that the text remains sharp when you scale or resize type, save a Photoshop PDF file, or print the image at high resolution. Also, you can easily change the characters of a text layer at any time.

2 You can create point type or paragraph type. Point type is anchored to a point created where you click a type tool. Paragraph type can contain multiple lines that can recompose as you resize their text container; you create it by dragging a type tool.

3 A clipping mask is an object or group that uses the visible pixels of one layer to mask another—you see only the areas of the layer that overlap the visible pixels of the clipping mask. To use a text layer as a clipping mask, make sure the layer you want to reveal is directly above the text layer, select the layer you want to show through the letters, and apply the Create Clipping Mask command (found on the Layer menu, the Layers panel menu, or the layer's context menu).

4 Inner Shadow is a layer style, which you can select from the Add a Layer Style button menu on the Layers panel, or on the Layer > Layer Styles submenu.

8 VECTOR DRAWING TECHNIQUES

Lesson overview

In this lesson, you'll learn how to do the following:

- Understand the difference between bitmap and vector graphics.
- Draw straight and curved paths using the Pen tool.
- Save paths.
- Draw and edit shape layers.
- Draw custom shapes.
- Use Smart Guides.

This lesson will take about 90 minutes to complete. To get the lesson files used in this chapter, download them from the web page for this book at peachpit.com/PhotoshopCIB2025. For more information, see "Accessing the lesson files and Web Edition" in the Getting Started section at the beginning of this book.

As you work on this lesson, you'll preserve the start files. If you need to restore the start files, download them from your Account page.

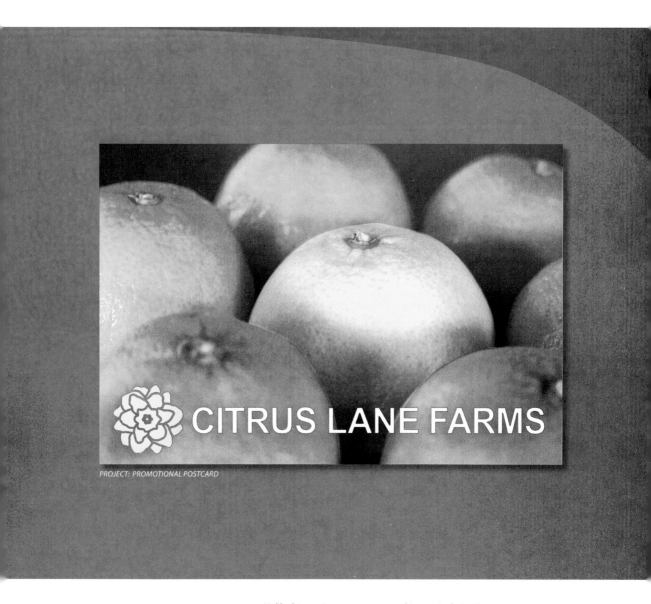

PROJECT: PROMOTIONAL POSTCARD

Unlike bitmap images, vector graphics retain their crisp
edges when you enlarge them to any size. You can draw
vector shapes and paths in your Photoshop images and
add vector masks to control what is shown in an image.

About bitmap images and vector graphics

Before working with vector shapes and vector paths, it's important to understand the basic differences between the two main categories of computer graphics: *bitmap images* and *vector graphics*. You can use Photoshop to work with either kind of graphic; in fact, you can combine both bitmap and vector data in an individual Photoshop image file.

Bitmap images, technically called *raster images*, are based on a grid of dots known as *pixels*. Each pixel is assigned a specific location and color value. In working with bitmap images, you edit groups of pixels rather than objects or shapes. Because bitmap graphics can represent subtle gradations of shade and color, they are appropriate for continuous-tone images such as photographs or artwork created in painting programs. A disadvantage of bitmap graphics is that they contain a fixed number of pixels. As a result, they can lose detail and appear jagged when scaled up onscreen or printed at a lower resolution than they were created for.

Vector graphics are made up of lines and curves defined by mathematical objects called *vectors*. These graphics retain their crispness whether they are moved, resized, or have their color changed. Vector graphics are appropriate for illustrations, type, and graphics such as logos that may be scaled to different sizes.

In the lessons so far, you've worked with bitmap images on Photoshop layers. A different type of layer—a shape layer—contains vector graphics in Photoshop.

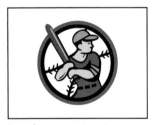 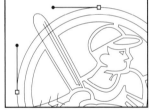

Logo drawn as vector art.

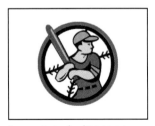 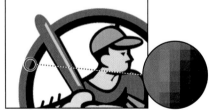

Logo rasterized as bitmap art.

About paths and the Pen tool

In Photoshop, the outline of a vector shape is called a *path*. A path is a curved or straight line segment you draw using the Pen tool, the Freeform Pen tool, the Curvature Pen tool, or a shape tool. The Pen and Curvature Pen tools draw paths with great precision; shape tools create rectangles, ellipses, and other shape paths; and the Freeform Pen tool draws paths as if you were drawing with a pen on paper.

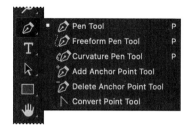

Paths can be open or closed. An open path (such as a wavy line) has two distinct endpoints. A closed path (such as a circle) is continuous. The type of path you draw affects how it can be selected and adjusted.

Unlike the pixels created by the painting tools, a path doesn't make a printable mark on its own. A path is more like a selection marquee in vector form, so you can use a path to mark an area of a layer with pixels using a *fill* (color, pattern, or other content) or a *stroke* (outline). To use a path as a vector object that you can fill, stroke, print, export, and continue to edit as a vector object, create it as a *shape* layer.

Julieanne Kost is an official Adobe Photoshop evangelist.

Tool tips from the Photoshop evangelist

Accessing tools quickly

Each tool in the Tools panel has a single-letter keyboard shortcut. Type the letter, get the tool. Press Shift with the shortcut key to cycle through any nested tools in a group. For example, press P to select the Pen tool, and press Shift+P to toggle between the Pen, Freeform Pen, and Curvature Pen tools.

Getting started with vector drawing

In this lesson, you'll create a postcard that will help promote a citrus fruit farm. You've been given an image of oranges, but because the farm wants to convey the idea that they grow more than just oranges, it's been decided that one of the oranges will be recolored to look like a lemon. Recoloring one item requires isolating it by creating a mask of its outline, and one quick and precise way to create a clean outline of that item is using the Pen tool to draw a vector path.

Before you begin, view the image you'll be creating.

1 Start Photoshop, and then simultaneously hold down Ctrl+Alt+Shift (Windows) or Command+Option+Shift (macOS) to restore the default preferences. (See "Restoring default preferences" on page 5.)

2 When prompted, click Yes to delete the Adobe Photoshop Settings file.

3 Choose File > Browse In Bridge.

4 In the Favorites panel, click the Lessons folder, and then double-click the Lesson08 folder in the Content panel.

5 Select the 08End.psd file, and press the spacebar to see it in full-screen view.

To create this postcard, you'll trace an image and use that tracing to make a vector mask that lets you change the color of one of the oranges. First, you'll practice making paths and selections using the Pen tool.

6 When you've finished looking at the 08End.psd file, press the spacebar again. Then double-click the 08Practice_Start.psd file to open it in Photoshop, and close any messages that appear about new features.

7 Choose File > Save As, rename the file **08Practice_Working.psd**, and click Save. If the Photoshop Format Options dialog box appears, click OK.

● **Note:** If Bridge isn't installed, the File > Browse In Bridge command in Photoshop will start the Creative Cloud desktop app, which will download and install Bridge. After installation completes, you can start Bridge. For more information, see page 3.

● **Note:** If Photoshop displays a dialog box telling you about the difference between saving to Cloud Documents and On Your Computer, click Save On Your Computer. You can also select Don't Show Again, but that setting will deselect after you reset Photoshop preferences.

Drawing a shape with the Pen tool

The Pen tool is commonly used for creating vector graphics on a computer. You'll find the Pen tool in many applications, including Adobe Illustrator (which first featured the Pen tool in 1987), Adobe Photoshop, and Adobe InDesign. Video applications such as Adobe Premiere Pro and Adobe After Effects also include the Pen tool, because you can use it to quickly draw precise shapes, masks, and paths for motion graphics and visual effects. The Pen tool can be a challenge to learn, but trust us: Knowing how to use the Pen tool is worth the effort and investment to learn, because it's a marketable skill across many creative digital disciplines.

▶ **Tip:** The Curvature Pen tool offers a potentially simpler way to draw precise vector paths; consider learning it if you find the Pen tool to be challenging to use. The Pen tool is taught in this lesson because it's a traditional and industry-standard tool for precisely drawing vector graphics.

To achieve its high precision and control, the Pen tool works differently than a brush or pencil tool. We've created a practice file that you'll use to learn how to draw a straight path, a simple curve, and an S-curve with the Pen tool.

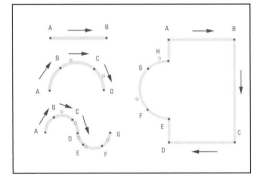

Creating paths with the Pen tool

You can use the Pen tool to create paths that are straight or curved, open or closed. If you're unfamiliar with the Pen tool, it can be confusing to use at first. Understanding the elements of a path and how to create those elements with the Pen tool makes paths much easier to draw.

To create a straight path, click the mouse button. The first time you click, you set the first *anchor point*. Each time that you click thereafter, a straight line is drawn between the previous anchor point and the current one. To draw complex straight-segment paths with the Pen tool, click each time you want to add a new segment.

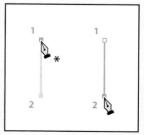

Creating a straight line.

To create a curved path, drag to both place an anchor point and extend a direction line for that point, and then click or drag to place the next anchor point. Each direction line ends in two direction points; the positions of direction lines and points determine the size and shape of the curved segment. Moving the direction lines and points reshapes the curves in a path.

Smooth curves are connected by anchor points called *smooth points*. Sharply curved paths are connected by *corner points*. When you move a direction line on a smooth point, the curved segments on both sides of the point adjust simultaneously, but when you move a direction line on a corner point, only the curve on the same side of the point as the direction line is adjusted.

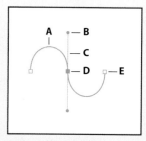

A. Curved line segment
B. Direction point
C. Direction line
D. Selected anchor point
E. Unselected anchor point

You can move path segments and anchor points, either individually or as a group. When a path contains multiple segments, you can drag individual anchor points to adjust individual segments of the path, or select all anchor points in a path to edit the entire path. Use the Direct Selection tool (⟡) to select and adjust an anchor point, a path segment, or an entire path.

Creating a closed path differs from creating an open path, in the way that you end it. To end an open path, press Enter or Return. To create a closed path, position the Pen tool pointer over the starting point, and click. Closing a path automatically ends the path. After the path closes, the Pen tool pointer appears with a small *, indicating that your next click will start a new path.

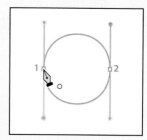

Creating a closed path.

When you first draw a path, it appears in the Paths panel as a Work Path, which is only temporary. Save any work path you want to use again in the future, especially if you want to use multiple paths in the same document. To save a work path, double-click it in the Paths panel, type a name in the Save Path dialog box, and click OK. It's added as a new named path in the Paths panel and remains selected. If you don't save a work path, it's lost as soon as you deselect it and then start drawing again. (Saving the path isn't necessary when you draw a path as a shape, because a shape is created as a named layer.)

First, you'll configure the Pen tool options and the work area.

1 In the Tools panel, select the Pen tool (✐).

2 In the options bar, select or verify the following settings:

- Choose Shape from the Tool Mode pop-up menu.

- In the Path Options menu, make sure that Rubber Band is not selected.

- Make sure that Auto Add/Delete is selected.

- Choose No Color from the Fill pop-up menu.

- Choose a green color from the Stroke pop-up menu. We used the green swatch in the CMYK presets group.

- Enter **4 pt** for the stroke width.

- In the Stroke Options window, choose Center (the second option) from the Align menu.

Tip: The Align stroke option controls whether the stroke width sits entirely to one side of a path or the other or is centered over the path.

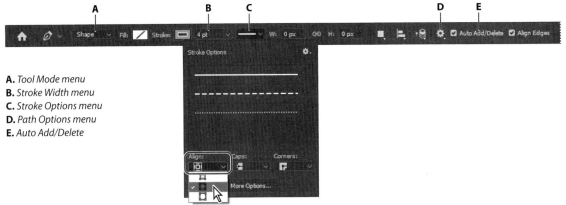

A. *Tool Mode menu*
B. *Stroke Width menu*
C. *Stroke Options menu*
D. *Path Options menu*
E. *Auto Add/Delete*

Drawing a straight line

You'll start by drawing a straight line. Anchor points mark the ends of path segments; the straight line you'll draw is a single path segment with two anchor points.

1 Drag the Paths panel tab out of the Layers panel group so that you can see both it and the Layers panel at the same time. You can dock the Paths panel with another panel group.

The Paths panel displays thumbnail previews of the paths you draw. Currently, the panel is empty, because you haven't started drawing.

2 If necessary, zoom in so that you can easily see the lettered points and red circles on the shape template. Make sure you can see the whole template in the document window, and after you zoom, make sure the Pen tool is selected.

3 On the first shape, click point A, and release the mouse button. You've created an anchor point.

4 Click point B. You've created a perfectly straight line with two anchor points.

5 Press Enter or Return to stop drawing.

Note: If a tutorial pops up for the Curvature Pen tool, you don't need to read it at this time. It will probably close on its own, or you can close it.

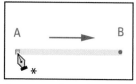 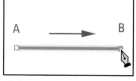 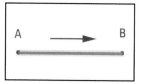

Create an anchor point.   *Click to create a straight line.*   *Complete the path.*

The path you drew appears in the Paths panel and as a new layer in the Layers panel.

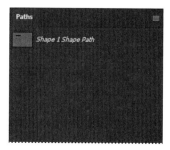 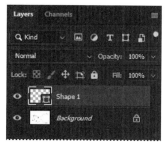

Note: The new path appears in both the Paths and Layers panels because the Tool Mode menu in the options bar is set to Shape, so drawing a new path also creates a new shape layer. If the Tool Mode menu was set to Path, the new path would be added to the Paths panel only.

Drawing curves

On curved segments, selecting an anchor point displays one or two direction lines, depending on the shapes of adjacent segments. You adjust the shape of a curved segment by dragging the direction point at the end of a direction line, and the direction line shapes the curve. You'll create curved lines, using smooth points.

1 Click point A, and release the mouse to create the first anchor point.

2 Click point B, but don't release the mouse button. Instead, drag to the open red circle to the right of point B to create a curved path segment and a smooth anchor point. Then release the mouse button.

Tip: The red circles indicate where you should stop dragging an anchor point's direction point to form the desired shape of the curve. If you drag the direction point to a different location, the curve will have a different shape.

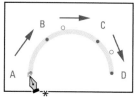 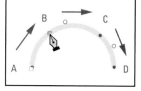 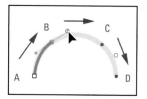

Create an anchor point.   *Click and hold.*   *Drag to curve the path segment.*

Smooth anchor points have two linked direction lines. When you move one, the curved segments on both sides of the path adjust simultaneously.

3 Position the pointer over point C, click and drag down to the open red circle below, and then release the mouse button. You've created a second curved path segment and another smooth point.

4 Click point D, and release the mouse to create the final anchor point. Press Enter or Return to complete the path.

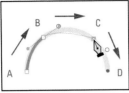 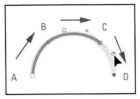 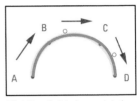

Click C to create a point.   *Drag to curve the segment.*   *Click D to finish the semicircle.*

Tip: What's the advantage of drawing paths using points and handles, instead of drawing directly as with a real pen or pencil? For most people, it's difficult to draw curves and straight lines without bumps or other errors. Points and handles let you draw perfect curves and straight lines. If you prefer to draw normally, you can use the Freeform Pen tool.

When you draw your own paths using the Pen tool, use as few points as possible to create the shape you want. The fewer points you use, the smoother the curves are, and the easier it is to edit the shape later.

Using the same techniques, you'll draw an S-shaped curve.

5 Click point A, and then click and drag from point B to its open red circle.

6 Continue with points C, D, E, and F, in each case clicking the point and then dragging to the corresponding open red circle.

7 Click point G to create the final anchor point, and then press Enter or Return to complete the path.

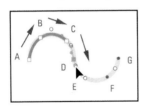 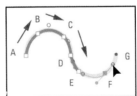 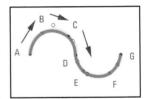

Each of the three shapes is on its own layer in the Layers panel. Only one path is in the Paths panel, because the Paths panel shows only the Shape Path for the layer that's currently selected in the Layers panel.

Notice that the curves you drew with the Pen tool are much smoother and easier to precisely control than if you had drawn them freehand.

Drawing a more complex shape

Now that you've got the idea, you'll draw a more complex object.

1 Click point A on the shape on the right side to set the first anchor point.

2 Press the Shift key as you click point B. Pressing the Shift key constrains the line to 45-degree angles, which in this case ensures you'll get a horizontal line.

3 Press the Shift key as you click points C, D, and E to create straight path segments.

4 Click point F, and drag to the open red circle to create a curve. Then release the mouse button.

5 Click point G, and drag to the open red circle to create another curve. Then release the mouse button.

6 Click point H to create a corner point.

When you move a direction line on a corner point, only the curve on the same side of the point as the direction line is adjusted, so you can create a sharp transition between two segments.

7 Click point A to draw the final path segment and close the path. Closing a path automatically ends the drawing; if you click or drag the Pen tool, it will create a new path. After you close a path, you don't need to press Enter or Return unless you also want to deselect the path.

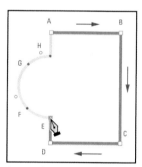 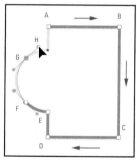 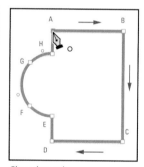

Start with straight segments. *Drag to create a curve.* *Close the path.*

▶ **Tip:** If you notice that you slightly missed the red dot on the template while dragging a curve point, you can reposition the point without starting over. Keeping the mouse button down, hold down the spacebar and drag until the point is in the right place. Then release the spacebar to continue dragging the direction lines of that anchor point.

8 Close the file (you don't have to save changes for this exercise). You have successfully used the Pen tool to draw both curves and straight lines.

ADOBE PHOTOSHOP CLASSROOM IN A BOOK 2025 RELEASE **213**

Drawing a path traced from a photo

Now you're ready to draw a path around a real object. You'll use the techniques you've practiced to draw a path around the edge of one orange out of several. The path you draw will later be converted into a layer mask so that you can change the color of that orange. The orange is partially covered by surrounding oranges, so the path you draw will be a combination of curved and straight segments, like the shapes you've practiced on. Later, you'll combine the altered image with text and a shape layer to create a promotional postcard for a citrus farm.

1 From Photoshop or Bridge, open the 08Start.psd file.

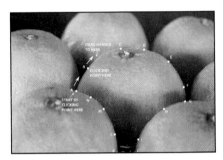

The image includes two layers: the background layer and a template layer named Path Guide that you will trace to draw the path.

2 Choose File > Save As, rename the file **08Working.psd**, and click Save. If the Photoshop Format Options dialog box appears, click OK.

3 Select the Pen tool, and then, in the options bar, choose Path from the Tool Mode pop-up menu.

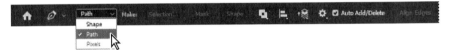

Because Path is now selected in the options bar instead of Shape, what you see when you draw will be different than in the practice exercise. You'll be drawing a path, not a shape. The path you draw will appear as a temporary work path in the Paths panel, and a shape layer won't be created.

The reason you're switching to a path is because you won't need to print or export the path you're about to draw. You'll use the path as a starting point for creating a mask, so the path itself doesn't need to be a visible part of the final document. For more information about shapes and paths, see the sidebar "Comparing shapes, paths, and pixels."

Comparing shapes, paths, and pixels

When you use the Pen tool or the tools grouped with it, or the Rectangle tool or any of the tools grouped with it, a menu in the options bar lets you choose whether you want the tool to draw a shape, a path, or, in some cases, pixels.

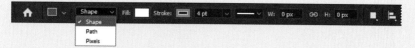

This is an important decision, because each option has different advantages:

Shape. A shape is a vector object created on its own layer in the Layers panel. You can apply the same layer effects, masks, and other properties that you would to a pixel layer. The difference is that you can continue to edit the shape as a vector path, using path editing tools such as the Pen tool and the Direct Selection tool. You can't edit a shape layer using pixel-based tools such as brushes. You can change a shape layer's fill and stroke. Because a shape is a layer, when its layer visibility is enabled, it's visible and will print and export.

A selected shape layer also displays its path in the Paths panel.

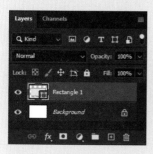
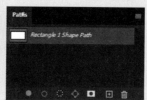

Path. A path is a vector object that doesn't display, print, or export, so it doesn't appear in the Layers panel; you'll find it in the Paths panel. A path is useful for creating type along a path, clipping paths, and in other "backstage" roles where editing a vector path saves time. For example, sometimes it's faster to create a selection by first drawing and editing a path and then converting that to a selection.

Because a path is not a layer, it's visible in the document window only when it's selected in the Paths panel, and it can't have a stroke and fill. If it's hard to see, you can improve its visibility by clicking the Path Options menu (the gear) in the options bar and adjusting the path's Thickness and Color. Because a path isn't visible in a printed or exported image, those options affect only the visibility of the path while drawing in Photoshop.

Pixels. Some tools, such as the Rectangle tool and the tools grouped with it, also offer a Pixels option. Drawing with the Pixels option creates pixels on the currently selected layer, without creating a vector path or shape layer.

The Pixels option creates a pixel layer, so you won't be able to edit the resulting layer using path editing tools. Instead, edit it with pixel-based tools such as the brushes, eraser, and selection tools.

4 With the Pen tool selected, click point A. A new temporary Work Path appears in the Paths panel.

5 Click point B, and drag to the open circle on the right to create the initial curve.

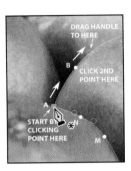
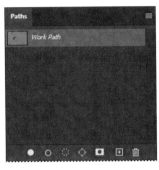
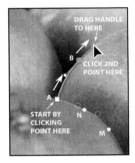

6 Click point C, and drag to the open circle to its right.

7 Continue tracing the orange, clicking and dragging curve segments for points D through F.

8 Click point G (do not drag). This creates the corner at point G.

▶ **Tip:** When tracing along a well-defined edge, the Pen tool is not the only useful tool. For some shapes and edges, you might find it easier to use the Magic Lasso tool, the Object Selection tool, or the Quick Selection tool.

9 At points H and I, click and drag to their corresponding open circles to create their curved segments.

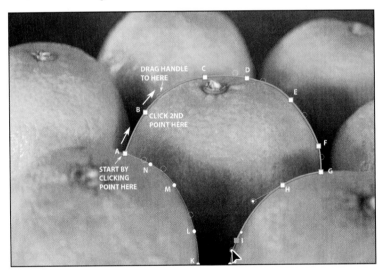

10 Click point J to create a corner.

11 Hold down Shift to create a perfectly level segment as you click point K.

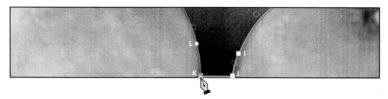

12 At points L, M, and N, click and drag to their corresponding open circles to create their curved segments.

13 Position the pointer over point A, and when you see a small circle by the Pen tool pointer, click to close the path. The circle indicates that the pointer is close enough to close the path.

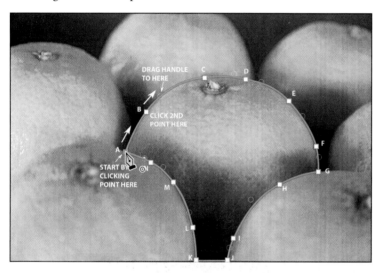

14 Evaluate your path. If you want to adjust any segments, do step 15; otherwise skip to step 16.

15 Select the Direct Selection tool (⟍) (grouped with the Path Selection tool (⟍)), and then press the Esc key (or click in the document window away from the path) so that no points are selected but you can still see the path. Then do any of the following with the Direct Selection tool as needed:

- To reposition a point or a straight segment, drag it.

- To change the shape of a curved segment between two points, drag the segment (not points).

- To change the shape of a curved segment extending from a point, drag its direction point to adjust the angle of that direction line.

16 When you're done, leave the path selected, and save your work so far.

▶ **Tip:** To move the entire path, drag it with the Path Selection tool, grouped with the Direct Selection tool.

Converting a path to a selection and a layer mask

Tip: If you'd prefer to create a mask that you can always edit as a path, create a vector mask for the layer instead. Skip step 2, and then, in step 4, make sure the Lemon path is selected in the Paths panel when you add the new Hue/Saturation adjustment layer.

Using the Pen tool made it easy to create a precise outline of the orange in the center of the image. But the goal is to change the color of that orange without changing the others, through a layer mask. Creating the layer mask requires making a selection. Fortunately, it's easy to convert a path to a selection.

The path is a work path, which is temporary; it will be replaced if you draw another path. You can still create a selection from a work path, but first, it's a good practice to save any path you might want to use again in the future.

1 In the Paths panel, double-click Work Path. In the Save Path dialog box, type **Lemon** for the name, and click OK.

2 Make sure the Lemon path is selected in the Paths panel, and then click the Load Path as a Selection button (⋮⋮) at the bottom of the Paths panel.

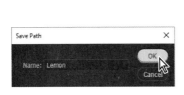
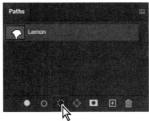

Photoshop creates a selection from the path. You'll change the color of the selected orange to lemon yellow, using a Hue/Saturation adjustment layer through a layer mask of the orange. The selection you just created will make it quick and easy to create the layer mask, because an active selection is automatically converted to a layer mask when you add an adjustment layer.

Tip: It's just as easy to convert a selection into a path. When a selection is active, click the Make Work Path from Selection button in the Paths panel; it's the button to the right of the one you clicked in step 2.

3 In the Layers panel, hide the Path Guide layer, because you no longer need it, and select the Background layer.

4 In the Adjustments panel, in the Single Adjustments list click Hue/Saturation (⊞). A new Hue/Saturation adjustment layer appears in the Layers panel, and the selection becomes a mask for that new adjustment layer.

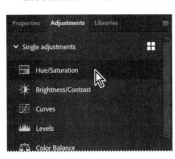
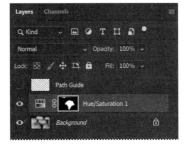

5 In the Properties panel, change the Hue setting so that the orange in the center changes to a lemon yellow color. We entered a Hue value of **+17**.

6 Save the document.

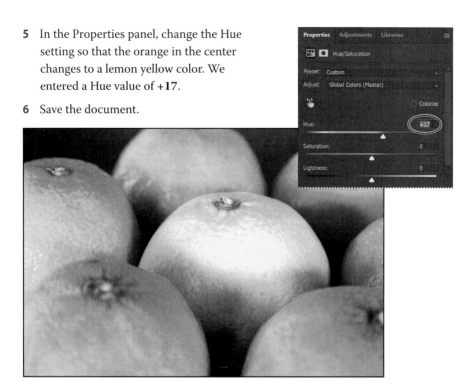

▶ **Tip:** After you change the color of the center orange, you may notice minor errors along the edges of the layer mask. Remember that you can edit a layer mask: Click the layer mask thumbnail in the Layers panel to select it, and then use the Brush tool to paint white where you want the color applied by the adjustment layer to be visible, or paint black where you want the color of the Background layer to be visible. (If it was still a vector mask, you would edit it using the Direct Selection tool and Pen tool.)

You used the Pen tool to quickly and precisely draw a path that traced the outline of an object in an image. You converted the path into a selection so that when you added a new adjustment layer, the selection became a layer mask that isolated the object for the adjustment layer. Well done!

Creating a logo with text and a custom shape

Now you'll create a logo that will overlay the image, using text and a shape layer.

1 If the rulers aren't visible, choose View > Rulers to display them.

2 Right-click (Windows) or Control-click (macOS) the rulers, and if they are currently displaying in pixels, choose Inches. This document will become a printed postcard, and Inches is an appropriate unit of measure for print.

3 In the Layers panel, make sure the Hue/Saturation adjustment layer is selected so that the layer you're about to create will be added above it.

Tip: For step 4, a quick way to find a font is to type **bold** or **heavy** into the font menu. The list will display only font names containing the word you entered, so all you have to do is pick one.

4   Select the Horizontal Type tool (**T**), and, in the options bar, do the following:

- Choose a bold or heavy typeface from the Font Family pop-up menu. We used Arial Bold; you can choose another font that looks good as a logo.
- Click the Right Align Text button, because you'll soon add a graphic element to the left of the text.
- Click the color swatch and set the text color to white.
- Type **55 pt** for the Size, and press Enter or Return.

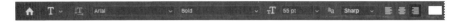

5   Drag the Horizontal Type tool to create a text layer across the bottom of the canvas, inset about half an inch away from the sides and bottom. Ours is about 9 inches wide by 1 inch tall.

6   Type **Citrus Lane Farms** to replace the placeholder text, click the Commit button (✓) in the options bar, and leave the text layer selected in the Layers panel.

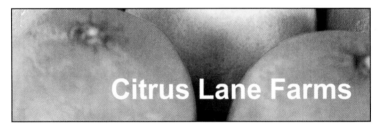

7   This font looks better with tighter letter spacing. With the text selected, in the Character or Properties panel, apply a negative Tracking value; for our font we used −25.

8   In the Properties panel, select the All Caps button (**TT**) in the Type Options group. If you don't see this option, scroll down in the Properties panel.

9   If needed, use the Move tool to reposition the text layer so that it looks better relative to the bottom and right sides. Leave space to the left of the text for a graphic you're about to add.

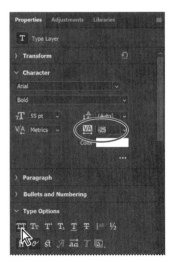

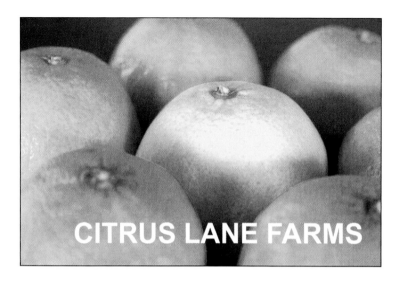

Adding a preset shape

When you need a shape such as a symbol or object, one place you can turn to is the Shapes panel, which contains a wide selection of premade graphics. When you add a shape to a document, it becomes a shape layer.

A shape is a vector object drawn using paths, which has two advantages. You can edit it using the same techniques you used to edit the paths you drew earlier in this lesson. Also, like a text layer, a path is resolution-independent, so it will always be as smooth and detailed as the document resolution allows.

You find shapes in the Shapes panel. It's easy to use, because it works like the other Photoshop panels that contain preset effects, such as the Swatches, Gradients, and Brushes panels: You see small visual previews of each preset, you can organize them in groups (folders), and you can create your own.

1 Choose Window > Shapes to open the Shapes panel. The Shapes panel includes groups of shape presets.

2 Expand the Flowers presets group.

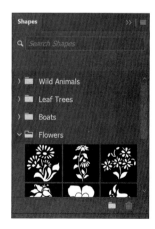

Tip: Photoshop includes more preset groups than you see by default in a presets panel list. In the panel menu, choose Legacy Shapes and More to load additional preset groups, including presets that were available in older versions of Photoshop.

Extra credit

Using Creative Cloud Libraries with linked Smart Objects

When you organize and share your design assets using Creative Cloud Libraries, you and your team can use those library items in many Creative Cloud desktop and mobile apps. Let's take a look:

1   Open 08End.psd. If the Libraries panel isn't open, choose Window > Libraries.

2   Click the Add Libraries button (+), click Create New Library, name it **Citrus Lane Farms**, and click Create.

3   In the Layers panel, select the Flower layer, and then hold down Shift as you click the Citrus Lane Farms text layer so that the two layers are selected.

4   Click the Add Elements button (+), and choose Graphic to add both layers as a single library item.

After the Libraries panel syncs the logo to Creative Cloud, it will be available in Creative Cloud desktop and mobile apps that use Creative Cloud Libraries.

The appearance of the Citrus Lane Farms text layer was adjusted to look good over the image of the oranges; it should be tested over a wide range of backgrounds and edited as needed for readability. A library item is a Smart Object linked to Creative Cloud, so you can edit it in Photoshop by double-clicking it in the Libraries panel. When you save changes, it updates in all documents that use it.

Adding a color

A library can store colors for use across Adobe applications.

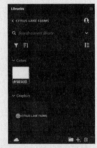

1   With the Eyedropper tool, click the flower in the document window so that its yellow color becomes the foreground swatch in the Tools panel.

2   At the bottom of the Libraries panel, click the Add Elements button (+), and click the Foreground Color swatch, adding it to the current library.

Collaborating

When you share a Creative Cloud Library, your team always has the current version of those assets. In the Libraries panel menu, choose Invite People. The Creative Cloud desktop app opens; fill in the Invite screen that appears. When the people you invited are signed into their Creative Cloud accounts, they will see your shared library in their Creative Cloud applications.

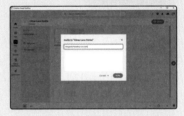

Adding assets to libraries using Adobe mobile apps

Use Adobe mobile apps—such as Adobe Capture—to use your phone or tablet camera to record color themes, shapes, and brushes from real life and add them to your Creative Cloud libraries. Library assets you add with mobile apps automatically sync to your Creative Cloud account, so you'll see the new assets in your Libraries panel when you return to your computer.

3 Drag the last shape preset, and drop it to the left of the Citrus Lane Farms logo.

The flower shape now appears in the Layers panel, but it isn't fully committed to the document yet; if the Contextual Task Bar is visible, you can see that it has Cancel and Done buttons. The shape has a box of transform controls around it, which you will now use to make adjustments to the new shape layer's size and position before committing it to the document.

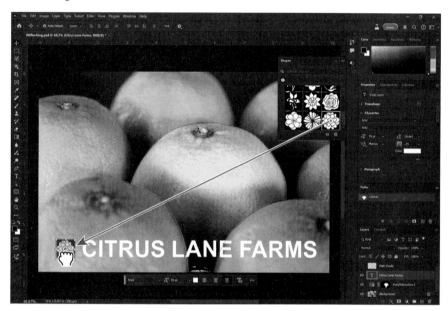

> **Tip:** Want to save your own shape preset? Draw a path or shape, select it with the Path Selection tool, choose Edit > Define Custom Shape, name it, and click OK. It's added to the Shapes panel; if a shape group is active, it's added to that group.

4 Drag any handle on the shape to resize it to be about 1.5 inches tall.

5 Drag the flower to position it between the left edge of the document and the Citrus Lane Farms text.

6 Click Done in the Contextual Task Bar, or press Enter or Return, or click the Commit Transform button (✓) in the options bar if it's visible.

A shape is added using the current fill and stroke settings for shapes, which were the ones set for the practice shape earlier. The flower shape is intended to have a solid yellow fill. That change could not be done before the new shape was committed to the document, but now that it is, the colors can be changed.

7 Make sure the flower shape is still selected in the Layers panel.

8 In the Layers panel, double-click the name of the shape layer, type **Flower**, and press Return or Enter to rename the layer.

9 In the Contextual Task Bar, click the Fill swatch, expand the RGB swatch presets group that appears in the drop-down menu, click the yellow swatch, and close the menu by pressing Enter or Return.

> **Tip:** If the magenta Smart Guides prevent you from making precise adjustments, hold down the Control key as you drag.

> **Tip:** Do you wish one of the preset shapes was slightly different? All shapes are paths, so after you add a shape to the document, you can edit it by using the Direct Selection tool, the Pen tool, or any of the tools grouped with the Pen tool.

10 In the Contextual Task Bar, click the Stroke swatch, set it to No Color, and close the menu.

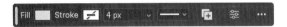

11 Choose Select > Deselect Layers. Now you can see the flower shape without its path being highlighted.

12 If needed, use the Move tool to reposition the flower and text, composing them relative to each other as a logo and relative to the edges of the document.

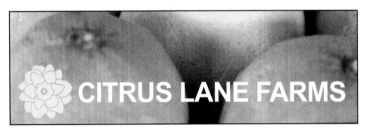

13 Save your work, and close the document.

You've combined an image, a color adjustment layer masked with the help of a path you drew by hand, a pre-made shape, and a text layer. The postcard is ready to go!

About vector layers and document resolution

Photoshop is fundamentally a pixel graphics editor, and shape layers and type layers are both forms of vector graphics. This difference affects the resolution of shape and type layers.

Shape and type layers always render at the full resolution of a Photoshop document, even if you scale them up. However, the pixel width and height of a Photoshop document limit every kind of layer in it. Shape layers and type appear as sharp as, but never sharper than, pixel layers in the same document. If a web button graphic is 120 × 90 pixels, that is all the pixels that shape and type layers can use.

The pixel dimensions of a Photoshop document are also the limit of how sharp it can be when printed. For example, if a 2400 × 3000 pixel Photoshop document is printed at 8 × 10 inches, the effective resolution of everything in the document — even its shape and type layers — is 300 pixels per inch (3000 pixels divided by 10 inches), even if the printer can print at a much higher resolution.

By comparison, applications based on vector graphics, such as Adobe Illustrator and Adobe InDesign, can render at the full resolution of a display or printer. For example, if an 8 × 10 inch document made in Illustrator is sent to a 2400 dpi printer, vector graphics and type will print at 2400 dpi. For this reason, it's common for designers to lay out high-resolution print projects in Illustrator or InDesign, and any non-vector elements (such as photos) are created in Photoshop and imported into those apps.

Extra credit

Quickly adding color and effects using presets

You can use presets to quickly enhance the look of both the text and the flower in the logo. The way that you do this is similar to how you added the flower shape with the Shapes panel and changed its color using the Swatches panel.

1   Open 08Working.psd (if it isn't already open), and save it as **08StylePresets.psd**.

2   Start by applying a preset to the flower. In the Styles panel (Window > Styles), expand the Basics preset group.

3   Drag the second preset from the Basics group, and drop it on the flower in the document window. The style is applied to the flower shape layer. Then drag the same style and drop it on the text.

You can apply a preset by dragging and dropping it on a layer or by clicking a preset when the layer is selected. Either way is fine.

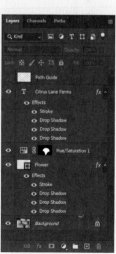

In this example, the Basic style applies a simple stroke and drop shadow. But the possibilities are much wider. Explore your design options by freely editing the presets in the Styles, Gradients, Patterns, and Swatches panels and applying them to layers until you get the look you want. And you can add your own presets to those panels.

You can see that the effects have been applied in the Layers panel, and you can fine-tune those effects in different ways:

•   Click the eye icon for different layer effects to disable or enable them.

•   Double-click an effect name to open the Layer Style dialog box, where you can edit effects.

•   If you try to apply a style and it doesn't seem to change the layer, you may first need to delete effects already applied to the layer: In the Layers panel, drag that layer's Effects heading to the Delete (trash can) icon at the bottom of the Layers panel. Note that a preset may also alter a layer's Opacity and Fill Opacity, so you may have to set those back to the default of 100%.

•   If you don't see any effects listed after a layer after applying a style, the preset may have been applied as a fill or stroke instead of a layer style. To edit it, double-click the shape layer thumbnail (not the name).

•   If you applied a preset to a shape, select any shape tool, such as the Rectangle tool, to display shape options in the options bar. Click the Fill or Stroke swatch to edit the preset.

Extra credit

Using Smart Guides to maintain alignment and equal spacing

You can use the Citrus Lane Farms logo to make a repeated motif for packaging or other signage. Smart Guides can help you position the images evenly.

1   Open 08End.psd, and save it as **08SmartGuides.psd**. Choose View > Show, and make sure there is a check mark next to the Smart Guides command, indicating that it's enabled. If not, select the Smart Guides command to enable it.

2   Select the Flower layer. Then select the Move tool, hold down the Alt (Windows) or Option (macOS) key as you drag a copy of the Flower layer up until the value in the magenta box indicates that it's about 3 inches away from the original, and then release the mouse button. Notice that the magenta Smart Guides help keep the Flower copy perfectly aligned with the original. Without Smart Guides, you'd have to also press Shift to keep the copy aligned. The Alt or Option key copies the selected layer.

3   In the Layers panel, change the Opacity of the Flower copy layer to 50%.

4   Make sure the Move tool and Flower copy layer are still selected. Hold down the Alt (Windows) or Option (macOS) key as you use the Move tool to drag a copy of the Flower copy layer to the right, until the magenta values indicate that the layer and its copy are about 1 inch apart and still aligned. Then release the mouse button.

5   This time, with the Flower copy 2 layer still selected, hold down Alt or Option as you drag the Flower copy 2 layer to the right; release the mouse when two transformation values boxes appear between the three flower layers across the top. The boxes let you know that the distance between the three flower layers is now equal. Using Smart Guides is a fast and easy way to make sure layers you drag are evenly spaced, without having to do math or use a distribution command.

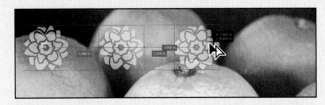

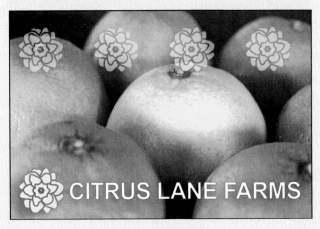

6   Repeat step 4 so that you have four equally spaced flowers.

Review questions

1 What is the difference between a bitmap image and a vector graphic?

2 After using the Pen tool to add an anchor point to a path, how do you make sure the next path segment is a curve?

3 How can you add a preset shape to the document?

4 For paths and shapes, why would you use the Direct Selection tool instead of the Selection tool?

5 What are some ways to change the shape of a curved path segment?

Review answers

1 Bitmap, or raster, images are based on a grid of pixels and are appropriate for continuous-tone images such as photographs or artwork created in painting programs. Vector graphics are made up of shapes based on mathematical expressions and are appropriate for illustrations, type, and drawings that require clear, smooth lines.

2 Drag (instead of clicking) to create the next point with the Pen tool.

3 To add a preset shape, open the Shapes panel, find the shape, and drag it into the document window.

4 The Direct Selection tool lets you edit the points, segments, and direction lines of a path or shape. The Selection tool lets you move and resize an entire path or shape.

5 You can change the shape of a curved path segment by using the Direct Selection tool to drag either of a curved segment's two anchor points, the direction points for either anchor point, or the curved segment itself.

9 ADVANCED COMPOSITING

Lesson overview

In this lesson, you'll learn how to do the following:

- Apply and edit Smart Filters.

- Use the Liquify filter to creatively distort an image.

- Apply color effects to selected areas of an image.

- Apply filters to create various effects.

- Use the History panel to return to a previous state.

- Upscale a low-resolution image while maintaining quality.

This lesson will take about an hour to complete. To get the lesson files used in this chapter, download them from the web page for this book at peachpit.com/PhotoshopCIB2025. For more information, see "Accessing the lesson files and Web Edition" in the Getting Started section at the beginning of this book.

As you work on this lesson, you'll preserve the start files. If you need to restore the start files, download them from your Account page.

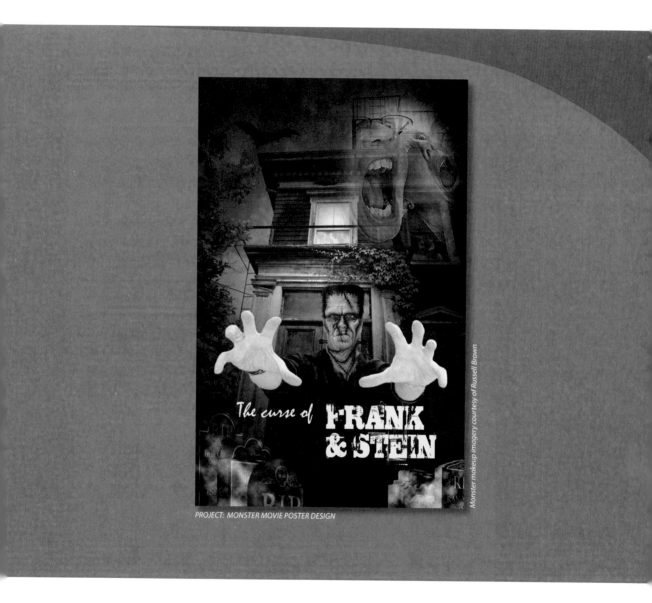

PROJECT: MONSTER MOVIE POSTER DESIGN

Filters can transform ordinary images into extraordinary digital artwork. Smart Filters let you edit those transformations at any time. The wide variety of features in Photoshop lets you be as creative as you want to be.

Getting started

In this lesson, you'll assemble a montage of images for a movie poster as you explore filters in Photoshop. First, look at the final project to see what you'll be creating.

1   Start Photoshop, and then simultaneously hold down Ctrl+Alt+Shift (Windows) or Command+Option+Shift (macOS) to restore the default preferences. (See "Restoring default preferences" on page 5.)

2   When prompted, click Yes to delete the Adobe Photoshop Settings file.

3   Choose File > Browse In Bridge.

Note: If Bridge isn't installed, the File > Browse In Bridge command in Photoshop will start the Creative Cloud desktop app, which will download and install Bridge. After installation completes, you can start Bridge.

4   In Bridge, choose Favorites from the menu on the left, and then click the Lessons folder. Double-click the Lesson09 folder.

5   View the 09_End.psd thumbnail. Move the slider at the bottom of the Bridge window if you need to zoom in to see the thumbnail more clearly.

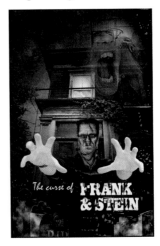

This file is a movie poster that comprises a background, a monster image, and several smaller images. Each image has had one or more filters or effects applied to it.

The monster is composed of an image of a perfectly normal (though slightly threatening) guy with several ghoulish images applied. These monstrous additions are courtesy of Russell Brown, with illustration by John Connell.

6   In Bridge, navigate to the Lesson09/Monster_Makeup folder, and open it.

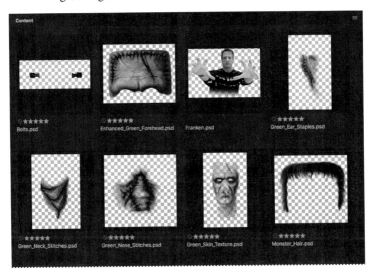

7 Shift-click the first and last items to select all the files in the Monster_Makeup folder, then choose Tools > Photoshop > Load Files Into Photoshop Layers, and close any messages that appear about new features.

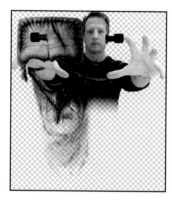
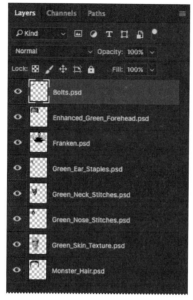

Photoshop imports all the selected files as individual layers in a new Photoshop file. The designer used a red layer color to indicate components of the monster's look.

8 In Photoshop, choose File > Save As. Choose Photoshop for the Format, and name the new file **09Working.psd**. Save it in the Lesson09 folder. Click OK in the Photoshop Format Options dialog box.

● **Note:** If Photoshop displays a dialog box telling you about the difference between saving to Cloud Documents and On Your Computer, click Save On Your Computer. You can also select Don't Show Again, but that setting will deselect after you reset Photoshop preferences.

Arranging layers

Your image file contains eight layers, imported in alphabetical order. In their current positions, they don't make a very convincing monster. You'll rearrange the layer order and resize their contents as you start to build your monster.

1 Zoom out or scroll so that you can see the entire document canvas. Also, if you can't see all of the layers in the Layers panel at once, drag the top edge of the Layers panel to make it taller.

2 In the Layers panel, drag the Monster_Hair layer to the top of the layer stack, if it isn't already on top.

3 Drag the Franken layer to the bottom of the layer stack.

● **Note:** If the wrong layer becomes selected when you try to drag the Franken layer to the bottom of the image, deselect Auto-Select in the options bar.

4 Select the Move tool (✛), and then in the document window, drag the Franken layer (the image of the person) to the bottom of the canvas.

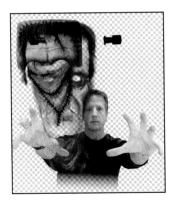

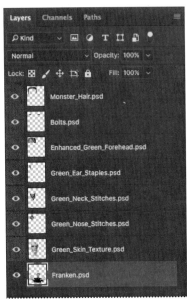

▶ **Tip:** The keyboard shortcut for Free Transform is Ctrl+T (Windows) or Command+T (macOS). This is a good all-in-one shortcut to learn because you can use it to move, scale, or rotate selected layers.

5 In the Layers panel, Shift-select every layer except the Franken layer, and choose Edit > Free Transform.

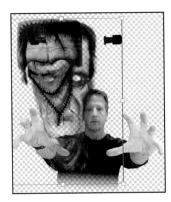

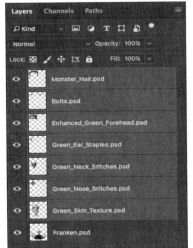

6 Drag down from a corner of the selection to resize all the selected layers to about 50% of their original size. (Watch the width and height percentages in the options bar.)

7 With the Free Transform bounding box still active, position the layers over the head of the Franken layer. Then press Enter or Return to commit the transformation.

Note: If the Free Transform bounding box and handles remain after committing a transformation, that means the Show Transform Controls option is enabled. When it's enabled you don't have to choose Edit > Free Transform. To better match the lesson steps, select the Move tool, and in the options bar deselect Show Transform Controls.

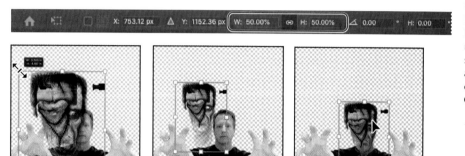

8 Zoom in to see the head area clearly.

9 Hide all layers except the Green_Skin_Texture and Franken layers.

10 Select only the Green_Skin_Texture layer, and use the Move tool to center it over the face.

Tip: If magenta Smart Guides appear as you drag, making it difficult to position the Green_Skin_Texture layer, hold down the Control key to temporarily suppress snapping to Smart Guides as you drag. Or permanently disable them by deselecting the View > Show > Smart Guides command.

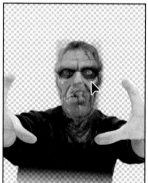

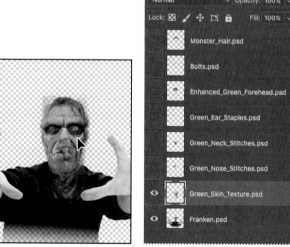

Tip: For more detailed control over how the texture fits the face, choose Edit > Transform > Warp, drag the transform grid or handles, and then press Return or Enter to commit the changes.

11 Choose Edit > Free Transform again to adjust the fit of the texture to the face. Using the eyes and mouth as a guide, press arrow keys to nudge the entire layer into position. Drag handles on the bounding box to adjust the width and height. (To adjust without preserving proportions, Shift-drag a handle.) When you've positioned the skin texture, press Enter or Return to commit the transformation.

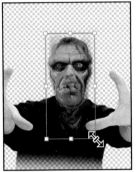 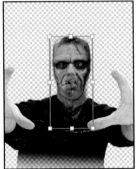 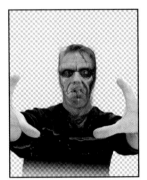

12 Save your file.

Using Smart Filters

When you apply a filter (any command on the Filter menu), it permanently changes layer pixels. To be able to edit, hide, or remove filter settings at any time after applying the filter, you can apply a filter to a Smart Object layer, making it a nondestructive Smart Filter.

Applying the Liquify filter

You'll use the Liquify filter to tighten the eye openings and change the shape of the monster's face. To be able to adjust the filter settings later, you'll apply the Liquify filter as a Smart Filter. To make that possible, you'll first convert the Green_Skin_Texture layer to a Smart Object.

Tip: In the Layers panel, the thumbnail icon for the Green_Skin_Texture layer now displays a small badge in the bottom-right corner to indicate that it is a Smart Object.

1 Make sure the Green_Skin_Texture layer is selected in the Layers panel, and then choose Filter > Convert For Smart Filters. This creates a Smart Object. Click OK if you're asked to confirm the conversion to a Smart Object.

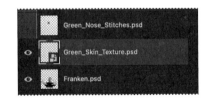

2 Choose Filter > Liquify.

Photoshop displays the layer in the Liquify dialog box.

3 In the Liquify dialog box, if the Face-Aware Liquify group of options is expanded, click the disclosure triangle next to it to collapse the group.

You already explored Face-Aware Liquify in Lesson 5. While Face-Aware Liquify is a quick and powerful way to modify facial features, the amount of face editing you can do with those options is limited. In this lesson, you'll try some manual Liquify techniques, which you may prefer when you want to create a more expressive face. Hiding the Face-Aware Liquify options makes it easier to concentrate on the other options in the Liquify dialog box.

Note: Step 4 doesn't change the document; it just changes how much you see of other layers while you work on the layer that was selected when you entered the Liquify dialog box.

4 Select Show Backdrop, and then choose Behind from the Mode menu. Set the Opacity to **75**.

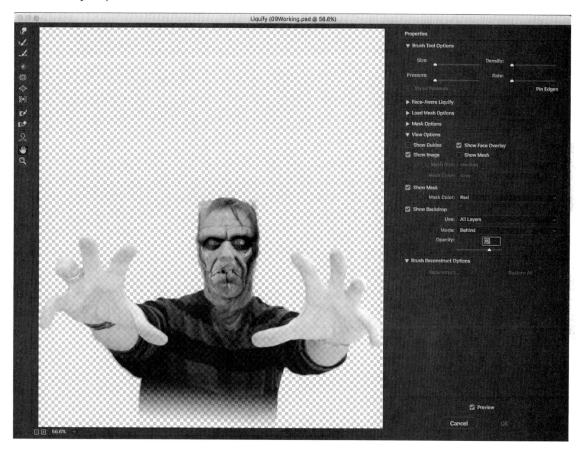

5 Select the Zoom tool (🔍) from the Tools panel on the left side of the dialog box, and zoom in to the eye area.

6 Select the Forward Warp tool (〰️) (the first tool).

The Forward Warp tool pushes pixels forward as you drag.

7 In the Brush Tool Options area, set Size to **150** and Pressure to **75**.

8 With the Forward Warp tool, pull the monster makeup's right eyebrow down to close the eye opening. Then pull up from under the eye.

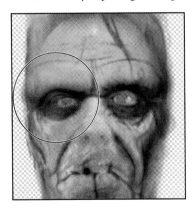
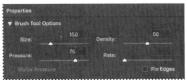

9 Repeat step 8 on the left eyebrow and under-eye area. You might prefer to use the Forward Warp tool differently for each eye, to create an even scarier face.

10 When you've closed the gap around the eyes, click OK.

Because you've applied the Liquify filter as a Smart Filter, you can freely remove or change your Liquify edits later without losing image quality, by double-clicking the Liquify effect applied to the Smart Object in the Layers panel.

Positioning other layers

Now that you've got the skin texture in place, you'll move the other layers into position, working up from the lowest layers in the Layers panel.

1 Make the Green_Nose_Stitches layer visible, and select it in the Layers panel.

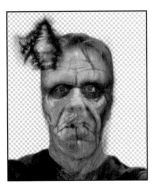
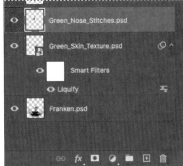

2 Choose Edit > Free Transform, and then position the layer over the nose, resizing it as necessary. Press Enter or Return to commit the transformation.

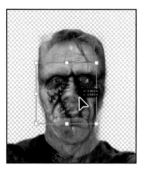 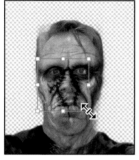 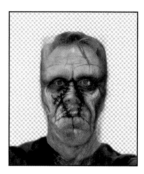

Tip: To resize from the center of a selection, hold down Alt (Windows) or Option (macOS) as you drag a bounding box handle.

You'll repeat the process to position the rest of the layers.

3 Make the Green_Neck_Stitches layer visible, and select it. Then move it over the neck. If you need to adjust it, choose Edit > Free Transform, resize it, and press Enter or Return.

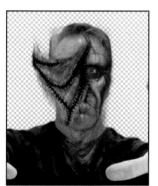
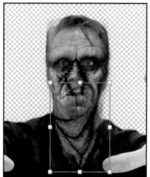

Tip: If you only need to move a layer, you can simply drag it with the Move tool. In these steps, choosing Edit > Free Transform lets you both move and resize a layer.

4 Make the Green_Ear_Staples layer visible, and select it. Move the staples over his right ear. Choose Edit > Free Transform, resize and reposition the staples, and then press Enter or Return.

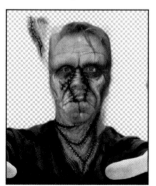
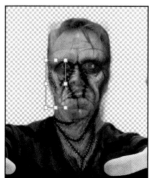

Tip: Remember that you can position and size a selected layer using any combination of the Move tool, the Edit > Free Transform command, and the arrow keys. Use whatever tools get the job done!

5   Make the Enhanced_Green_Forehead layer visible, and select it. Move it over the forehead; it's probably a bit large. Choose Edit > Free Transform, resize the forehead to fit his head, and press Enter or Return.

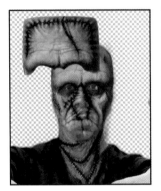 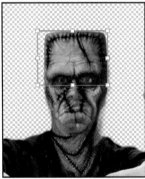

6   Make the Bolts layer visible, and select it. Drag the bolts so they're positioned on both sides of the neck. Choose Edit > Free Transform, and resize them so that they fit snugly against the neck. When you have them in position, press Enter or Return to commit the transformation.

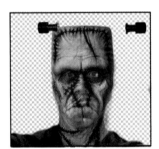 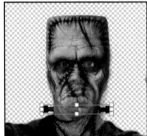

7   Finally, make the Monster_Hair layer visible, and select it. Move it over the forehead. Choose Edit > Free Transform, and then resize the hair so it fits properly against the forehead. Press Enter or Return to commit the change.

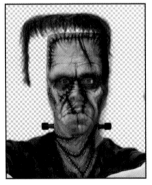 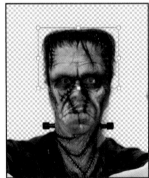

8   Save your work so far.

Editing a Smart Filter

With all the layers in position, you can further refine the eye openings and experiment with the bulges in the eyebrows. You'll return to the Liquify filter to make those adjustments.

1 In the Layers panel, double-click Liquify, listed under Smart Filters in the Green_Skin_Texture layer.

Photoshop opens the Liquify dialog box again. This time, all the layers are visible in Photoshop, so when Show Backdrop is selected, you see them all. Sometimes it's easier to make changes without a backdrop to distract you. Other times, it's useful to see your edits in context.

2 Zoom in to see the eyes more closely.

3 Select the Pucker tool (🖫) in the Tools panel, and click on the outer corner of each eye.

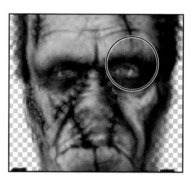

The Pucker tool moves pixels toward the center of the brush as you click or hold the mouse button, or drag.

4 Select the Bloat tool (◈), and click the outer edge of an eyebrow to expand it; do the same for the other eyebrow.

The Bloat tool moves pixels away from the center of the brush as you click or drag.

5 Experiment with the Pucker, Bloat, and other tools in the Liquify filter to customize the monster's face.

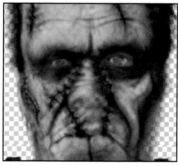

Remember that you can change the brush size and other settings. You can undo individual steps using the Undo keyboard shortcut (Ctrl+Z on Windows and Command+Z on Mac) if the Edit menu isn't available. If you want to discard all current changes and start over, hold down the Alt (Windows) or Option (macOS) key to change the Cancel button into a Reset button, and click Reset.

6 When you're happy with the monster's face, click OK, and save your work.

▶ **Tip:** The Pucker, Bloat, and other tools on the left side of the Liquify panel provide more control over Liquify distortions than the Face-Aware Liquify options, and they work on any part of an image. But Face-Aware Liquify is easier for quick and subtle adjustments to facial features.

Painting a layer

There are many ways to paint objects and layers in Photoshop. One of the simplest is to paint with the Brush tool on a layer set to the Color blending mode. You'll use this method to paint the exposed skin green on your monster.

1 Select the Franken layer in the Layers panel.

2 Click the Create A New Layer button (⊞) at the bottom of the Layers panel.

Photoshop creates a new layer, named Layer 1.

▶ **Tip:** Be sure to distinguish the blending mode of a layer (shown in the Layers panel) from the blending mode of a tool (shown in the options bar). To learn more about blending modes, including a description of each one, see "Blending modes" in Photoshop Help.

3 With Layer 1 selected, choose Color from the Blending Mode menu at the top of the Layers panel.

The Color blending mode combines the luminance of the base color (the color already on the layer) with the hue and saturation of the color you're applying. It's a good blending mode to use when you're coloring monochrome images or tinting color images.

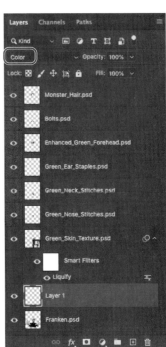

4 In the Tools panel, select the Brush tool (✐). In the options bar, select a **60**-pixel brush with a Hardness of **0**.

5 Hold down Alt or Option (to temporarily switch to the Eyedropper tool) as you click the forehead to sample a green color there. Then release the Alt or Option key to return to the Brush tool.

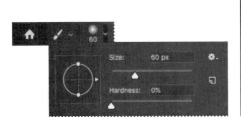
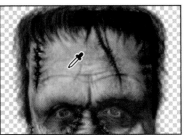

The sampled color becomes the new Foreground color, loaded into the Brush tool.

6 Ctrl-click (Windows) or Command-click (macOS) the thumbnail in the Franken layer to select its contents. Notice that a selection marquee appears on the layer.

▶ **Tip:** Step 6 selects nontransparent areas of a layer. The goal here is to recolor the skin, so another approach is to choose Select > Color Range and choose Skin Tones from the Select menu. That would specifically select the skin and not the shirt.

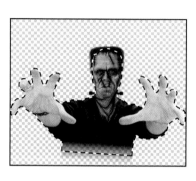
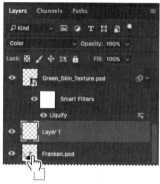

Clicking a layer in the Layers panel selects Layer 1 for painting, but the goal here is to paint only over the exposed skin on the Franken layer. Ctrl-clicking (Windows) or Command-clicking (macOS) the Franken layer thumbnail is a quick way to create a selection based on the Franken layer's non-transparent pixels.

7 Make sure Layer 1 is still selected in the Layers panel, and then use the Brush tool to paint over the hands and arms. You can paint quickly where the hands are against transparent areas, because the selection restricts the paintable area. However, remember that the shirt is part of the selection, so as you paint the skin close to the shirt color, take care to paint only the skin and not the shirt.

▶ **Tip:** To change the brush size as you paint, press the bracket keys on your keyboard. The Left Bracket key ([) decreases the brush size; the Right Bracket (]) increases it.

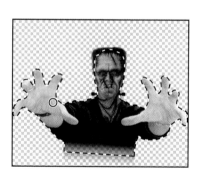
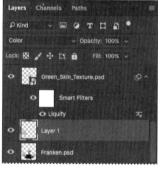

8 Paint any areas of the face or neck where the original flesh color shows through the Green_Skin_Texture layer.

9 When you're happy with the green skin, choose Select > Deselect. Save your work.

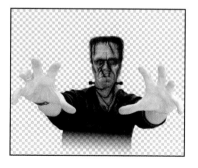

▶ **Tip:** If you paint over clothes accidentally, you can reverse the mistake by choosing Edit > Undo or by selecting the Eraser tool and dragging it on Layer 1 over the areas of paint you need to delete.

Adding a background

You've got a good-looking monster. Now it's time to put him in his spooky environment. To easily move the monster onto a background, you'll first merge the layers.

▶ **Tip:** Merging or flattening layers permanently combines them into a single layer. That also reduces the file size of the Photoshop document. If you want to preserve the ability to edit selected layers separately, select layers and choose New Group from Layers instead of Merge Visible in step 1. Then, in step 6, drag that layer group from the Layers panel to the other document.

1 Make sure all the layers are visible. Then choose Layer > Merge Visible.

Photoshop merges all the visible layers into one. It's named Layer 1 because that was the selected layer at the time of the merge.

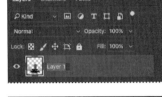

2 In the Layers panel, double-click the name of Layer 1, and rename it **Monster**.

3 Choose File > Open. Navigate to and open the Backdrop.psd file in the Lesson09 folder.

4 Choose Window > Arrange > 2-Up Vertical to display both the monster and backdrop files.

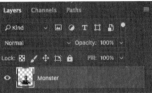

5 Click the 09Working.psd file to make it active.

6 Select the Move tool (✛), drag the Monster layer, and then drop it onto the Backdrop.psd file. Position the monster so his hands are just above the movie title.

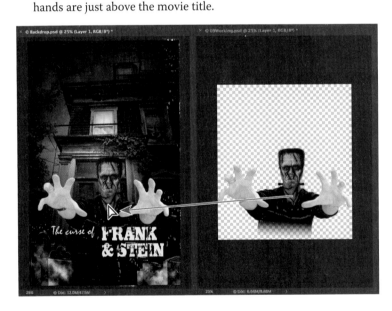

7 Close the 09Working.psd file, saving changes when prompted.

From now on, you'll work on the movie poster file itself.

8 Choose File > Save As, and save the file with the name **Movie-Poster.psd**. Click Save, and then click OK in the Photoshop Format Options dialog box.

Using the History panel to undo edits

You've used the Edit > Undo command to back out of the last change you applied. You can also choose Edit > Redo to reapply a change you just undid. Repeatedly choosing either command steps you back or forward through multiple edits.

For a before/after comparison of just your last edit, choose Edit > Toggle Last State, or press its keyboard shortcut: Ctrl+Alt+Z (Windows) or Command+Option+Z (macOS). This is a quick way to undo/redo with one command instead of two.

A more visual way to step backward and forward through your changes is to use the History panel; choose Window > History to see it. The History panel shows you a list of your changes. To go back to a certain edit (for example, four steps ago), just select it in the History panel, and continue working from that point.

To show how you can use the History panel, you'll first apply some steps that you can then back out of using the History panel.

Applying an adjustment to part of an image

In Lesson 2, you learned how you can use an adjustment layer to apply a tone or color correction to a document. In Lesson 6, you learned how a layer mask can hide part of an image. You can combine those techniques: A mask can also hide part of an adjustment layer; for example, if you want a Levels adjustment to apply to just some parts of a layer, you can mask the layer areas where you don't want the adjustment to appear, and you'll try that next.

Traditionally, this is done by adding an adjustment layer first, then restricting the adjustment area by painting in a mask. In Photoshop, the Adjustment Brush tool can save some of those steps.

> **Tip:** Masked adjustment layers are a popular technique for lightening or darkening specific areas of an image, with more control than the Dodge and Burn tools offer.

You'll add a tombstone to the poster, and you'll experiment with the Adjustment Brush tool, and then you'll use the History panel to back up to an earlier edit state.

1 In Photoshop, choose File > Open.

2 Navigate to the Lesson09 folder, and double-click the T1.psd file to open it. If an Embedded Profile Mismatch message appears, click OK.

The tombstone image is plain, but you'll add some visual interest to it. You'll start by adding a little atmospheric texture to the tombstone.

3 Press the D key to reset the default foreground and background colors.

4 Choose Filter > Render > Difference Clouds.

> **Tip:** The D key is a shortcut for clicking the Default Foreground and Background Colors icon (⬛) in the Tools panel. The foreground and background colors are set because in step 4, Difference Clouds will use those colors.

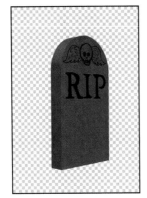

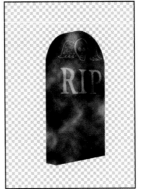

The original is dull. *Clouds add drama.*

● **Note:** The Difference Clouds result you get may not match the figure shown; Difference Clouds renders uniquely each time you run it.

You'll paint an adjustment over parts of the tombstone to make it look like moonlight is coming through trees.

5 In the Tools panel, select the Adjustment Brush tool (🖌).

6 In the options bar click the Brush Preset picker and set the brush size to 300.

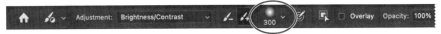

7 In the options bar, click the Adjustment menu and choose Levels. When you use the Adjustment Brush tool, you need to select an adjustment before you paint.

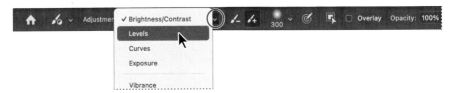

8 Drag the Adjustment Brush tool to paint a few irregular strokes over the middle of the top half of the tombstone, as if moonlight is coming through trees.

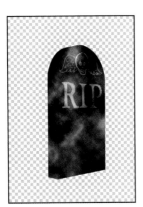

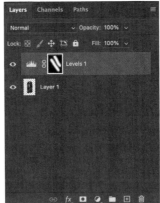

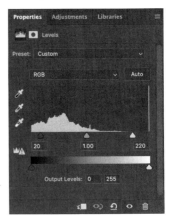

In the Layers panel, a new adjustment layer named Levels 1 was created and became selected the moment you started painting with the Adjustment Brush tool. In the mask icon for that adjustment layer, the white area shows you where you painted. The Properties panel displays the current settings of that Levels adjustment layer.

Tip: To toggle the view of just the mask, hold down the Alt (Windows) or Option (macOS) key as you click the layer mask thumbnail icon. To toggle hiding and showing the mask, hold down the Shift key as you click the layer mask thumbnail icon.

9 In the Properties panel, drag the black point input slider to 0, and drag the midtone slider to 1.30. The area you painted lightens.

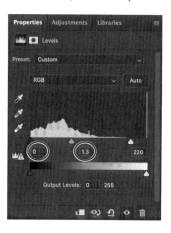

10 In the Properties panel, click the RGB menu and choose Red; then drag the midpoint gray slider to 0.70. Then choose Green from the RGB menu and set the midpoint gray slider to 0.80. These edits to the RGB channels give the adjustment a blue cast that better matches the other tombstones on the poster, and makes it look as if it's lit by spooky moonlight.

11 With the Levels 1 adjustment layer still selected, paint a few more brush strokes in the lower part of the tombstone. The tombstone lightens and appears more blue where you paint.

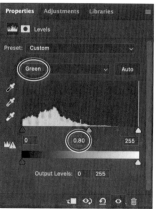

12 In the Contextual Task Bar, click Add New Adjustment, choose Color Balance, and paint over the word "RIP." This adds a color balance adjustment, and a second adjustment layer named Color Balance 1 appears in the Layers panel.

Adding this color edit doesn't improve the look of the tombstone, so you'll soon decide how far back to go in your edits.

Because the Adjustment Brush tool creates an adjustment layer, you can hide its edit by hiding that layer. And because the adjustment is applied through a layer mask, you can control which areas show the adjustment by painting white into the mask, and you control which areas hide the adjustment by painting black into the mask.

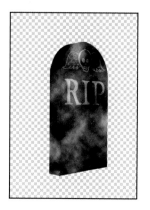

Undoing multiple steps

The tombstone certainly looks different than it did when you started, but the last color edit doesn't quite match the tombstones that are already in the poster. You'll use the History panel to revisit the steps you've taken.

1   If the History panel isn't already open, choose Window > History. Drag the bottom edge of the panel down so that you can see the entire list.

Note: The History panel lists the steps you have done in the current session only. The list is reset when you close a document, so when you open a document, the History panel is empty.

The History panel records the recent steps you've performed on the image. The current state is selected.

2   Click the Difference Clouds state in the History panel.

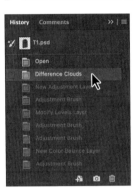 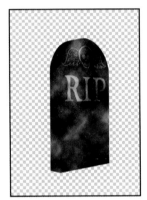

The History states below the selected state are dimmed, and the image has changed. At the selected History state, the Difference Clouds filter was run, but the Layers panel doesn't show the Levels adjustment layer because the current History state is before you added the Levels edit with the Adjustment Brush tool.

3   Click the last Modify Levels Layer state in the History panel.

More history states are restored. The color has returned, along with the Levels adjustment, and you again see the Levels adjustment layer in the Layers panel. However, the states below the one you selected remain dimmed, because this is before you painted the adjustments into the lower part of the tombstone.

You'll return almost to the beginning to apply different effects to the tombstone.

4 Click the Adjustment Brush step that's just before New Color Balance Layer.

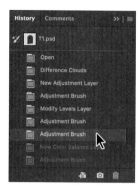 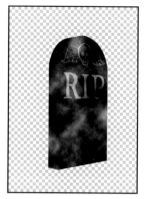

In the History panel, everything after that state is dimmed.

5 Choose Layer > Merge Visible, and name the resulting layer **Tombstone**.

6 Choose Filter > Noise > Add Noise.

Adding noise will give the tombstone a more stone-like texture.

7 In the Add Noise dialog box, set the Amount to **3**%, select Gaussian, and select Monochromatic. Then click OK.

Note: Unlike the Flatten command, the Merge Visible command preserves the transparent background, which is needed for compositing the tombstone with the movie poster later. The Flatten command would result in a solid white background.

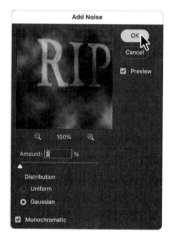 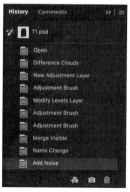 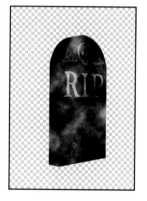

Tip: If the Noise adjustments are hard to see, click the right magnifying glass icon in the Add Noise dialog box.

The states that were dimmed after the state you selected (Adjustment Brush) are no longer in the History panel. They were replaced by the tasks you just performed (Merge Visible, Name Change, and Add Noise). You can click any state to return to that point in the process, but as soon as you perform a new task, Photoshop replaces all dimmed states.

The tombstone is ready to join the others in your movie poster.

8 Choose Window > Arrange > Tile All Vertically.

9 With the Move tool, drag the tombstone you just created to the Movie-Poster.psd file. Click OK if you see a color management warning.

10 Drag the tombstone to the bottom-left corner, with the top third of it showing.

11 Choose File > Save to save the Movie-Poster.psd file. Then close the T1.psd file without saving it.

Note: A Paste Profile Mismatch dialog box may appear when you drag a layer between documents with different document color profiles. For this lesson, clicking OK is fine because it will convert the layer colors to match the destination document.

You've had a chance to try the Adjustment Brush tool and to use the History panel to backtrack. By default, the History panel retains only the last 50 states. You can change the number of levels in the History panel by choosing Edit > Preferences > Performance (Windows) or Photoshop > Settings > Performance (macOS) and entering a different value for History States.

Note: Setting the number of History states involves a trade-off. Maintaining more History states may cause Photoshop to use more memory or create a larger temporary scratch file.

Note: If you're using macOS 12 or earlier, the Settings command is named Preferences.

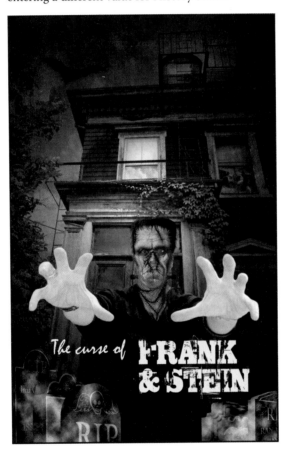

Improving a low-resolution image

You'll add another image to the movie poster. However, the pixel dimensions (width and height) of the only version available are very low, which may work for web pages and social media but will appear too coarse for high-quality printing. To address this, Photoshop can *resample* the image—change its pixel dimensions by creating or deleting new pixels based on existing ones. Increasing pixel dimensions is called *upsampling*, and decreasing them is called *downsampling*.

The Super Zoom Neural Filter can upsample a low-resolution image using machine learning that can be more effective than older Photoshop resampling options. You'll use Super Zoom to improve a low-resolution image for the movie poster.

1 Choose File > Open, navigate to the Lesson09 folder, and open the Faces.jpg file.

2 Zoom in to 300% or more. At this magnification, pixels should be visible. If the Status Bar at the bottom of the document window is set to Document Dimensions, it will show that the pixel dimensions are 216 × 288 px—a very low number of pixels. (You can also verify this by choosing Image > Image Size.)

3 Choose Filter > Neural Filters. If a Welcome to Neural Filters message appears, click Skip Tour.

4 In the All Filters list, click Super Zoom to select it, and click its toggle switch to enable it. If the filter is not loaded in the panel on the right, click Download.

5 At the bottom of the Neural Filters workspace, make sure the Output menu is set to New Document.

6 Under the Super Zoom preview on the right, click the Zoom In icon (⊕) until the label next to it says Zoom image (3x). Notice that the resolution on the large preview on the left improves as you increase the scaling factor.

7 Make sure Enhance Image Details, Remove JPEG Artifacts, and Enhance Face Details are selected, and set Noise Reduction to **3**.

● **Note:** For typical resampling tasks, you can use one of the options in the Resample menu in the Image > Image Size dialog box. But the traditional Resample options are less effective at enhancing this very low resolution example, so the Super Zoom Neural Filter is used instead.

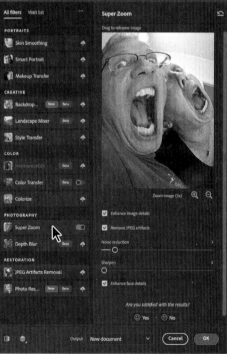

● **Note:** When Output is set to New Layer, the Zoom Image option maintains the current pixel dimensions and enlarges an enhanced portion of it. Here, you want to create a more detailed version of the image at larger pixel dimensions, and that requires choosing New Document in the Output menu.

8 Click the Show Original button to view the image as it is before opening Neural Filters, and then click it again to toggle back to previewing the image with the current options for all enabled Neural Filters.

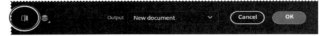

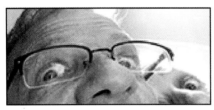
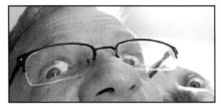

Original image.   *Preview of Super Zoom settings.*

9 Click OK. Super Zoom creates a new, untitled document tab with the results. Its pixel dimensions are now 648 × 864 px, or 3x the original width and height.

10 Choose Select > All, and then choose Edit > Copy.

11 Select the Movie-Poster.psd tab to bring it to the front, and then select the Elliptical Marquee tool (◯), hidden under the Rectangular Marquee tool (▭).

Tip: You can drag to recompose the pasted image behind its layer mask because the layer and its mask are unlinked. When you want to transform the layer and its mask together, in the Layers panel click the space between the layer and mask icons to enable the link icon, which is visible when enabled.

12 In the options bar, enter **50 px** for Feather to soften the edge of the pasted image.

13 Draw an oval in the upper-right corner of the poster, above the monster's head. The oval should overlap the window and fire escape.

14 Make sure the Tombstone layer is selected, and then choose Edit > Paste Special > Paste Into. If the Paste Profile Mismatch dialog box appears, click OK.

15 Select the Move tool (✛), and center the pasted image in the feathered area.

16 In the Layers panel, choose Luminosity from the Blending Mode menu, and move the Opacity slider to **50**%.

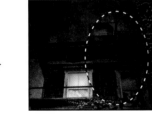
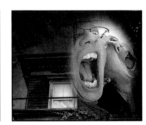
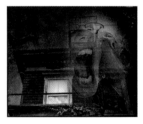

Tip: If you wanted to distribute this poster in a way that makes it easy for others to print and preserves its quality, a widely accepted method is to choose File > Save A Copy, for Format choose Photoshop PDF, and in the Save Adobe PDF dialog box, select a PDF preset such as High Quality Print.

In the Layers panel, you'll see that Layer 1 is the image you just pasted, and that layer has a layer mask with a feathered elliptical mask shape. When you used the Edit > Paste Into command, Photoshop created the layer mask from the feathered elliptical selection you drew.

17 You've finished the poster! Close the Movie-Poster.psd document, saving changes. Then close the Faces.jpg file and its untitled copy without saving them.

Review questions

1 What are the differences between using a Smart Filter and a regular filter to apply effects to an image?

2 What do the Bloat and Pucker tools in the Liquify filter do?

3 What does the History panel do?

4 What is the Adjustment Brush tool for, and in what way is it convenient?

5 What is the relationship of the Undo and Redo commands to the History panel?

Review answers

1 Smart Filters are nondestructive: They can be adjusted, enabled and disabled, and deleted at any time without altering original layer pixels. In contrast, regular filters permanently change a layer; once applied, the original state of that layer can't be restored (except by using the Edit > Undo command). A Smart Filter is a filter applied to a Smart Object layer.

2 The Bloat tool moves pixels away from the center of the brush; the Pucker tool moves pixels toward the center of the brush.

3 The History panel records recent steps you've performed in Photoshop during the current session. You can return to an earlier step by selecting it in the History panel.

4 The Adjustment Brush tool restricts an adjustment to the area where you paint, by automatically creating a masked adjustment layer. To do the same thing without the Adjustment Brush tool, you must first set up a masked adjustment layer yourself and then restrict the adjustment by painting with the Brush tool in that layer's mask.

5 The Undo and Redo commands move back or forward, respectively, through the steps in the History panel.

10 PAINTING WITH THE MIXER BRUSH

Lesson overview

In this lesson, you'll learn how to do the following:

- Customize brush settings.

- Clean the brush.

- Mix colors.

- Create a custom brush preset.

- Use wet and dry brushes to blend color.

 This lesson will take about an hour to complete. To get the lesson files used in this chapter, download them from the web page for this book at peachpit.com/PhotoshopCIB2025. For more information, see "Accessing the lesson files and Web Edition" in the Getting Started section at the beginning of this book.

As you work on this lesson, you'll preserve the start files. If you need to restore the start files, download them from your Account page.

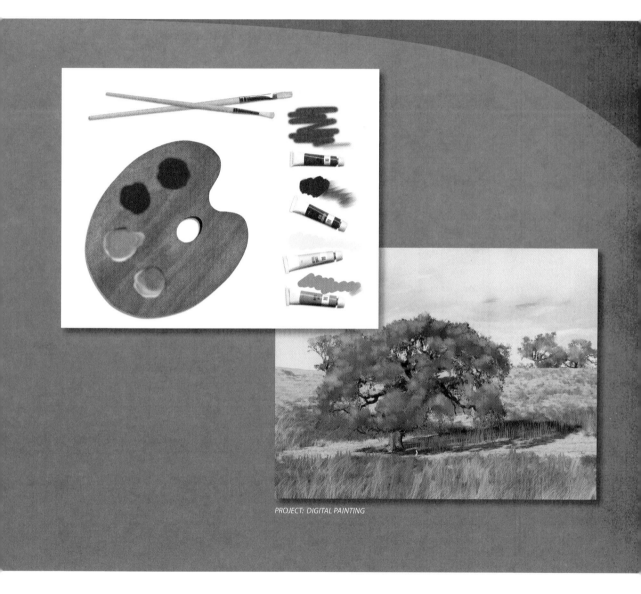

PROJECT: DIGITAL PAINTING

The Mixer Brush tool gives you flexibility, color-mixing
abilities, and brush strokes as if you were painting on
a physical canvas.

About the Mixer Brush

In previous lessons, you've used brushes in Photoshop to perform various tasks. The Mixer Brush is unlike other brushes in that it lets you mix colors with each other. You can change the wetness of the brush and how it mixes the brush color with the color already on the canvas.

Some Photoshop brush types can have realistic bristles, so you can add textures that resemble those in paintings you might create in the physical world. While this is a great feature in general, it's particularly useful when you're using the Mixer Brush. Combining different bristle settings and brush tips with different wetness, paint-load, and paint-mixing settings gives you opportunities to create exactly the look you want.

Getting started

In this lesson, you'll get acquainted with the Mixer Brush as well as the brush tip and bristle options available in Photoshop. Start by taking a look at the final projects you'll create.

1 Start Photoshop, and then simultaneously hold down Ctrl+Alt+Shift (Windows) or Command+Option+Shift (macOS) to restore the default preferences. (See "Restoring default preferences" on page 5.)

Note: If Bridge isn't installed, the File > Browse In Bridge command in Photoshop will start the Creative Cloud desktop app, which will download and install Bridge. After installation completes, you can start Bridge.

2 When prompted, click Yes to delete the Adobe Photoshop Settings file.

3 Choose File > Browse In Bridge to open Adobe Bridge.

4 In Bridge, click Lessons in the Favorites panel. Double-click the Lesson10 folder in the Content panel.

5 Preview the Lesson10 end files.

You'll use the palette image to explore brush options and learn to mix colors. You'll then apply what you've learned to transform the landscape image into a painting.

Note: If Photoshop displays a dialog box telling you about the difference between saving to Cloud Documents and On Your Computer, click Save On Your Computer. You can also select Don't Show Again, but that setting will deselect after you reset Photoshop preferences.

6 Double-click 10Palette_Start.psd to open the file in Photoshop.

7 Choose File > Save As, and name the file **10Palette_Working.psd**. Click OK if the Photoshop Format Options dialog box appears.

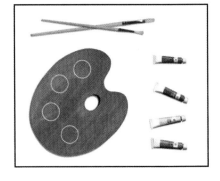

8 Click the Choose a Workspace icon at the top-right corner of the application frame, and choose the Painting workspace. This changes the Tools panel and the panels that are visible.

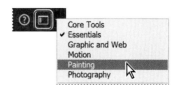

Note: You can paint more naturally and expressively by using a stylus and a graphics tablet. If the stylus can sense attributes such as pressure and angle, you can set up Photoshop brush options so that your brush strokes respond like a real brush.

Selecting brush settings

The practice image includes a palette and four tubes of color, which you'll use to sample the colors you're working with. You'll change settings as you paint different colors, exploring brush tip settings and wetness options.

1 Select the Zoom tool (🔍), and zoom in on the four tubes of paint, leaving some empty space above the red tube.

2 Select the Eyedropper tool (🖉), and click the red tube to sample its color.

The foreground color changes to red.

3 Select the Mixer Brush tool (🖌) in the Tools panel. (When another workspace is selected, you may find the Mixer Brush hidden under the Brush tool [🖌].)

Note: When you hold down the Eyedropper tool on the image, Photoshop displays a sampling ring that previews the color you're selecting. The sampling ring is available if Photoshop can use the graphics processor on your computer (see the Performance panel in Photoshop preferences).

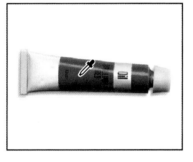

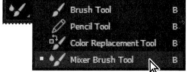

4 Choose Window > Brush Settings to open the Brush Settings panel. Select the first brush.

The Brush Settings panel contains brush presets and several options for customizing brushes.

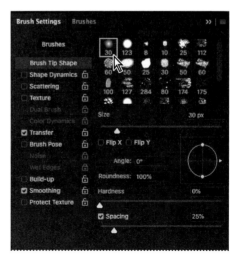

Tip: Looking for a specific brush name in the Brush Settings panel? Hover the pointer over a brush thumbnail, and its name will pop up in a tool tip.

Experimenting with wetness options and brushes

The effect of the brush is determined by the Wet, Load, and Mix fields in the options bar. *Wet* controls how much paint the brush picks up from the canvas. *Load* controls how much paint the brush holds when you begin painting (as with a physical brush, it runs out of paint as you paint with it). *Mix* controls the ratio of paint from the canvas and paint from the brush.

You can change these settings separately. However, it's faster to select a standard combination from the pop-up menu.

1   In the options bar, choose Dry from the pop-up menu of blending brush combinations.

When you select Dry, Wet is set to 0%, Load to 50%, and Mix is not applicable. With the Dry preset, you paint opaque color; you can't mix colors on a dry canvas.

2   Paint one continuous zigzag stroke in the area above the red tube. As you continue painting without releasing the mouse, the red paint eventually fades and runs out.

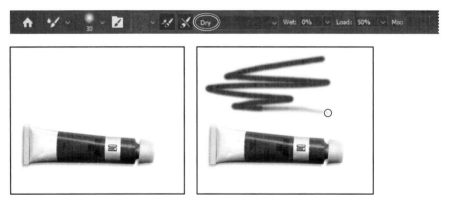

● **Note:** You can also sample paint by Alt-clicking or Option-clicking the Mixer Brush tool. This samples the area within the brush size as an image, unless you selected Load Solid Colors Only in the Current Brush Load menu in the options bar.

3   With the Eyedropper tool, sample the blue color from the blue tube of paint.

4   Select the Mixer Brush. For the blue paint, in the Brush Settings panel we chose the Round Sketch Ballpoint Pen brush (the first brush in the second row).

5   Choose Wet from the pop-up menu in the options bar.

If the brush you select doesn't match the one shown here, resize the Brush Settings panel so that the brush thumbnails display six columns across.

6   Paint above the blue tube. The paint mixes with the white background.

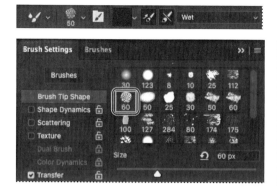

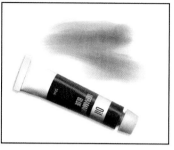

Note: If you aren't getting the same results from the brushes, make sure the Background layer is selected in the Layers panel.

7   Choose Dry from the menu in the options bar, and then paint again above the blue tube. A much darker, more opaque blue appears and doesn't mix with the white background.

8   Sample the yellow color from the yellow paint tube, and then select the Mixer Brush. For the yellow paint, in the Brush Settings panel we chose the Pencil KTW 1 brush (the fourth brush in the second row). Choose Dry from the menu in the options bar, and then paint in the area over the yellow paint tube.

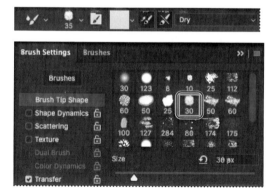

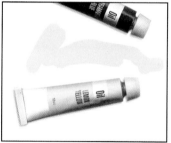

Note: If the brushes in your Brush Settings panel don't match the ones shown in this lesson, open the Brushes panel, Shift-select all brushes and brush folders in the list, click the Delete Brush button (🗑), click OK to confirm, and then choose Restore Default Brushes from the Brushes panel menu.

9   Choose Very Wet from the menu in the options bar, and then paint some more. Now the yellow mixes with the white background.

10 Sample the green color from the green paint tube, and then select the Mixer Brush. For the green paint, in the Brush Settings panel we chose the Hard Round 30 brush (the sixth brush in the fifth row). Choose Dry from the menu in the options bar.

11 Paint a brush stroke above the green paint tube. Experiment on your own, painting over the green stroke with a different color, using different Mixer Brush settings, particularly the Wet amount.

Mixing colors

● **Note:** Depending on the complexity of your project and the performance of your computer, you may need to be patient. Mixing colors can be an intensive process.

You've used wet and dry brushes, changed brush settings, and mixed the paint with the background color. Now, you'll focus more on mixing colors with each other as you add paint to the painter's palette.

1 Zoom out just enough to see the full palette and the paint tubes.

2 Select the Paint mix layer in the Layers panel so the color you paint won't blend with the brown palette on the Background layer.

The Mixer Brush tool mixes colors only on the active layer unless you select Sample All Layers in the options bar.

3 Use the Eyedropper tool to sample the red color from the red paint tube, and then select the Mixer Brush. In the Brush Settings panel, select the Soft Round 30 brush (the first brush in the first row). Then choose Wet from the pop-up menu in the options bar, and paint in the top circle on the palette.

4 Click the Clean The Brush After Each Stroke icon (✖) in the options bar to deselect it.

▶ **Tip:** If the paint tubes are covered by the Brush Settings panel, feel free to rearrange your workspace to make room. For example, collapse or close panels you aren't using. But make sure you can still see the Layers panel.

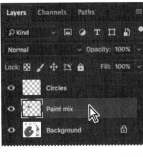
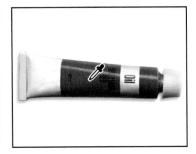

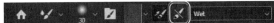

▶ **Tip:** You can use the Eyedropper tool to sample a color even if the layer that contains the color isn't selected.

5 Use the Eyedropper tool to sample the blue color from the blue paint tube, and then use the Mixer Brush tool to paint in the same circle, mixing the red with the blue until the color becomes purple.

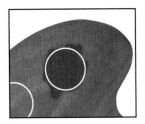
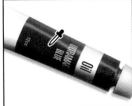
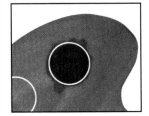

6 Use the Eyedropper tool to sample the purple color from the circle you just painted, and then paint in the next circle.

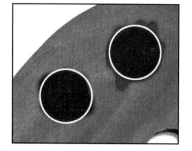

▶ **Tip:** Use the Eyedropper tool to sample the color, since it's on a different layer.

7 In the options bar, choose Clean Brush from the Current Brush Load pop-up menu. The preview changes to indicate transparency, meaning the brush has no paint loaded.

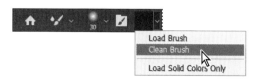

To remove the paint load from a brush, you can choose Clean Brush in the options bar. To replace the paint load in a brush, sample a different color.

If you want Photoshop to clean the brush after each stroke, select the Clean The Brush After Each Stroke icon (✗) in the options bar. To load the brush with the foreground color after each stroke, select the Load The Brush After Each Stroke icon (✔) in the options bar. By default, both of these options are selected.

8 Use the Eyedropper tool to sample the blue color from the blue paint tube, and then use the Mixer Brush to paint blue in half of the next circle.

9 Sample the yellow color from the yellow paint tube, and slowly paint over the blue with a wet brush to mix the two colors.

▶ **Tip:** When switching tools often as in these steps, it's useful to watch the pointer icon to make sure the active tool is the one you currently want.

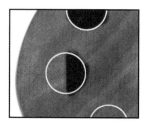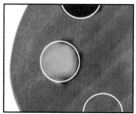

10 Fill the last circle with yellow and red paint, mixing the two with a wet brush to create an orange color.

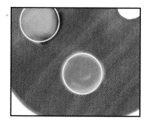

11 Hide the Circles layer in the Layers panel to remove the outlines on the palette. You've mixed paint colors on a digital palette!

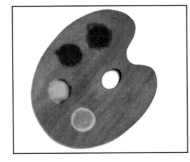 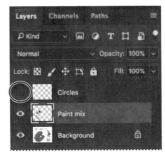

In your own projects, you can use these techniques to paint colors that you sample from any documents open in Photoshop. It's also common to load a brush with color by setting the foreground color using the Color panel, Swatches panel, or the foreground swatch in the Tools panel.

12 Choose File > Save, and close the document.

Julieanne Kost is an official Adobe Photoshop evangelist.

Tool tips from the Photoshop evangelist

Mixer Brush shortcuts

There are no default keyboard shortcuts for the Mixer Brush tool, but you can create your own.

To create custom keyboard shortcuts:

1   Choose Edit > Keyboard Shortcuts.

2   Choose Tools from the Shortcuts For menu.

3   Scroll down to the bottom of the list.

4   Select a command, and then enter a custom shortcut. You can create shortcuts for the following commands:

- Load Mixer Brush
- Clean Mixer Brush
- Toggle Mixer Brush Auto-Load
- Toggle Mixer Brush Auto-Clean
- Toggle Mixer Brush Sample All Layers
- Sharpen Erodible Tips

Mixing colors with a photograph

When you come up with a great brush, you probably want to save all of its settings so that you can use that brush again in a later project. While Photoshop already has a tool preset feature that lets you save tool settings, brushes have more options than most tools. For this reason, Photoshop has convenient brush presets that can remember everything about a brush.

Earlier, you mixed colors with a white background and with each other. Now, you'll use a photograph as your canvas. You'll add colors and mix them with each other and with the background colors to transform a photograph of a landscape into a painting.

1 Choose File > Open. Double-click the 10Landscape_Start.jpg file in the Lesson10 folder to open it.

2 Choose File > Save As. Rename the file **10Landscape_Working.jpg**, and click Save. Click OK in the JPEG Options dialog box.

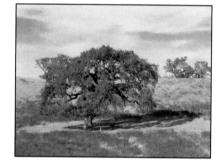

Photoshop includes numerous brush presets, which are very handy. But if you need a different brush for your project, you might find it easier to create your own brush preset or download brush presets that another artist has created and shared online. In the following exercises, you'll load, edit, and save custom brush presets.

Loading custom brush presets

The Brushes panel displays visual samples of the strokes created by different brushes. If you already know the name of the brush you want to use, it can be easier to display the brushes by name. You'll list them by name now, so you can find your preset for the next exercise.

1 In the Brushes panel (choose Window > Brushes if it's not open), expand one of the brush preset groups to see how the brushes are organized.

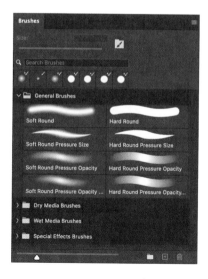

▶ **Tip:** If you have enough space on your screen, you can see more brushes at once by making the Brushes panel wider or taller.

Now you'll load brush presets that you'll use for this exercise. Loading brush presets is how you use brush presets that you've downloaded or purchased.

2 Click the Brushes panel menu, and choose Import Brushes.

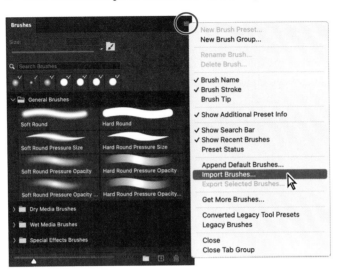

Tip: If you want
to share your custom
brushes with others or
back them up, select
the brushes or brush
groups, and choose
Export Selected Brushes
from the Brushes panel
menu.

3 Navigate to the Lesson10 folder, select CiB Landscape Brushes.abr, and
click Open or Load. The CiB Landscape Brushes group appears at the end of the
Brushes panel list.

4 Click to expand the CiB Landscape Brushes group, revealing the brushes
it contains.

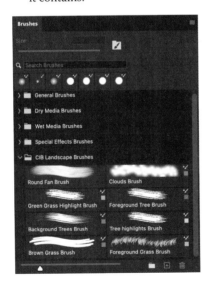

Some of the presets contain not only a stroke preview and a name, but also a color
swatch. That's because a color can be part of a brush preset.

Creating a custom brush preset

For the next exercise, you'll create and save a variation on a brush preset that exists in the CiB Landscape Brushes you just imported.

1 Select the Mixer Brush, and then, in the CiB Landscape Brushes group in the Brushes panel, select the Round Fan Brush. You'll use this brush preset as the starting point for the brush preset you'll create.

2 Change the following settings in the Brush Settings panel:

- Size: **36** px

- Shape: Round Fan

- Bristles: **35%**

- Length: **32%**

- Thickness: **2%**

- Stiffness: **75%**

- Angle: **0°**

- Spacing: **2%**

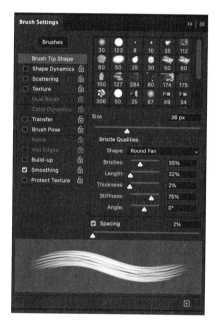

▶ **Tip:** In the Brush Settings panel, the Brush Tip Shape options include the Angle setting, which simulates the rotation angle at which you hold the brush handle. Some graphics tablets can use a stylus that lets you rotate the brush tip as you paint, by rotating the stylus. If you don't have such a stylus, you can rotate the brush tip angle by one degree as you paint, by pressing the Left Arrow or Right Arrow keys. Add the Shift key to rotate in 15-degree increments. The current brush angle is displayed at the end of the options bar.

3 Click the Foreground color swatch in the Tools panel. Select a medium-light blue color (we chose R=86, G=201, B=252), and click OK.

4 Choose Dry from the pop-up menu in the options bar.

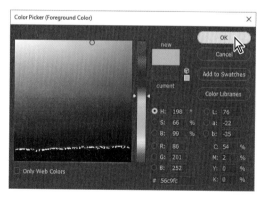

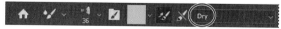

Now it's time to save the settings as a brush preset.

5 Choose New Brush Preset from the Brush Settings panel menu.

Tip: The options in the New Brush dialog box make it possible to save the brush size, the tool settings, and the brush color in the preset.

6 Name the brush **Sky Brush**, select all of the options in the New Brush dialog box, and then click OK.

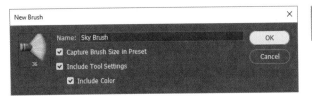
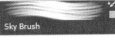

Your new brush is saved in the CiB Landscape Brushes group because it was based on a brush preset from that group. Feel free to reorganize your brush presets any way you like by dragging and dropping presets into brush preset groups within the Brushes panel. You can create a brush preset group by clicking the Create A New Group button (▢) at the bottom of the Brushes panel. You can change the order of the Brushes panel list and organize brush preset groups into subgroups.

Using brush presets to paint and mix colors

Now you'll use brush presets to interpret an existing image using your own painting style. You'll paint the sky first, using the brush preset you just created.

1 Select the Sky Brush from the Brushes panel.

Presets are saved on your system, so once added, they are always available.

2 Paint over the sky, moving in close to the trees. Because you're using a dry brush, the blue paint isn't mixing with the colors beneath it.

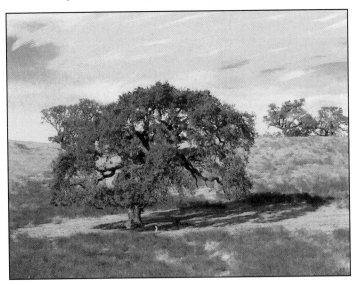

3 Select the Clouds Brush.

4 Use this brush to scrub diagonally in the upper-right corner of the sky, blending the color in the wet brush preset with the existing color on the layer.

Tip: When using different brush presets, observe how brush behavior is affected by the settings in both the options bar and the Brush Settings panel. It's a good way to learn how to create your own brush presets.

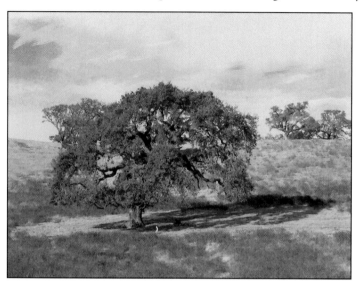

When you're satisfied with the sky, move on to the grass and trees.

5 Select the Green Grass Highlight Brush. Then paint short vertical strokes over the darker green grass areas to add some bright green grass.

Tip: Notice how Mixer Brush strokes look different depending on the colors under the brush when you start dragging. Experiment with painting blades of grass starting from the bottom compared to starting at the top.

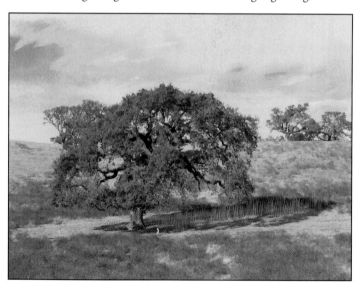

Tip: If you're using a stylus that senses angle, notice how the angle of some brush tips changes depending on how you hold the stylus. With those brush types, how your brush strokes look depends on the direction you drag relative to the brush tip angle.

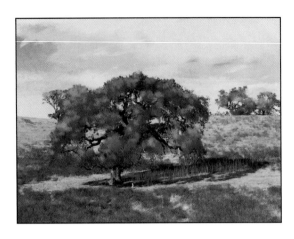

▶ **Tip:** You can paint brush strokes that are shorter and lighter for a more representational and textured image, or you can paint longer, more intensive strokes to create a bolder, more expressive image.

6   Select the Tree Brush, and then paint the darker areas of the tree. Then select the Background Trees Brush, and paint the two smaller trees on the right side of the painting. Select the Tree Highlights Brush, and paint the lighter areas of the trees. These are Wet brushes so that you can blend colors.

So far, so good. Now you can add some detail to the grasses.

▶ **Tip:** Experiment by changing the brush size or options in the Brush Settings panel. If you're using a stylus that senses pressure or angle, experiment by varying them as you paint. Use the full range of Mixer Brush settings and techniques to create your personal painting style!

7   Select the Brown Grass Brush. Paint along the brown grass with up-and-down strokes for the look of a field. Use the same brush to paint the trunk of the tree.

8   Select the Foreground Grass Brush. Then paint using diagonal strokes to blend the colors in the grass.

9   Choose File > Save, and close the document.

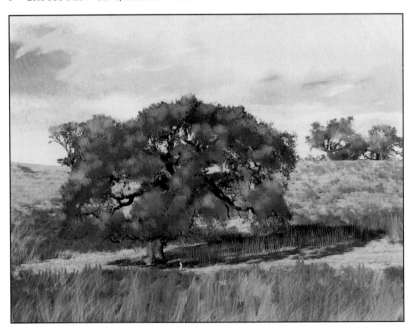

Voilà! You've created a masterpiece with your paints and brushes, and there's no mess to clean up.

Brushes from Kyle T. Webster

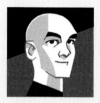

You can add brush collections by Kyle T. Webster to Photoshop. Kyle has drawn for *The New Yorker*, *TIME*, *The New York Times*, *The Wall Street Journal*, *The Atlantic*, *Entertainment Weekly*, Scholastic, Nike, IDEO, and many other distinguished editorial, advertising, publishing, and institutional clients. His illustration work has been recognized by the Society of Illustrators, Communications Arts, and American Illustration.

To add the Kyle T. Webster brushes to Photoshop, open the Brushes panel (Window > Brushes), and choose Get More Brushes from the Brushes panel menu. After you download a brush pack and with Photoshop running, double-click the downloaded ABR file to add its brushes as a new group in the Brushes panel.

Painting with symmetry

If you're painting a design that uses symmetry, try the Paint Symmetry brush option. When a brush type that supports Paint Symmetry is selected, you'll see the Paint Symmetry icon (🦋) in the options bar. Click that icon, and select the type of symmetry axis you want; it appears as a guide object in the document. Move, scale, or rotate the guide if you want, and then press Enter or Return. As you paint with Paint Symmetry, each of your brush strokes is repeated across the axes you set up.

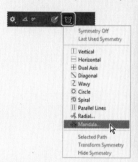
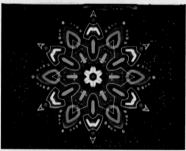

You might use a single axis for simple mirror symmetry, but you can also use multiple axes arranged in different ways. For example, you can use horizontal and vertical axes to design tiles, or radial axes to design mandalas.

The axes are actually paths, so you can see and edit them in the Paths panel. You can even create your own custom axis. Draw with a tool such as the Pen, Curvature Pen, or Custom Shape tool in Path mode (not Shape mode). With the path selected in the Paths panel, choose Make Symmetry Path from the Paths panel menu.

Painting gallery

The painting tools and brush tips in Photoshop let you create all kinds of painting effects.

The following pages show examples of art created with the brush tips and tools in Photoshop.

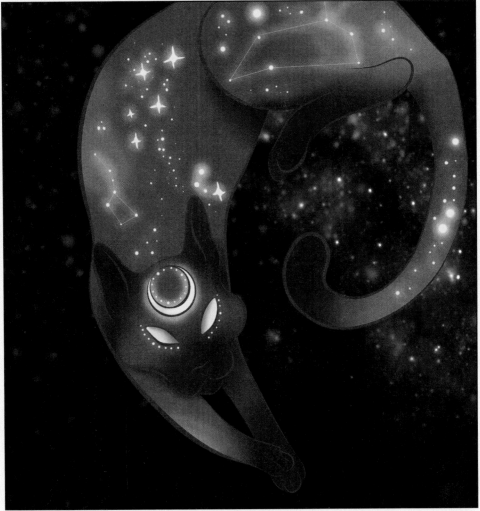

Image © Megan Lee, www.megan-lee.com

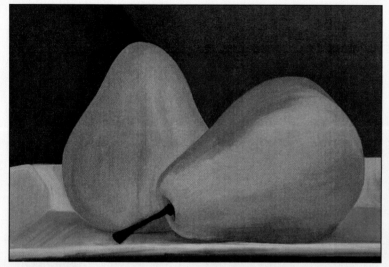

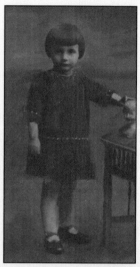

Image © Victoria Pavlov, victoriapavlovart.com

Image © sholby, www.sholby.net

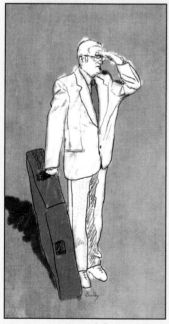

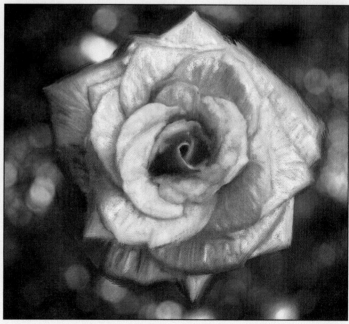

Image © sholby, www.sholby.net

Image © sholby, www.sholby.net

Continues on next page

Painting gallery (continued)

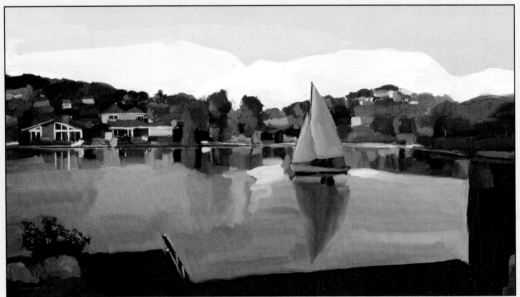

Image © Andrew Faulkner, www.andrew-faulkner.com

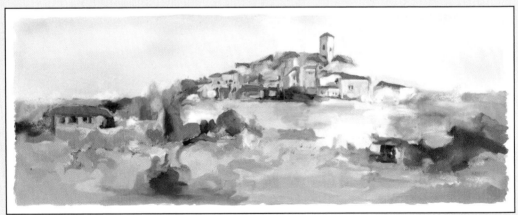

Image © Lynette Kent, www.LynetteKent.com

Review questions

1 What does the Mixer Brush do that other brushes don't?

2 How do you load a Mixer Brush with color?

3 How do you clean a brush?

4 What is the name of the panel that you use to customize a brush?

5 What is the name of the panel that you use to manage and select brush presets?

6 If the Mixer Brush and brush panels are not visible in the workspace, what single step makes all of them visible?

Review answers

1 The Mixer Brush mixes the current brush color with existing colors on a layer.

2 You can load color on a Mixer Brush by sampling a color with the Eyedropper tool or changing the Foreground color. If the brush is clean, you can choose Load Brush from the pop-up menu in the options bar to load the brush with the foreground color.

3 To clean a brush, choose Clean Brush from the pop-up menu in the options bar.

4 You customize a brush in the Brush Settings panel.

5 You manage and select brush presets in the Brushes panel.

6 Switch to the Painting workspace, using the Choose a Workspace button (or by choosing Window > Workspace > Painting).

11 EDITING VIDEO

Lesson overview

In this lesson, you'll learn how to do the following:

- Use the Timeline panel to create a video that animates a layered Photoshop document and combines it with video and audio clips.

- Sequence and trim video files in the Timeline panel.

- Add motion to still layers.

- Add transitions between video clips.

- Animate layers using keyframes.

- Add audio to a video.

- Render a finished video.

 This lesson will take about 90 minutes to complete. To get the lesson files used in this chapter, download them from the web page for this book at peachpit.com/PhotoshopCIB2025. For more information, see "Accessing the lesson files and Web Edition" in the Getting Started section at the beginning of this book.

As you work on this lesson, you'll preserve the start files. If you need to restore the start files, download them from your Account page.

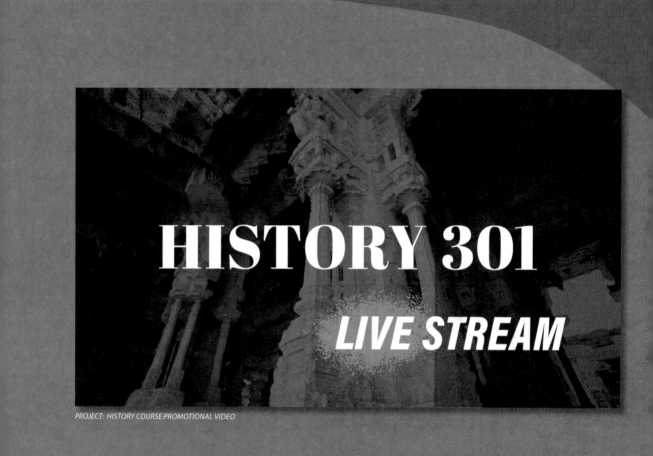

PROJECT: HISTORY COURSE PROMOTIONAL VIDEO

You can edit video files in Photoshop using many of the same effects you use to edit image files. You can create a movie from video files, still images, Smart Objects, audio files, and type layers; apply transitions; and animate effects using keyframes.

About video and animation in Photoshop

A Photoshop document can contain still, animated, and video layers. In this lesson, you'll use the Timeline panel to add video clips, edit them as a sequence, overlay still layers that you animate, and add background music.

You can use Photoshop to create basic to moderately complex video projects. If you need more precision and flexibility, or better ways to work efficiently with longer videos or many layers and clips, consider using an application such as Adobe Premiere® Pro for video editing, and Adobe After Effects® for motion graphics.

Photoshop works with many commonly used video and audio formats, including video captured using smartphones and professional digital cameras. In Lesson 1, you created a still frame that announces and promotes a live video stream. In this lesson, you'll build a video version of that design that includes video and audio and animates its layers. First, look at the final video to see what you'll create.

1 Start Photoshop, and then simultaneously hold down Ctrl+Alt+Shift (Windows) or Command+Option+Shift (macOS) to restore the default preferences. (See "Restoring default preferences" on page 5.)

2 When prompted, click Yes to delete the Adobe Photoshop Settings file.

3 Choose File > Browse In Bridge.

Note: If Bridge isn't installed, the File > Browse In Bridge command in Photoshop will start the Creative Cloud desktop app, which will download and install Bridge. After installation completes, you can start Bridge.

4 In Bridge, select the Lessons folder in the Favorites panel. Then, double-click the Lesson11 folder in the Content panel, and select the 11End.mp4 file.

5 In the Preview panel, click the Play (▶) button to view the final video.

Bridge offers other ways to play a video file. You can also choose View > Full Screen Preview, or you can double-click the file to open it in the default video player on your system, such as QuickTime Player (macOS) or Movies & TV (Windows).

Tip: When a video is selected in Bridge and the Preview panel is open, press the spacebar as a shortcut for the Play button.

It's a short clip that introduces a live stream, combining multiple video clips, animated text and rectangles, and music. It's 10 seconds long.

6 Double-click the 11End.psd file to open it in Photoshop.

Using the Timeline panel

If you've used a video-editing application, you might already be familiar with a video timeline, where you can arrange video clips, still images, and audio files as a sequence. In Photoshop you do this in the Timeline panel.

1 Choose Window > Timeline to open the Timeline panel.

In the Timeline panel you see the same vertical stack of content as in the Layers panel, with the additional ability to lay out video clips, still images, and audio files horizontally (in time), and with controls specific to time and motion. Video clips are blue, and image files are purple. Audio tracks are green, appear at the bottom of the Timeline panel stack, and don't appear in the Layers panel.

Tip: If the Timeline is too short to display both video groups and the audio track all at once, make the Timeline panel taller by dragging its top border up.

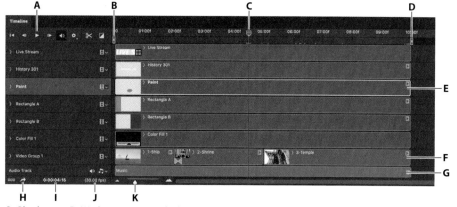

A. *Play button* **B.** *Work area start* **C.** *Playhead* **D.** *Work area end* **E.** *Image layer* **F.** *Video clip* **G.** *Audio track* **H.** *Render Video button* **I.** *Current time* **J.** *Frame rate* **K.** *Control Timeline Magnification slider*

The timeline contents should appear visible as in the figure above. If they're collapsed against the left side so that content titles and previews aren't visible, drag the magnification slider (below the timeline) to the right to see time in more detail. If you can't see all of the tracks, drag the top edge of the Timeline panel upward to make the panel taller.

2 In the Timeline panel, click the Play button (▶) to play back the timeline.

The playhead moves across the time ruler, displaying each frame of the timeline. The Play button appears as a Stop button when the timeline is playing. The movie automatically stops playing when the playhead reaches the work area end marker.

Tip: The spacebar is a keyboard shortcut for the Play/Stop button.

3 Click the Stop button in the Timeline panel.

4 Drag the playhead to another point in the time ruler.

The playhead's time location determines what appears in the document window.

When a document is created from a video preset, Photoshop displays cyan guides across the document window. Some older televisions might crop the picture, and some video players might overlay their own graphics around the edges. To minimize

Tip: If you don't want to see the guides, choose View > Show > Guides and deselect that command.

the chance that your content near edges will be cut off or covered, keep important content within the center area marked by the guides. Guides don't appear in exported video.

5   Leave the 11End.psd file open so that you can refer to it as you work.

Getting started

In this lesson you'll start with the graphic you created in Lesson 1, because the brief for this project is to create an animated version of it.

1   Choose File > Browse In Bridge to switch back to Adobe Bridge.

2   In the Lesson11 folder, double-click the 11Start.psd file to open it in Photoshop. Close any messages that appear about new features.

Note: If Photoshop displays a dialog box telling you about the difference between saving to Cloud Documents and On Your Computer, click Save On Your Computer. You can also select Don't Show Again, but that setting will deselect after you reset Photoshop preferences.

3   Choose File > Save As, rename the file **11Working.psd**, and click Save. Click OK if you see the Photoshop Format Options dialog box.

You'll notice that the Timeline panel is empty in the start file; you'll create a video timeline soon. Also, we converted the History 301 and Live Stream type layers to shape (outline) layers (using Type > Convert to Shape) to preserve their appearance if you aren't able to install the fonts they used. There's no difference between animating type layers and other layers. However, type layers converted to shapes can no longer be edited using a type tool.

The colored rectangles that were on the same layer in Lesson 1 are now on separate layers named Rectangle A and Rectangle B. We separated them into two layers because the motion design idea is to animate each rectangle individually.

Adding video

▶ **Tip:** For your own projects, if the video must meet a specific frame rate, do this after the video timeline is created: Choose Set Timeline Frame Rate from the Timeline panel menu, enter the frame rate you need, and then click OK.

The design requires replacing the still image Arch layer with video clips fitting the same history theme. Using video requires a video timeline, so you'll create that first.

1   Choose View > Fit On Screen to show the entire canvas above the Timeline panel.

2   In the Timeline panel, click Create Video Timeline.

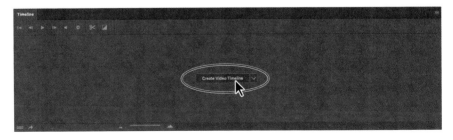

Layers panel content now also appears in the Timeline, as *tracks*.

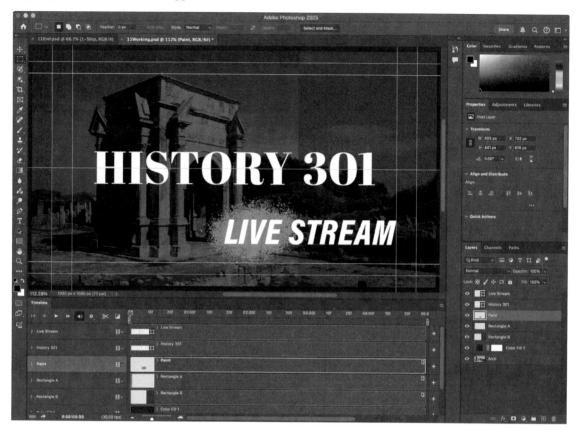

Adjusting the total duration of a timeline

If you play the timeline, you'll notice that the still layers aren't animated yet, and play stops after five seconds because that's when every track ends. The 01End file shows that the total sequence length needs to be 10 seconds, so before adding more content, you'll set the *duration* (time length) of all media to 10 seconds.

1 Drag the Control Timeline Magnification slider at the bottom of the Timeline panel until the existing tracks fill about half of the Timeline panel horizontally. You want to be able to see a thumbnail of each clip and enough detail in the time ruler that you can accurately change the duration of each clip.

Tip: If the Control Timeline Magnification slider is hard to control, click the magnification icons to the left and right of the slider.

2   Drag the right edge of the first clip (Live Stream) to 10:00 (ten seconds and zero frames) on the time ruler. Because the clip starts at 0:00, ending it at 10:00 sets its duration to 10:00. As you drag, the clip End time and Duration display next to the pointer so that you can see when it's time to release the mouse button.

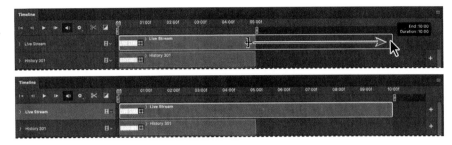

3   Repeat step 2 with all other tracks so that they all end at 10:00.

Adding to a video group

In Photoshop, video exists in a special layer type called a *video group*, which makes it possible to arrange video and still content as a sequence in time. When you created this video timeline, each layer was converted into a video group. You'll add video clips to the Arch layer.

1   Click the Video menu in the Arch track, and choose New Video Group.

Video Group 1 appears above the Arch track. Video Group 1 is empty for now.

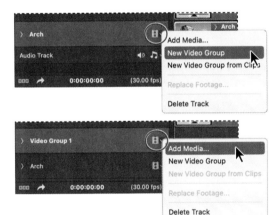

2   Click the Video menu in the Video Group 1 track, and choose Add Media.

3   Navigate to the Lesson11 folder, and open the Media folder.

4   Shift-select the video assets numbered 1–3, and click Open.

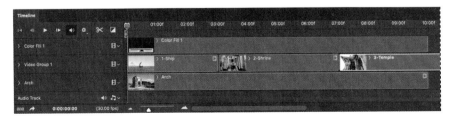

Photoshop imports all three of the assets you selected onto the Video Group 1 track, in sequence. The Timeline displays video clips with a blue background, unlike the purple background of still content. The total duration of Video Group 1 is longer than 10 seconds, but you'll change that soon. First you'll delete the still Arch layer, which is no longer needed.

5   In the Layers panel, select the Arch layer, and click the Delete Layer button (🗑) at the bottom of the panel. Click Yes to confirm the deletion.

Note: If the media appear in reverse order in the timeline, choose Edit > Undo, and when you choose Add Media again, make sure you select 1-Ship.mp4 first and then Shift-select 3-Temple.mp4. Also, it will be easiest to Shift-select the media if the files are sorted by name. It's normal for the media to appear in reverse order in the Layers panel, where the bottom layer is considered the first.

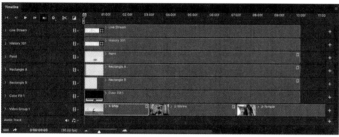
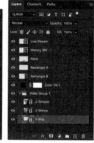

6   If the playhead isn't at the beginning of the time ruler, click the Go To First Frame button (◄).

7   Click the Play button (▶) to see how the sequence looks so far.

In this lesson, when you're asked to play the timeline, play it from the beginning as you did in this step so that you can evaluate the entire 10 seconds.

8   Choose File > Save.

Adding audio

Before you adjust the clip durations in Video Group 1, you'll import a music clip that plays for the entire duration of the sequence. The audio needs to be added now, because you'll sync clip durations to key points in the music.

1   Click the musical-note icon at the end of the Audio Track header, and choose Add Audio.

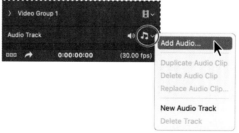

2   In the Lesson 11/Media folder, select the file Music.mp3, and click Open.

Tip: You can also add an audio track by clicking the + sign at the far-right end of the track in the Timeline panel.

3   Play the timeline from the beginning.

The audio file is longer than the timeline duration, so you'll shorten it to match. Playing it back revealed that it's the end of a song, so you'll edit it from its beginning.

4 Drag the left edge of the Music clip in the Audio Track until the Duration next to the pointer says 10:00. The audio clip remains anchored to the start of the sequence, so its end now matches up with the rest of the timeline at 10 seconds.

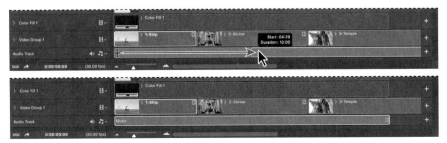

5 Click the small triangle at the right edge of the audio clip to open the Audio panel. Then enter **0.25** seconds for Fade In and **0.5** seconds for Fade Out.

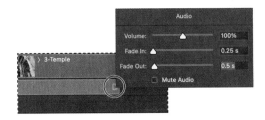

6 Click an empty area of the Timeline panel to close the Audio panel.

Changing clip durations in a video group

The clips on Video Group 1 need to be timed to cut from one to the other at chord changes in the music. As you might have noticed when playing back to hear the audio track, they are not currently synced up with chord changes, so you'll adjust their timing.

1 Play the timeline, and notice when the music changes. The first chord change is at 02:00, and the second is at 05:00.

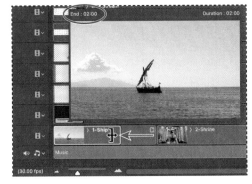

2 Drag the right edge of the first clip (1-Ship) until the End time is 02:00. Notice that the End time and Duration are both displayed in the preview that appears as you drag the edge.

3 Drag the right edge of the second clip (2-Shrine) until the End time is 5:00.

The last video clip extends beyond the end of the sequence, so trim its end.

4 Drag the right edge of the third clip (3-Temple) until the End time is 10:00. You may have to scroll the Timeline panel or adjust its magnification to see the end.

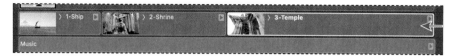

Tip: As you adjust the duration of one clip in a video group, the clips after it shift so that there is no gap in the sequence. You can override this by dragging any clip along the timeline.

5 Play the timeline to check your work, and then save the file.

Animating with keyframes

Keyframes let you control animation, effects, and other changes that happen over time. A keyframe marks a point in time where you can make a layer look a certain way, such as setting its position, size, or opacity. Creating a change over time requires at least two keyframes: one for the state at the beginning of the change and one for the state at the end. Photoshop interpolates the values for the positions in between so that the change happens gradually over time. You'll use keyframes to create the layer animations you saw in the 11End.psd file.

Tip: As you work in a timeline, keep in mind that what you see on the canvas depends on where the playhead is in time.

All layers are currently in position for the last frame of the video, so for each layer you'll animate, it's easiest to begin by adding a keyframe at that time. Then you'll add another keyframe at the time that layer starts animating to set how it looks then.

Animating position (moving a layer over time)

You'll start by animating the Live Stream layer and then the colored rectangles. The Live Stream layer needs to start moving at 04:00 so that it takes one second to slide in and arrive at its final position at 5:00. To do that, you'll set two keyframes.

1 Move the playhead to 05:00, the time of the last chord change in the music.

2 Click the triangle next to the name of the Live Stream track to expand its properties, and click the stopwatch icon (⏱) next to the Vector Mask Position property to set an initial keyframe for the layer.

The keyframe appears as a yellow diamond, indicating that it's selected. A hollow keyframe indicates that it isn't selected. Now you'll add the second keyframe.

Tip: Photoshop displays the playhead's current time in the lower-left corner of the Timeline panel.

Note: For the Live Stream track, Vector Mask Position is animated because it's a vector shape layer. For pixel layers and video clips you would animate position using the Position property instead. For editable type layers and Smart Objects, you'd animate the Transform property.

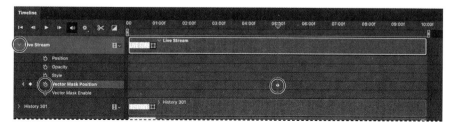

3 Move the playhead to 04:00.

4 Change the view to reveal more of the area outside the right side of the canvas.

▶ **Tip:** Dragging layers in this lesson may be easier if you disable Auto-Select in the options bar for the Move tool.

5 Select the Move tool (✛), and then on the canvas, press the Shift key as you drag the Live Stream layer to the right until it's slightly beyond the canvas edge.

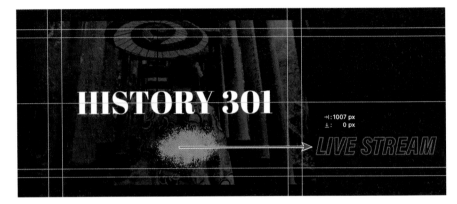

Photoshop creates a keyframe at the current time, recording the layer's position.

6 Play the timeline. The Live Stream layer should move into position by 05:00.

7 In the Timeline panel, click the triangle to the left of the Live Stream layer name to close its attributes, and then save your work.

▶ **Tip:** You can move to the next keyframe by clicking the right triangle next to the attribute (in this case, Transform) in the Timeline panel. Click the left triangle to move to the previous keyframe.

8 Animate the position of the two rectangles the same way: Repeat steps 1 through 7 to add their ending and starting keyframes, but use the following settings:

- For Rectangle A, set the playhead at 05:00, and click its Position property stopwatch icon to add the keyframe for its ending position. Move the playhead to 0:00, and then Shift-drag the Rectangle A layer to the right until it's slightly beyond the right canvas edge, creating the keyframe for its starting position.

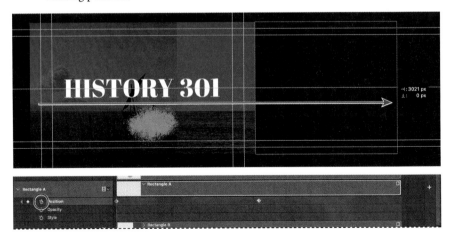

- For Rectangle B, set the playhead at 05:00, and click its Position property stopwatch icon to add the keyframe for its ending position. Move the playhead to 0:00, and then Shift-drag the Rectangle B layer to the left until its left edge is aligned with the left canvas edge, creating the keyframe for its starting position.

9 Play the timeline. The two rectangles should enter the frame from opposite sides, pass each other, and end at their final positions.

Animating size

The 11End.psd file shows that the History 301 layer appears to zoom in. This is done by animating its size.

1 Move the playhead to 05:00, where all animations are planned to stop.

2 Click the triangle next to the History 301 track name to expand its properties.

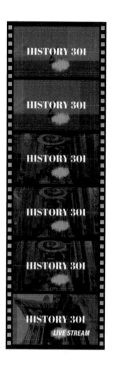

You want to animate its scale (size), but no property of that type is available. One solution is to convert the layer to a Smart Object.

3 Make sure the History 301 track is selected, and then choose Layer > Smart Objects > Convert to Smart Object.

4 Expand the properties for the History 301 track, and now there is a Transform property, so click its stopwatch icon to create an initial keyframe at 05:00. The keyframe records the layer's current transform values, including its 100% scale.

Note: Different layer types (such as type layers, pixel layers, shape layers, and Smart Objects) may offer slightly different Timeline properties.

5 Move the playhead to 00:00.

6 Choose Edit > Free Transform, and in the options bar, enter 1% in the W field, and then press Enter or Return twice (one to commit the value, and one to commit and exit Free Transform mode).

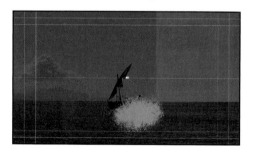

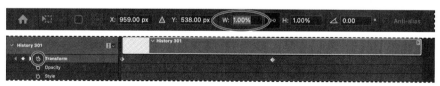

7 Play the timeline. The History 301 layer should grow until it reaches its final size.

Animating opacity

The final animation animates the opacity of the Paint layer. Its keyframe timing should sync with the Live Stream layer that arrives over it.

1   Move the playhead to 05:00, where all animations are planned to stop.

2   Click the triangle next to the name of the Paint track to expand its properties, and click the stopwatch icon (⏱) next to the Opacity property to set an initial keyframe for the layer. The keyframe records the current 100% Opacity value.

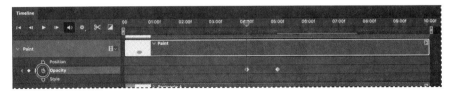

3   Move the playhead to 04:00, and in the Layers panel, set the Opacity value to 0%. This creates a keyframe that records the 0% Opacity value.

4   Drag the playhead between 04:00 and 05:00 to see how the animation looks.

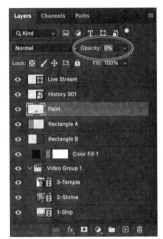

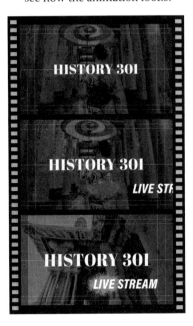

▶ **Tip:** You can add keyframes in any order. For this sequence, it was easier to add the first keyframes to the last frame because all of the layers were already in the correct states for the end of the video.

For each animated layer in this timeline, you added one keyframe at the end time of the animation and one keyframe at the start. In your own work, you can create more complex animations by adding keyframes between the first and last ones.

Using Motion panel animation shortcuts

If you want to apply a quick animation such as a zoom, you might not need to add keyframes. Photoshop provides pre-built effects in the Motion panel, which you open by clicking the triangle at the top-right corner of a video clip. Five animation effects are available: Pan & Zoom, Pan, Zoom, Rotate, and Rotate & Zoom.

When a Motion panel effect is applied, you can customize it using the options in the Motion panel. Applying a Motion panel effect also adds keyframes to that clip, so if you want to customize the effect further, expand that clip's properties and edit the values at each keyframe as needed.

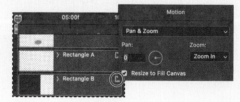

Adding transitions

You'll add a brief cross-fade transition between the first and second clips. Adding a transition is a simple drag-and-drop step.

1 Click the Transition button (▧) near the upper-left corner of the Timeline panel. Select Cross Fade, and change the Duration value to **.25 s** (a quarter of a second).

2 Drag the Cross Fade transition and drop it where the 1-Ship and 2-Shrine clips meet. A black rectangle appears when it's OK to drop it.

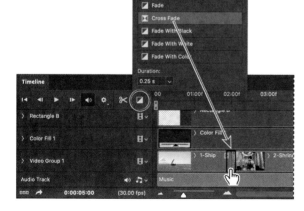
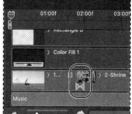

Photoshop adjusts the ends of the clips to apply the transition and adds a white transition icon in the lower-left corner of the second clip.

Notice that after adding the transition, Video Group 1 is no longer 10 seconds long. That's because adding a 0.25-second cross fade means the two clips must now overlap by 0.25 seconds to allow for the transition, so the following clips were shifted earlier in time by 0.25 seconds to create that overlap. This means the sequence edits might no longer sync to the music. You'll address this by adjusting the first edit by enough frames to make the sequence 10 seconds long again.

3   Select the 1-Ship layer, and position the pointer over the out point (end) of the clip, and only when the out point indicator (⊕) appears, drag to the right until the Duration in the preview reads 2:08.

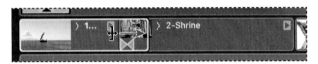

You release the mouse button when the duration becomes 2:08 because the 0.25 second transition left the sequence 8 frames short of 10 seconds, so to compensate, you increased its duration from 2:00 to 2:08.

In this video group, you won't add a transition between the second and third clips because it's designed to be a straight cut synced with the dramatic last chord change in the music. In your own projects, you can drop a transition at each edit between clips. You can also fade from black at the beginning of the sequence by adding a Fade With Black transition to the start of the first clip, or fade to black using the same transition at the end of the last clip.

4   Play back the entire sequence, making sure that you're satisfied with the timing.

5   If you think any of the edit timings or animations could be improved, make those changes, and save the document.

Rendering the timeline as a finished video file

You're ready to render the timeline contents as a single file in a video format that others can play. Rendering video can involve many complex options, but Photoshop simplifies this by offering appropriate presets for different types of video delivery, such as YouTube. Just choose the right preset to set many options correctly.

1   Choose File > Export > Render Video, or click the Render Video button (↗) in the lower-left corner of the Timeline panel.

2   Name the file **11Final.mp4**.

3   Click Select Folder, navigate to the Lesson11 folder, and click OK or Choose.

4   From the Preset menu, choose YouTube HD 1080p 29.97.

5   Click Render.

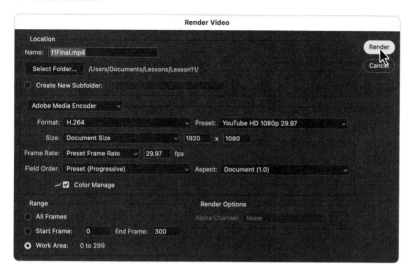

Note: If the Preset menu doesn't list presets for YouTube, check the other menus in the Render Video dialog box. YouTube presets are available if the Format menu is set to H.264, and H.264 is available when the menu for that options group is set to Adobe Media Encoder (not Photoshop Image Sequence).

Photoshop displays a progress bar as it exports the video. Depending on your system, rendering the video may take several minutes.

6   Save your work, and close the 11Working.psd and (if open) the 11End.psd file.

7   Locate the 11Final.mp4 file in the Lesson11 folder in Bridge, and play back the video you made in Photoshop!

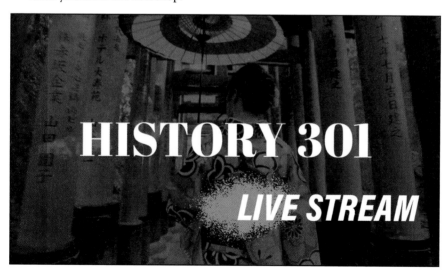

Tip: To mark a range of frames to export, in the Timeline drag the work area start and end markers to the first and last frames to export, respectively. Then, in the Render Video dialog box, select Work Area in the Range options.

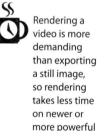

Rendering a video is more demanding than exporting a still image, so rendering takes less time on newer or more powerful computers.

Extra credit: Frame animation

In this lesson, you use the Timeline panel in Video Timeline mode to animate using keyframes. Frame Animation mode is also available: You animate frame by frame, similar to hand-painting each frame in old film animations. One typical use is to make a looping GIF animation for a website.

1   In the Lesson11 folder, open the Frame Animation folder, open the file 11Frames_Start.psd, and save it as 11Frames_Working.psd. You'll animate this Photoshop design to match the 11Frames_End.psd and 11Frames_End.gif files in the same folder.

2   In the Timeline panel, click the arrow next to the Create Video Timeline button, choose Create Frame Animation, and then click the Create Frame Animation button. The timeline converts the document into a timeline with one frame. You'll soon add more.

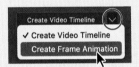

3   In the Layers panel, hide the Vinyl layer. Later you'll make it appear in the last frame.

4   In the Timeline panel, click the Duplicates Selected Frames button (⊞). A copy appears.

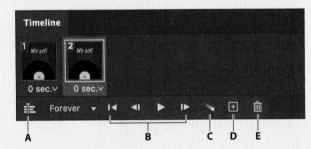

A. *Convert between video timeline and frame animation*
B. *Playback controls*
C. *Tweens Animation Frames*
D. *Duplicates Selected Frames*
E. *Deletes Selected Frames*

5   Select the LP Record layer group in the Layers panel, and with frame 2 selected in the Timeline panel, use the Move tool to drag the LP Record layer group down to hide most of it. (If only the LP Record vinyl layer moves, undo, in the options bar deselect Auto-Select, and try this step again.)

6   In the Timeline panel menu, choose Reverse Frames. Click each frame to view it.

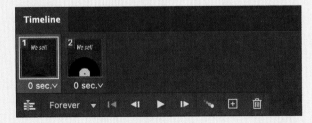

7　Select the second frame, and click the Tweens Animation Frames button ( ). For Tween With, choose Previous Frame. For Frames to Add, enter **10**. Make sure All Layers is selected, and click OK. Tweening creates 10 new frames that fill in the changes to the LP Record layer group position.

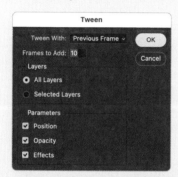

8　Select the last frame in the timeline, and in the Layers panel, show the Vinyl layer.

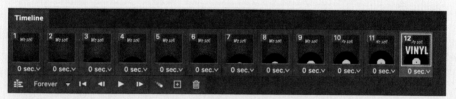

9　Play the timeline. The animation loops too quickly. Stop playback.

10　Click the time delay menu under the last frame, and choose 5.0 seconds to hold that frame.

11　Play the timeline again. The last frame now holds for five seconds.

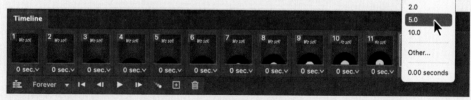

12　Choose File > Save a Copy, and for Format choose GIF. Name it 11_Final.gif, navigate to the Frame Animation folder, and click Save. In the GIF Save Options dialog box that appears, click OK.

13　Play back 11_Final.gif using Bridge or a web browser.

Tips for working with video in Photoshop

Here are a few more ways to create the video you want by using Photoshop efficiently.

Verify the frame size. If the video must fit a specific type of screen, such as a standard high-definition television, choose Image > Canvas Size or Image > Image Size, and make sure the frame dimensions in pixels are correct before you start editing or animating a Photoshop document. In the New Document dialog box, the Film & Video presets offer standard video frame sizes.

Adjusting video clip size. If a video clip is too large or small, resize it using the same methods you use for non-video layers: Choose Edit > Free Transform, and edit using the handles or the options bar.

Adjusting video clip appearance. You can edit the tone and color of a video clip in the Layers panel using the same features you've used for non-video layers, such as adjustment layers and layer styles. To apply an effect such as a filter, you might first need to convert the video layer to a Smart Object. Photoshop can't animate adjustment layers or effects; use a video editing application to do that.

"Cropping" a video. To hide parts of a video, apply a mask of any shape to it in the Layers panel.

Creating a picture-in-picture effect. To superimpose one video over another, put the superimposed video in a separate video group higher up in the Layers panel stack. If they're the same dimensions the upper clip will completely cover the lower clip, so either reduce the size of the upper clip or add a mask to it.

Creating a time-lapse video. On the desktop, fill a folder with images with filenames numbered in sequence. In Photoshop, choose File > Open, select the first image in the folder, and select Image Sequence, and all of the folder's images import as a single video in the Timeline.

Animation presets. You might not have to manually set up keyframes for common animations such as panning, zooming, and rotating, because presets for those effects are included in the Motion panel. See the sidebar "Using Motion panel animation shortcuts" in this lesson.

More features in menus. Although many video features are visible in the Timeline panel, you'll find more in the Timeline panel menu and in the Layer > Video Layers submenu.

Review questions

1 What are keyframes, and how do you use them to create an animation?

2 How do you add a transition between clips?

3 How do you render a video?

Review answers

1 A keyframe marks the point in time where you specify a value, such as a position, size, or style. To create a change over time, you must have at least two keyframes: one for the state at the beginning of the change and one for the state at the end. To create an initial keyframe, click the stopwatch icon next to the attribute you want to animate for the layer. When you change the value of that attribute at a different playhead time position, Photoshop creates a new keyframe to record the change at that time.

2 To add a transition, click the Transition button near the upper-left corner of the Timeline panel, and then drag a transition onto a clip.

3 To render a video, choose File > Export > Render Video, or click the Render Video button in the lower-left corner of the Timeline panel. Then select the video settings that are appropriate for the online service or device on which you'll show the video.

12 WORKING WITH CAMERA RAW

Lesson overview

In this lesson, you'll learn how to do the following:

- Open a camera raw image in Adobe Camera Raw.

- Adjust tone and color in a raw image.

- Sharpen an image in Camera Raw.

- Synchronize settings across multiple images.

- Retouch a portrait in Camera Raw using masked adjustments.

This lesson will take about 90 minutes to complete. To get the lesson files used in this chapter, download them from the web page for this book at peachpit.com/PhotoshopCIB2025. For more information, see "Accessing the lesson files and Web Edition" in the Getting Started section at the beginning of this book.

As you work on this lesson, you'll preserve the start files. If you need to restore the start files, download them from your Account page.

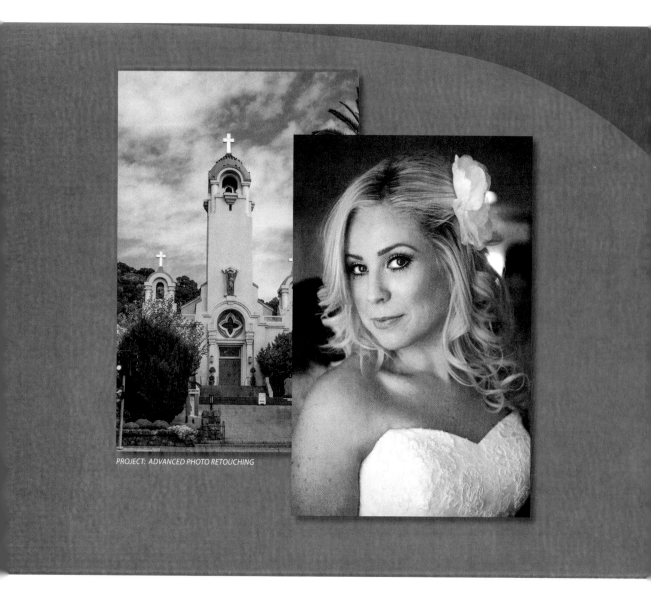

PROJECT: ADVANCED PHOTO RETOUCHING

Camera raw files give you greater flexibility, especially for adjusting color and tone, when compared to editing JPEG format files from a camera. You can tap into that potential by using Adobe Camera Raw, an application integrated with Photoshop and Bridge.

Getting started

In this lesson, you'll edit several digital images using Adobe Camera Raw, a plug-in application you can use from within Photoshop or Bridge. You'll use a variety of techniques to touch up and improve the appearance of digital photographs. You'll start by viewing the before and after images in Adobe Bridge.

1 Start Photoshop, and then simultaneously hold down Ctrl+Alt+Shift (Windows) or Command+Option+Shift (macOS) to restore the default preferences. (See "Restoring default preferences" on page 5.)

2 When prompted, click Yes to delete the Adobe Photoshop Settings file.

3 Choose File > Browse In Bridge to open Adobe Bridge.

● **Note:** If Bridge isn't installed, the File > Browse In Bridge command in Photoshop will start the Creative Cloud desktop app, which will download and install Bridge. After installation completes, you can start Bridge.

4 In the Favorites panel in Bridge, click the Lessons folder. Then, in the Content panel, double-click the Lesson12 folder to open it.

5 Adjust the thumbnail slider, if necessary, so that you can see the thumbnail previews clearly. Then look at the 12A_Start.crw and 12A_End.psd files.

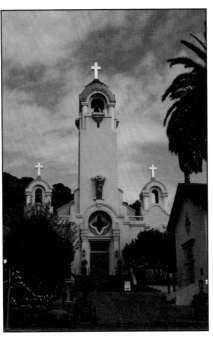

12A_Start.crw.

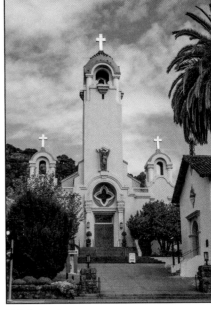

12A_End.psd.

● **Note:** We used Adobe Camera Raw 17, which was the current version at the time of publication. Adobe updates Camera Raw frequently; if you're using a later version, some of the steps in this lesson may not match what you see.

The original photograph of a Spanish-style church is a camera raw file, so it doesn't have the usual .psd or .jpg file extension you've worked with so far in this book. It was shot with a Canon camera, and its document uses the Canon proprietary .crw file extension. You'll process this camera raw image to make it brighter, sharper, and clearer, and then save it both as a JPEG file for the web and as a PSD file so that you can work on it further in Photoshop.

6   Compare the 12B_Start.nef and 12B_End.psd thumbnail previews.

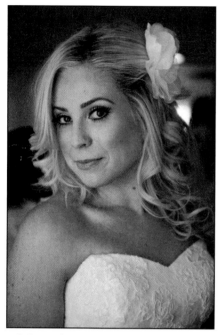
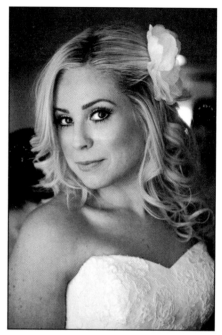

12B_Start.nef.   *12B_End.psd.*

This time, the start file was taken with a Nikon camera, and the raw image has an .nef extension. You'll perform color corrections and image enhancements in Camera Raw and Photoshop to achieve the end result.

About camera raw files

Many digital cameras can save images in *camera raw* format. A camera raw file contains unprocessed picture data from a digital camera's image sensor, somewhat like undeveloped film. Raw sensor data is not yet converted to a standard multiple-channel color image file. It's still one unprocessed channel of sensor data, and in that form, it is not yet viewable as an image. You might then wonder: How can you view raw files, such as those included with this lesson, on the back of the camera and on your computer before you open them? The answer is that a camera typically saves a raw file with an embedded preview image that represents the camera's settings and its interpretation of the raw data.

Raw processing software such as Adobe Camera Raw interprets the unprocessed raw data into the multiple color channels (such as three RGB channels) that photo editing software such as Photoshop can edit. Camera raw files let you interpret the original image data in your own way, giving you more flexibility than when you edit a JPEG file saved by the camera with its interpretation of the raw data. You can use Adobe Camera Raw to make larger changes to white balance, tonal range, contrast, color saturation, noise reduction, and sharpening than you could if the raw data was already converted to RGB. You can reprocess a raw file at any time, without degrading the original image data.

To create camera raw files, set your digital camera to save files in raw format instead of JPEG format. A raw file has a manufacturer-specific filename extension such as .nef (from Nikon) or .crw (from Canon). In Bridge or Photoshop, you can process camera raw files from a myriad of supported digital cameras from Canon, Fuji, Leica, Nikon, and other makers. You can then export the proprietary camera raw files to DNG, JPEG, TIFF, or PSD file format.

Should you always capture camera raw images instead of JPEG images? If you want maximum editing flexibility, then yes. However, camera raw images require more space to store and more processing power to edit. If images from your camera don't need much editing, you can decide to capture and edit JPEG images instead.

> **Note:** Camera raw files are typically unique to each camera model's sensor. If you have CRW files from three different Canon camera models and NEF files from three Nikon models, chances are those represent six different types of sensor data. If you buy a new camera, you might need an Adobe Camera Raw update that adds support for its specific raw data.

Processing files in Camera Raw

When you make adjustments to an image in Camera Raw, such as straightening or cropping the image, Photoshop and Bridge store your edits separately from the original file. You can edit the image as needed, export an edited version, and keep the original intact for different or improved adjustments in the future.

Opening images in Camera Raw

> **Tip:** You can open and edit TIFF and JPEG images in Camera Raw, if those formats are enabled in the File Handling preferences for Camera Raw. But those formats don't provide the same range of adjustments as a camera raw file.

You can open Camera Raw from either Bridge or Photoshop. You can edit multiple images in Camera Raw and apply the same edits to multiple files simultaneously. That's useful if you're working with images that were all shot in the same environment and therefore need similar adjustments.

Camera Raw provides extensive controls for adjusting white balance, exposure, contrast, sharpness, tone curves, and much more. In this exercise, you'll edit one image and then apply the settings to similar images. But first you'll make sure Camera Raw preferences are reset to their default settings.

1   In Bridge, hold down the Alt (Windows) or Option (macOS) key as you choose Edit > Camera Raw Preferences (Windows) or Bridge > Camera Raw Preferences (macOS). Click Yes when you see the alert that says "Delete the Camera Raw Preferences?" and then click OK to close the Camera Preferences dialog box.

2 In Bridge, open the Lessons/Lesson12/Mission folder, which contains three shots of the Spanish church you previewed earlier.

3 Shift-click to select all of the images—Mission01.crw, Mission02.crw, and Mission03.crw—and then choose File > Open In Camera Raw.

4 If a Welcome to Camera Raw 17.0 screen appears, click Get Started.

Both the Set Up Camera Raw and Welcome to Camera Raw 17.0 screens appear only the first time you start Camera Raw 17 or the first time after you reset Camera Raw preferences (which are separate from Photoshop preferences).

Note: If a Set Up Camera Raw screen appears, make sure New ACR Default is selected, and click OK.

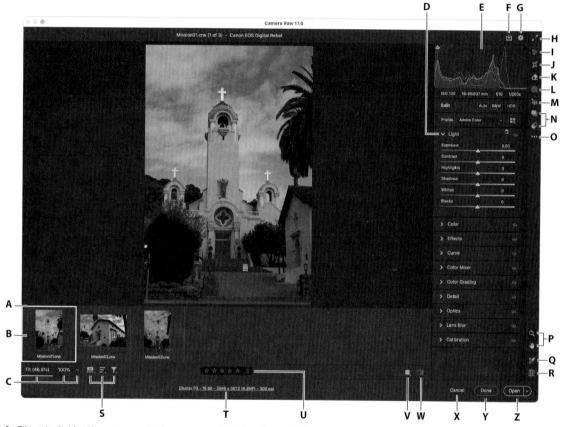

A. Filmstrip divider (drag to adjust)
B. Filmstrip
C. Fit and Zoom buttons, and magnification menu
D. Collapsible adjustments panels (in Edit mode; other modes display other options)
E. Histogram

F. Save a copy, with edits, of selected images
G. Camera Raw preference settings
H. Toggle Full Screen mode
I. Edit (image adjustments)
J. Crop & rotate
K. Remove, Heal, and Clone
L. Masking (local) adjustments
M. Red Eye removal

N. Snapshots and Presets
O. More Image Settings menu
P. Zoom and Hand tools
Q. Toggle Sampler Overlay
R. Toggle Grid Overlay
S. Filmstrip, Sort, and Filter menus
T. Workflow preference settings
U. Rate, and mark for deletion

V. Before/After Views (click to cycle through options, click and hold for options)
W. Toggle between default and current settings
X. Exit and don't save changes
Y. Exit and save changes
Z. Exit, save changes, and open in Photoshop

5　If the photos appear in a vertical strip along the left side of the Adobe Camera Raw window, click and hold the filmstrip menu button (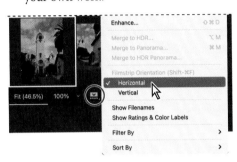) and choose Horizontal from the menu that appears. This is so that the layout matches the figures in this lesson. If you prefer the vertical filmstrip, you may use it for your own work.

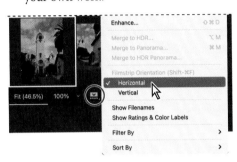

Note: If more than one image is selected in Camera Raw, in the filmstrip the thumbnails for the selected images display a gray border, and the currently previewed image displays a white border.

Note: When you first open a raw format image in Camera Raw, its appearance may seem to change. This is normal. Camera Raw renders a new preview using its settings, replacing the preview generated by the camera and its settings.

Note: If the filmstrip disappears, it's because you clicked the filmstrip menu button instead of clicking and holding. Click it again to display the filmstrip.

The Camera Raw dialog box displays a large preview of the selected image, and a filmstrip displays all open images. The histogram in the upper-right corner shows the tonal range of the selected image. The workflow options below the preview window control the selected image's color space, bit depth, size, and resolution, which you can click to change. Tools along the right side of the dialog box let you zoom, pan, crop, straighten, and make other adjustments to the image.

In the default mode (Edit), Camera Raw displays a stack of collapsible panels under the histogram. You can expand individual panels to edit the selected image's color, tone, detail (sharpening and noise reduction); correct lens distortions; and more. You can also save settings as a preset so that you can apply them to other images.

The Camera Raw options within the Edit mode are intentionally organized so that you can get good results by using the tabbed panels from top to bottom. But it's okay to adjust the options in any order, and you don't have to adjust every option.

You will explore these controls now as you edit the first image file.

6　For this lesson it will be useful to see the filenames for each image. Click and hold the filmstrip menu button (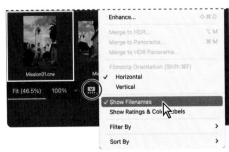), and choose Show Filenames.

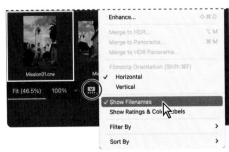

7 Click each thumbnail in the filmstrip to preview each image before you begin. When you've seen all three, select the Mission01.crw image.

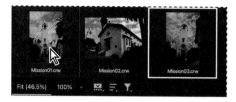

Choosing an Adobe Raw profile

An *Adobe Raw profile* affects how Camera Raw interprets the original raw data. This initial rendering is a visual starting point for the edits you make in Camera Raw. If the currently selected raw profile produces a look that's far from what you want, another raw profile may be a better starting point that saves you time.

1 If the Profile panel isn't already displayed under the histogram, click the Edit button (⚞). The Profile panel is above the controls, so if it isn't visible, it might be scrolled out of view; scroll the panel stack until you can see the top.

2 Choose Adobe Landscape from the Profile menu.

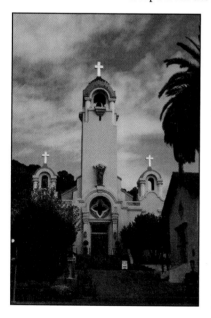

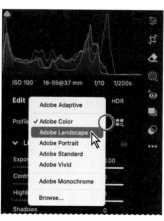

The default raw profile, Adobe Color, is good for general use. Adobe Landscape emphasizes colors in nature, like trees and skies, and is a better starting point for this image. The goal of the Adobe Portrait profile is a natural representation of skin tones, and Adobe Vivid adds punchy color contrast. Adobe Monochrome provides a high-quality conversion to black and white.

▶ **Tip:** You can also move among filmstrip images by pressing the Left Arrow or Right Arrow key. But if you clicked an option's field to edit its value, arrow keys move within the text, so add the Ctrl (Windows) or Command (macOS) key to view other images (for example, press Ctrl/Command-Right Arrow).

▶ **Tip:** If you want the image to look more like the preview generated by the camera, click the Browse Profiles icon to the right of the Profile menu, scroll down to see the list of profile categories, and try a profile from the Camera Matching category.

● **Note:** Adobe Raw profiles are different than the ICC color profiles used by your display or printer. Raw profiles affect only how camera raw data is converted to a conventional image.

Adjusting white balance

Tip: You can use Creative profiles to apply a visual style to an image. Click the Browse Profiles icon (■■) to the right of the Profile menu, scroll down to see the list of profile categories (such as Artistic, B&W, Modern, and Vintage), select one, and then click Back.

An image's white balance represents the color conditions under which it was captured. A digital camera records the white balance at the time of exposure; this is the value that initially appears in the Camera Raw dialog box image preview.

White balance comprises two components. The first is *temperature*, which is measured in kelvins and determines the level of "coolness" or "warmth" of the image—that is, its cool blue-green tones or warm yellow-red tones. The second component is *tint*, which compensates for magenta or green color casts.

Depending on the settings you're using on your camera and the environment in which you're shooting (for example, with artificial light or mixed light sources), you may want to adjust the white balance for the image.

By default, As Shot is selected in the White Balance menu, applying the white balance settings that were in your camera at the time of exposure. If you think you could improve on the current white balance setting, Camera Raw includes other White Balance presets that you can try.

1   If you can't see White Balance options under the Profile menu, click the Color panel heading to expand it.

2   Choose Cloudy from the White Balance menu.

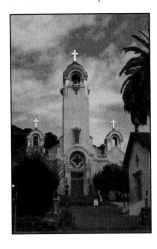
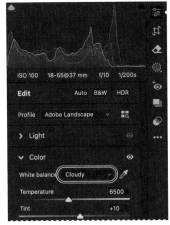

Tip: Adjusting white balance is easiest when there is only one light source. When a scene is lit by multiple light sources with different color characteristics, you may have to manually choose a white balance setting and also make masked color corrections over specific areas.

Camera Raw adjusts the temperature and tint for a cloudy day. Sometimes a preset is an instant fix. In this case, though, the image still has a color cast. You'll adjust the white balance manually.

3   Select the White Balance tool (✐) to the right of the White Balance menu.

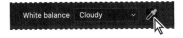

To set an accurate white balance, select an object that should be white or gray. The spot where you click becomes a reference for neutral white balance; Camera Raw shifts the image colors accordingly.

4   Click the white clouds in the image. The color balance of the image changes.

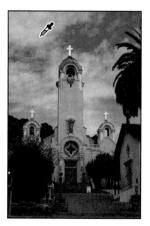 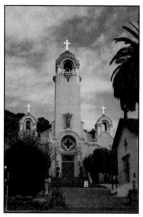

5   Click a different area of the clouds. The color balance shifts again, because that area of the clouds has slightly different color values.

To find the best color balance quickly and easily, click the White Balance tool on an area that should be neutral. Clouds are not always a neutral color, depending on the weather and time of day. In Camera Raw, clicking different areas changes color balance without altering the original image file, so you can experiment freely.

6   Click the white area of the small sign in front of the church. This removes most of the color casts.

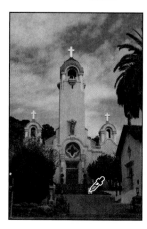 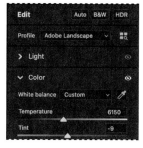

▶ **Tip:** Clicking a known neutral area, such as the sign in step 6, applies White Balance values that result in a neutral image, with unwanted color casts removed. You are then free to use options such as White Balance expressively. For example, apply a higher Temperature value to make a scene appear shot closer to sunset, or simply to evoke a warmer mood.

▶ **Tip:** To toggle between current and default settings with the keyboard, press the backslash (\) key. To cycle through the Before/After Views menu, press Q.

7 To see the changes you've made, click and hold the Before/After Views button (■) at the bottom of the window, and choose Before/After Left/Right from the pop-up menu. (If you only click without holding, it cycles to the next option.)

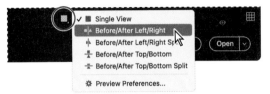

▶ **Tip:** To expand Camera Raw to fill the screen, click the Toggle Full Screen Mode button (↙↗) near the top-right corner of the window, or press F.

Camera Raw displays the Before image on the left and the After image on the right so you can compare them.

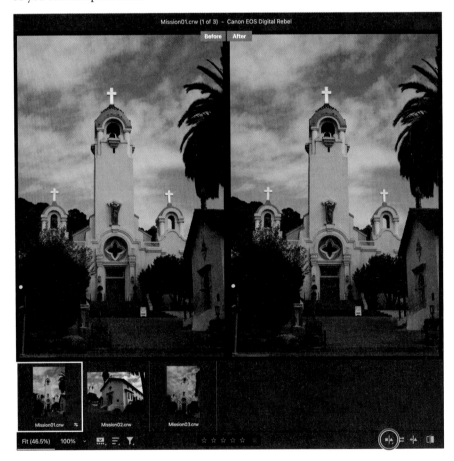

8 To see only the After image again, click and hold the Before/After Views menu and choose Single View. Or, if you prefer, you can leave both views visible so you can see how the image changes as you continue to alter it.

Making basic tonal adjustments in Camera Raw

The group of options in the Light panel affects how tones are distributed from dark to light in the image. Except for Contrast, moving a slider to the right lightens the areas of the image that it affects, and moving it to the left darkens those areas. Exposure sets the overall brightness of the image. The Highlights and Shadows options control detail in near-white and near-black tones, respectively. The Whites option defines the *white point*, or the lightest tone of the image; tones above its value are made white. Conversely, the Blacks option sets the *black point*, or the darkest tone in the image; tones above its value are made black.

Dragging the Contrast slider to the right moves darker and lighter midtones away from the midtone; dragging left moves those tones toward the midtone. In the Effects panel, you can use the Clarity and Texture sliders to apply more nuanced adjustments to local contrast, but these options are best used sparingly.

▶ **Tip:** To apply Clarity properly, increase the Clarity slider until you see halos near the edge details, and then reduce the setting until the halos are not distracting.

In the Color panel, the Saturation option adjusts the intensity of all colors in the image equally. The Vibrance option is often more useful because it has a greater effect on undersaturated colors. For example, you can use Vibrance to bring life to an image without oversaturating any skin tones in it.

Now you'll try some basic adjustments to the selected image.

1   Click Auto at the top of the Edit mode panel stack.

▶ **Tip:** Clicking Auto again toggles between default settings and Auto settings.

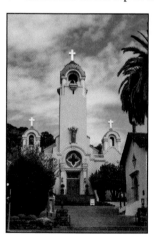
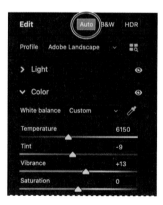

The Auto button changes several settings in the Light and Color panels, and the image is greatly improved. Auto correction may produce a useful image right away, because it's based on advanced Adobe Sensei machine learning technology, which is trained using a wide variety of professionally corrected sample images. This makes Auto a quick way to reach a good starting point for your own edits. If you like the results, you can study and learn from the adjustments made by Auto. You can choose to keep some Auto adjustments and change others. Or you can enter your own adjustments, as you are about to do.

Tip: When adjusting tones, watch out for highlight or shadow clipping (loss of detail from over-adjustment). One way to preview clipping is to hold down the Alt (Windows) or Option (macOS) key while dragging a slider for Exposure, Highlights, Shadows, Whites, or Blacks. When Alt/ Option-dragging those sliders, pixels are OK if they appear black (for Exposure, Highlights, and Whites) or white (for Shadows and Blacks); otherwise, they are clipped.

2   In the Light panel, set the options as follows:

- Exposure: +**0.50**

- Contrast: +**0**

- Highlights: -**20**

- Shadows: +**70**

- Whites: +**20**

- Blacks: −**10**

3   In the Color panel, set Vibrance to +**20**, and in the Effects panel, set Clarity to +**20**.

These settings brighten the image, especially the dark shadow areas, and boost color without oversaturating it. The Shadows option helps open up the dark foliage.

Tip: Expanding a panel collapses others, by default. You can keep multiple panels open simultaneously, as shown in the figure for step 3. To enable that, right-click (Windows) or Control-click (macOS) any panel heading, and choose Multiple Mode. This makes better use of a large display.

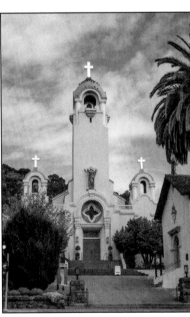

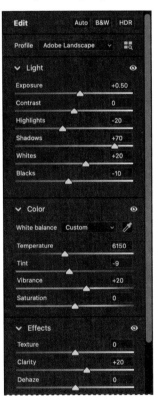

About adjusting color in Adobe Camera Raw

If you capture a raw image properly in camera, in Adobe Camera Raw you may not need to do much more than apply an appropriate raw profile, White Balance setting, and Auto correction. When you need to solve more complex color issues in a camera raw file, performing major color edits in Camera Raw may be more forgiving and better preserve original image quality compared to making those edits in Photoshop. Adobe Camera Raw offers a wide range of advanced color controls:

Masked adjustment tools. To apply different color or tone settings to specific areas of an image, click the Masking icon. To save time, Camera Raw offers some automatically generated masks, such as Select Subject, Select Sky, Select Background, and Select People. The Luminance Range Mask and Color Range Mask are valuable for making color changes within specific tonal ranges or colors. For more information, see the sidebar "About Camera Raw mask types" on page 328.

Curve panel. Like Curves in Photoshop, you can use the Curve panel in Camera Raw to edit the tone curve of each color channel separately. This is one way to compensate for color casts that vary across highlights, midtones, and shadows, but it can be more challenging to control than other methods.

Mixer. In the Color Mixer panel, the Mixer tab lets you adjust specific preset colors by hue, saturation, or luminance. When you click the B&W button at the top of the Edit mode panel stack, you can use the Color Mixer to customize a color to black-and-white conversion similar to how you did in Photoshop at the end of Lesson 2.

Point Color. In the Color Mixer panel, use the Point Color tab when you need more precision than the Mixer tab provides. Point Color offers fine control over the hue, saturation, and luminance ranges of both a color you sample and your adjustments to it. You can sample and alter multiple colors per adjustment.

Color Grading panel. In the Color Grading panel you can use color wheels to adjust the hue, saturation, and luminance separately for midtones, shadows, and highlights. This type of tool is familiar to video editors. Although you can use it for color correction, conventional color grading is typically a creative step applied after color correction to create an expressive color palette for a "look" or for a split toning effect.

Custom raw profiles. It's possible to use Photoshop to create a custom color lookup table (color LUT or CLUT). A color LUT can be the basis for your own creative profile that you can select in the Profile menu or browser in Camera Raw.

Calibration panel. The Calibration panel adjusts the fundamental color conversion from camera raw format, which affects the range of adjustment that's possible with the rest of the panel. Today, raw profiles are a more convenient way to tune that conversion, so now the Calibration panel tends to be used as a creative option for altering color relationships within an image.

Details about using these tools are outside the scope of this book, but when you are in Photoshop (not Camera Raw), you can learn more about them in the Search panel (Edit > Search), which also contains interactive tutorials and help documents.

▶ **Tip:** For even more precision, after targeting a specific tonal range or color with a Luminance Range Mask or Color Range Mask, you can apply Point Color adjustments through the mask. Range masks are not covered in this lesson, but basic masking in Camera Raw is covered starting on page 320.

About the Camera Raw histogram

Tip: Indications of clipped shadows or highlights don't always mean you've overcorrected an image. For example, a clipped specular highlight (such as a reflection of the sun or a studio light on metal) is acceptable, because a specular highlight has no detail to lose.

The histogram in the upper-right corner of the Camera Raw dialog box simultaneously shows the red, green, and blue channels of the selected image and updates interactively as you adjust settings. As you move any tool over the preview image, the RGB values for the area under the pointer appear in the histogram. Selecting the icons at the top corners enables image overlays that indicate clipping. A red overlay marks clipped highlight detail, and blue marks clipped shadow detail.

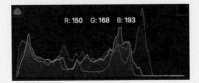

Tip: Sharpening enhances the finest details of an image. The Clarity option in the Effects panel can help emphasize relatively large details. The Texture slider can bring out details that are between the size ranges handled by Sharpening and Clarity. Texture is typically best applied to specific areas using a masked adjustment tool to avoid emphasizing noise in broad areas.

Applying sharpening

Photoshop offers several ways to sharpen, but when an image is in raw format, it's good to apply basic sharpening in the Detail panel in Camera Raw. To see the best preview of sharpening, view the image at 100% or greater magnification.

1   Click the Zoom Levels menu (⌄) near the bottom-left corner of the window, and choose 100%. Then select the Hand tool (🖑), and drag the image preview to pan (slide) it down until you see the cross at the top of the mission tower.

2   In the Edit mode panel stack under the histogram, scroll down until you see the Detail panel, and click its heading to expand it.

Tip: You can use keyboard shortcuts to go to an Edit panel directly, to reduce scrolling. Press the Ctrl (Windows) or Command (macOS) key along with a number key; the panels are numbered from the Light panel down. For example, the Effects panel is the third one, so to open it press Ctrl-3 (Windows) or Command-3 (macOS).

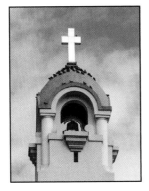

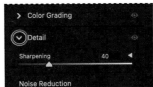

The Sharpening option determines how much Camera Raw emphasizes fine details. One approach is to exaggerate the Sharpening value at first to more easily see the effect of other sharpening options, and after those settings are tuned, reduce the Sharpening value back down to a more realistic level.

3 Change the Sharpening value to **100**.

4 If necessary, click the disclosure triangle above the right end of the Sharpening slider to reveal more options.

Many Camera Raw features have advanced options that are hidden to save space. If you see a disclosure triangle along the right side, you know there are more options available there if you need them.

5 Change the Radius value to **0.9**.

Tip: The Noise Reduction section offers the Denoise option and other AI options. Raw Details enhances sharpness, and Super Resolution increases pixel dimensions by using AI upscaling. For more information about the Denoise and Manual Noise Reduction options, see the sidebar "About Camera Raw noise reduction" on page 328.

The Radius option determines how far out from a pixel that sharpening is applied. For properly focused images without motion blur, a Radius value of 1 pixel works well to start. You might decrease the Radius value for images with fine details that are precisely focused or increase Radius to help sharpen blurred details.

6 Change the Detail value to **25**, unless it's already set that way.

The Detail option controls the balance between sharpening edges and textures for images with fine details. Lower values draw sharpening toward edges leaving broad areas smoother; higher values can bring out textures in broad areas.

7 Change the Masking value to **61**.

Tip: Want to see what Masking is actually doing? Press Alt (Windows) or Option (macOS) as you drag the Masking slider. White indicates areas Camera Raw will sharpen; black areas aren't changed.

The Masking slider is similar to the Detail slider in that it helps keep sharpening constrained along content edges, but Masking is more generally useful because it isn't just for fine details. A higher Masking value makes it easier to increase the Sharpening value without oversharpening noise and textures in broad areas of the image that should look smooth, such as a face or the sky. Lower the Masking value when you want Sharpening to emphasize details in broad areas, such as the weave of threads in fabric.

After you've adjusted the Radius, Detail, and Masking sliders, you can lower the Sharpening slider to a more reasonable final value.

8 Decrease the Sharpening slider to **70**.

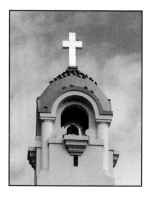

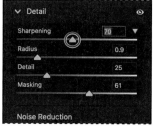

Camera Raw doesn't save changes into an original raw file, because raw files are intended to be read-only. Your Camera Raw edits are saved in XMP format "sidecar" files that are stored in the same folder as the original file and have the same base filename with an .xmp filename extension. If you also added masked (local) adjustments, in the image's folder on the desktop you may also see an .acr sidecar file with the same base filename. When you move a raw image edited in Adobe Camera Raw to another computer or storage medium, be sure to move its XMP file (and ACR file, if present) with it. Adobe Camera Raw can include edits in the same file as the raw image when exporting to the open Adobe DNG raw format.

Synchronizing settings across images

All three of the church images were shot at the same time under the same lighting conditions. Now that you've made the first one look great, you can automatically apply the same settings to the other two images using the Synchronize command.

1   Click and hold the filmstrip menu button (▣), and choose Select All to select all of the images in the filmstrip.

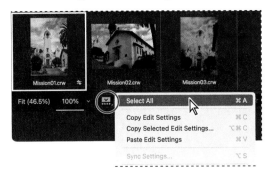

▶ **Tip:** When more than one image is selected in the filmstrip, editing an option affects all selected images. That's one way to apply the same edit to multiple images. Sync Settings is a better option when you already made edits to one image and want to apply them to others.

2   Click and hold the filmstrip menu button again, and choose Sync Settings.

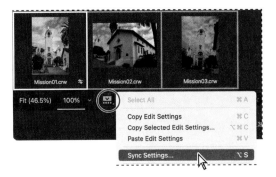

The Synchronize dialog box appears, listing all the settings you can apply to the images. By default, some options are not selected. For this project, you can accept the default selections, even though you didn't change all the settings.

3 Click OK in the Synchronize dialog box.

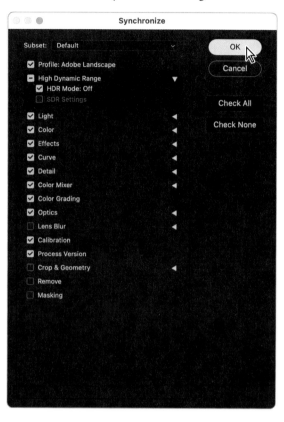

Note: A yellow alert triangle may temporarily appear over a preview or thumbnail image while Camera Raw is synchronizing settings to that image. When the triangle goes away, the preview or thumbnail is up to date.

Note: Synchronizing edits across images may take longer if any Synchronize options are selected that use AI, such as Denoise or AI-generated masks.

When you synchronize the settings across all of the selected images, the thumbnails update to reflect the changes you made. To review the changed images, click each thumbnail in the filmstrip.

Saving Camera Raw changes as new files

Many applications don't read raw files, so it's typically necessary to save raw image edits in a more common image file format. First, you'll save the images with adjustments as low-resolution JPEG files that you can share on the web. Then, you'll save one image, Mission01, as a Photoshop file that you can open as a Smart Object in Photoshop. When you open an image as a Smart Object in Photoshop, you can return to Camera Raw at any time to make further adjustments.

Note: It's always a good idea to review images altered by synchronizing settings. Some images may have slight variations in tone and color that may require a few more minor adjustments.

1 If all images in the filmstrip are not selected, click the filmstrip menu button and choose Select All.

2 Click the Convert And Save Selected Images button (⏏) near the top-right corner of the Camera Raw window.

3 In the Save Options dialog box, do the following:

- Choose Save In Same Location from the Destination menu.
- In the File Naming area, leave "Document Name" in the first box.
- Choose JPEG from the Format menu, and set the Quality level to High (8–9).
- In the Color Space area, choose sRGB IEC61966-2.1 from the Space menu.
- In the Image Sizing area, select Resize To Fit, and then choose Long Side from the Resize To Fit menu.
- In the field below Resize to Fit, enter **800** pixels. This will set the long side of an image to 800 pixels whether it's a portrait (tall) or landscape (wide) image. When you choose Long Side, the dimension of the short side will automatically be adjusted proportionally.
- Type **72** pixels/inch for the Resolution value.

▶ **Tip:** The four fields at the top of the File Naming section let you rename the saved copies using a name that you build using the options in each field's drop-down list (such as a sequence number), or you can type your own text into a field.

▶ **Tip:** If your images contain metadata that you consider private, you can restrict what metadata is included when you save copies from Camera Raw. For example, if your images contain camera information, keywords such as names of people, a copyright notice, and other metadata you entered in Bridge, choose Copyright Only from the Metadata menu to include only the copyright notice.

These settings will save your corrected images as smaller, downsampled JPEG files, which you can share with colleagues on the web. They'll be resized so that most viewers won't need to scroll to see the entire image when it opens. Your files will be named Mission01.jpg, Mission02.jpg, and Mission03.jpg.

4 Click Save.

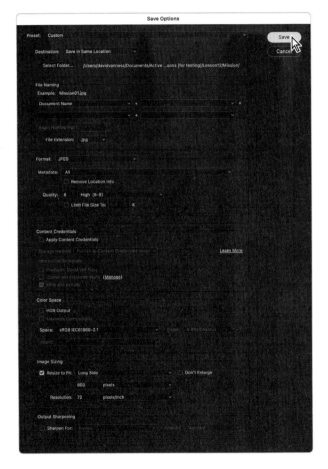

In the Camera Raw dialog box, a readout in the bottom-left corner indicates how many images have been processed until all the images have been saved. The CRW thumbnails still appear in the Camera Raw dialog box. However, in the Mission folder, you now also have JPEG versions as well as the original raw image files, which you can continue to edit or leave for another time.

Now you'll open a copy of the Mission01 image in Photoshop.

5   In the filmstrip, select just the Mission01.crw image thumbnail. Then click the menu of options to the right of the Open button, and choose Open as Object. Close any messages that appear about new features.

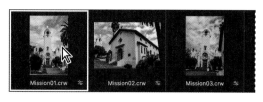
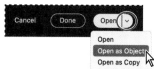

The Open as Object button opens the image as a Smart Object layer in Photoshop: Instead of converting the camera raw file to Photoshop format, the Smart Object preserves it in camera raw format inside the Photoshop document. This lets you continue making raw-based adjustments at any time, by double-clicking the Smart Object thumbnail in the Layers panel to open Camera Raw. If, instead, you had clicked Open, the image would be permanently converted into a normal Photoshop layer, and no more raw format edits would be possible.

Note: If you see a message that says "Skip loading optional and third-party plug-ins?" click No. The message appears if the Shift key is held down when Photoshop starts up.

Tip: To change the Open button so that it's always an Open Object button, click the underlined workflow options link at the bottom of the Camera Raw dialog box, select Open In Photoshop As Smart Object, and click OK.

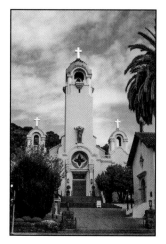
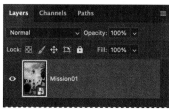

Note: If Photoshop displays a dialog box telling you about the difference between saving to Cloud Documents and On Your Computer, click Save On Your Computer. You can also select Don't Show Again, but that setting will deselect after you reset Photoshop preferences.

6   In Photoshop, choose File > Save As. In the Save As dialog box, choose Photoshop for the format, rename the file **Mission_Final.psd**, navigate to the Lesson12 folder, and click Save. Click OK if the Photoshop Format Options dialog box appears. Then close the file.

A photographer for more than 25 years, Jay Graham began his career designing and building custom homes. Today, Graham has clients in the advertising, architectural, editorial, and travel industries.

See Jay Graham's portfolio on the web at jaygraham.com.

Pro photo workflow

Good habits make all the difference

A sensible workflow and good work habits will keep you enthusiastic about digital photography, help your images shine, and save you from the night terrors of losing work you never backed up. Here's an outline of the basic workflow for digital images from a professional photographer with more than 25 years' experience. To help you get the most from the images you shoot, Jay Graham offers guidelines for setting up your camera, creating a basic color workflow, selecting file formats, organizing images, and showing off your work.

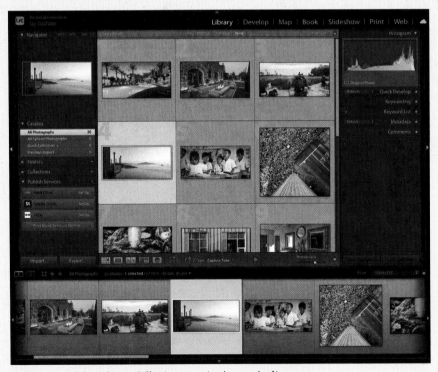

Graham uses Adobe Lightroom® Classic to organize thousands of images.

"The biggest complaint from people is they've lost their image. Where is it? What does it look like?" says Graham. "So naming is important."

Start out right by setting up your camera preferences

If your camera has the option, it's generally best to shoot in its camera raw file format, which captures all the image information you need. With one camera raw photo, says Graham, "you can go from daylight to an indoor tungsten image without degradation" when it's reproduced. If it makes more sense to shoot in JPEG for your project, use fine compression and high resolution.

Start with the best material

Get all the data when you capture—at fine compression and high resolution. You can't go back later.

Organize your files

"If the camera names files, eventually it resets and produces multiple files with the same name," says Graham. The Import dialog box in Lightroom Classic catalog lets you apply a naming convention to all incoming images. In the Library module, you can rename, rank, and add metadata to the photos you plan to keep; take advantage of the Reject flag to quickly cull images you don't want to keep.

Graham names his files by date (and possibly subject). For example, for a series of photos taken October 18, 2017, at Stinson Beach, he would store them in a folder named 171018_stinson. Within the folder, he names each image incrementally; for example, the first image would be named 171018_stinson_01. This should result in a truly unique filename for each image. "That way, it lines up on the hard drive really easily," he says. Follow naming conventions that allow filenames to be usable on any platform: 32 characters maximum; only using numbers, letters, underscores, and hyphens.

Keep a full quality source image

If you convert a raw file to a Photoshop document to do edits that aren't possible in a raw processor such as Lightroom Classic or Adobe Camera Raw, save your original in PSD, PSB, or TIFF format, which can preserve all Photoshop layers and features. If you store originals in a format such as JPEG, Photoshop layers can't be preserved, and the format may limit how much editing you can do before the image degrades, due to constraints related to how the format stores or compresses the image.

Show off to clients and friends

When you prepare your work for delivery, choose the appropriate color space for the destination. Convert the image to that color space's profile, rather than assigning the profile. The sRGB color space is generally best for electronic viewing or for printing from most online printing services. Adobe RGB may be a better color space for RGB images destined for traditionally printed materials such as brochures. Adobe RGB and ProPhoto RGB work well for printing on inkjet printers.

Back up your images

You've devoted a lot of time and effort to your images: Don't lose them. To protect your photos against a range of potential disasters, it's best to have backups on multiple media such as external storage and a cloud backup service, set to back up automatically. "The question is not if your [internal] hard drive is going to crash," says Graham, reciting a common adage. "It's when."

About saving files from Camera Raw to other formats

Note: The Camera Raw dialog box doesn't have a traditional Save command (remember, its Save button actually exports a copy of each selected image). Your changes are saved when you click Done or Open, but that closes Camera Raw. The Cancel button discards all changes made during a Camera Raw session, so take care not to click the Cancel button unless you really want to start over. Avoid pressing the Esc key, a shortcut for the Cancel button.

Most websites, applications, and social media apps can't read a camera raw file or its corresponding metadata file that contains image edits, keywords, and other information you added. One way to prepare a camera raw file for other applications is to click the Open button in Adobe Camera Raw so that the image opens in Photoshop, where you can save or export the file using Photoshop commands.

If you don't need to edit the image further using Photoshop features, you can skip the step of continuing on to Photoshop. In Camera Raw you can use the Convert And Save Image button (📥) to convert selected images to the Adobe DNG, JPEG, TIFF, or PSD format, and save those images to new files in that format.

- The **DNG (Adobe Digital Negative)** format contains raw image data from a digital camera along with metadata that defines how the image data should look. DNG is intended to be an industry-wide standard format for raw image data, helping photographers manage the variety of proprietary raw formats and providing a compatible archival format. (You can save this format only from the Camera Raw dialog box.)

- The **JPEG (Joint Photographic Experts Group)** file format is commonly used to display photographs and other continuous-tone RGB images on the web. JPEG compresses file size by selectively discarding data, starting with the visual information that our eyes are least likely to notice. The greater the compression, the lower the image quality.

- **TIFF (Tagged Image File Format)** is a flexible format supported by virtually all paint, image-editing, and page layout applications. It can save Photoshop layers. TIFF images can also be produced by most applications that control image capture hardware such as scanners.

- **PSD format** is the Photoshop native file format. Because of the tight integration between Adobe products, other Adobe applications such as Adobe Illustrator, Adobe InDesign, and Adobe After Effects can directly import PSD files and preserve many Photoshop features.

- **JPEG XL** and **AVIF (AV1 Image File Format)** can preserve the additional tonal range available when using HDR editing. See the sidebar "About HDR and panoramas in Camera Raw" on page 315.

If you click the Open button in Camera Raw to convert and open a raw file in Photoshop, you can save a copy of or export it in the additional formats that Photoshop offers, including Large Document Format (PSB), Photoshop PDF, GIF, or PNG. You may also see the Photoshop Raw format (RAW), a specialized technical file format that is not commonly used by photographers and designers—do not confuse Photoshop Raw format with camera raw files.

For more information about file formats in Camera Raw and Photoshop, see Photoshop Help.

About HDR and panoramas in Camera Raw

When you select multiple images in Camera Raw, you can choose Merge To HDR or Merge To Panorama by clicking and holding the filmstrip menu button. HDR (high dynamic range) requires darker and lighter exposures of the same composition, while a panorama requires multiple exposures as tiles of a larger scene. Photoshop also has HDR merge and panorama features, but the Camera Raw versions are simpler, provide a preview, can process in the background, and produce a DNG file that you can edit in Camera Raw with the flexibility of a raw format image.

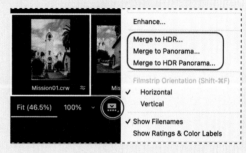

Comparing HDR Merge and HDR Editing

Camera Raw can work with HDR images in two ways:

HDR merge. You select multiple images of different exposures and merge them into one. The original dynamic range of the images is merged and mapped down to a standard dynamic range (SDR) image. This is the method used in the Merge To HDR command in Camera Raw. You can edit an HDR merge on any supported computer or device and export a copy to a commonly used file format such as JPEG.

HDR editing. You edit an image using a wider dynamic range than SDR supports, particularly in the highlights. Seeing the full dynamic range requires graphics hardware that meets the DisplayHDR 1000 standard, such as an Apple display with "XDR" in its name.

In Camera Raw, you enable HDR editing by clicking the HDR button (HDR) at the top of the Edit controls. Also, enabling the HDR button reveals additional options for editing and export (not covered in this lesson) that are necessary to properly monitor and export HDR edits. In Photoshop, HDR controls and monitoring are available when an image is set to Image > Mode > 32 Bits/Channel.

To preserve the extra dynamic range outside of Adobe Camera Raw or Photoshop, for further editing save the image in Photoshop or TIFF format at 32 bits per channel. For sharing, save a copy in JPEG format with the HDR Output option selected, or save it in JPEG XL or AVIF format. At the time this book was written, relatively few applications support HDR in images.

If you're planning to print an HDR image, the dynamic range of print is so low compared to an HDR display that the full tonal range of HDR editing cannot be reproduced by ink on paper. Images intended only for print should be edited normally (SDR), not as HDR. To print an HDR image, its HDR tonal range must be remapped within the dynamic range of the printing conditions.

HDR editing is an advanced workflow that's beyond the scope of this book, but it's important to understand the difference between an HDR merge to an SDR image, and the capabilities of HDR editing on HDR-capable displays.

For more information, see the Adobe article High Dynamic Range Explained: blog.adobe.com/en/publish/2023/10/10/hdr-explained.

Retouching a portrait in Camera Raw

The image editing features in Camera Raw are deep enough that it's possible to perform most correction tasks at the raw level, using Photoshop only when you need to do more advanced retouching or masking. When you don't need to continue on to Photoshop, you can simply save finished images directly from Camera Raw. You'll use a range of Camera Raw tools to improve a raw image of a bride.

Making initial corrections

The default rendering of the raw image uses the Adobe Color profile and has a slight color cast. You'll get started by correcting both.

1 In Bridge, navigate to the Lesson12 folder. Select the 12B_Start.nef file, and choose File > Open In Camera Raw.

2 In the Edit options, choose Adobe Portrait from the Profile menu to apply a more portrait-friendly initial rendering.

3 In the Color panel in Camera Raw, select the White Balance tool (🖋), and then click a white area in the model's dress to remove a green color cast.

> **Tip:** You can try other profiles to see if they work better. For this image, Adobe Color produces a similar result to Adobe Portrait, but other profiles may be too garish or contrasty for skin tones.

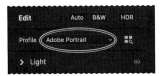
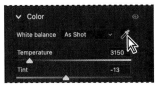

> **Tip:** It may work better to click a white area of the dress that is directly lit rather than in shade. The white balance of a neutral area facing the light source is more likely to be consistent with the white balance of the light source. A neutral area in shadow might be shifted by the color of light reflected by nearby surfaces.

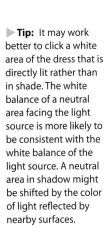
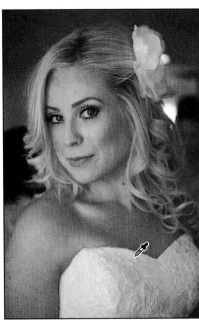
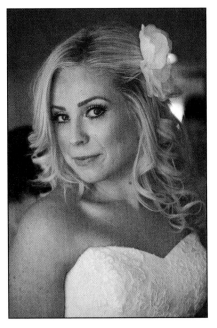

4 If the filmstrip is still showing, click the filmstrip menu button (▦) to hide it. With only one file open, you don't need to use the filmstrip. Hiding it frees up more space for viewing the image.

5 In the Edit options, click Auto.

The Auto corrections improve the image; the automatic Highlights adjustment reveals more detail in the white dress and lace hair piece. However, some of the changes go too far, so you'll edit certain settings.

6 Adjust specific Light panel options:

- Double-click the slider control for Exposure to reset its value to **0**. Double-clicking is a shortcut for resetting an option to its default value.

- Set Contrast to **−20**.

7 In the Effects panel, set Clarity to **+8**.

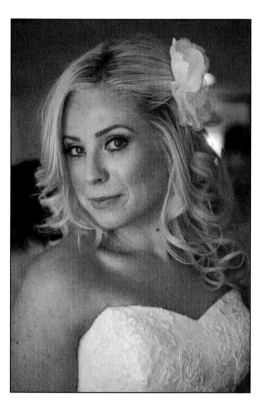

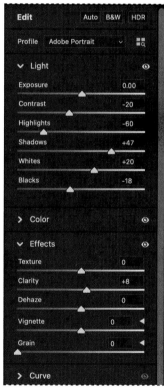

▶ **Tip:** Be careful when applying Clarity or Texture to a portrait. Higher values may emphasize skin texture and surface characteristics such as freckles and wrinkles. Apply higher Clarity and Texture values only to specific areas, by using the masked adjustment tools covered later.

Using the Remove tool to correct blemishes

▶ **Tip:** In Lesson 2, you used the Spot Healing Brush and Patch tool in Photoshop. Camera Raw offers similar tools when you want to make similar edits to a camera raw image.

● **Note:** In step 1, if a message appears asking you to agree to Generative AI User Guidelines and you accept, make sure Use Generative AI is not selected for the Remove tool.

Now you're ready to give the model's face some focused attention. You'll use the Remove tool to hide blemishes and smooth the skin.

1 In the toolbar along the right edge of the Camera Raw window, click the Remove icon (🩹). Under the Histogram, Remove tools replace the Edit tools.

2 In the Remove options, make sure the Remove tool (🩹) is selected, and make sure Use Generative AI is deselected.

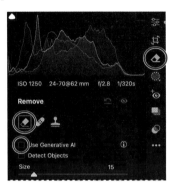

The Remove tool can delete content such as skin blemishes and seamlessly fill them in with surrounding content. It's similar to the Spot Healing Brush tool you used in Photoshop in Lesson 2.

3 Set the view magnification to 100%.

4 In the Remove options, set Size to **15**.

About Camera Raw remove tools

What are the differences between the three Remove tools in Camera Raw? They're similar to the differences among the Remove tool, healing tools, and cloning tools in Photoshop.

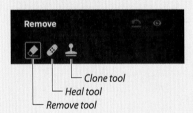

└── Clone tool
└── Heal tool
└── Remove tool

Remove tool. Deletes content you brush over and intelligently replaces it with content from surrounding areas. All you have to do is brush over what you want to remove. It's possible to sample a specific content source if needed. Selecting the Use Generative AI option can give you much better results, but takes more time.

Heal tool. Replaces content you brush over with content sampled from another part of the image, but blended in so that it's seamlessly healed.

Clone tool. Replaces content you brush over with content sampled from another part of the image, but without blending it in. Similar to the Clone Stamp tool in Photoshop, use the Clone tool in Camera Raw when you want to paint content exactly as it is in another part of the image.

The Heal and Clone tools let you change the sampling point for filled-in content. The Remove tool fills in the area you paint by analyzing nearby image areas.

5 Click one of the spots on the face. The Remove tool fills in the spot you clicked using the content around it.

6 If Show Overlay is enabled in the Remove tools, click to disable it so that you can better see the results of your corrections.

▶ **Tip:** You can toggle Show Controls with the keyboard by pressing the V key.

When Show Overlay is enabled, you can see the locations of that tool's edits on the image, represented by icons. This lets you select and then change or delete your edits. When an edit draws from source content elsewhere in the image (more common when using the Heal or Clone tool), Show Overlay shows you where the source is and lets you drag the source to change its location.

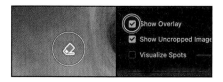
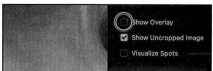

7 Drag the Remove tool over the dark blemish on the neck. Dragging is useful here because the current Size setting may not be able to remove the entire blemish in one click.

▶ **Tip:** When a Remove edit is selected, a section named Selected appears below the Remove options. If you want to adjust that edit, you can try different options in the Selected section. But if you like the results, you don't have to change any options in the Selected section.

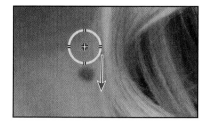
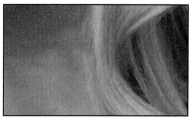

8 Brush over fine lines around the eyes and mouth. You can also brush away freckles and minor blemishes on her face, neck, arms, and chest. Experiment with simply clicking, using very short strokes, and creating longer brush strokes.

Remove distracting lines and blemishes, but leave enough that the face retains its character. You can practice by removing the jewelry on the nose, but on a real job, it may be preferable to leave the jewelry visible if it's meaningful to the subject and part of their character. This might also be true for beauty spots and birthmarks. The safe thing to do is to ask the subject before removing significant identifying marks or jewelry.

▶ **Tip:** If the area filled by the Remove tool is not seamless because it used nearby content that's visually inconsistent, as long as that edit is selected you can Ctrl-drag (Windows) or Command-drag (macOS) somewhere else in the image to define a different source for that edit.

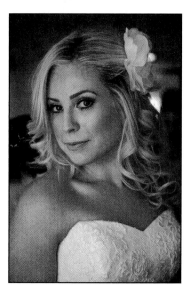

What about the Heal and Clone tools? Use the Heal tool when you want to paint an area to seamlessly fill it from another specific area of the image. Use the Clone tool to fill by copying pixels exactly from another image area without blending them in.

Enhancing the face with masked adjustments

You'll use masked adjustments to brighten the eyes and lips. A mask constrains the adjustment to a specific area. Applying a Camera Raw masked adjustment is similar to painting white in an adjustment layer mask in Photoshop.

1 Use the Hand tool to change the view so that you can see the eyes.

2 Click the Masking icon (🌑), and then click Brush. The Masking panel appears, listing a New Mask and New Brush in italic because they have not yet been created. They will be created as soon as you use the brush.

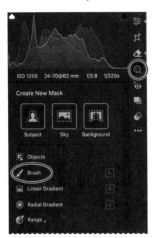 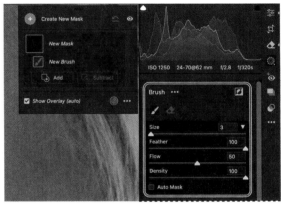

Notice that the Edit settings that were under the histogram are now under a Brush heading. When a masked adjustment is selected in the masks panel, the settings shown are for that selected adjustment—not for the entire image. You'll change Brush settings to set up what this Brush adjustment will do. You want it to increase the saturation of whatever you brush, in this case the irises of the eyes.

3 In the Brush options, change settings as follows:

- Size: **2**

- Feather: **100**

- Flow: **50**

- Density: **100**

- Auto Mask: **Off**

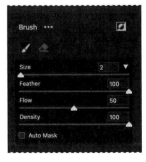

4 Scroll the Brush settings until you see the Color panel, and set Saturation to **+70**.

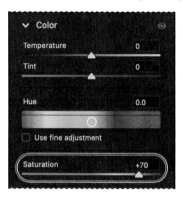

5 Drag the Brush tool over the irises in the eyes to increase their saturation.

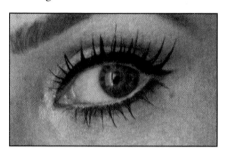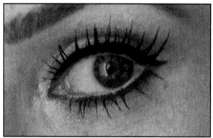

6 If you think the irises are oversaturated, make sure Brush 1 is still selected in the masks panel, and then reduce the Saturation value until it looks reasonable.

Mask 1 no longer appears in italics because the mask was created after you brushed. If you make many masks, naming them helps you identify them later.

7 In the masks panel, double-click Mask 1, rename it **Eye Irises**, and click OK.

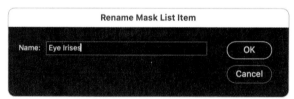

8 In the masks panel, select the Show Overlay option to enable it.

A red overlay appears, showing you where you brushed. If you see areas you did not intend to brush with the current adjustment, as long as the brush mask is selected in the masks panel you can subtract areas from the mask by holding down the Alt (Windows) or Option (macOS) key as you brush.

Now you'll create another brush mask to desaturate the red corners of the eye.

▶ **Tip:** When you hold down the Alt or Option key to use the Brush adjustment in Erase mode, the Brush settings may change. That's because Erase mode can have different Brush settings.

notice the Add button
within the Eye Irises
mask. The reason you do
not click Add in step 9
is that Add creates
another submask within
Eye Irises. Eye Irises
adds Saturation, and
all submasks within
Eye Irises would do
the same. But now you
want to desaturate, so
you need to create a
different mask, not a
submask of Eye Irises.
Add is useful when you
want to control multiple
submasks using the
same settings.

9 In the masks panel, click the blue Create New Mask button, and choose Brush.

10 In the Color panel, set Saturation to −50, and brush the red corners of the eyes.

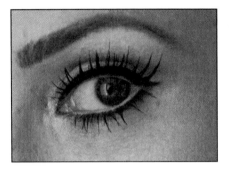 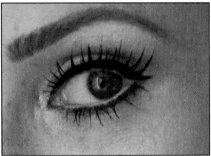

11 In the masks panel, double-click Mask 1, rename it **Eye Corners**, and click OK.

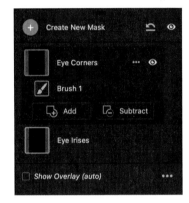

Now you'll use another brush adjustment to brighten other areas around the eyes.

12 In the masks panel, click the blue Create New Mask button, and choose Brush.

13 Scroll the Brush settings until you see the Light panel, and set Exposure to **+.50**.

14 Brush over the white areas of the eyes, the irises, and the shadows above the eye.

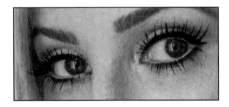 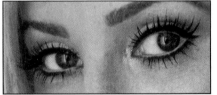

15 In the masks panel, double-click Mask 1, rename it **Eye Brighten**, and click OK.

Now step back and review your work.

16 In the masks panel, click the eye icon for the Eye Brighten mask to hide it; then click it again to show it. Evaluate whether you need to adjust anything, and make any needed adjustments to that mask while it is selected.

▶ **Tip:** To save clicks, you can do a simpler before/after: Position the pointer over a mask's eye icon and hold down (instead of clicking) the mouse button. The mask is temporarily hidden only as long as you hold down the mouse button; when you release the mouse button, the mask is permanently restored.

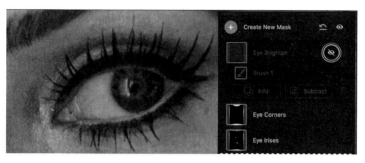

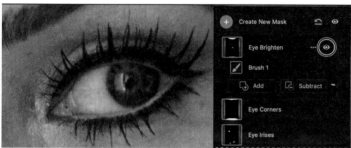

For example, if Exposure is too strong, make sure the Eye Brighten mask is selected in the masks panel and reduce the Exposure value. You can experiment with how other Light settings affect this mask, such as Shadows and Whites, to find the right combination. Or create more brush masks with different settings for each area.

Using Camera Raw as a filter

In this lesson, Camera Raw is used to preprocess a camera raw file before saving a converted copy in a standard file format, or opening the camera raw file in Photoshop after converting it to a Photoshop document.

Some features in Camera Raw, such as Texture and Clarity, are not available in Photoshop. But you can use those features in Photoshop by using Camera Raw as a filter on a selected Photoshop layer. For example, if you're working on a document in Photoshop and you want to use the Texture or Clarity options on a layer, select that layer in the Layers panel, and choose Filter > Camera Raw Filter. That opens the layer in Camera Raw, where you can apply Texture or Clarity. When you click OK to close Camera Raw, the Photoshop layer is updated with the Camera Raw changes.

Some Camera Raw features, such as the Crop tool and Save option, are not available when you use Camera Raw as a filter. It's usually because the missing features are intended to work with an entire document, but when used as a filter, Camera Raw is operating only on a layer within a Photoshop document.

▶ **Tip:** As with other filters, if you want to be able to edit Camera Raw Filter changes at any time in the future, first convert the Photoshop layer to a Smart Object (such as by choosing Filter > Convert for Smart Filters) and apply the Camera Raw Filter to that Smart Object.

Smoothing skin texture

● **Note:** If Select People isn't available, check the specifications of your computer. Select People requires at least 2GB of memory available to the graphics processor. Some older or lower-priced computers may not meet this requirement.

In Camera Raw you can use a masked adjustment that automatically recognizes skin on people so that it's easier to retouch skin without affecting the entire raw image.

1   Set the view magnification to Fit In View.

2   In the masks panel, click the Create New Mask button, and choose Select People.

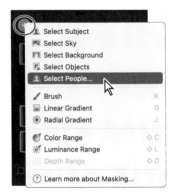

Camera Raw searches for people in the image, which may take a few moments. Then, under Person Mask Options, a list of identified people appears. In this image, there is only one person. Mask 1 appears in the masks panel; this is the current mask. A red overlay for Mask 1 appears over the image.

3   In Person Mask Options, if options are not active, click the circular Person thumbnail to select it.

4   Make sure that Facial Skin and Body Skin are selected and that all the other options are deselected, and click Create.

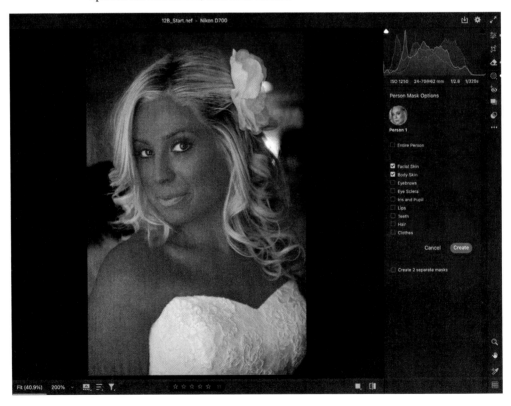

Camera Raw automatically isolates face and body skin areas and creates masks for those areas—you didn't have to do any manual masking. It creates a new Mask 1 with separate Body Skin and Facial Skin submasks for the person (named Person 1).

Tip: You can also select a color range and skin tones when an image is open in Photoshop. Choose Select > Color Range, and in the Color Range dialog box, choose Skin Tones from the Select pop-up menu.

5   Make sure Mask 1 is selected.

6   You'll need to see skin details, so set the view magnification to 100%.

7   In the options for Mask 1, scroll until you see the Effects panel, and set the Texture value to **−30**.

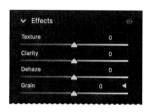
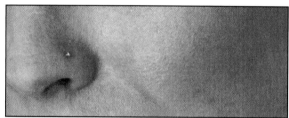

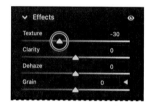
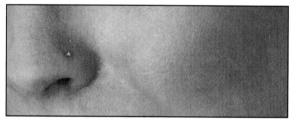

You should see the skin texture become smoother, because a negative Texture value de-emphasizes detail. (If you didn't notice the change, toggle the eye icon for Mask 1 in the masks panel.) Again, if you think the adjustment is too much or too little, go ahead and adjust the Texture value while Mask 1 is selected in the masks panel.

While the skin mask is selected, it's a good time to also make any other skin tone or color adjustments you think are needed. For example, if there is a color cast to remove from the skin, try adjusting options in Mask 1 panels such as Color and Curve. (If you want to correct a color cast across the entire image, after step 8 click the Edit button to exit masking; then adjust options in the general Edit panels.)

8   In the masks panel, double-click Mask 1, rename it **Skin**, and click OK.

9   Click the Edit button (⚏) to close the masks panel, and set the view magnification to Fit In View so that you can review the entire image.

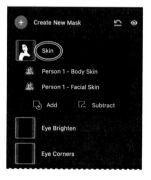

You opened an image from Bridge into Camera Raw and performed portrait retouching, without opening Photoshop. If you need a finished copy to distribute, you can click the Save icon (⬇) as you did with the mission buildings earlier in this lesson. If you want to apply more advanced retouching techniques that Camera Raw can't do, you can click Open to convert the image into a Photoshop document and continue editing in Photoshop. But for now, let's make sure all of the work you did in Camera Raw is saved.

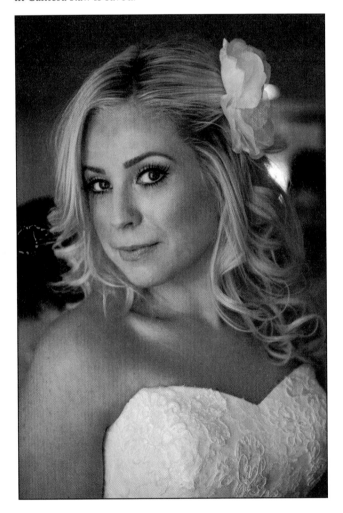

10 Click Done. Great work! The Done button saves your changes and closes Camera Raw, returning you to Bridge.

Secrets of the More Image Settings menu

In Adobe Camera Raw, the More Image Settings menu is not always noticed, but it offers powerful features, some of which aren't visible in the Camera Raw window. To open this menu, click the More Image Settings button (…), the last button in the button group at the upper-right corner of the Camera Raw window.

Here are some of the more useful commands in the More Image Settings menu. For more information about them, see Camera Raw online help.

Reset to Open and Reset to Default. These discard edits so you can start over. Reset to Open reverts an image to its state at the time you opened it in Camera Raw, and Reset to Default reverts to default Camera Raw settings, which you can customize (see Set Raw Defaults below).

Commands for managing snapshots and presets. These work with the Snapshots and Presets panels; their buttons are above the More Image Settings menu.

Commands for copying and pasting settings. Use these to transfer edits to other images in the filmstrip, similar to the Sync Settings command shown in this lesson.

Load Settings and Save Settings. Normally, Camera Raw reads edits from and writes edits to an XMP metadata file in the same folder as the current camera raw file. These commands let you load edits from or save them as an XMP file in another folder, or using a different filename.

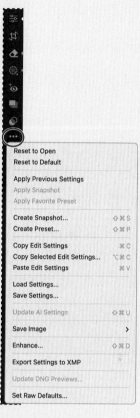

Save Image. This is the same as the Save button (⤓) near the upper-right corner of the Camera Raw window. Its submenu applies Save presets, skipping the dialog box.

Enhance. This opens the Enhance dialog box, which uses machine learning to apply AI-powered Denoise noise reduction, Raw Details detail improvement, and Super Resolution upscaling, producing an enhanced DNG copy of the image file.

Set Raw Defaults. If you wish Camera Raw options had different starting values, use this command to customize Camera Raw default settings.

Many of these commands are also available on the Camera Raw filmstrip menu, or in the context menu that appears when you right-click (Windows) or Control-click (macOS) an image or its filmstrip thumbnail.

About Camera Raw mask types

Masking corrections in Camera Raw can potentially save you a trip to Photoshop. Camera Raw offers more mask types than the ones you used in this lesson.

Subject, Sky, Background, and People.
Camera Raw uses machine learning to recognize specific types of content and create a mask for them. The difference between Subject and People is that Subject works on non-human subjects.

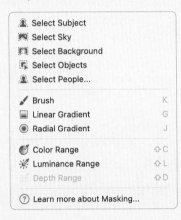

Objects. When Select Subject doesn't select what you want, drag the Select Objects masking tool around a specific object to select it more precisely.

Linear Gradient and Radial Gradient.
These create a mask that fades out gradually from one end to the other (for a Linear Gradient) or from the center of an ellipse outward (for a Radial Gradient). A Linear Gradient can be useful for equalizing tone or color differences on different sides of an image. A Radial Gradient is useful for emphasizing a spot within an image or creating an off-center vignette.

Color Range, Luminance Range, and Depth Range. A range mask is defined by a range of colors (Color Range), tones (Luminance Range), or distances (Depth Range) that you specify. For example, if you specify a Luminance Range mask that targets just the shadow tones in an image, you can then increase Exposure and reduce Noise across that range of tones only. Or you can create a Color Range mask that targets skin tones.

The Depth Range mask is available only if a camera embedded depth metadata into the image, as some smartphone cameras do.

About AI noise reduction

When an image has a lot of visual noise, such as an image taken in dim light, you can try Noise Reduction options in the Detail panel of Camera Raw.

The Denoise option applies AI-powered noise reduction, which can be surprisingly effective on very noisy images. Denoise is also easy to use, because it offers only one adjustment that controls the amount of noise reduction. Denoise works best on a recent computer that has a powerful graphics processing unit (GPU).

If Denoise takes too long on your computer, or if you want to refine the results of Denoise, use the Manual Noise Reduction controls further down in the Detail panel. Start by setting the Luminance and Color options to low values, and work your way up, keeping a balance between reducing noise and preserving detail.

Review questions

1 How is editing a camera raw image different than editing a photo in a format such as JPEG or Photoshop file format?

2 What is the advantage of the Adobe Digital Negative (DNG) file format?

3 How can you apply the same settings to multiple images in Camera Raw?

4 How do you apply a Camera Raw edit to specific areas of an image?

Review answers

1 A camera raw file contains unprocessed picture data from a digital camera's image sensor, like unprocessed film. Camera raw files give photographers control over interpreting the image data from the beginning, rather than letting the camera apply an initial conversion and adjustments. When you edit the image in Camera Raw, it stores the edits separately so that the original raw file is not altered. This way, you can edit the image the way you want, export it, and keep the original intact for future re-interpretation, re-editing with future improved software, or for other adjustments.

2 The Adobe Digital Negative (DNG) file format contains the raw image data from a digital camera as well as metadata that defines what the image data means. DNG is an industry-wide standard for camera raw image data. DNG can help photographers manage proprietary camera raw file formats using an openly available standard, and it provides a compatible archival format that includes edits.

3 To apply the same settings to multiple images in Camera Raw, select the images in the filmstrip, click the filmstrip menu button, and choose Sync Settings. Then select the settings you want to apply, and click OK.

4 To apply a Camera Raw edit to specific areas of an image, click the Masking icon, and create a new mask that isolates the areas you want to edit.

13 PREPARING FILES FOR THE WEB

Lesson overview

In this lesson, you'll learn how to do the following:

- Use the Frame tool to create a placeholder for a layout.

- Create and stylize a button for a website.

- Use layer groups and artboards.

- Optimize design assets for the web.

- Record an action to automate a series of steps.

- Play an action to affect multiple images.

- Save entire layouts and individual assets using Export As.

- Design for multiple screen sizes with multiple artboards.

 This lesson will take about an hour to complete. To get the lesson files used in this chapter, download them from the web page for this book at peachpit.com/PhotoshopCIB2025. For more information, see "Accessing the lesson files and Web Edition" in the Getting Started section at the beginning of this book.

As you work on this lesson, you'll preserve the start files. If you need to restore the start files, download them from your Account page.

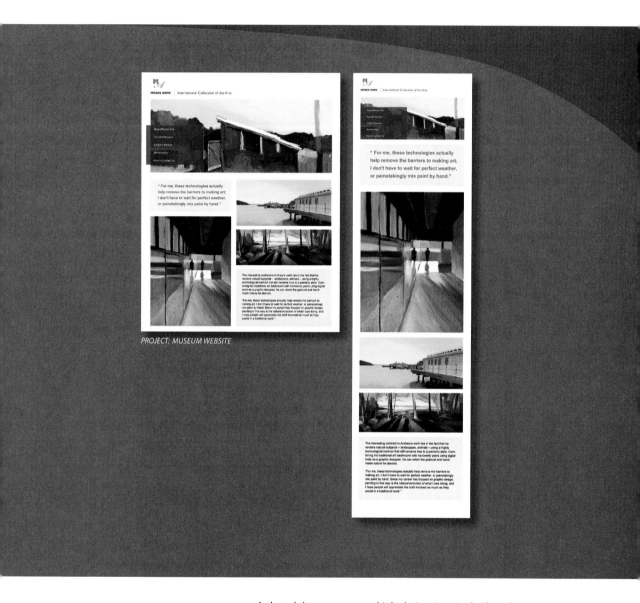

PROJECT: MUSEUM WEBSITE

Artboards let you create multiple designs in a single Photoshop document. For example, you can consistently design both the mobile and desktop versions of a website. When it's ready, the Export As workflow makes it easy to save layers, layer groups, and artboards as separate image assets that you can deliver to a web developer, or for review.

Getting started

In this lesson, you will build buttons for the home page of an art museum's website and then generate appropriate graphics files for each button. You'll use layer groups to assemble the buttons and then create actions to prepare a set of images for use as a second group of buttons. First, you'll view the final web design.

1   Start Photoshop, and then simultaneously hold down Ctrl+Alt+Shift (Windows) or Command+Option+Shift (macOS) to restore the default preferences. (See "Restoring default preferences" on page 5.)

2   When prompted, click Yes to delete the Adobe Photoshop Settings file.

3   Choose File > Browse In Bridge.

Note: If Bridge isn't installed, the File > Browse In Bridge command in Photoshop will start the Creative Cloud desktop app, which will download and install Bridge. After installation completes, you can start Bridge. For more information, see page 3.

4   In Bridge, click Lessons in the Favorites panel. Double-click the Lesson13 folder in the Content panel.

5   View the 13End.psd file in Bridge.

There are eight buttons at the bottom of the page, arranged in two rows. You'll transform images into buttons for the top row and use an action to prepare the buttons for the second row.

6   Double-click the 13Start.psd thumbnail to open the file in Photoshop. Click OK if you see the Missing Profile dialog box, and close any messages that appear about new features.

Note: If Photoshop displays a dialog box telling you about the difference between saving to Cloud Documents and On Your Computer, click Save On Your Computer. You can also select Don't Show Again, but that setting will deselect after you reset Photoshop preferences.

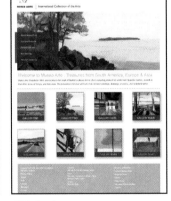

13Start.psd.   *13End.psd.*

7   Choose File > Save As, rename the file **13Working.psd**, and click Save. Click OK in the Photoshop Format Options dialog box.

Creating placeholders with the Frame tool

When you create a print, web, or mobile device project, it's common to design the layout before you have the final graphics for it. You could add temporary graphics that you plan to replace later with final graphics, but then you must manage more files. One way to simplify the design process is to create placeholder shapes, called *frames*, during the early stages of design. As you refine the design and as final graphics become available, it's easy to place the final graphics directly into placeholder frames. Designing with placeholder frames is common in page layout applications such as Adobe InDesign.

You create frames using the Frame tool. A frame can contain an imported graphic, a Smart Object, or a pixel layer. When you create a frame, it appears in the Layers panel, because a frame is like a layer group with a vector mask.

The document 13Working.psd contains empty gray boxes. The gray boxes exist only to help you position new frames that you'll create for this lesson. When you create your own designs, you can design using the Frame tool alone.

1   Choose Edit > Preferences > Units & Rulers (Windows) or Photoshop > Settings > Units & Rulers (macOS). In the Units area of the dialog box, make sure Pixels is selected in the Rulers menu, and then click OK.

Note: If you're using macOS 12 or earlier, the Settings command is named Preferences.

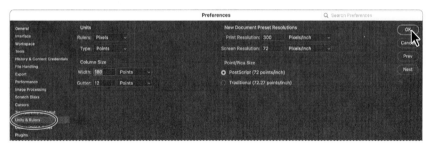

You want to work in pixels because this document is intended to be a web page.

2   Choose Window > Info to open the Info panel.

The Info panel displays information dynamically as you move the pointer or make selections. Which information it displays depends on the tool that is selected. You'll use it to determine the position of the ruler guide (based on the Y coordinate) and the size of an area you select (based on the width and height). It's also handy for seeing the values of colors under the pointer.

3   If the rulers aren't visible, choose View > Rulers.

Tip: A quick way to change the unit of measure is to right-click (Windows) or Control-click (macOS) the rulers.

Tip: To customize the Info panel display of the color values under the pointer, click an eyedropper or crosshair icon in the Info panel, and then choose the display option you want.

Tip: The keyboard shortcut for showing or hiding rulers is Ctrl+R (Windows) or Command+R (macOS).

Adding a frame

A frame is easy to add, because you create one the same way you'd create a shape such as a rectangle or circle.

▶ **Tip:** You can create an elliptical or circular frame by selecting the Elliptical Frame icon in the options bar for the Frame tool.

1   In the Tools panel, select the Frame tool (⊠).

2   Drag to create a rectangular frame over the large gray rectangle at the top of the document.

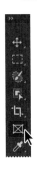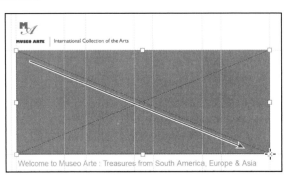

▶ **Tip:** To create a frame of any shape, such as a star, first draw the shape using a Pen tool or a shape tool. Then, with the shape layer selected in the Layers panel, choose Layer > New > Convert To Frame.

The frame appears as a rectangle with an X inside it. The X indicates that it's not just a vector shape, but also a placeholder frame. As a placeholder, it's ready to contain a graphic at any time.

Adding a graphic to a frame

When you finalize the images and other graphics that go into a document, you can add them to the placeholder frames you've created.

1   In the Layers panel, make sure the Frame 1 layer is still selected.

2   Choose File > Place Linked.

3   Navigate to the Lesson13/Art folder, select the NorthShore.jpg file, and click Place.

The image appears inside the selected frame and automatically resizes to fill the frame.

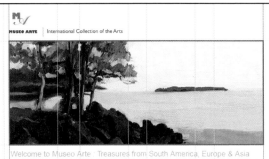

You can also drag an image from Bridge or the desktop and drop it into a frame in a Photoshop document window. This embeds the image—it makes a complete copy of it inside the Photoshop document. To have the frame link instead, so that it always loads the current version of the image from outside the Photoshop document, hold down Alt or Option as you drag.

Editing frame attributes with the Properties panel

When a frame is selected in the Layers panel, you can see and edit frame attributes in the Properties panel so that you can change a frame after you create it.

1 With the Frame tool, draw a rectangle frame between the row of four gray squares and the bottom of the document. The exact size and position aren't important, because you're about to edit them.

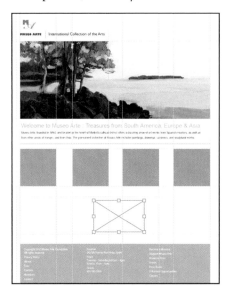

2 With the frame selected, enter the following values in the Properties panel (if it isn't already open, choose Window > Properties):

- Width: **180**

- Height: **180**

- X: **40**

- Y: **648**

► **Tip:** As in the options bar, you can change the unit of measure in a Properties panel field by right-clicking (Windows) or Control-clicking (macOS) the field. Or you can override a field's unit of measure by typing the unit after the value, for example, **4 in**.

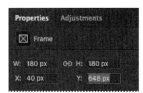
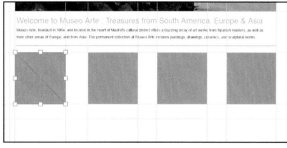

The frame should change after you apply each value. After you enter all four values, the size and position of the frame should now match the first gray square.

Duplicating frames

The other three squares in the row are the same size, so instead of drawing all four squares manually, you can simply duplicate them. Duplicating a frame is similar to duplicating a layer, because frames appear in the Layers panel.

1   In the Layers panel, drag the Frame 1 layer, and drop it on the Create A New Layer button (⊞). The duplicate layer, Frame 1 Copy, appears in the Layers panel.

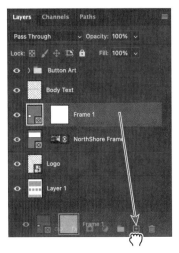 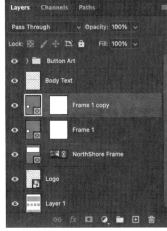

2   With the Frame 1 Copy layer selected, in the Properties panel change the X value to **300**. This makes the duplicate square frame line up with the second gray square.

▶ **Tip:** It's always your choice to size and position a selected layer by dragging or by precisely editing values in the Properties panel or options bar.

3   Repeat step 1 to create two more duplicate frames. In the Properties panel, change the X value of the third frame to **550** and the X value of the fourth frame to **800**.

You've created a complete row of four placeholder frames.

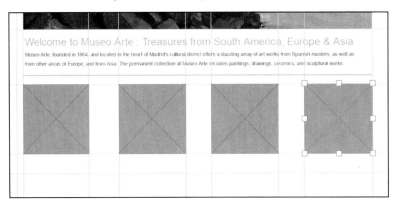

Adding images to frames

When graphics become available to use in the layout, you can quickly add them to each frame. One convenient way is by using the Properties panel.

1 Make sure the first square frame (Frame 1) is selected.

2 In the Properties panel, click the Inset Image menu, and choose Place From Local Disk - Linked.

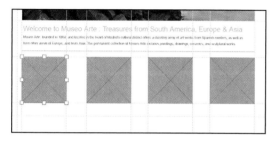 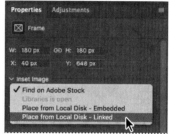

3 Navigate to the Lesson13/Art folder, select the Beach.jpg file, and click Place.

The Beach.jpg file is scaled to fit the frame, the name of the frame changes to Beach Frame, and the Properties panel displays the folder path to the linked document that's placed in the frame.

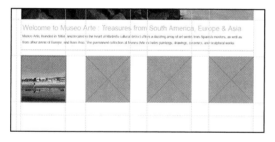 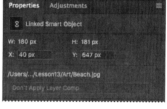

4 Repeat step 2 for the other three square frames, placing the files NorthShore.jpg, DeYoung.jpg, and MaineOne.jpg.

Tip: Remember that another way to add a linked image to a frame is to Alt-drag (Windows) or Option-drag (macOS) an image from the desktop or Bridge and drop it into a frame.

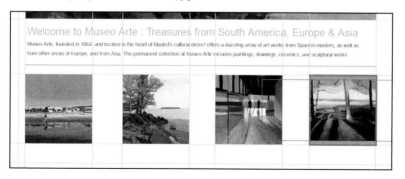

5   In the Layers panel, click to select the frame layer thumbnail (the right thumbnail with the link icon) of the MaineOne Frame layer. This selects just the contents of the frame. (Clicking the left thumbnail would select the frame.)

6   Choose Edit > Free Transform, drag the image or any of its edge handles to improve the composition of the image within the frame, and press Enter or Return when you're done.

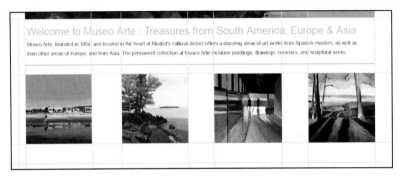

Note: If you can't select a frame or its contents on the canvas with the Move tool, make sure Auto-Select Layer is enabled in the options bar when the Move tool is selected. When Auto-Select Layer is not enabled, you must click the thumbnail of the frame or the contents in the Layers panel.

After adding graphics to frames, it's always a good idea to inspect all of the frames to make sure the graphics are well-composed within them. Feel free to adjust any of the other images within their frames.

Using layer groups to create button graphics

Layer groups make it easier to organize and work with layers in complex images, especially when there are sets of layers that work together. You'll use layer groups to assemble the layers that make up each button, and this organization will make things easier later, when you export them as website assets.

The four frames you created now serve as the basis for buttons. You'll add a label to each, identifying the gallery it represents, and then add a drop shadow and a stroke.

1   If the Info panel isn't already open, choose Window > Info to open it.

Tip: If you have trouble positioning the horizontal ruler guide precisely, hold down the Shift key to constrain the increments. If that doesn't snap to 795 pixels, zoom in, because the Shift key snap interval is smaller at higher magnifications.

2   Position the Move tool pointer over the horizontal ruler, and drag a ruler guide down until the Y value in the Info panel is 795 pixels.

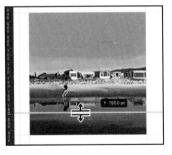
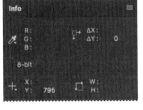

You'll use this guide to draw a band across the bottom of the image for the label.

3 Zoom in on the first square image, of the man on the beach. Then select Beach Frame in the Layers panel.

You'll use this image to design the first button.

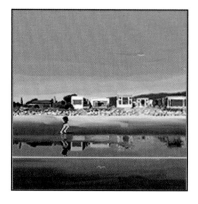 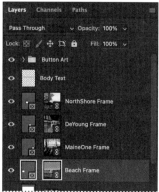

4 Select the Rectangle tool (▭) in the Tools panel. Then, drag to create a rectangle shape across the bottom of the image, aligned with the guides and image edges. The shape should be 180 pixels wide and 33 pixels high. Press Enter or Return to commit the new shape, which is named Rectangle 1. Rename it **Band**.

► **Tip:** Remember that the quickest way to rename a layer is to double-click its name in the Layers panel.

5 With the Band layer selected, click the Fill swatch in the Contextual Task Bar, click the Color Picker icon, and then select a dark blue; we entered the hex color **194879**. Click OK to close the Color Picker, and then press Enter or Return to close the Fill options.

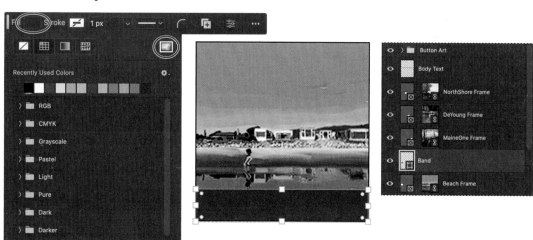

6 Click the Stroke swatch in the Contextual Task bar, click No Color (▱), and close the Stroke options.

The new shape appears as a dark blue band at the bottom of the first image. You'll add text to it next.

7   Select the Horizontal Type tool, and select the following settings in the options bar:

- Font Family: Myriad Pro

- Font Style: Regular

- Anti-aliasing: Strong

- Alignment: Center

- Color: White

- Font Size: **18** pt

Tip: As you position the text layer, if it snaps to a vertical magenta Smart Guide that appears in the middle of the Beach Frame and Blue Band layers, that means the text layer is centered in front of those layers.

8   Click in the center of the blue band, and type **GALLERY ONE**. Use the Move tool to adjust the position of the type layer if necessary.

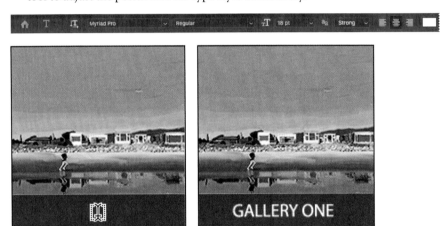

Tip: When multiple layers are selected in the Layers panel, you can also create a layer group from them by clicking the New Group button or by pressing the keyboard shortcut Ctrl+G (Windows) or Command+G (macOS).

9   Select both the GALLERY ONE and Band layers in the Layers panel, and choose Layer > Group Layers.

Photoshop creates a group named Group 1.

10 Double-click the Group 1 layer group, and rename it **Gallery 1**. Then expand the group. The layers you selected are indented, indicating they're part of that group.

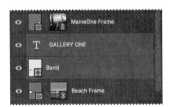
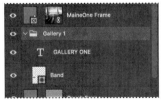

11 Drag the Gallery 1 layer group up so that it's above all of the frame layers.

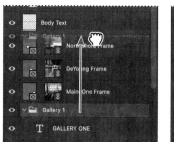 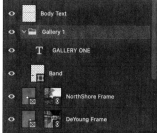

12 Choose File > Save.

Duplicating button bands and text

You've designed the label for one button. You could go through all those steps again to create the band and text for each of the other buttons, but it's faster to duplicate the layer group you created for the first band and text and then edit the copies.

1 In the Layers panel, make sure the Gallery 1 layer group is selected.

2 With the Move tool selected, make sure Auto-Select is not selected in the options bar.

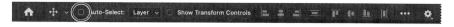

3 With the Move tool, hold down the Alt (Windows) or Option (macOS) key as you drag the Gallery One button to the right, and drop it when it snaps into alignment with the second square frame and its guides.

● **Note:** In the Layers panel, moving a selected layer group moves all layers in it, even if the group's individual layers don't appear selected in the Layers panel. What's important is that the group is selected.

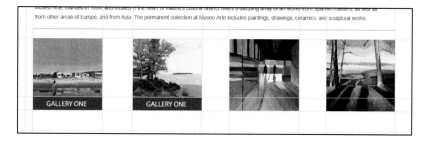

Holding down Alt or Option creates a copy of the selected layer group as you drag it with the Move tool. When you release the mouse button, the copy (Gallery 1 copy) should be selected in the Layers panel.

4 Repeat step 3 by Alt-dragging (Windows) or Option-dragging (macOS) a copy of the second button over the third square frame, and then do it one more time to copy the third button over the fourth square frame, completing the row.

Now edit the text in the three copies to match their images.

5 With the Horizontal Text tool, select the ONE text in the second button, and change ONE so that it now says **GALLERY TWO**.

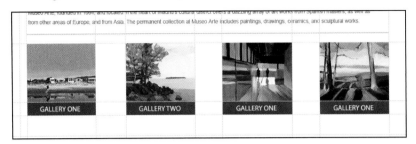

6 Repeat step 5 for the third and fourth buttons so that they say **GALLERY THREE** and **GALLERY FOUR**, respectively.

7 After you finish editing the GALLERY FOUR text, commit the last text edit by selecting the Move tool.

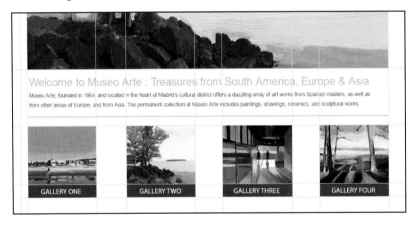

8 In the Layers panel, rename the layer groups to be consistent with their contents:

▶ **Tip:** These steps are easier if you make the Layers panel taller so that you can see multiple expanded layer groups at once.

- Double-click the name of the "Gallery 1 copy" layer group, and name it **Gallery 2**.

- Double-click the name of the "Gallery 1 copy 2" layer group, and name it **Gallery 3**.

- Double-click the name of the "Gallery 1 copy 3" layer group, and name it **Gallery 4**.

Now move each button image into its layer group.

9 In the Layers panel, do the following:

- Drag the Beach Frame layer into the Gallery 1 layer group, below the GALLERY ONE and Band layers.

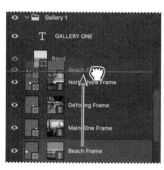 Note: When dragging layers in step 9, position the pointer over the layer name, not the thumbnails, before dragging.

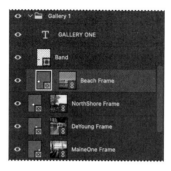

- Drag the upper NorthShore Frame layer into the Gallery 2 layer group, below the GALLERY TWO and Band layers.

- Drag the DeYoung Frame layer into the Gallery 3 layer group, below the GALLERY THREE and Band layers.

- Drag the MaineOne Frame layer into the Gallery 4 layer group, below the GALLERY FOUR and Band layers.

10 Click the arrow next to each of the Gallery layer group icons to collapse them, simplifying the Layers panel display.

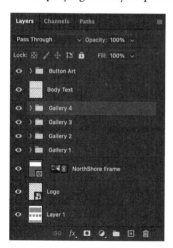

Now you'll add a drop shadow and stroke to improve the appearance of the button.

11 Select the Gallery 1 layer group in the Layers panel. Then, click the Add A Layer Style button (*fx*) at the bottom of the Layers panel, and choose Drop Shadow.

Tip: When you apply a layer style to a group, it applies to all layers in that group. In this book you have now tried applying a layer style to one layer and also to a layer group.

12 In the Layer Style dialog box, change the following settings in the Structure area:

- Opacity: **27**%

- Distance: **9** px

- Spread: **19**%

- Size: **18** px

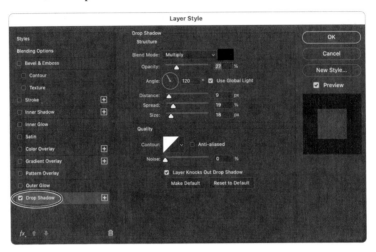

Note: Be sure to click the word "Stroke." If you click only the checkbox, Photoshop applies the layer style with its default settings, but you won't see the options.

13 With the Layer Style dialog box still open, select Stroke on the left, making sure that it's enabled, and apply the following settings:

- Size: **1** px

- Position: Inside

- Color: Click the color swatch to open the Color Picker. Move the pointer outside the Color Picker dialog box so that the pointer becomes a sampler icon (✐), click the blue band to sample its color values and load them into the Color Picker, and click OK.

Tip: The stroke and drop shadow that you applied to the layer group are now listed with that layer group in the Layers panel.

14 Click OK to apply both layer styles and close the Layer Style dialog box.

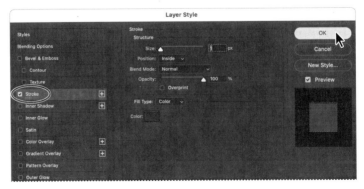

15 In the Layers panel, position the pointer over the fx icon next to the Gallery 1 layer group. Then hold down the Alt (Windows) or Option (macOS) key as you drag the fx icon and drop it on the Gallery 2 layer group. This is a quick way to copy layer effects to another layer or layer group.

▶ **Tip:** Another way to transfer the effects of one layer or layer group to another is to drag its Effects header. That does the same thing as dragging the fx icon.

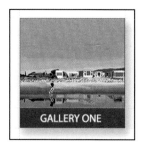
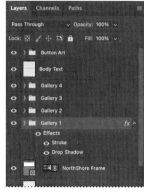
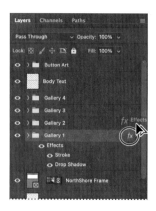

16 Repeat step 15 to copy the layer effects to the Gallery 3 and Gallery 4 layer groups.

17 In the Layers panel, expand the Button Art layer group, and then click the eye icon for the Navigation layer to make it visible. Then collapse the Button Art layer group.

This layer represents the navigation among sections of the museum website.

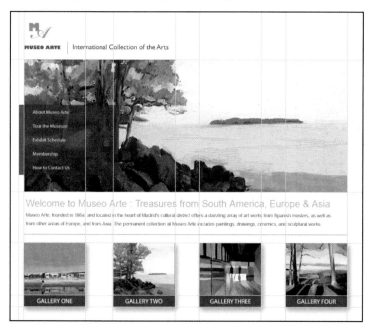

18 Save the file, and then close it.

Automating a multistep task

You can record a set of one or more commands and play it back to apply to a single file or a batch of files. In Photoshop this feature is called an *action*. (Some applications call this kind of feature a *macro*.) In this exercise, you'll create an action that prepares a set of images to serve as buttons for additional galleries on the web page you're designing.

Recording an action

▶ **Tip:** Actions are easy to use, but limited in scope. To automate Photoshop with more control, you can write a script. Photoshop can run scripts written in VBScript (Windows), AppleScript (macOS), or JavaScript (Windows and macOS).

You'll start by recording an action that resizes an image, changes its canvas size, and adds layer styles so that the additional buttons match the ones you've already created. You use the Actions panel to record, play, edit, and delete individual actions. You also use the Actions panel to save and load action files.

There are four images in the Buttons folder that will serve as the basis for new gallery buttons on your website. The images are large, so the first thing you'll need to do is resize them to match the existing buttons. You'll perform each of the steps on the Gallery5.jpg file as you record the action. You'll then play the action to make the same changes on the other images in the folder automatically.

1   Choose File > Open, and navigate to the Lesson13/Buttons folder. Double-click the Gallery5.jpg file to open it in Photoshop.

2   Choose Window > Actions to open the Actions panel. Close the Default Actions set (folder); you'll create and use your own set for this lesson.

3   Click the Create New Set button (□) at the bottom of the Actions panel. In the New Set dialog box, name the set **Buttons**, and click OK.

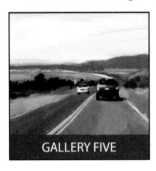
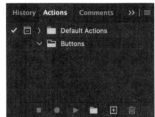

The Default Actions set includes prerecorded sample actions that you can use and study. As you build your own actions, you can organize them by creating action sets.

4   Click the Create New Action button (⊞) at the bottom of the Actions panel. Name the action **Resizing and Styling Images**, and click Record.

It's a good idea to name actions in a way that makes it clear what the actions do so you can find them easily later.

At the bottom of the Actions panel, the Begin
Recording button turns red to let you know that
recording is in progress.

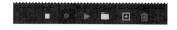

Even though you're recording, there's no need to rush. Take all the time you need
to perform the procedure accurately. Actions don't record in real time; they record
steps as you complete them, but they play them back as quickly as possible.

You'll start by resizing and sharpening the image.

5 Choose Image > Image Size, and do the following:

   • Make sure Resample is selected.

   • For Width, choose Pixels from the units menu, and then change the Width to
     180.

   • Confirm that the Height has changed to **180** pixels. It should, because
     original proportions are preserved using the Constrain Aspect Ratio link icon
     to the left of the Width and Height values, which is selected by default.

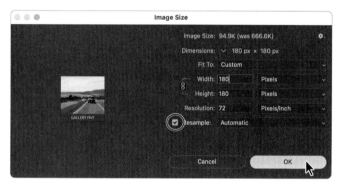

6 Click OK.

7 Choose Filter > Sharpen > Smart Sharpen, apply the following settings, and
   click OK:

   • Amount: **100**%

   • Radius: **1.0** px

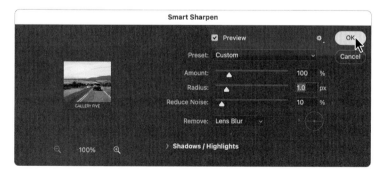

You need to make some additional changes to the image that you can't make as long as the Background layer is locked. You'll convert it to a regular layer.

8 Double-click the Background layer name in the Layers panel. In the New Layer dialog box, name the layer **Button**, and click OK.

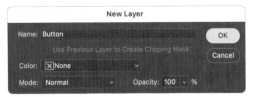 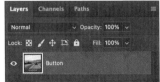

▶ **Tip:** If you want to convert a background layer to a regular layer and you don't need to name it, simply click the Background layer's lock icon in the Layers panel.

When you rename a Background layer, you're converting it to a regular layer, so Photoshop displays the New Layer dialog box. But no layers are added; the Background layer becomes the new layer.

Now that you've converted the Background layer, you can change the canvas size and add layer styles.

9 Choose Image > Canvas Size, and do the following:

▶ **Tip:** Use Canvas Size when you want to add area to or remove area from a document; use Image Size when you want to resample, change the physical dimensions, or change the resolution of a document.

- Make sure the unit of measure is set to Pixels.

- Change the Width to **220** pixels and the Height to **220** pixels.

- Click the center square in the anchor area to ensure the canvas is extended evenly on all sides.

- Click OK.

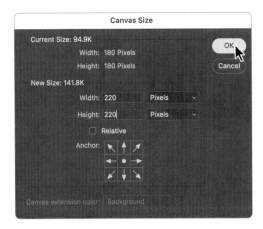 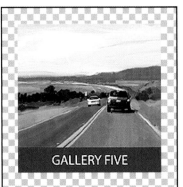

10 Choose Layer > Layer Style > Drop Shadow.

11 In the Layer Style dialog box, apply the following settings:

- Opacity: **27**%

- Angle: **120°**

- Distance: **9** px

- Spread: **19**%

- Size: **18** px

▶ **Tip:** Stay on task while the Actions panel is recording. It records any Photoshop image edits, so if you record unwanted steps, you'll have to edit them out later. The Actions panel doesn't record view changes such as scrolling and zooming.

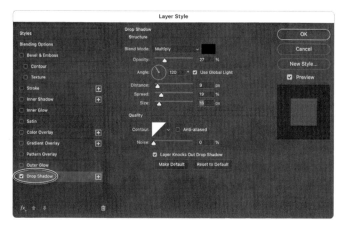

12 With the Layer Style dialog box still open, select Stroke on the left, and apply the following settings:

- Size: **1** px

- Position: Inside

- Color: If the color swatch doesn't already match the other blue band you made, click the color swatch and sample the blue band as you did earlier.

● **Note:** Be sure to click the word "Stroke." If you click only the checkbox, Photoshop applies the layer style with its default settings, but you won't see the options.

13 Click OK to apply both layer styles.

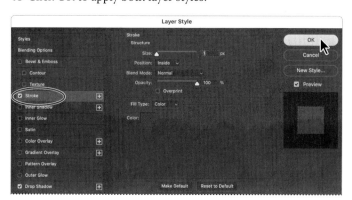

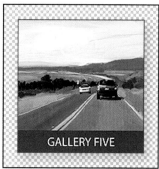

14 Choose File > Save As, choose Photoshop for the Format, and click Save. Click OK if the Photoshop Format Options dialog box appears.

15 Close the file. The Home screen appears, so click the Photoshop icon so that you can see the Actions panel again.

16 Click the Stop Playing/Recording button at the bottom of the Actions panel.

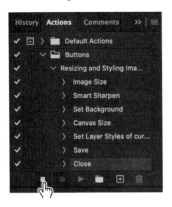

▶ **Tip:** As you review an action, you can edit the sequence by dragging steps, edit steps by double-clicking them (if applicable), or remove unneeded steps by deleting them.

The action you just recorded (Resizing and Styling Images) is now saved in the Buttons set in the Actions panel. Click the arrows to expand different sets of steps. You can examine each recorded step and the specific edits you made.

Batch-playing an action

Applying actions is a timesaving process for performing routine tasks on files, but you can streamline your work even further by applying actions to multiple files at once. You'll apply the action you've created to the three remaining images.

1 Choose File > Open, and navigate to the Lesson13/Buttons folder. Ctrl-select (Windows) or Command-select (macOS) the Gallery6.jpg, Gallery7.jpg, and Gallery8.jpg files, and click Open. They open as tabs in the document window.

2 Choose File > Automate > Batch.

▶ **Tip:** You can create conditional actions that change their behavior based on criteria you define. To do this, choose Insert Conditional from the Actions panel menu.

3 In the Batch dialog box, do the following:
- Confirm that Buttons is chosen in the Set menu and that Resizing and Styling Images—the action you just created—is chosen in the Action menu.
- Choose Opened Files from the Source menu.
- Make sure None is chosen for the Destination.
- Click OK.

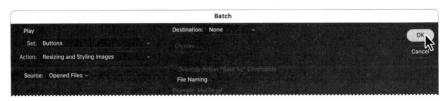

Photoshop plays the action, applying its steps to all the files that are open. You can also apply an action to an entire folder of images without opening them.

Because you saved the file and closed it while you were recording the action, Photoshop saves each of the images as a PSD file in its original folder and then closes the file. After Photoshop closes the last file, the Home screen appears.

Note: If you get an error when running an action, click Stop. There may be a problem with the action that was recorded, especially if you had to correct a mistake while recording. Try troubleshooting or re-recording the action.

Placing files in Photoshop

The four additional button images are ready to be placed into the design. You probably noticed that each already has a blue band with its gallery name included in the image, so you don't need to perform those steps. They're ready to go.

1   If the file 13Working.psd is in the Recent list in the Home screen, click its name to reopen it. If not, choose File > Open to open it.

2   In the Layers panel, select the Gallery 4 layer group name. This ensures that the files about to be placed are not added inside any layer groups, because new layers are added above the selected layer.

3   Choose File > Place Embedded.

You'll place these files as embedded Smart Objects. Because they're embedded, the entire image is copied into the Photoshop file.

4   In the Place Embedded dialog box, navigate to the Lesson13/Buttons folder, and double-click the Gallery5.psd file.

Photoshop places the Gallery5.psd file in the center of the 13Working.psd file. But that's not where you want it to go, so you'll move it.

5   Drag the image into position below the Gallery One button. Use the guides to align the image with the one above. When it's in position, commit the change by pressing Enter or Return.

Note: The bounding box of the placed image is larger than the button, because the bounding box includes the complete extent of the drop shadow.

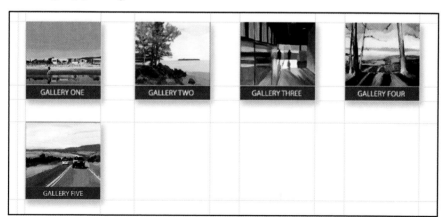

Tip: You can also place embedded files by dragging them into the Photoshop document from the desktop or from other applications. You can drag multiple images to place at once; after you commit one image, the next will be placed.

6 Repeat steps 3–5 to place the Gallery6.psd, Gallery7.psd, and Gallery8.psd files, aligning them below the Gallery Two, Gallery Three, and Gallery Four buttons.

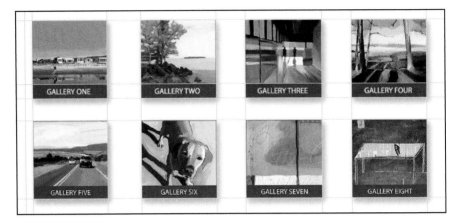

7 You've completed the web page design! Save your work and close the file.

Designing with artboards

Tip: If you want automatic export of layers for web and mobile user interfaces, you might try Adobe Generator. When Adobe Generator is on, Photoshop exports layers to image assets as you work. A layer naming convention controls the specs of the exported assets.

When you're designing websites or user interfaces for mobile devices, you may need to create separate image files for buttons and other content. In Photoshop, you can use the Export As feature to export an entire document or individual layers to web- and mobile-friendly formats including PNG, JPEG, or GIF. In addition to being able to export multiple layers to individual files at once, Export As makes it possible to export to multiple sizes at once if you need to produce sets of images for low- and high-resolution displays.

You may need to coordinate different ideas for a single design, or design variations for different display sizes. This is easier when you use artboards, which are like multiple canvases in a single Photoshop document. You can also use Export As to export entire artboards.

Tip: You may notice or have been taught to use the older Save For Web command in Photoshop. Although that command is still available under File > Export > Save For Web (Legacy), Save For Web can't export multiple layers, artboards, or scaling factors, while Export As can.

With Export As, you control what exports by selecting artboards or layers in the Layers panel.

Duplicating an artboard

You'll use artboards to adapt the design of the museum website for a different screen size. Later, you'll export both designs at once.

1 In the Photoshop Home screen, click Open. Navigate to the Lesson13 folder, and open the file 13Museo.psd.

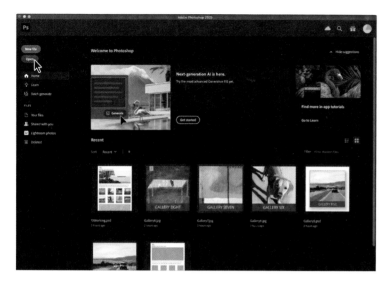

2 Choose File > Save As, rename the file **13Museo_Working.psd**, and click Save. Click OK in the Photoshop Format Options dialog box.

This is a web page that's being adapted for a responsive web design so that it will work well on display sizes from desktops to smartphones.

3 Choose Select > All Layers.

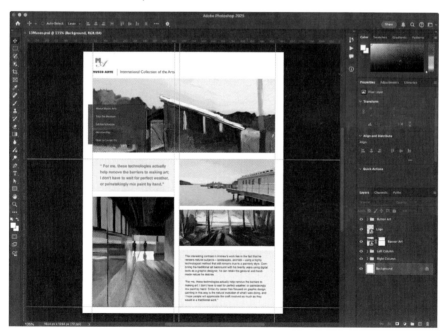

Note: Select > All Layers doesn't select the Background layer, because it's locked by default. However, you will find that step 4 converts the Background layer to Layer 0.

4 Choose Layer > New > Artboard From Layers, name the new artboard **Desktop**, and click OK. The artboard name appears above the new artboard and also on its new artboard group in the Layers panel.

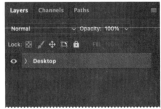

5 Make sure the Artboard tool (⌐) is selected; it's grouped with the Move tool in the Tools panel. Then Alt/Option-click the Add Artboard button to the right of the artboard to duplicate both the Desktop artboard and its contents.

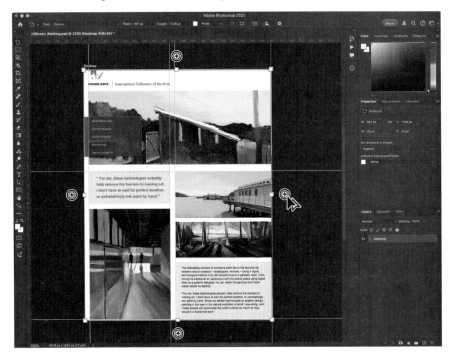

6 In the Layers panel, double-click the name of the duplicate Desktop Copy artboard, and name it **iPhone**.

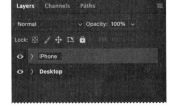

7 In the Properties panel, click the Set Artboard to Preset menu, and choose **iPhone 8/7/6**. That artboard preset applies the pixel dimensions of an iPhone 8, iPhone 7, and iPhone 6 (750 pixels wide by 1334 pixels tall). Now you can develop a design for that iPhone size, using the elements of the Desktop design. It will also be easier to maintain design consistency, because both the desktop and mobile designs are in the same document.

8 Save your work.

Tip: You can choose artboard presets from the Size menu in the options bar when the Artboard tool is selected. If none of the artboard presets matches the display you're designing for, such as a newer model, you can enter your own values for Width and Height in the options bar or Properties panel.

Creating a design variation with artboards

You now have different artboards for desktop and smartphone display sizes; the next task is to fit the desktop-sized objects within the width of the smartphone display's pixel dimensions.

1   In the Layers panel, expand the iPhone artboard, and Shift-select the first and last layers in that artboard only. Don't select the artboard name itself.

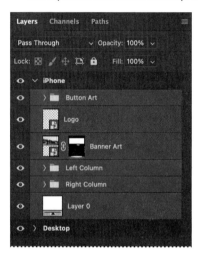

2   Make sure the Artboard tool is selected in the Tools panel, and choose Edit > Free Transform.

3   In the options bar, do the following:

- Click the Toggle Reference Point checkbox to select it; this makes the reference point visible in the transformation bounding box and makes it possible for you to reposition the reference point.

- Select the top-left square of the reference point location option. Scaling, rotating, or other transformations will now be performed from the top-left corner of the bounding box (instead of the center).

- Make sure the Maintain Aspect Ratio button (the link icon) is selected so that the selected layers will scale proportionally.

- Enter **726px** for W (Width).

> **Tip:** You can position the reference point anywhere inside or outside the transformation bounding box by dragging it.

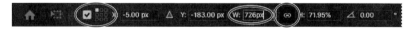

4   Press Enter or Return to apply the new settings to all selected layers as a unit. (Press Enter or Return only once to apply the value in the options bar. If you press Enter or Return a second time, it will commit the transformation.)

Those settings proportionally scale the selected layers to 726 pixels wide, from the top-left corner of the selection, to better fit the artboard.

5 Position the pointer inside the Free Transform bounding box, and then Shift-drag the selected layers down until you can see the entire Museo Arts logo at the top of the page.

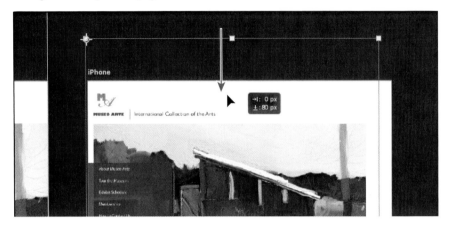

6 Press Enter or Return to exit Free Transform mode, and choose Select > Deselect Layers.

7 In the Layers panel, select the Logo layer, and choose Edit > Free Transform.

8 Drag the bottom-right handle on the Free Transform bounding box until the transformation values next to the pointer indicate that the logo is 672 pixels wide, matching the width of the other elements. Then press Enter or Return. Enlarging the logo makes it more readable on a smartphone screen.

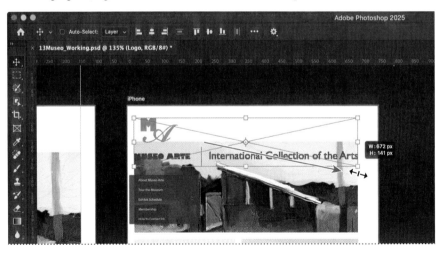

9 In the Layers panel, select the Banner Art, Left Column, and Right Column layers.

10 With the Move tool, Shift-drag the selected layers down until the top is even with the top of the blue button stack on the left.

▶ **Tip:** Remember that you can also nudge selected layers using the arrow keys if that makes it easier to precisely align them with the top of the blue button stack.

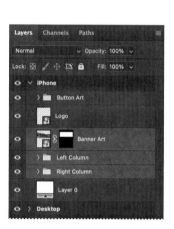

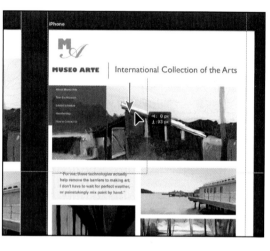

Now you'll take the two-column layout and make each column fill the width of the artboard. But first you'll need to accommodate them by making the artboard taller.

11 Select the iPhone artboard in the Layers panel, and then, with the Artboard tool, drag the bottom handle of the iPhone artboard until the transformation values next to the pointer indicate that it's 2800 px tall.

▶ **Tip:** You can also change the height of an artboard by entering a new Height in the Properties panel when an artboard is selected.

● **Note:** If a document uses artboards, resize them using only the Artboard tool. The Image > Image Size and Image > Canvas Size commands work best with a Photoshop document that doesn't use artboards.

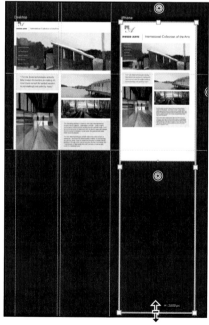

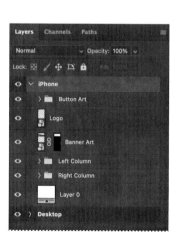

12 Select the Right Column layer group in the Layers panel, and then choose Edit > Free Transform.

13 In the options bar, do the following:

- Make sure the Toggle Reference Point checkbox is selected, and then select the top-right square of the reference point location option.

- Make sure the Maintain Aspect Ratio (link) button is selected, and enter **672px** for Width.

- Press Enter or Return to apply the new width.

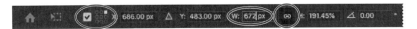

14 Position the pointer inside the Free Transform bounding box, and then Shift-drag the selected layer group down until the transformation values next to the pointer indicate a vertical move of 1200 px (the Y value in the options bar should say about 1680 px when the top-right square of the reference point locator is selected). Press Enter or Return to commit and exit the transformation.

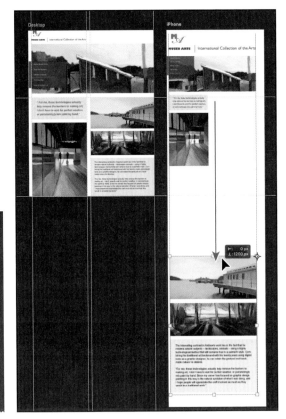

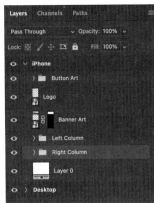

15 Select the Left Column layer group in the Layers panel, and then choose Edit > Free Transform.

16 In the options bar, do the following:

- Make sure the Toggle Reference Point checkbox is selected, and then select the top-left square of the reference point location option.

- Make sure the Maintain Aspect Ratio (link) button is selected, and enter **672px** for Width.

- Press Enter or Return to apply the new width.

- Then press Enter or Return to commit and exit the transformation.

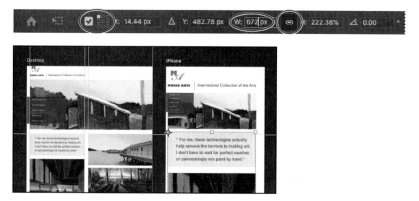

Feel free to adjust the positioning and the vertical spacing among the layer groups and layers.

17 Choose View > Fit On Screen to see both artboards at once, and then save your work.

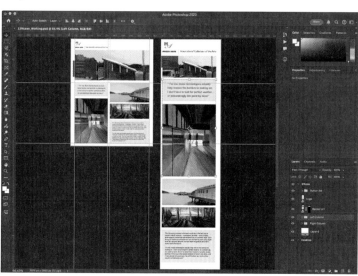

▶ **Tip:** To nudge selected layers or layer groups when the Move tool is active, press the arrow keys. When Free Transform is active, you can also nudge by clicking in a number field and pressing the up arrow or down arrow key.

You've adapted a desktop-sized, multicolumn web page layout for a single-column smartphone layout. Both layouts exist on two artboards in the same document.

Exporting artboards with Export As (File menu)

When it's time to have a client review your designs, you can use the Export As command to easily export any artboard, layer, or layer group into its own file. You'll export the complete desktop and smartphone artboards, and then you'll export the layers of each artboard to their own folder.

1   Choose File > Export > Export As. This command exports each whole artboard so you see each artboard in the list on the left side of the Export As dialog box.

Note: The Export As dialog box doesn't preview multiple Scale All options. Artboards are previewed at 1x.

You can preview the exported dimensions and file size of each item; the preview is determined by the settings on the right side of the Export As dialog box.

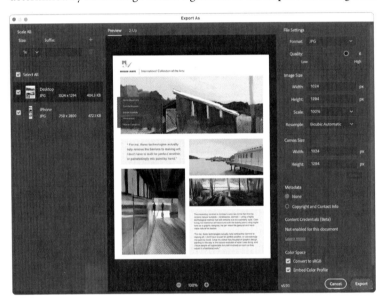

Tip: Not sure about the best combination of format, compression, and visual quality? Click the 2-up tab at the top of the Export As dialog box to see two views. Select one view and change the settings; then select the other view and change its settings. Now you can compare their quality, and you can see the resulting file size below each preview.

2   In the list on the left, click the Desktop artboard to highlight it, and then set the Export As options to the following:

- In the Scale All section, make sure Size is set to 1x and Suffix is empty.
- In the File Settings section, choose JPG from the Format menu, and make sure Quality is set to **6**.
- In the Color Space section, make sure Convert To sRGB is selected.
- Other settings can be left at the defaults.

3   In the list on the left, click the iPhone artboard to highlight it, and apply the same settings as in step 2.

4 Make sure Select All is selected, click Export, navigate to the Assets folder inside the Lesson13 folder, and then click Save or Open.

Tip: If you often use the Export As command with the same settings, choose File > Export > Export Preferences, and specify the settings you use the most. Now you can export to those settings in one step by choosing File > Export > Quick Export As or choosing Quick Export As (*Format*) from the Layers panel menu.

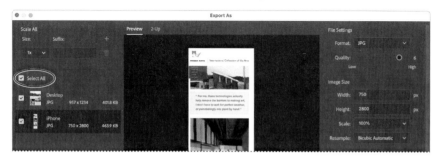

5 Switch to the desktop or Bridge, and open the Assets folder in the Lesson13 folder to see the Desktop.jpg and iPhone.jpg files representing each artboard. The filenames are based on the artboard names. You can send those files for review by a client or web development team.

6 Switch back to Photoshop.

Exporting layers as assets with Export As (Layer menu)

If the reviewers approve the design, you can then use Export As to create separate files for each layer on each artboard, such as images or buttons. Those assets can be used by a web or application developer who executes the design in code.

1 In the Layers panel, Shift-select all layers of the Desktop artboard.

2 Choose Layer > Export As. (Do not choose File > Export As.)

Notice that in the Export As dialog box, each layer is listed separately, because they will export separately.

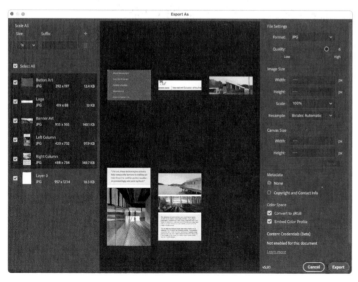

3 Click Button Art to highlight it; then hold down Shift and click Right Column to highlight the five top layers. Now when you adjust settings in the following steps, those changes will affect all highlighted layers.

4 In the Export As dialog box, enter the same settings as you did in step 2 of the previous section (on page 360).

5 Deselect the checkbox for Layer 0 so that it will not export. It's a solid white background that should be implemented through the web page code itself.

6 Click Export, navigate to the Assets_Desktop folder in the Lesson13 folder, and click Open or Save.

You have exported all assets for the Desktop artboard into a single folder.

7 Repeat steps 1–4 for the iPhone artboard.

8 Click Export, navigate to the Assets_iPhone folder in the Lesson13 folder, and click Open or Save.

▶ **Tip:** If a developer asks for assets at multiple scale factors (for Retina/HiDPI display resolutions), in the Export As dialog box click the plus button in the Scale All section to add and specify additional scale factors (Size) such as 2x or 3x. Those will be exported at the same time. Be sure to specify the proper option in the Suffix field for each scale factor.

9 In Photoshop, choose File > Browse In Bridge.

10 Navigate to the Assets_Desktop folder in the Lesson13 folder, and inspect the images by browsing each file with the Preview panel open. If you want, you can also inspect the assets you exported to the Assets_iPhone folder.

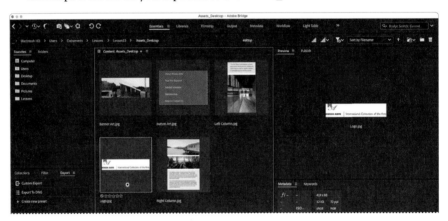

Each layer you exported is in its own file. You were able to quickly produce two different sets of files for two different screen sizes:

- By using the file-based Export As command (File > Export > Export As), you created JPG images of the complete desktop and iPhone artboards.

- By using the layer-based Export As command (on the Layers panel menu or Layer > Export As), you created assets from the individual layers of each artboard.

11 In Photoshop, save your changes, and close the document.

Review questions

1 What is a layer group?

2 What is an action? How do you create one?

3 How can you create assets from layers and layer groups in Photoshop?

Review answers

1 A layer group is a set of layers organized as a unit in the Layers panel. Layer groups make it easier to work with layers in complex images, especially when there are sets of layers that need to stay together when moved or scaled.

2 An action is a set of one or more commands that you record and then play back to apply to a single file or a batch of files. To create one, click the Create New Action button in the Actions panel, name the action, and click Record. Then perform the tasks you want to include in your action. When you've finished, click the Stop Recording button at the bottom of the Actions panel.

3 Use the Export As command to create assets from artboards, layers, and layer groups in Photoshop. To create images of each whole artboard, choose the Export As command on the File menu (File > Export > Export As). To create assets from selected layers and layer groups, choose the Export As on the Layers panel menu or Layer menu (Layer > Export As).

14 EDITING FOR CONSISTENT COLOR

Lesson overview

In this lesson, you'll learn how to do the following:

- Set up basic color management settings.

- Understand how color reproduction differs across media such as printers, presses, and displays.

- Inspect and edit image colors while viewing a document through a simulation of printable colors.

- Prepare an image to print on a color printer.

- Save an image as a Photoshop PDF file for commercial printing.

This lesson will take less than an hour to complete. To get the lesson files used in this chapter, download them from the web page for this book at peachpit.com/PhotoshopCIB2025. For more information, see "Accessing the lesson files and Web Edition" in the Getting Started section at the beginning of this book.

As you work on this lesson, you'll preserve the start files. If you need to restore the start files, download them from your Account page.

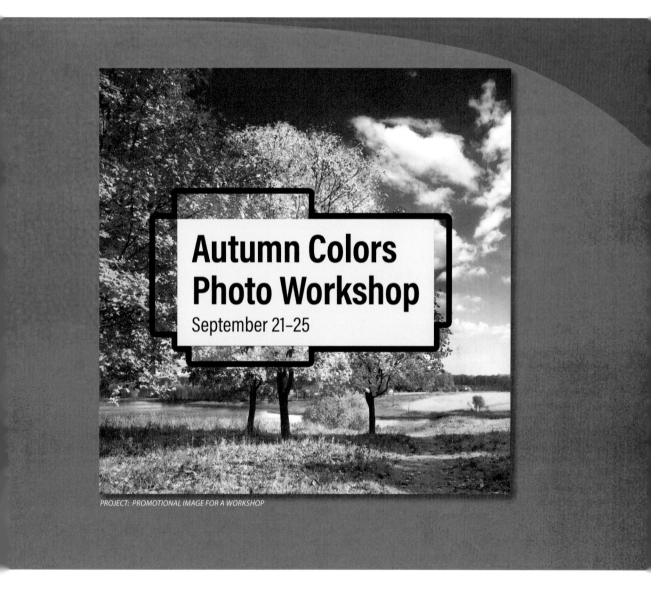

**Autumn Colors
Photo Workshop**
September 21–25

PROJECT: PROMOTIONAL IMAGE FOR A WORKSHOP

How colors appear can vary depending on the media that reproduces it, from different desktop and mobile displays to printers and traditional printing presses. To produce consistent color, edit in a standard color space that's consistent with your final delivery media, and use soft-proofing to simulate and preview what those colors look like on different media.

Understanding digital color reproduction

It's natural to assume that if you specify a certain color value, such as a sky blue or a neon green, it will look the same everywhere. But it won't. In reality, the way a color looks depends on the limitations of the media reproducing that color, such as a display or ink on paper. You've seen this if you've gone shopping for televisions, when you see the same program is shown on twenty TVs on a store shelf but the colors are different on various TVs.

For a computer display, television, or smartphone, color reproduction depends on the color range that can be reproduced by a specific model and its settings.

● **Note:** Print professionals often talk in terms of a *substrate* because ink is not always printed on paper. Sometimes ink is printed on a vinyl banner or clothing or metal such as a beverage can.

For prints, color reproduction depends on the color range that can be reproduced by a specific combination of printer, ink, and substrate such as paper.

It can be frustrating when a color created on a computer screen doesn't look that way on a smartphone or in print. Some media is less capable of reproducing color, and some very vivid colors can't be reproduced in all media. Photoshop has tools that can help you simulate how colors look in different media so that you can adjust colors as much as you can for the limitations of various media.

Getting started

You'll prepare a document for reproduction on various media, including a CMYK press. First, start Photoshop, and restore its default preferences.

1   Start Photoshop, and then simultaneously hold down Ctrl+Alt+Shift (Windows) or Command+Option+Shift (Mac) to restore the default preferences. (See "Restoring default preferences" on page 5.)

2   When prompted, click Yes to delete the Adobe Photoshop Settings file.

3   Choose File > Open, navigate to the Lesson14 folder, and double-click the 14Start.psd file. Close any messages that appear about new features.

● **Note:** If Photoshop displays a dialog box telling you about the difference between saving to Cloud Documents and On Your Computer, click Save On Your Computer. You can also select Don't Show Again, but that setting will deselect after you reset Photoshop preferences.

4   Choose File > Save As, navigate to the Lesson14 folder, and save the file as **14Working.psd**. Click OK if the Photoshop Format Options dialog box appears.

This document is a promotional image for a photography workshop. The designer chose an autumn scene using many colors that are vivid to start with, and amplified them using blending modes and by increasing saturation. The square image is intended to be posted on social media and printed as a postcard and poster. On the screen it looks great, but you'll check it against how well its colors can be reproduced in different media, adjust it as needed, and then learn about printing it and exporting it for different media while maintaining color consistency.

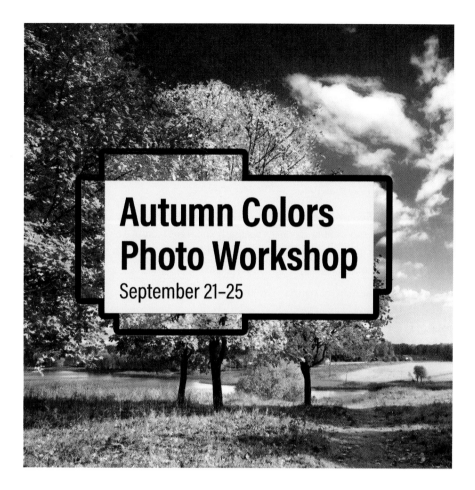

About color management

It's good to first understand a technology that helps maintain consistent color across software and devices. That technology is called *color management*, and it's built into many operating systems and applications.

Color management is necessary because of the very different ways that various devices and media reproduce color. Some media, such as displays, use the RGB color model, and other media such as printing presses use CMYK. The RGB and CMYK color models use different methods to display colors, so each reproduces a different color *gamut* (color range). RGB creates color using transmitted light such as in a backlit digital display or TV, and CMYK creates color through the way that an ink and paper combination reflects and absorbs light. These differences determine the gamut each color model can reproduce. In general, RGB can reproduce more colors than CMYK; for example CMYK is not large enough to reproduce highly saturated blue or neon green. However, both color models can reproduce certain color ranges that the other cannot.

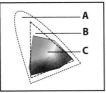

A. *Natural color gamut*
B. *RGB color gamut*
C. *CMYK color gamut*

RGB color model.

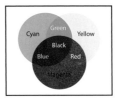

CMYK color model.

Tip: Some color spaces are specific to a device or output conditions, such as a printer. Other color spaces, such as Adobe RGB, are designed to accommodate the color ranges of different media and devices, and to be flexible for editing.

Note: Your monitor may have been factory-calibrated, but you may not know how precisely and to what standard. For example, if your print service provider recommends that your monitor use the common prepress standard of a D65 white point, how do you know how well your monitor meets that standard? To make sure, calibrate and profile your monitor with D65 set as the target standard.

There are also differences within RGB and CMYK. Each monitor and printer model is built differently, so each reproduces a slightly different gamut. For example, one brand of monitor may produce slightly brighter blues than another, so each has a slightly different native *color space* within the RGB color model.

The color management system in Windows, macOS, and Photoshop uses International Color Consortium (ICC) *color profiles*. A color profile describes a color space, such as a common RGB editing space, the color space of your display, and the CMYK color space of a press standard. Color profiles make it easy to use all of these different color spaces at the same time because they work like translators,

RGB color model

Much of the visible color spectrum can be represented by mixing red, green, and blue (RGB) colored light in various proportions and intensities. Where the colors overlap, they create cyan, magenta, yellow, and white.

Because the RGB colors combine to create white, they are also called *additive* colors. Adding all colors together creates white—that is, all light is transmitted back to the eye. Additive colors are used for lighting, video, and monitors. For example, an LCD monitor creates color by emitting its backlight through red, green, and blue filters.

CMYK color model

The CMYK model is based on the light-absorbing quality of ink printed on a substrate (surface) such as paper or packaging. As white light strikes translucent inks, part of the spectrum is absorbed, while other parts are reflected back to your eyes.

In theory, pure cyan (C), magenta (M), and yellow (Y) pigments should combine to absorb all color and produce black. For this reason, these colors are called *subtractive* colors. But because all printing inks contain some impurities, these three inks actually produce a muddy brown and must be combined with black (K) ink to produce a denser black. (K is used instead of B to avoid confusion with blue.) These are called *process colors* because they are used in four-color process printing.

helping to keep color appearance consistent as the document's color values are reproduced by the color spaces of your document, different displays, and different printers. You can use Photoshop to embed a profile into an image file so that other applications can consistently interpret the colors of your images.

Which color space should you use for your images?

You might have heard of sRGB, Adobe RGB, and P3, which are commonly used color spaces. Many cameras and smartphones save images using these color spaces, and for many projects it's acceptable to edit in any of those color spaces. You're more likely to leave an image in its original color space and edit it in that, and convert to different color spaces when exporting or saving copies for different media.

If an image is intended to take advantage of high-end displays, TVs, or printers that can display a wider range of colors, you have the option of creating and editing it using what's called a *wide gamut* color space such as Adobe RGB, P3, or ProPhoto RGB. Working with wide gamut color works best when you understand how the entire workflow will handle wide gamut color; for example, you may need to work with the document set to 16 bits per channel instead of 8 bits per channel, and edit while viewing images on a wide gamut display (which is becoming more common).

Setting up color management defaults for Photoshop

In Photoshop, the Color Settings dialog box is initially set up for frequently used RGB-based workflows such as production for the web, social media, and general printing. If those are the media you usually edit for, you might not need to change anything in Color Settings. Sometimes, when preparing artwork for printing on a CMYK press, a printing company might require you to change specific settings to be consistent with their CMYK-based prepress requirements. When you have special production requirements, override the default options in Color Settings as needed.

When a color profile is embedded in a document, Photoshop uses that profile as the document working space instead of the Working Space setting. Color Settings options apply mostly when you start a new empty document or when you open an image that doesn't contain an embedded profile.

You'll temporarily change the default color settings to a preset designed for more traditional CMYK prepress workflows.

1   Choose Edit > Color Settings to open the Color Settings dialog box.

2   Without clicking (don't change settings), hover the pointer over each part of the dialog box, including the names of sections (such as Working Spaces), the menu names, and the menu options. As you move the pointer, Photoshop displays information about each item in the Description area at the bottom of the Color Settings dialog box.

Note: ICC color profiles are widely used for print production, and to a lesser extent for web and other digital media. Video production and other non-print workflows may use other color systems to maintain consistent color.

Tip: If you need to specify a combination of Color Settings that doesn't match any of the built-in Settings presets, set up Color Settings the way you want and click the Save button to save the preset. To load a preset file, such as one provided to you by a printing company, click the Load button.

Tip: The Color Settings dialog box can seem complex. Remember that the only thing you usually need to do is pick the Settings preset that most closely matches your current workflow. Each Settings preset changes the other options for you. If you're working with a print service provider, they might recommend specific settings that work best with their equipment.

3 Choose the North America Prepress 2 preset from the Settings menu. Notice that many of the settings for working spaces and color-management policies change, such as how Photoshop handles color for imported or pasted content.

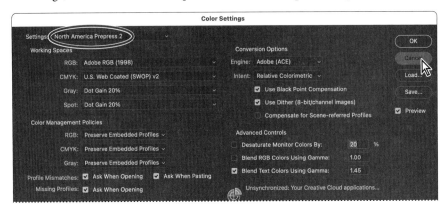

● **Note:** If you clicked OK in step 4, choose Edit > Color Settings, then in the Settings menu choose North America General Purpose 2, and then click OK.

You won't save this change, because leaving it set to North America Prepress 2 may display warnings you aren't expecting if you don't normally use that workflow.

4 Click Cancel so that the settings aren't permanently changed.

About calibration and profiling

Calibration means adjusting a device to meet a standard, like making sure a monitor displays neutral gray when neutral gray color values are sent to it. A *profile* describes whether the device meets a standard and, if not, how far off it is so that a color management system can correct for the difference and show image colors accurately.

To get the most out of color management, calibrate and profile your monitor so that you evaluate color on a screen using an accurate display profile. You can use calibration/profiling software that drives a color measurement device. The software uses the device to measure the colors produced by your screen and corrects for inaccuracies by creating a customized ICC display profile of your monitor. Your system uses this display profile to show colors accurately in any software that is color-managed, such as Photoshop and most other Adobe graphics software.

▶ **Tip:** When you're concerned about how a color might reproduce on press, you can ask your prepress service provider about seeing a *hard proof*, a test print calibrated for the exact press conditions.

Checking colors for the final medium

The color range covered by typical CMYK printing can reproduce many but not all of the colors in an RGB image from a digital camera or scanner. For example, colored LED lights or vivid flowers may produce colors that are outside the gamut that a CMYK printer can reproduce. Those colors may print with less detail and saturation than expected. Some intense blue colors in RGB can shift toward purple in CMYK.

You'll view an onscreen simulation of what the open document's colors will look like when printed. Choosing a profile that properly represents the final output lets you proof on the screen (*soft-proof*). This simulation is based on a *proof setup*, which defines the output conditions (in this case, the printing conditions). Photoshop provides settings that can help you proof images for different uses, such as for different printers and devices. For this lesson, you'll create a custom proof setup. You can then save the settings for use on other images that will be output the same way.

Tip: If a document has no embedded profile, the status bar says "Untagged" and it displays colors using the Working Space in Color Settings.

It's useful to understand what color space your document currently uses; this is the same as asking if a document has an embedded color profile. The quickest way to see this is to change what's showing in the status bar.

1   In the status area at the bottom of the document window, click the arrow there and choose Document Profile from the pop-up menu that appears.

Tip: The status bar is especially useful when you have multiple documents open and each has a different color profile, because the status bar can show you each document's profile at a glance.

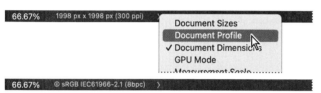

The status bar now says "© sRGB IEC61966-2.1 (8bpc)". Similar to the document tab, it displays multiple types of information in one line:

© indicates that the document contains copyright metadata, which you can inspect by choosing File > File Info.

sRGB IEC61966-2.1 is the full name of the document color profile; for simplicity it's usually called just "sRGB".

(8bpc) indicates that the document is 8 bits per channel.

Tip: Inexpensive home/office printers might not install print profiles; for those devices soft proofing may not be useful. Print profiles are generally available for high-end color printers intended for photography and graphic design and for commercial print service providers.

2   Choose View > Proof Setup > Custom. The Customize Proof Condition dialog box opens. Make sure Preview is selected.

3   From the Device To Simulate menu, choose the profile Working CMYK–U.S. Web Coated (SWOP) v2 as an example for this lesson. For your own work, choose a profile that represents your own project's output conditions, such as a profile for a specific combination of printer, ink, and paper.

4   Make sure Preserve Numbers is *not* selected. This option is more for advanced color conversions and isn't typically used for normal printing

Tip: When the Customize Proof Condition dialog box isn't open, you can view the document with or without the current proof settings by selecting or deselecting the View > Proof Colors command.

5 Make sure Relative Colorimetric is selected for Rendering Intent.

A rendering intent determines how the color is converted from one color space to another. Relative Colorimetric is commonly used because it preserves color relationships while minimizing color shifts. Perceptual is the second most commonly used and sometimes provides a better color conversion; you can try both.

6 Select Simulate Black Ink if it's available for the profile you chose. Then deselect it and select Simulate Paper Color; selecting this option automatically selects Simulate Black Ink.

When the Preview option is enabled, the blue sky and many of the highly saturated autumn colors simulate the color gamut limits in the CMYK profile selected in the Device To Simulate menu. The settings can also make the image appear to lose contrast. Most paper is not pure white; Paper Color simulates that. Most black ink is not perfectly solid or neutral black, so Black Ink simulates the actual ink. Both get that information from the selected profile in Proof Setup.

> ▶ **Tip:** You might wonder how the colors in CMYK-printed posters and magazines look so vivid if they are subject to the same CMYK limitations. One answer is that the CMYK colors would not look as good if you were able to see the original full range images next to them.

Don't be alarmed by the loss of saturation and contrast. The image might look worse, but the soft-proofing simulation is just being honest about how the image will actually print; light reflecting off of paper and ink simply cannot reproduce the same range of tones and colors as a display that emits its own light. Choosing higher-quality paper stock and inks can help a printed image look more like it's shown on a screen.

> ● **Note:** Soft-proofing is most commonly done for jobs intended for print, but you can also soft-proof any non-print profile that's listed, such as sRGB or the video standard rec.709. For example, this can be useful when you want to see how colors in an image using a wide gamut such as Adobe RGB will change when exported to a smaller non-print color gamut such as the widely used sRGB gamut.

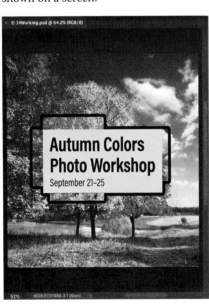

Original RGB image.

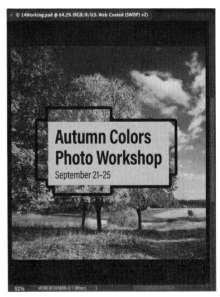

Image with Proof Setup options for a CMYK print.

7 Toggle the Preview option to see the difference between the image as it is displayed onscreen and as it will print, based on the profile you selected. Then click OK.

About gamut warnings

In Photoshop, the command View > Gamut Warning displays a gray highlight where an image color is outside (can't be reproduced by) the gamut of the color profile that's set up in the View > Proof Setup submenu. If you enable the Gamut Warning command and significant image areas are marked as out of gamut, you may want to inspect those areas using a soft proof (on screen) or hard proof (calibrated test print). If the proof visually indicates that meaningful color details will be lost in the out of gamut areas, then you can decide to adjust those areas. However, before making edits, verify that the current Proof Setup profile represents the final medium you're checking against (such as an inkjet printer or a press), because what the gamut warning marks is based on that profile's color space.

You don't always have to spend time adjusting colors indicated as out of gamut, as long as those colors look acceptable in a proof and don't lose important detail. It's a higher priority to address meaningful out-of-gamut colors, such as brand colors. A soft proof or hard proof is much more important than a gamut warning, because you can see how colors marked as out-of-gamut actually look.

If you use the Gamut Warning command and want to customize the highlight color, adjust the Gamut Warning color in the Transparency & Gamut panel of the Preferences dialog box in Photoshop.

▶ **Tip:** Quickly toggle the View > Proof Colors command by using its keyboard shortcut: Press Ctrl-Y (Windows) or Command-Y (macOS). Remember to make sure an appropriate output profile is set up in the View > Proof Setup > Custom command.

8   Click the View menu, and if the Proof Colors command is enabled, choose that command to disable it. This is a quick way to enable or disable the soft-proof settings that you set up in the Customize Proof Condition dialog box.

Inspecting document color values

If you'll be editing images for print, it's useful to know how to find out about color values in important areas of the document and how they change for final output. First you'll save and edit a copy of the document intended only to be sent for printing under the conditions described by the current Proof Setup profile.

1   Choose File > Save As, navigate to the Lesson14 folder, and save the file as **14Press.psd**. Click OK if the Photoshop Format Options dialog box appears.

2   Choose Window > Arrange > New Window For 14Press.psd. Another document tab appears. This isn't a new document, it's a second view of the same document.

3   Choose Window > Arrange > 2 Up Vertical so that the two views are side-by-side.

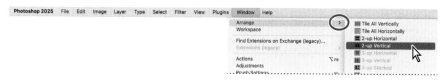

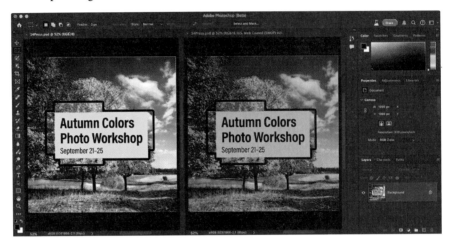

> **Tip:** If you're not sure which tab has Proof Colors enabled, remember to check each document tab; the one ending in a profile name uses Proof Colors.

4 If View > Proof Colors is currently set the same way for both views, toggle the command in either view so that one view shows the document's native RGB tones and colors, and the other view simulates colors through the current Proof Setup settings.

Inspecting color values under the pointer

You can use the Info panel to inspect the color values of the pixels under the pointer, and you can customize how it reports those color values.

1 If the Info panel isn't open, choose Window > Info.

The Info panel is useful for showing you the color values under the pointer. The top of the Info panel shows two color readouts at the current pointer position. You can customize what they report.

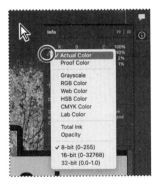

> **Tip:** Remember that the Info panel can help when you precisely edit tones and colors in different color modes. For example, if you often edit grayscale ("black and white") photos, you might want to set an Info panel readout to Grayscale.

2 In the Info panel, click the first eyedropper, and on the menu that appears, make sure Actual Color is selected. Notice the many types of color values it can display. This document is in RGB mode, so Actual Color shows RGB values.

3 In the Info panel, click the second eyedropper, and on the menu that appears, make sure Proof Color is selected. This will now display the color values in the color space of the profile that's selected in the Proof Setup dialog box.

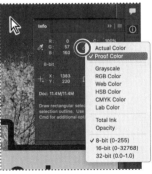

As you hover the pointer over different areas of the active document canvas, the two color readouts in the Info panel now let you immediately compare the original color values at that position with what the color values will be if it's converted to the color space in Proof Setup. For example, the RGB blue in the sky converts to mostly cyan and magenta in CMYK. This information can be useful if a print service provider is helping you resolve a color reproduction issue.

If the Info panel isn't changing during these exercises, make sure the pointer is in the active document. For this exercise it doesn't matter whether you do the steps in the left or right document tab; what's important is that you're working in the active document (the highlighted document tab).

Adding color samplers to track color values continuously

When you want to keep an eye on color values in specific positions in the image as you work, you can add color samplers that stay where you add them.

1   In the Tools panel, select the Eyedropper tool (🖋), position it in the active document in the blue sky above the letter "u" in the word "Autumn," and hold down Shift as you click to add a new color sampler there.

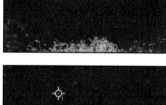

▶ **Tip:** To delete a color sampler, hold down Alt and Shift (Windows) or Option and Shift (macOS) as you hover the pointer over a sampler. When a scissors (cut) pointer appears next to the pointer, click the color sampler to delete it.

Notice that when you hold down Shift, a plus sign appears next to the Eyedropper tool pointer, indicating that clicking will add a new sampler there.

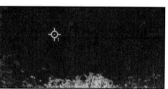

After you click, a new readout labeled "#1" appears in the Info panel below the X/Y coordinate readout. The new readout represents the color sampler you just added.

2   Position the Eyedropper tool over the darker tree leaves above the letter "u" in the word "Autumn" on the canvas, and Shift-click to add another color sampler.

In the Info panel, color samplers #1 and #2 now track color values in the sky and leaves, respectively.

3   In the Info panel, click the eyedropper icon for color sampler #1 and set it to Proof Color; repeat this for color sampler #2.

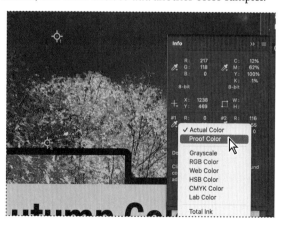

▶ **Tip:** If a print service provider advises you to keep CMYK colors below a certain ink limit percentage, you can set an Info panel color sampler readout to Total Ink. Keeping the Total Ink value below the printer's ink limit prevents a situation where excessive ink levels saturate the paper, making the job print badly or the paper falls apart in the press.

Editing while simulating final output

You don't necessarily have to live with the soft-proofing result as it is. You can try to optimize the colors of a document for its specific output conditions. That will be easier now that you've set up both a visual simulation (soft proof) and color value readouts (from the color samplers) that tell you how colors should translate to the profile selected in the Proof Colors dialog box. You'll see how saturation affects the original and CMYK versions of the image.

▶ **Tip:** When you compare views side-by-side, you can change both views at the same time. When using the Zoom tool, in the options bar select Zoom All Windows; when using the Hand tool, in the options bar select Scroll All Windows.

1 In the Adjustments panel, in the Single Adjustments list click Vibrance. A new Vibrance adjustment layer appears in the Layers panel, and the Properties panel now displays options for Vibrance and Saturation.

2 Zoom in and reposition both views so that you can clearly see the two color samplers and the areas around them, side-by-side.

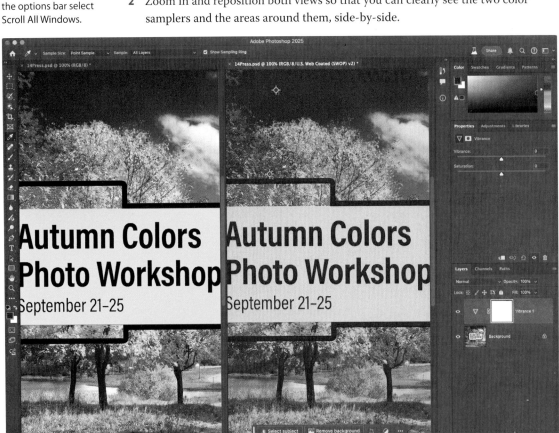

3 Keep an eye on the details in the darker tree leaves in the image as you slowly drag the Saturation slider back and forth between 0 and about 50.

What you should see is that there is a Saturation value above which color details in the dark leaves disappear; they all become the same flat color because they're hitting the wall of the color space. That's as saturated as they can get, the colors are being *clipped* by the limit of the color gamut. Notice that the clipping happens sooner in the view where Proof Colors is on, because the currently selected profile, U.S. Web Coated (SWOP) v2, cannot reproduce as much of those colors' saturation as sRGB.

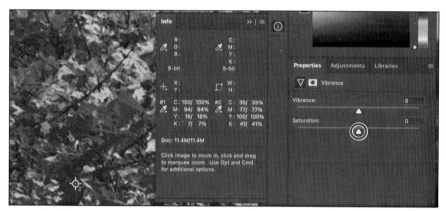

Leaves have detail.

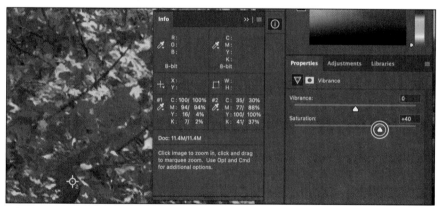

Color detail lost, leaves now look flat.

4 Continue moving the Saturation slider between 0 and 50 as you watch the readouts for color samplers #1 and #2. Notice that one reason the CMYK values can't go as high is because inks such as cyan and magenta are already at 100%.

5 You can decide how far to push Saturation or Vibrance without losing color detail. We chose to leave both values at **0** because the colors are already quite saturated and near the edge of the color gamut of the profile selected for Proof Colors.

If you are working on a project that will be printed on a press and you're not satisfied with how the colors look through a soft-proof simulation of the press profile, your print service provider may be able to suggest adjustments that work well on their equipment.

▶ **Tip:** If you want to adjust just some colors, choose Select > Color Range to create a selection from a specific range of colors or tones. If you apply Color Range when the mask of an adjustment is selected, the range selection edits that mask.

Preparing files for printing

Whether you'll print the document on your own printer or send it to a printing service, you should perform the following tasks before printing.

- Understand how the printing conditions affect how you prepare your image, ideally before the work is complete. If you're going to send your work to a print service provider, ask in advance about their technical requirements, such as any color limitations and what file format they prefer. In some cases, they may request a file exported to a specific Adobe Portable Document Format (PDF) standard or preset.

- Verify that the image resolution is appropriate. For professional printing, a good guideline is 300 ppi at an image's final printed dimensions. This value can be different depending on factors such as the screening method used for the press, or the grade of paper. To determine the best print resolution for your project, consult your production team, print service provider, or printer user manual.

- Do a "zoom test": Zoom into the image to check and correct sharpness, color correction, noise, and other issues that can affect the final printed image quality.

- If you want any part of a design to print all the way to the edge of the page, set up a *bleed* (extending the artwork past the page edge) for the document. A bleed ensures that there isn't an unprinted gap at the page edge if the page is trimmed a little wide of the crop marks. You may need to extend the canvas and the design on all sides, typically by ¼ inch. For files you send out, your print service provider can recommend the bleed amount that works best on their equipment. When printing on a desktop printer that offers a "borderless" option, the printer driver software typically creates the bleed by slightly enlarging the print to extend it beyond the edges of the selected paper size.

- Keep images in their original color space, such as Adobe RGB (see "About Color Management" on page 367), unless your print service provider instructs you to convert them. If you do, convert copies of the images, not the originals. Today, many prepress workflows keep content in its original color space throughout editing to preserve color flexibility as long as possible, converting images and documents to CMYK automatically during printing.

- Before flattening Photoshop documents, always ask your production team first. Some workflows may depend on preserving, not flattening, Photoshop layers so that other applications, such as Adobe InDesign, can control the visibility of imported Photoshop layers from within their documents.

- Soft-proof the image to simulate onscreen how the colors will print.

Converting an image to CMYK

So far, you've been working with a document that is in the RGB color mode and only being previewed through a CMYK color profile. If you are asked to convert the final version to CMYK, it's generally a good idea to work in RGB mode as long as possible so that your edits can take advantage of the larger RGB color gamut. Also, some filters and other features work in RGB mode but not in CMYK mode. So if the original document is in RGB mode keep it that way while editing, especially if you also want to output the image to an inkjet printer or distribute it digitally later.

Tip: If you aren't sure if or when you should convert images to CMYK, ask the print service provider that will output your job. They can recommend the image preparation steps that work best with their prepress equipment.

1   Close the document tab where Proof Colors is enabled (the one with the profile name in the document tab). You'll work with the usual single view of the document with Proof Colors disabled.

2   Choose View > Fit on Screen.

3   Click the Channels tab to bring the Channels panel to the front.

The image is currently in RGB mode, so three channels are listed: red, green, and blue. The RGB channel is not actually a channel, but a composite of all three. You also see a channel named Vibrance 1 Mask; this channel contains the mask information for the layer currently selected in the Layers panel.

4   Choose Image > Mode > CMYK Color.

5   Click Flatten in the message that warns you that you might lose some adjustment layers. Flattening the layers helps preserve the appearance of colors.

Another message appears, saying: "You are about to convert to CMYK using the 'U.S. Web Coated (SWOP) v2' profile. This may not be what you intend. To choose a different profile, use Edit > Convert To Profile." This message lets you know that the active CMYK profile is U.S. Web Coated (SWOP) v2, the Photoshop default profile for CMYK color. That profile might not represent the actual prepress specification or proofing standard that will be used.

In a real job, you would ask the print service provider which CMYK profile to use for color conversions; they may be able to provide a custom profile that accurately represents how their equipment reproduces tones and colors. You would then load that custom CMYK profile into your operating system's standard location for ICC profiles so that you can select it as the CMYK Working Space in the Edit > Color Settings dialog box or so you can select it when converting the image to CMYK using the more advanced and precise Edit > Convert To Profile command.

6 Click OK in the message about the color profile used in the conversion.

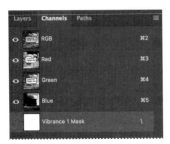 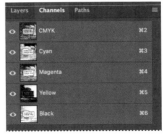

The Channels panel now displays four channels: cyan, magenta, yellow, and black. On top, it lists the composite view of all CMYK channels together. The layers were merged during conversion, so there is only one layer in the Layers panel. The document now appears as it did when you soft-proofed the RGB document to this profile, but because the conversion is permanent, now the original RGB color gamut can't be recovered (except by using the Edit > Undo command or the History panel).

7 In the Channels panel, see what each ink will print by clicking each of the channels in turn: Cyan, Magenta, Yellow, and Black. When you're done, click CMYK to return to the composite view of all channels together.

8 Save the document.

About CMYK color separations

When a document is sent to a CMYK press, each of the CMYK channels becomes *color separated*—sent to its own printing plate. As the paper moves through the press, each of the four plates prints its ink on the paper. Your eyes combine the four inks and see a full color image.

In Photoshop, the Print dialog box includes options that let you print separations for a CMYK document. However, this is usually not useful for previewing a job. A desktop printer's resolution, precision, and *screen* method (how it uses ink dots to build colors) are different than a prepress platesetter. The color separation options in the Photoshop print dialog box are intended to be used by those operating prepress equipment.

If you just want to know on which plate certain elements of your document will print, you can view each CMYK channel in the Channels panel.

Saving the image as Photoshop PDF

When print jobs are submitted in various document formats, components such as type, fonts, and transparency might not be included or might be handled in different ways. To solve this problem, some print service providers may request that you submit a print job in PDF format, which is popular because it can consistently preserve many document attributes that are important for high-quality printing on press.

1   Choose File > Save A Copy.

2   In the Save A Copy dialog box, navigate to the Lesson14 folder, choose Photoshop PDF from the Format menu, name the file **14Print.pdf**, and then click Save.

3   Click OK if a message appears about Save Adobe PDF settings.

4   In the Save Adobe PDF dialog box, choose [PDF/X-4:2008] from the Adobe PDF Preset menu. How do you know which preset to choose? Ask your print service provider which preset best matches their printing workflow.

▶ **Tip:** PDF/X is an industry standard for storing printing information for high-quality reproduction on press. Newer PDF/X standards support more printing features.

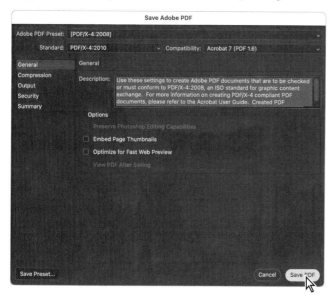

The five panels you can select from the list on the left side of the Save Adobe PDF dialog box (General, Compression, etc.) contain many PDF options. Fortunately, if you know or have been told which Adobe PDF Preset to choose, you don't have to think about any of those options, because choosing a preset sets those options for you.

5   Click Save PDF. Photoshop saves the PDF copy.

If you want, you can open the Lesson14 folder in Adobe Bridge or on the desktop and double-click the 14Print.pdf file. It opens in the default PDF application on your computer. If Adobe Acrobat is installed, it may open in that application.

Note: This exercise requires a printer connected to your computer and requires that its printer driver software is installed on your computer.

Printing to a desktop color printer

Many color inkjet printers make high-quality prints of photographs and other image files. However, they reproduce color differently than a press. You'll get the best results if you do the following:

- Make sure the printer's driver software is installed and up to date.

- Use the appropriate paper for your intended use, such as coated paper for photographs, high-quality matte for graphic design, or textured for digital paintings. Plain paper and inexpensive office-grade paper may not reproduce color and detail with the quality you want for photographs and graphic art.

- Don't convert an RGB image to CMYK to print on a desktop color printer. Most desktop printers are designed to receive RGB color data. The printer driver software converts from RGB to the specific ink set used in that printer. For example, a pro inkjet printer that uses eight inks to reproduce a wider color gamut needs to convert RGB to the specific eight ink colors that it uses, not the four CMYK ink colors that a press uses.

Tip: Want to see more print settings at once? Resize the Photoshop Print Settings window by dragging a corner or edge.

1 Choose File > Print.

2 In the Printer Setup section, select a printer from the Printer menu.

3 Click Print Settings, set the appropriate paper size and any other options needed for the print job, and click Save to return to Photoshop Print Settings.

Tip: If Scale to Fit Media isn't selected, you can enter dimensions in the Scale section, and position and scale the image in the print preview on the left.

It's not possible to cover the Print Settings button in more detail, because the settings and layout differ depending on whether you are using macOS or Windows, and which printer you're using. The driver software for each printer adds options specific to that printer brand and model. Typically, it's important to set the paper/ media type, paper size, and color management settings in Print Settings. For more information, consult the help files for your operating system and your printer.

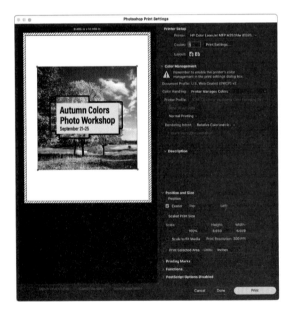

Color for online viewing

Correcting color for print is challenging because colors can reproduce differently depending on the specific combination of paper, inks, and printer or press. It's also true that computer, TV, and mobile screens are not all the same, but newer models tend to reproduce color more closely to specific color standards. The sRGB color space is now widely supported by consumer devices, so it's a safe choice as the color space to use when exporting for the web, social media, and mobile devices.

Photoshop has commands for exporting to the web and social media, such as the File > Export and File > Export > Save for Web (Legacy) commands. In the dialog boxes for these commands are two options: Convert to sRGB and Embed Color Profile. Typically, you'll want to select both options for more consistent color reproduction across devices. However, how image colors look on a specific screen is still influenced by settings the viewer can change, such as brightness or blue light reduction.

Some digital workflows, such as professional video production, may require delivering media in a specific color space. For those, you can choose Edit > Convert to Profile before saving or exporting a copy of the document for delivery.

4 In the Color Management section, for general-purpose color printers set Color Handling to Printer Manages Colors. For professional photo or fine art printers, you may get better results by setting Color Handling to Photoshop Manages Colors; selecting a color profile for your combination of printer, ink, and paper from the Printer Profile menu; and making sure color management is disabled in the printer driver settings.

5 Check the preview on the left to see if the document print size and position is correct relative to the paper size. If not, change options in the Position and Size section, or change the paper size by clicking the Print Settings button at the top.

The border with diagonal lines shows the non-printable margins. The margin widths are provided to Photoshop by the printer driver software, so the margins are determined by the printer and paper selected in Print Settings.

6 If you need any marks printed outside the image area, such as crop marks or print information, set them up in the Printing Marks and Functions sections. For marks to have room to print outside the image, the paper size must be larger than the image size.

7 If you want to print, click Print. If you don't want to print now and you want to save the changes you made for when you print later, click Done.

Congratulations … you've learned a lot about preparing a document to be printed!

Note: If you set Color Handling to Photoshop Manages Colors, you typically want to disable color management in the printer driver settings to avoid double color management. Either the printer or Photoshop should control print colors, but not both.

Note: The PostScript Options section is not covered here because it's typically used by print service providers, not with common desktop printers.

Extra credit

Sharing your work on Adobe Portfolio

Part of Adobe Creative Cloud, Adobe Portfolio lets you quickly create a well-designed and functional website that showcases your creations, with one-click connections to your social media presence (such as your Instagram, Facebook, and X feeds) and a prebuilt contact form that makes it easy for potential clients and customers to get in touch with you.

The Portfolio user interface you see may vary as Adobe updates the service. Some of the following steps may appear only when creating a Portfolio website for the first time.

1 In a web browser, go to myportfolio.com, the web address for Adobe Portfolio.

2 At the top of the Adobe Portfolio home page, if necessary click Sign In, enter your Adobe ID email address and password, and click Sign In.

3 On the next screen, click to select the type of site you want to create: Full Portfolio or Welcome Page. We clicked Full Portfolio and scrolled down to pick the Rose theme.

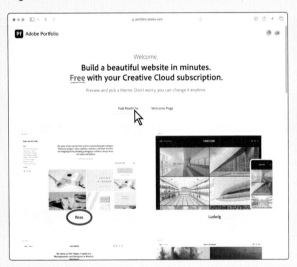

4 Explore the interactive preview that appears, and then click Use This Theme. You can change the theme at any time.

Portfolio creates an empty version of the site, showing its home page. Each empty rectangle represents a gallery, so you need to create at least one gallery.

5 Click Add Page, click Page, and then in the New Page dialog box, enter a Page Title of **Student Projects**, and click Create Page.

You can add many types of creative media including Lightroom photos (on cloud storage), and you can embed content from the web. For this page, you'll upload images you already have.

6   Click Photo Grid, click Upload Files, navigate to the Assets folder inside the Lesson14 folder, select all of the files in the Assets folder, and then click Choose, Open, or Upload (the button name depends on the web browser you use). Portfolio builds a photo grid on the page.

7   Hover over the bottom of the photo grid, and when a circle with a plus sign appears, click it to reveal a menu. You don't need to click anything in the menu right now, but if you wanted, you could click an icon to add more content to the page, such as text or other media.

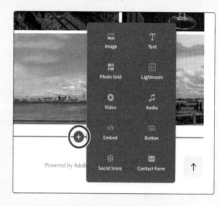

You can also add content before the photo grid by hovering over any of its other edges. If you add content to the left or right sides, you add a second column next to the existing content.

8   Click Preview to view an interactive simulation of how the website will be seen by others. The buttons at the bottom of the preview simulate how the page will look on different device displays and orientations, such as a smartphone held vertically or horizontally.

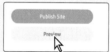

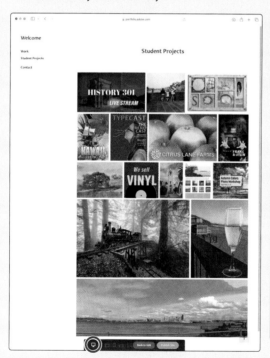

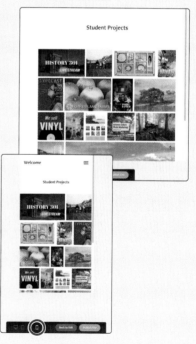

Continues on next page

9 Click Back To Edit to continue customizing the website.

As needed, use the options along the left side of the Portfolio editor to add or organize pages, customize the design (including the theme, fonts, and page backgrounds), or set options for the entire website such as password protection. If you need to make other common changes:

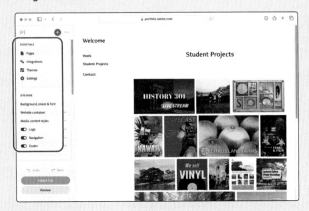

- To edit the photo grid, hover the pointer over it and click the blue tab that appears, then choose from the menu that opens from the tab.

- To edit the text at the top of the home page, click it.

- To edit other pages listed in the top left page corner such as Work or Contact, click them.

- To see the website from its top level, click the name at the top left corner (which is marked Logo when you hover the pointer over it).

- To edit the name at the top left corner, in the Portfolio editor under Site-Wide expand Logo, click Site Name/Logo, and edit the Text field.

If your site looks good and you want the world to see it, click Publish Site. It's live! (If you don't publish the website, it stays hidden from public view on the web.)

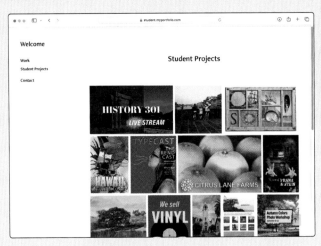

If you have your own Internet domain name, you can easily connect it to Adobe Portfolio so that your website's address is fully consistent with your brand. To do this, click Settings, and then edit settings in the Domain Name panel. You can create and manage multiple Adobe Portfolio websites.

If you don't use a custom domain name, your website address is a subdomain of myportfolio.com. You can customize this by clicking Settings > Domain Name and editing the Site Subdomain. For example, if you enter "student" as the Site Subdomain, then student.myportfolio.com is the web address.

Review questions

1 What steps should you follow to reproduce color consistently?

2 What is a gamut?

3 What is a color profile?

4 What are color separations?

5 What are two reasons it is typically not necessary to convert an RGB image to CMYK before printing it?

Review answers

1 To reproduce color consistently, first calibrate and profile your monitor, and verify that the Edit > Color Settings dialog box is set up properly for your workflow. You can then soft-proof the image to check out-of-gamut colors, and adjust colors as needed.

2 A gamut is the range of colors that can be reproduced by a color model or real-world device. For example, the RGB and CMYK color models have different gamuts. Within each color model, various printers, printing standards, and device displays reproduce different gamuts.

3 A color profile is a description of a color space, such as the CMYK color space of a particular printer. Applications such as Photoshop can read the color profiles representing different applications, platforms, and devices, to maintain consistent color across them.

4 Color separations are separate plates for each ink used in a document being reproduced on press, such as the four color separations required to print the cyan, magenta, yellow, and black process colors on a press.

5 For prepress jobs, many workflows now convert RGB to CMYK in the equipment at the print service provider. For desktop color printing, RGB is converted to CMYK by the printer driver software because the ink or toner colors used by many desktop printers do not exactly match the inks used on press.

15 EXPLORING GENERATIVE AI

Lesson overview

In this lesson, you'll learn how to do the following:

- Create and enhance images using generative AI features.

- Refine the results of generative AI to get the image you want.

- Use different types of generative AI features in Photoshop.

- Understand how Adobe Firefly generative AI handles issues related to generative AI, such as rights and credits.

 This lesson will take about 30 minutes to complete. To get the lesson files used in this chapter, download them from the web page for this book at peachpit.com/PhotoshopCIB2025. For more information, see "Accessing the lesson files and Web Edition" in the Getting Started section at the beginning of this book.

As you work on this lesson, you'll preserve the start files. If you need to restore the start files, download them from your Account page.

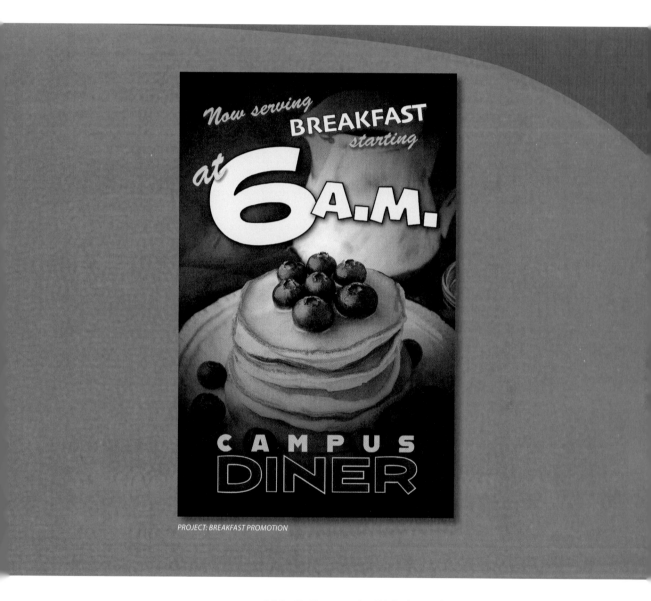

PROJECT: BREAKFAST PROMOTION

Adobe Firefly generative AI is built into Photoshop so that you can quickly explore visual ideas and create photorealistic or illustrative images simply by describing what you want.

About Adobe Firefly generative AI

The term *artificial intelligence*, or *AI*, isn't new; you've probably been hearing it for years, and it's been around for decades. For most of that time, AI has been about calculating results or analyses that seem unusually advanced. More recently, AI has been extended to include visual recognition such as being able to identify faces and read text in images.

Generative AI is much newer, and it's called "generative" because it isn't just about calculating or recognizing — it can create entirely new content. You saw this in Lesson 1 when you used Generative Fill to extend a photo into an empty area, convincingly, in seconds. Traditionally, you'd do this kind of image extension by hand using a cloning tool to copy image content to the empty area, but there was always the risk of areas being obvious repetitions of something else in the image, and it took a significant amount of time.

The ability of generative AI to seemingly invent completely new photorealistic images or write new text or music seems miraculous or magical, but in reality, generative AI only knows what to create based on its model of the problem and how well that model has been trained. Generative AI models are trained using very large sets of examples. Generative AI in Photoshop is trained on hundreds of millions of images. Because the quality of generative AI depends on its training, generative AI is constantly improving as the models are trained on more examples.

Generative AI is used not only in Photoshop but throughout many Adobe applications and services. For example, anyone can try generative AI in Adobe Express, a set of easy-to-use creative tools that work in a mobile app or web browser. Adobe gave their overall generative AI technology its own name, Adobe Firefly, and added Firefly capabilities into many of their applications including Photoshop.

There are some guidelines and restrictions for using Firefly generative AI; see www.adobe.com/legal/licenses-terms/adobe-gen-ai-user-guidelines.html.

How does Photoshop use generative AI?

Adobe Firefly generative AI is so useful that it appears in different forms throughout Photoshop so that it can help solve a range of challenges. You'll find generative AI in places including:

Contextual Task Bar. After you create a selection marquee using any tool or method, the Contextual Task Bar offers a button such as Generative Fill or Generate Image; you learned this in Lesson 2. When the Contextual Task Bar is hidden or when the document context (such as the layer type selected in the Layers panel) doesn't display generative AI options, generative AI features are still available in other ways.

Edit menu. On the Edit menu, you'll find the Generative Fill, Generate Image, and (in some versions) Generative Workspace commands. You'll learn about all three of those later in this lesson.

Options bar. Some tools contain generative AI options. The Remove tool you tried in Lesson 2 has a Mode menu that includes generative AI options that can improve the results. In Lesson 5, you learned that the Crop tool has a Generative Expand option for filling empty areas created by cropping and straightening.

Many of these features didn't exist a few years ago, and people are finding new uses for generative AI all the time. Don't be surprised if there are even more generative AI features in Photoshop by the time you read this.

In earlier lessons, you used generative AI to repair or extend images. That use of generative AI is as a production tool to improve images you created or already have. Now it's time to try using generative AI the other way: to create whole new images!

Getting started

You'll use generative AI to complete a document that helps promote an earlier start time for breakfast service at a restaurant. The document needs to be easy to adapt for the different ways the restaurant wants to promote the service, so it's been designed as a tall, narrow document so that it can easily be exported for posting on vertical format social media feeds, and it also matches a common size for an ad in a print publication.

Note: If Bridge isn't installed, the File > Browse In Bridge command in Photoshop will start the Creative Cloud desktop app, which will download and install Bridge. After installation completes, you can start Bridge. For more information, see page 3.

1 Start Photoshop, and then simultaneously hold down Ctrl+Alt+Shift (Windows) or Command+Option+Shift (macOS) to restore the default preferences. (See "Restoring default preferences" on page 5.)

2 When prompted, click Yes to delete the Adobe Photoshop Settings file.

3 Choose File > Browse In Bridge to open Adobe Bridge.

4 In Bridge, click Lessons in the Favorites panel. Double-click the Lesson15 folder in the Content panel.

5 Compare the files 15_Start.psd and 15_End.psd.

6 In Bridge, double-click the 15_Start.psd file to open it in Photoshop. If the Embedded Profile Mismatch dialog box appears, click OK.

7 Save the document as **15_Working.psd** in the Lesson15 folder. If the Photoshop Format Options dialog box appears, click OK.

Note: If Photoshop displays a dialog box telling you about the difference between saving to Cloud Documents and On Your Computer, click Save On Your Computer. You can also select Don't Show Again, but that setting will deselect after you reset Photoshop preferences.

Generating a complete image

Note: The examples of generative AI images in this lesson may differ from the results you get, in part because, over time, Adobe Firefly generative AI is likely to be updated and trained with more images to improve the results.

In earlier lessons, you used generative AI to enhance existing images. Another popular use of generative AI is to create entirely new images. The 15_Start.psd document needs an appealing image of a breakfast.

You do have to think about how appropriate generative AI is for the project you're working on. This project promotes a general breakfast service and not a specific named dish, so a generative AI image may be acceptable; but always check with the client. If the promotion was about a specific item on the menu, it would be much better to commission a photograph of what that menu item actually looks like.

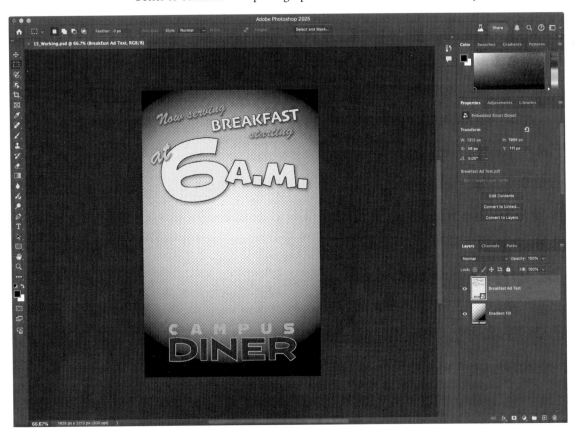

The lesson file has two layers. The bottom layer, Gradient Fill, is a radial gradient that goes from transparent in the center to black at the edge. If you want to inspect how it's set up, in the Layers panel select the Gradient Fill layer, and then in the Tools panel select the Gradient tool so that the Properties panel displays Gradient Adjustment options. The gradient is transparent in the center so that after you generate an image and move it to the bottom of the layer stack, you'll be able to see the image through the gradient.

The top layer, Breakfast Ad Text, was created in Photoshop as a separate document and saved as a Photoshop PDF to maintain its vector outlines. It was then brought into this lesson file using the File > Place Embedded command, which adds it to the Layers panel as an embedded Smart Object.

Tip: Because the vector text outlines in the Breakfast Ad Text layer are preserved in Photoshop PDF format, the text edges remain smooth if you scale up that Smart Object layer.

If the document contained a pixel layer and it was selected, the Contextual Task Bar might offer a Generate Image button. Neither of the existing layers is a pixel layer (one is an embedded Smart Object layer and the other is a gradient fill layer), but that's not a problem; you can still use generative AI from the Edit menu.

1 Choose Edit > Generate Image.

2 In the Generate Image dialog box, click in the "Describe..." prompt box, type **healthy breakfast** to describe the image for it to generate, and then click Generate. If a message appears asking you to read and agree to the Generative AI User Guidelines, click Agree when you're ready.

Tip: The prompt in step 2 uses just two words, but it's common for a prompt to use more words to get the image you want.

Generating images may take some time. When it finishes, you'll see that:

- On the canvas, the empty selection is replaced with new content.

- In the Layers panel, a new Generative Layer was created, and the name of the layer is the prompt you entered.

- In the Properties panel, as long as a generative layer is selected, a Variations section offers alternatives you can click to try. The selected variation is the one you see on the canvas.

Note: If you don't see the Variations section, it may be out of view, especially on a smaller display. Try scrolling the Properties panel to bring the Variations panel up and into view.

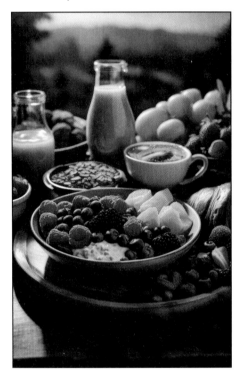

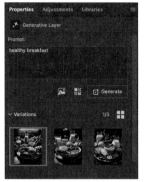

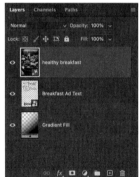

3 In the Layers panel, drag the Healthy Breakfast layer to the bottom of the layer stack so that you can see the design working as intended, showing the text and radial gradient in front of the image.

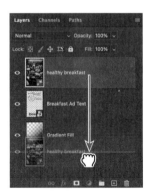

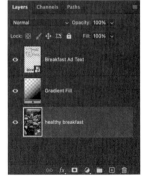

4 In the Variations section of the Properties panel, click the other variations in turn, and leave selected the variation you think is the best.

▶ **Tip:** Variations are saved with the document, so if you think the document file size is too large, delete any variations you are sure you don't want to keep.

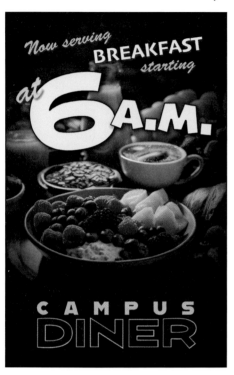

5 Save the document.

Refining a generative layer

It's common for the first results of a prompt to be too far from the image you actually want. Photoshop offers ways to make the results closer to what you want.

1 In the Variations section of the Properties panel, hover over the first variation and click the ellipsis (…) menu. You don't have to click any of the options, but note what they are:

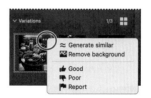

- Generate Similar creates another set of variations for the same prompt.

- Remove Background attempts to isolate the subject and erase the background. However, manually selecting and removing the background might work better.

- Good, Poor, and Report don't change the current variation but are a way of providing feedback to Adobe about the quality of the results of generative AI.

Another way to change the results is to change the prompt.

▶ **Tip:** The Enter or Return key is a shortcut for clicking the Generate button.

2 In the Properties panel, click in the Prompt box, enter a variation on "healthy breakfast" by adding descriptive words, click Generate, and select the variation you like the most. We entered **healthy breakfast with pancakes and blueberries**.

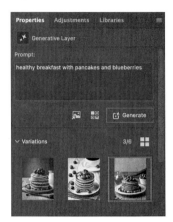

So far the variations are photorealistic. Next you'll choose a more illustrative style that you can customize.

3 Click the second icon below the Prompt box to open style options, select Art, and select a specific look from the Effects category. We clicked All, and then selected Art Deco.

4 Click Generate and select the variation that works best with the design.

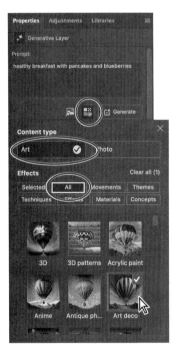

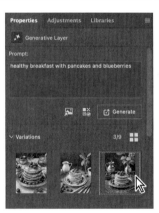

5   Click the first icon below the Prompt box to open Reference Image options. Select one of the images (we selected the first one), click Generate, and select the variation you like the most. These results were influenced by the style of the reference image you selected.

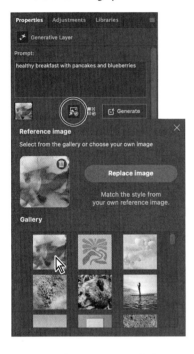 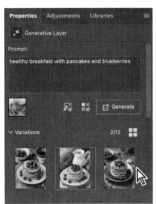

How is Reference Image different than the Effects? Selecting a reference image is a way for you to influence variations using any image. The images in the Gallery are simply examples, but a great use of Reference Image is for generating art based on your personal style. To do this, open Reference Image options, click the Replace Image button, and select an image that represents your style. Of course, you can also use Reference Image to generate art based on a style you want to emulate, such as a client's style.

Take a look at the icons for Reference Image and Style Effects and remember them, because they appear in other places in Photoshop where you can use generative AI. For example, those options are also available on the Contextual Task Bar for generative fill and in the Generative Workspace dialog box (see the sidebar "Save time with Generative Workspace" on page 399).

6 Feel free to continue to explore Firefly generative AI.

For 15_End.psd, we went with one of the photographic variations. Don't expect to match our results exactly because the Firefly model and training may change over time. Just create and select a variation that you think works the best for the promotional image.

7 When you're done, save and close the document.

The document is now ready to save or export copies for various media using workflows you've learned in earlier lessons, such as exporting for the web, printing on your own printer, or exporting for a print service provider.

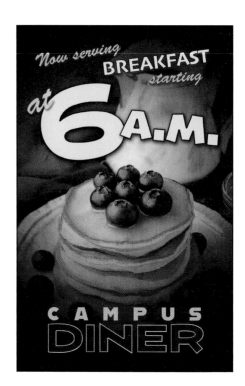

● **Note:** At the time this lesson is being written, the maximum pixel dimensions of a generative AI image in Photoshop is 2000 × 2000 pixels. If you use generative AI on larger areas, the 2000 × 2000 pixel result will be scaled up.

About generative credits

Generative AI requires significant computing power. Sometimes it can all be done on your computer. Other times, the fastest way to generate the results is for Photoshop to send the prompt and image to Adobe Firefly on a Creative Cloud server where the results are generated using a much more powerful computer, and then on your computer, Photoshop receives the results and integrates them with your Photoshop document.

It takes a lot of cloud computing power to run generative AI, so Adobe came up with a system to manage server usage called Generative Credits. Creative Cloud members receive a certain number of Generative Credits every month. The number of credits you get depends on the Creative Cloud plan used by you or your school or organization. If you run out of Generative Credits before the end of a month, you can continue to use Generative Fill, but it may run more slowly because your jobs will have a lower priority. If you need to restore performance priority, it's possible to purchase more credits. For more information, including how to see the number of generative credits you have in the current month, see helpx.adobe.com/firefly/using/generative-credits-faq.html.

Adobe continues to work out how to best provide generative AI services, so Generative Credits policies may change or improve over time.

Save time with Generative Workspace

Choose Edit > Generative Workspace to open a dialog box that offers a more efficient, streamlined way to create the images you want.

Check your work.
Generative Workspace remembers your prompts and results on a timeline, so if you want to better understand how you created a certain set of images, you can roll back the timeline to take a closer look at what you entered and how you refined it.

Generate in parallel.
You can quickly generate different sets of variations in parallel. Instead of waiting for the results of a prompt before trying another prompt, you can apply multiple prompts, and each set of variations appears in the timeline when they're ready.

Generate specific variations in a single prompt.
If you want to see slight variations on a prompt, you can type variables within brackets, separated by commas. For example, you could enter "breakfast [sausage, vegetarian, oatmeal, pancakes]" and Firefly will generate four breakfasts modified by each of the variables.

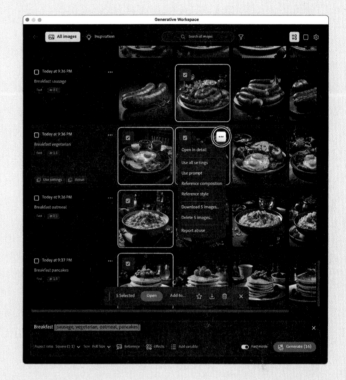

Easily open variations as documents or add to open documents. If you hover the pointer over a variation, a check box appears. Click the check box to select that variation. When at least one check box is selected, a Contextual Task Bar appears. Click Open to open the variation as a new Photoshop document, or click Add To to add the variation to an open Photoshop document as a layer.

Edit the timeline. Other buttons on the Contextual Task Bar, or that appear on a variation when you hover over it, offer other options such as liking, downloading, or deleting an image. A filter icon at the top lets you constrain the list to certain criteria; for example, you can filter the timeline to show you only images you liked.

Popular questions about generative AI

Generative AI is unlike most other software features because it raises many questions across a number of areas that aren't technical. This is largely because generative AI is not a simple program or algorithm. The fact that generative AI is trained on millions of images causes people to ask questions such as:

• Did the creators of the images in the training set give permission to use their images for generative AI training?

• Are the creators of the images in the training set compensated for the use of their images?

• Can generative AI images be used in commercial jobs?

• Is there a way to tell if generative AI was used to falsify part or all of an image?

Adobe Firefly generative AI and Photoshop address those questions as explained below so that you can create with confidence.

How rights are cleared for the training images

Generative imagery is created by training software models using large numbers of images. Some AI services may train using found images without securing appropriate usage rights. Rights issues may lead to legal liability, so some companies and organizations may avoid using work created by services that can't provide information on training image rights. Adobe Firefly generative AI is designed to be "commercial safe" in part because it's trained using images where usage rights are known, such as images from the Adobe Stock collection and images in the public domain. (Note: In the United States, the term *public domain* has a specific legal definition involving the intentional release or normal expiration of copyright and is not the same as a copyrighted image being publicly viewable online.) For more information, see helpx.adobe.com/firefly/faq.html#training-data.

Adobe does not train on any Creative Cloud subscriber's personal content.

At the enterprise level, Adobe offers intellectual property indemnity for Adobe Firefly. If you or an enterprise client are interested in more details about Firefly indemnity, do a web search for the document "Firefly Legal FAQs – Enterprise Customers" and download the one with the most recent date.

Compensating contributors to the training set

Adobe Stock is one of the sources used to train Firefly, and Adobe Stock images come from voluntary contributors. Submitting images to Adobe Stock requires agreeing to terms that give Adobe permission to create and train Firefly models with those images. In addition, an Adobe Stock bonus compensation plan provides a way for Adobe Stock contributors to be paid for the use of their images for generative AI training. For more information, see: helpx.adobe.com/stock/contributor/help/firefly-faq-for-adobe-stock-contributors.html

Detecting the use of generative AI

Another issue is being able to determine whether an image is original or contains generative AI content. Adobe is part of an industry-wide effort called the Content Authenticity Initiative (contentauthenticity.org). This includes an effort to create an open, global standard for sharing image metadata (information) that can include creator attribution, includes generative AI transparency (letting people know that generative AI was used for at least part of the image), and is tamper-evident (so you can know if the metadata was altered).

Adobe is developing a Content Credentials feature that supports the Content Authenticity Initiative. For more information and links about how Content Credentials work and how they relate to Photoshop, see helpx.adobe.com/creative-cloud/help/content-credentials.html.

For example, if you use Firefly generative AI in an image and choose File > Export > Export As, a Content Credentials section at the bottom right corner of the Export As dialog box tells you that a Content Credential will automatically be applied and lets you preview what it will say if someone else decides to inspect the credential.

Exploring the possibilities

This lesson is only an introduction to the power of Firefly generative AI. As you learn to use it, you'll probably think of more ways to use it to brainstorm, visualize, and possibly create finished art.

Remember that generative AI doesn't have to be completely synthetic. You can combine it with other images and photographs in Photoshop, and you can generate AI images where your own creativity still comes through. For example, you can apply a Reference Image of your work to a prompt, or you can generate an image and then stylize it yourself using Photoshop brushes as you did in Lesson 10. Have fun!

About Neural Filters

● **Note:** Adobe may update Neural Filters after this book is published, so the filter list and options you see may depend on the version of Photoshop you use.

Neural Filters are similar to generative AI but are more constrained and focused on specific tasks. To use them, choose Filter > Neural Filters. A list of filters appears; none is applied until you enable the toggle switch for a filter. It may be necessary to download some filters before using them. When a filter is enabled and selected, its options appear to the right of the filter list, and a large preview is to the left of the filter list. Some examples of Neural Filters are:

Smart Portrait can do things like change a smile or which ways eyes are looking.

Photo Restoration can quickly remove defects such as dust, creases, and scratches, and enhance old portraits.

Harmonization can help visually blend layers to look more consistent.

● **Note:** Some Neural Filters may be labeled Beta, which means they function but are still under development. You can use them, but when the finished version is released, those filters may produce different results or some options may be different.

Super Zoom can apply AI upscaling to create a higher resolution enlargement from a low resolution source image, with better quality than traditional upsampling.

At the bottom of the Neural Filters dialog box, the Output menu lets you use the results in different ways, such as a rendered layer, a Smart Filter, or a new document.

Neural Filters can be a lot of fun to play with, and may help you solve specific image editing challenges.

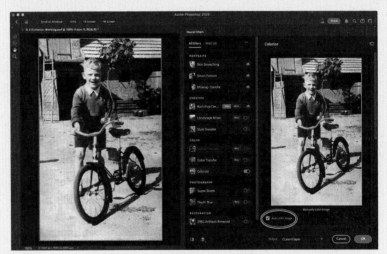

The Colorize Neural Filter is a quick way to add color to a scan of an old monochrome photograph.

Review questions

1 Where in Photoshop can you find generative AI features?

2 What feature/command name creates an entirely new picture (instead of altering an existing picture)?

3 What are at least three ways to improve a generative AI result that isn't quite right?

4 How can you make a generative AI result more like your own personal creative style?

5 Why are Adobe Firefly generative AI images called "commercial safe"?

Review answers

1 You can find generative AI features in the Contextual Task Bar (under certain conditions), on the Edit menu, and on the options bar when some tools are selected.

2 Generate Image.

3 You can select a different variation, change the prompt text, apply effects, and apply a reference image.

4 Apply a reference image using an image that represents your personal style.

5 Adobe Firefly images are trained on images where the rights either have been secured or are not an issue because the images are legally in the public domain.

INDEX

Curvature Pen tool 207, 208, 211

curved paths 209

Curve panel, in Camera Raw 305

Curves adjustment layer 51, 126

D

Darken blending mode 100

Darker Color blending mode 100

Decontaminate Colors option 173

defaults

    in Camera Raw 327

    resetting Photoshop 5, 10

Define Custom Shape command 223

Define Pattern command 179

Delete Cropped Pixels option 50

Denoise, in Camera Raw 327, 328

depth of field, extending 150

Deselect command 72

Detail panel, in Camera Raw 306

Difference blending mode 100

Difference Clouds filter 243

Direct Selection tool 209, 217

Discover panel 6

discretionary ligatures 201

distortions, correcting 153

DNG. *See* Adobe DNG (Digital Negative)
    file format

docking panels 30

document size, displaying 16, 118

document window

    fitting image to 81

    scrolling 20

    status bar 18

dots per inch (dpi) 49

drag-and-drop importing 103

Drop Shadow layer style 343, 348

drop shadows 110–111, 112

duplicating

    buttons 341–345

    images 119, 373

    layers 341

duration of video clips, changing 280

E

educators, resources for 7

Elliptical Marquee tool

    centering selection 80

    circular selection 74

    in Tools panel 66

emoji fonts 201

Enhance command 327

Enhance Edge option 71

Exclusion blending mode 100

Expand command 73

Export As command 360, 361

exporting

    Adobe Camera Raw edited version
        296, 309–315, 327

    artboards 360

    brushes 262

    layers as separate files 361

    video 286

Extras command 76

Eyedropper tool 31, 32, 255

eye icon, in the Layers panel 91

F

face adjustments

    with healing tools 318

    with Liquify filter 128, 234

Face-Aware Liquify filter 128

fading audio 280

Farrer, Lisa 424

Faulkner, Andrew 270

Feather command 76

feathering 76

Field Blur 130

file formats. *See* name of format

file size 49

fills

    foreground color 117

    gradient 106

M

machine learning 57, 66, 165, 202, 249, 303, 328

macros. *See* actions

Magic Wand tool 66, 70–71

Magnetic Lasso tool 66, 79–80

magnification. *See* Zoom tool

    document 18–20

    Timeline panel 277

magnifying glass. *See* Zoom tool

mandalas, painting 267

marching ants. *See* selection marquee

marquee tools 66

masks 162

    on adjustment layers 243

    in Adobe Camera Raw 320

    in Camera Raw 305

    channel 163

    creating 133, 163–166

    luminance 84

    overview 162

    refining 168–173

    compared to selections 162

    terminology 163

    vector 163

Match Font command 202

megapixels 48

merging

    images into a panorama 140

    images to extend depth of field 150

    images with different

        perspectives 153–156

    layers 118

mistakes, correcting 34–41

Mixer Brush tool

    about 254

    cleaning the brush 259

Mixer tab, in Camera Raw 305

mixing colors

    with a photograph 261

    with Mixer Brush tool 258

mobile devices

    designing for, with artboards 355

    using with libraries 222

monitor calibration 370

More Image Settings, in Camera Raw 327

motion blur effects 131

Motion panel 285

Move tool

    Auto-Select option 116

    moving selections 72

    scissors icon 81

moving

    layers. *See* Move tool

    panels 30

    selections 72–73

Multiply blending mode 100

muting audio 280–281

N

navigating

    in Camera Raw 297

    using the Navigator panel 20

Navigator panel 20

Neural Filters 129, 402

New Window command 373

noise reduction 327

noise reduction, in Camera Raw 328

nondestructive filters 234

notes. *See also* Note tool

    deleting 199

    Notes panel 197

Note tool 197

nudging layers 359

nudging selected pixels 75

O

Object Selection tool 73–74, 133

on-image adjustment tool. *See* targeted adjustment tool

opacity, changing 98–99

Production Notes

Adobe Photoshop Classroom in a Book 2025 Release was created electronically using Adobe InDesign. Art was produced using Adobe InDesign, Adobe Illustrator, and Adobe Photoshop. The Myriad Pro and Warnock Pro OpenType families of typefaces were used throughout this book. For information about OpenType and Adobe fonts, visit adobe.com/type/opentype/.

References to company names in the lessons are for demonstration purposes only and are not intended to refer to any actual organization or person.

Images

Photographic images and illustrations are intended for use with this book's lessons only.

Lesson 1 arch image: © Styve Reineck, Shutterstock

Lesson 2 autumn image: © gillmar, Shutterstock

Lesson 4 ukulele image from Adobe Stock, stock.adobe.com

Lesson 5 car image: @ Avpics, Alamy Ltd.

Lesson 11: Sailboat video © Openfinal, Shutterstock; Fushimi Inari Shrine video © Guitar photographer / Shutterstock; Vitala temple video © Krothapalli Ravindra Babu / 123RF; trailer music © Vladislav Litvinenko / 123RF; arch image: © Styve Reineck, Shutterstock

Team credits

The following individuals contributed to the development of *Adobe Photoshop Classroom in a Book 2025 Release*:

Writer and Designer: Conrad Chavez

Illustrator and Compositor: David Van Ness

Project Manager: Anne-Marie Praetzel

Copyeditor and Proofreader: Kim Wimpsett

Keystroke Reviewer: Megan Ahearn

Indexer: Conrad Chavez

Technical Reviewer: David Van Ness

Production Assistant: Thalita Di Domenico

Interior Design: Mimi Heft

Art Director: Conrad Chavez

Adobe Press Executive Editor: Laura Norman

Adobe Press Production Editor: Tracey Croom

Adobe Press Associate Editor: Anshul Sharma

Contributors

Jay Graham began his career designing and building custom homes. He has been a professional photographer for more than 25 years, with clients in the advertising, architectural, editorial, and travel industries. He contributed the "Pro photo workflow" tips in Lesson 12. www.jaygraham.com

Lisa Farrer is a photographer based in Marin County, CA. She contributed photography for Lesson 12.

Julieanne Kost is a veteran Adobe product evangelist.

Gawain Weaver has conserved and restored original works by artists ranging from Eadweard Muybridge to Man Ray, and from Ansel Adams to Cindy Sherman. He contributed to "Real-world photo restoration" in Lesson 2. www.gawainweaver.com

Special Thanks

We offer our sincere thanks to Stephen Nielson, Joel Baer, Russell Brown, Rikk Flohr, Steve Guilhamet, Meredith Payne Stotzner, Jeff Tranberry, and Pete Green for their support and help with this project. We couldn't have done it without you!

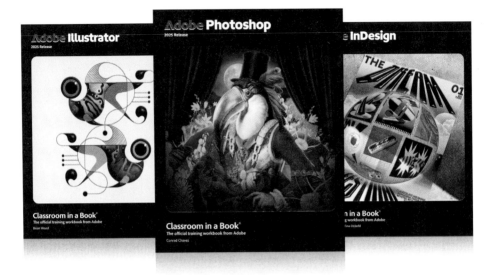

The fastest, easiest, most comprehensive way to learn
Adobe Creative Cloud

Classroom in a Book®, the best-selling series of hands-on software training books, helps you learn the features of Adobe software quickly and easily.

The **Classroom in a Book** series offers what no other book or training program does—an official training series from Adobe Systems, developed with the support of Adobe product experts.

To see a complete list of our titles in the Classroom in a Book series, go to: peachpit.com/CC2025

Adobe Press